ALTERNATIVE GLOBALIZATIONS

ALTERNATIVE GLOBALIZATIONS

Eastern Europe and the Postcolonial World

Edited by James Mark,
Artemy M. Kalinovsky, and
Steffi Marung

Indiana University Press

This book is a publication of

Indiana University Press
Office of Scholarly Publishing
Herman B Wells Library 350
1320 East 10th Street
Bloomington, Indiana 47405 USA

iupress.indiana.edu

Manufactured in the United States of America

Cataloging information is available from the Library of Congress.

ISBN 978-0-253-04650-5 (hdbk.)
ISBN 978-0-253-04651-2 (pbk.)
ISBN 978-0-253-04653-6 (web PDF)

1 2 3 4 5 25 24 23 22 21 20

Contents

Acknowledgments *vii*

Introduction / James Mark, Artemy M. Kalinovsky, and Steffi Marung *1*

Part I: Red Globalization?

1 The Soviet Union, Eastern Europe, and Alternative Visions of a Global Economy 1950s–1980s / James Mark and Yakov Feygin *35*

2 The Cold War in the Margins of Capital: The Soviet Union's Introduction to the Decolonized World, 1955–1961 / Oscar Sanchez-Sibony *59*

3 The Soviet Bloc and China's Global Opening-Up Policy during the Last Years of Mao Zedong / Péter Vámos *80*

4 From Socialist Assistance to National Self-Interest: Vietnamese Labor Migration into CMEA Countries / Alena K. Alamgir and Christina Schwenkel *100*

Part II: A Socialist Age of Development?

5 "Socialist Development" and East Germany in the Arab Middle East / Massimiliano Trentin *127*

6 Entangling Agrarian Modernities: The "Agrarian Question" through the Eyes of Soviet Africanists / Steffi Marung *145*

7 Socialist Worldmaking: Architecture and Global Urbanization in the Cold War / Łukasz Stanek *166*

Part III: Cultural Encounters: Discovering Similarities, Defining Difference, Creating Identities

8 Writing the Soviet South into the History of the Cold War and Decolonization / Artemy M. Kalinovsky *189*

9 Internationalizing the Thaw: Soviet Orientalists and the Contested Politics of Spiritual Solidarity in Asia 1954–1959 / Hanna Jansen *209*

10 Soviet Antiracism and Its Discontents: The Cold War Years / Maxim Matusevich *229*

11 Southeast by Global South: The Balkans, UNESCO, and the Cold War / Bogdan C. Iacob *251*

Part IV: Global Encounter and Challenges to State Socialism

12 A Prehistory of Postcolonialism in Socialist Poland / Adam F. Kola *273*

13 Competing Solidarities? Solidarność and the Global South during the 1980s / Kim Christiaens and Idesbald Goddeeris *288*

14 China Is Not Far! Alternative Internationalism and the Tiananmen Square Massacre in East Germany's 1989 / Quinn Slobodian *311*

Glossary *329*

Index *333*

Acknowledgments

We would like to express our thanks for the support of the Arts and Humanities Research Council (UK), whose support for the project "Socialism Goes Global: Cold War Connections Between the 'Second' and 'Third Worlds'" (grant: AH/M001830/1) underpinned the production of this volume. We would also like to express our gratitude to the Imre Kertész Kolleg at the University of Jena, who kindly hosted and provided support for the conference from which this volume emerged.

ALTERNATIVE GLOBALIZATIONS

Introduction

James Mark, Artemy M. Kalinovsky, and Steffi Marung

The Socialist World in the History of Globalization and Decolonization

Globalization is everywhere. For its champions, globalization is responsible for rising standards of living, greater equality between historically richer and poorer countries, and an unprecedented circulation of knowledge. For leftist critics, *globalization* is a byword for inequality, exploitation, accelerated environmental destruction, and cultural homogenization; for conservative ones, it is responsible for the erosion of morals and norms, the intrusion of unwanted migrants, and the collapse of traditional hierarchies and solidarities.

Historians, too, have been busy trying to make sense of globalization. Some have focused on how empire and technological change transformed economic and social life from the mid-nineteenth century until the First World War, pointing to the various political, economic, and cultural globalizing processes that increasingly question the centrality of Europe in that history. Others have focused on globalization as an economic process that took off in the 1970s with the collapse of the Bretton Woods system, the acceleration of cross-border capital flows, the evident increase in deterritorialized production, and ultimately the collapse of socialist states and their integration into the world market.

Most of these accounts, forged after a singular moment of capitalist triumphalism at the end of the Cold War, ignore the role socialist countries have played in these processes—at least until such countries abandoned state socialism.[1] And yet for the latter part of the twentieth century, an expanding socialist world worked to create its own networks and global links. Following the Second World War, the reach of socialism in the world expanded massively. Through varying combinations of Soviet power and popular revolution, state socialism came to Eastern Europe in the late 1940s—to be followed swiftly by the Chinese Communists' assumption of power in 1949. The rapid collapse of European empires in the 1950s hastened this process: elites in newly independent countries in Africa and Southeast Asia looked to various versions of socialism, or, at the very least, to noncapitalist development. The socialist world at the height of its expansion around 1980 encompassed roughly one-third of the world's population—stretching not only across the Eurasian landmass from Berlin to Pyongyang but also in dozens of states across four continents, including Cuba, Nicaragua, Chile, Vietnam, Laos, Cambodia, North Korea, Afghanistan, China, Ethiopia, Sri Lanka, Angola, and Mozambique.[2] Socialist states were party to all the major global conflicts and developments in the second half of the twentieth century; many of them were founding members of important international organizations. In the early 1970s the Soviet Union alone was a member of over two hundred political (e.g., the United Nations and its substructures) and nongovernmental (e.g., the Red Cross and the Olympic Committee) organizations. Within such organizations, shifting alliances of socialist states promoted new models for an anti-imperialist world economy and new conceptions of rights and world culture.[3] Restrictions of movement for their populations notwithstanding, socialist states became increasingly connected among themselves and with the rest of the world at multiple levels.

The idea of Western capitalism as the only engine of globalization bequeathed a distorted view of socialist and postcolonial states as inward looking, isolated, and cut off from global trends until the capitalist takeover in the 1980s and 1990s.[4] Such accounts ignore not only the agency of so-called peripheries in the creation of global interconnection but also the possibility that interconnection between peripheries might be considered a form of globalization similar to the intensification of interaction between "the West and the rest." Moreover, the study of these globalizing processes rested on excessively limited geographies. Certainly, new histories of globalization have been interested in contingency and have sought to distance themselves from totalizing and Eurocentric narratives on the emergence of the modern, globalized world, accepting that the challenge lies in the "recovery of the multiplicity of the world's pasts."[5] Many have sought to contribute to an understanding of the emergence of global integration "not as a set of procedures devised in the West and superimposed on the rest as if a compliant world waited for its victimization, but [. . . as . . .] carried forward, asymmetrically and unevenly, on a global scale."[6] This has resulted in a broad range of empirical and synthetic contributions[7] that have improved our understanding of these multifaceted global pasts, including the role of different world regions in these processes[8] and the position and function of empires for the shaping of globalization processes.[9] However, this literature so far has done little to suggest alternative geographies that go beyond the North-South axis and often focuses on the changing position of (Western) Europe vis à vis other world regions and onflows of people, goods, and ideas circulating among (Western) Europe, North America, and the Global South. Global integration in such historical narratives seems to be driven by the interactions of West European empires—France and

Britain most prominently—with their (post-) colonies. This literature thus runs the risk of reinforcing a geography it seeks to challenge.

Nor have histories of socialism taken up this challenge with enthusiasm: the understanding of how socialist projects across the globe were connected economically, politically, and culturally is still limited. The research remains fragmented: area studies specialists deal with socialism in their world regions so that, for example, African studies scholars investigate "African socialism." An ongoing division between postcommunist and postcolonial scholars has resulted in, until recently, little interest in bringing together stories of a broader socialist world.[10] Histories of socialism in Europe rarely take into consideration how the trajectories in other world regions and transregional connections are part of their histories, too. Scholarship in postsocialist regions has mainly been concerned with the search for a new national story after the experience of communist internationalism.[11] Those countries in particular that have turned toward the European Union have made little attempt to remember their socialist-era global engagements as they seek to constitute themselves primarily as members of the "European family." The declining prominence of the historiography of socialism in other world regions beyond Europe after the end of the Cold War is even more problematic, as we thus fail to understand trajectories of modernization and globalization projects, which are often deeply intertwined with the histories of socialism in non-European world regions.

Only historians of the Cold War have started to address these links in any real depth, questioning a bipolar account centered on the two superpowers that relegated the rest of the world to the status of "proxies" or "peripheries" and bringing the "Third World" in as a central actor in a drama now characterized as a multipolar conflict.[12] Some went further to suggest that the main cleavage in the world of the second half of the twentieth century was not the one between East and West but between colonial and anticolonial worlds.[13] The global history of the Cold War is increasingly reaching out into East-South connections, thereby also contributing to an understanding of the period as one of ambitious and interconnected nation-state building and modernization projects.[14]

By addressing the relationship between the Soviet Union and Eastern Europe and the decolonizing world in Africa and Asia—or between what Western contemporaries called the "Second" and "Third Worlds"—we hope to offer new insights into the processes and geographies of globalization after 1945. To what degree do histories of interactions between these so-called peripheries change the way in which we stitch together the postwar world? How do accounts of globalization shift if we see de-Stalinization and decolonization as formative moments in its history? To what extent was the postwar period characterized by different and competing models of globalization, and to what extent does the Cold War narrative of a divided world obscure the commonalities, connections, and transfers between capitalist and socialist states? How does the decline of state socialism relate to the globalizing forces of the postwar era, especially when one considers the socialist world a part of these processes rather than simply a victim of them? Do legacies of this moment of alternative interconnectedness remain? The authors, drawing for the most part on socialist engagements from the perspective of the "Global North"—from Berlin through Warsaw and Moscow to Central Asia and then Beijing—address these engagements and chronologies from the point of view of many sources: those of trade and cultural institutions that enabled exchange; produced within international organizations; from networks built by both state-supported and heterodox activists; through bilateral exchanges of experts or political elites; and from the experiences of socialist travelers and labor migrants. In the future, this conceptualization may be broadened to investigate the plurality of socialist globalizations from the perspective of a broader socialist camp, requiring the translation of the research agenda into the work of other area studies.

Some might find the term *globalization* problematic—deeming it a post-1989 invention born of capitalist triumphalism that only describes one form of (mainly economic) free market interconnectedness. Yet we seek to reclaim it. From the mid-nineteenth century the world saw the rise of what some historians have called "the global condition." From this moment, they argue, a specific quality of global interconnectedness developed that—beyond the mere increase in the extent and density of flows of goods and ideas—led to a situation in which no society had the capacity to withdraw completely from this web of interconnections.[15] Globalization may have started out as the deliberate project of empires, companies, or nonstate actors to address this global condition, but it took on a life of its own—in the sense of being appropriated and thus in effect coproduced by a multitude of actors who at first glance appear to be marginalized by bigger players. Their interactions and encounters helped to constitute an interconnected but heterogeneous world that is now known as "globalized." If one takes the term *globalization* to capture a plurality of cultural, social, political, and economic projects within this "global condition" as the result of the varied attempts of actors with their specific interests to deal with these intensifying flows and to attempt to regain control in and over them, then globalization can only be thought of in the plural, not simply attached to the forces of Western capitalism. The state played a major role in shaping and driving this socialist globalization, which was characterized by multiple tensions: between internationalism and nationalism; between far-reaching global ambitions and limited resources; between those circulations desired and those dreaded by regimes; and between efforts for regional cooperation and increasing competition and fissures in the socialist camp. These tensions resulted in particular patterns and logics in the state-socialist globalization project that are detailed below.

What Were Socialist Globalizations?

The heyday of socialist movements in Europe in the decades prior to the First World War coproduced what many historians consider the first era of globalization. Socialist activists of the time often thought in global terms. Karl Marx's famous slogan, "Workers of the World Unite!" pithily captures the starting premise of the communist emancipatory project: the realization that if capital and goods are global, the workers who are being exploited to produce them must be united as well. To this end, socialists formed their own transnational and international organizations and belonged to many more: within these, they began to address questions of global inequalities in a universalist language.[16] Nevertheless, since the 1860s the history of competing Socialist Internationals also demonstrated the dispute among the internationalist strategies of various socialist groups. The rise of nationalist movements in both European and extra-European empires provided fertile ground for the rise of socialism. Socialists of that era thus had to navigate between—or combine—the internationalist foundations of the movement with the growing attraction of the nation-state as the form in which to realize demands for social and economic equality and the expansion of political participation. Struggles over the role the nation-state should play in the formation of a socialist society and how international relations should be organized were hard-fought.[17] Such tensions became dramatically visible by the outbreak of the Great War, in which most socialist parties voted to support the war effort of their own nation and not unite with the proletariat of their allies and opponents; the support of workers for national governments emerging from the ruins of the Austro-Hungarian, Ottoman, and Russian empires further undermined hopes for workers' internationalism.

The idea of a socialist world order gained a second life with the success of the October Revolution in the USSR. The Bolsheviks understood that their workers' state could only survive in the long term if it enjoyed support around the world; hence a revived internationalism also became an instrument of Soviet foreign policy and of stabilizing the Soviet state.[18] Yet if a world revolution was not imminent, the Bolsheviks would have to build these links in other ways. One approach was to support workers' movements *within* capitalist countries and anticolonial movements where European empires still ruled: in Asia, Africa, and the Middle East. Yet this Soviet outreach ran parallel to the rise of communist internationalism across Europe and in the United States and to the emergence of Communist parties in the South, most notably in India, China, and South Africa. Thus interwar internationalism, embodied in the work of the "Third International" (1919–43), embedded Soviet actors in a much more diverse geography, and new themes such as anti-imperialism, anticolonial struggles, and race became a major part of its work.[19]

The young Soviet state also sought to secure its existence by establishing working relationships with the very regimes that the Bolsheviks hoped would be overthrown, so that they could acquire their technology and expertise. This led to increasing tensions within the Communist International, which were further exacerbated by the rise of Stalin: from the late 1920s, the Soviet leadership increasingly subordinated its former internationalism to the new realist—and cynical—version. "Socialism in one country," the slogan of the USSR under Stalin, did not denote Moscow's complete isolation from the world, but it did mean that any attempts to build an alternative global order were deferred. The revolution had to succeed in the USSR before it could be built elsewhere.

The attempt to launch an alternative globalization project was revived more than a decade after the Second World War. Many accounts of the most recent wave of globalization begin in the early 1970s with the rise of a deterritorialized finance capitalism led mainly by Western countries and institutions, in which the socialist world in general—and the USSR and Eastern Europe specifically—was viewed as a victim rather than an active coproducer. By shifting chronology, however, the perspective changes. First of all, rapid decolonization across Asia and Africa forced Soviet leaders and newly minted Communist regimes in Eastern Europe to rethink their earlier reluctance to engage with the non-European world—and to reconnect to prewar traditions of a socialist and nonsocialist kind. Second, the consolidation of Communist rule in China and Beijing's willingness to engage with anticolonial movements and postcolonial states forced Eastern Bloc states to return to their earlier internationalist ambitions and commitments. Finally, de-Stalinization in the Soviet Union and in other Eastern Bloc states meant that, while their policies would still be coordinated with Moscow, they were now encouraged to act more independently on the world stage. (Yugoslavia, which had split with the Soviet Union in 1948, was already doing so.)

The result was that from the 1950s a whole set of connections, interactions, trade links, and routes of circulation for ideas and people rapidly came into being. This new globalization should correctly be seen as a *project* of the USSR and other socialist states, and yet its actual shape cannot be attributed to the designs of Moscow or to any one actor alone. As was the case with prewar internationalism, the project was contested and plural from the outset. Furthermore, this new globalizing impulse did not take shape in isolation from the postwar capitalist order, which remained a source of emulation and trade; nor can it be considered separately from postcolonial efforts to create a nonaligned world order independent of the two superpowers and the former colonial empires. Rather, we can understand postwar state-socialist globalization as a process shaping and shaped by these other projects of connectivity.

Alliances between European socialist states and newly independent states in the Global South began to develop. These were based on common concerns for building economic sovereignty that kept the Leninist emphasis on national self-determination as a foundation for socialist internationalism; a shared sense of peripherality and backwardness that required a collective endeavor to be overcome, reconnecting to the anti-imperialism of earlier internationals; a shared respect for culture or tradition; and the struggle for equality and recognition in the global arena. It is in this period that we see the emergence of formal institutions to facilitate such links. These included organizations focused on trade and aid, such as the Council for Mutual Economic Assistance (CMEA, or Comecon) or the USSR's State Committee for Economic Cooperation (GKĖS), a rough parallel to Washington's US Agency for International Development (USAID). They also featured political and cultural organizations, such as Committees for Solidarity with the Peoples of Asia and Africa, which sprang up across the region. Socialist multinationals such as Yugoslavia's Energoinvest represented their state's socialist or nonaligned interests on the world stage. And they included the various cultural projects, festivals, and exchanges hosted by cities such as Moscow, Tashkent, Sofia, and Prague, which brought together artists and activists from the socialist and postcolonial worlds, setting up interactions that sometimes continued beyond and indeed outside the purview of official channels. International institutions were also essential: new alliances developed in organizations such as the United Nations, which, swelled by the ranks of newly decolonized nations, gave those previously excluded a new say in the shaping of the global economy and culture. Leftist international organizations, such as the World Peace Council or the World Federation of Trade Unions, provided other channels for exchange.

Many contributions analyze the way in which socialist states drove new forms of economic, political, and cultural interconnectedness. James Mark and Yakov Feygin explore the role that actors from the socialist world played in the swing back to an internationalization of trade in the late 1950s, after a period of isolationist economics from the 1930s. Soviet and Eastern European planning in particular can be considered one of the main globalizing forces of the mid- to late twentieth century. As China, the world's most populous nation, turned to socialism in 1949, one-third of all projects in its First Five-Year Plan were financed and executed by the USSR and East European states.[20] Tens of thousands of advisors and technicians from the socialist world flocked to all parts of the country. Odd Arne Westad called this transfer "history's biggest foreign assistance program."[21] Such expertise then proved attractive to decolonizing states in the Global South looking to build their own economic sovereignty in the late 1950s and 1960s.[22] The USSR's crash transformation from an agricultural country to one that could take on and defeat Nazi Germany, build nuclear weapons, and send rockets and humans into space—yet also develop a state in which multiple religions and nations could live together—proved an inspiration. Many postcolonial states, from Indonesia to Ghana, were thus influenced by the authoritarian socialism of the Soviet Union.[23] Smaller Eastern European states too, Łukasz Stanek shows, could be attractive models for leaders establishing new bureaucracies and modernizing their countries through central planning and social welfare. These states cleverly highlighted their own experiences of liberation from empires and of state building after the First and Second World Wars as they sought to render themselves attractive to decolonizing countries. Massimiliano Trentin explores how the German Democratic Republic (GDR), the most industrially advanced country in the bloc, promoted its expertise in agro-industrial development, an emphasis that converged with the reformist programs adopted by nationalist and left-leaning forces within the Arab world from the late fifties.

Nevertheless, we should be wary of viewing planning and development as simply an export story from North to South. Just as Moscow was not interested in a wholesale transfer of the Soviet system, the "recipient" countries were similarly intent on soliciting advice while preserving autonomy. Countries such as India and Afghanistan that experimented with five-year plans were not attracted by a Soviet-style planned economy in the narrow sense, but in ways to develop expertise and target plans accordingly.[24] Postcolonial leaders were interested in the specific techniques economists from around the world offered, and they selectively used the opinions of foreign experts to justify their own economic policies. Indeed, outreach from Eastern Europe was enmeshed in Cold War competition and as such could hand advantages over to the receiving side: locked in the struggle for international recognition with the rival Federal Republic of Germany, Berlin granted highly favorable conditions for credit and economic exchange in Syria and beyond.

Moreover, ideas and expertise flowed not only from Moscow and East European capitals and circulated between them but also from "recipient" countries back to the Eastern Bloc. Certainly the desire to export developmental visions—to show that one's system was better able to feed the vast rural populations of the Third World—was an important feature of early Cold War competition between the blocs.[25] At the same time, as David Engerman has argued for India, the "net effect of all the foreign advice" was close to zero. In this volume Steffi Marung shows that under Nikita Khrushchev the Soviet Union's ambition to modernize agriculture at home began to parallel similar processes emerging in the decolonizing states of Africa. As some African leaders turned to Moscow for support, so new opportunities for Soviet experts to prove the superiority of their own developmental vision emerged. The efficacy of Soviet agriculture in Africa, presented as the better, anti-imperialist alternative to Western blueprints for agrarian modernization, became a litmus test for the attractiveness of Soviet methods for other newly independent states. Yet these new transnational and transregional debates over culture and modernization between the socialist countries of the North and South also opened up new pathways of communication and possibilities for mutual influence, some of which could be disruptive. Such connections meant that the failures of collectivization in West Africa led some scholars to rethink their approach to the USSR's own agricultural problems and enabled African intellectuals to contribute to such debates in top Soviet journals.[26]

The appeal of the Eastern Bloc could be cultural as much as economic: Maxim Matusevich explores how Léopold Sédar Senghor, the first president of independent Senegal, was more fascinated by the potential of Russian literature and Slavic culture for African education than he was by Soviet economic models. It is important to note that Soviet claims regarding the superiority of their development model often lay in the assertion that it respected local heritage—and that preservation was part of the socialist package of modernization. Village cultures, some experts insisted, could only be saved by socialism in the face of the onslaught of capitalist modernization brought by the United States.[27] Hanna Jansen and Artemy Kalinovsky both highlight the importance of religion too: Soviet outreach in southern Asia used Islamic leaders to propagate the message that minority religious cultures were nurtured and that the USSR was an "authentic Asian power." The Soviets often appealed to minority emancipation and international solidarity rather than state-centered development projects. Such cultural diplomacy also played a role in the Sino-Soviet split. Under Khrushchev, the promotion of religious equality and appeals to a "common humanity" in Soviet diplomatic efforts to woo South Asia was understood by Beijing as Moscow's abandonment of revolution in favor of the values of Western imperialism. In the context of Tibetan rebellions of the late 1950s—when Beijing feared her Himalayan region might become "another Hungary"—Moscow's uncritical celebratory cultural universalism was seen to have the potential to inspire further uprisings on China's own ethnically and culturally distinct peripheries.

This communication was enabled in part because of the recognition of the similarities between regions in the Eastern Bloc and Global South deemed to be "peripheries"—defined as underdeveloped agricultural hinterlands far from the economic cores of the global economy. Artemy Kalinovsky and Steffi Marung draw attention to the role of the "Soviet South" (i.e., Central Asia and the Caucasus) in this regard. These now rapidly developing zones of the Soviet Union became showcases of Moscow's commitment to equitable and meaningful developmental programs. Specialists from these regions could be used to present evidence of Soviet policies of social mobility, and they claimed the climatic conditions meant that the forms of agriculture or medicine developed there would be more readily useable in South Asia or Africa. Bogdan Iacob emphasizes a similar phenomenon in Southeastern Europe, where Romanian and Bulgarian experts, as representatives from the more agrarian countries in the bloc, could present themselves not only as having experienced similar forms of economic marginalization within their own region but also possessing a more appropriate expertise to export.[28] Nevertheless, such claims were increasingly contested from the 1970s, in some cases even reshaping notions about the power of socialist development back home.

And there were further—and not exclusively economic—limitations to socialist internationalism and solidarity. The period of "socialism in one country" cast a long shadow in the form of xenophobia and suspicion that neither the USSR, nor China, nor other socialist states ever fully shed. Socialist states celebrated the connectedness of the laboring classes, but their state institutions were characterized by paranoia about the "wrong" kind of elements undermining domestic unity. This xenophobia reached its apogee with the "anticosmopolitan" campaign of the late 1940s, when ethnic Jews, who had been encouraged to use their family connections beyond the USSR to raise money for the Soviet war effort, became suspect for those same ties. But it persisted in other ways as well. Socialist countries were selective in whom they allowed to go abroad and whom they admitted. Travelers were taught to limit their enthusiasm for what they saw, particularly in capitalist countries. This xenophobia, however, was not restricted to state authorities—as Maxim Matusevich's chapter shows, it could also be reflected in popular perceptions. Creating vigilant citizens—always on the lookout for the alien and harmful but also internationalist and open to workers who looked, spoke, and acted differently—proved to be a delicate task.

Multiple Globalizations

As mentioned previously, multiple globalizing projects emerged from the socialist world. While research has so far focused on the Soviet version, contributors here stress the significant variation even within the Eastern Bloc. Most detail bilateral relationships between the GDR and Syria, the Soviet Union and West Africa and India, and China and East African countries, for instance. This is no accident of methodology: rather, it reflects the very nature of the project, which was characterized by an internationalism that drew from a Leninist legacy of self-determination that assigned a major role to the nation-state. Attempts to develop cooperation on a region-to-region basis through the United Nations often failed, and for the most part the substantial outreach was organized—often competitively—between individual socialist states. Eastern European nations at the United Nations preferred to work through the Industrial Development Organization—in which major bilateral deals to build dams or large factories could be brokered—rather than the Conference on Trade and Development (UNCTAD), in which representatives of the Global South advocated regional cooperation to break the monopoly of the great Western powers. Łukasz Stanek points to the inability of Comecon to coordinate technical assistance even with its own "less developed members"—Mongolia, Cuba, and Vietnam. Eastern Bloc countries could find themselves involved in competitive "proxy wars in expertise exports to the 'Third World.'"[29] Such bilateralism often enabled smaller Eastern European states to develop policies independently of Moscow, boosted by the legacies of their interwar engagement with a global economy that the Soviets lacked. At times the USSR encouraged this independence—particularly from the 1970s as it sought to wean bloc countries off cheap Soviet oil. Even enterprises within individual Eastern Bloc states might find themselves competing against each other. Yet as some argue here, this should not be viewed as a failure. The autarkic self-sufficiency model of national development advocated by Eastern Bloc states that refused to cooperate in their own backyard was attractive precisely for these reasons: it appealed to newly independent states outside Europe that sought economic sovereignty and admired strong autarkic states that could stand on their own. Recipients also appreciated such bilateralism as it enabled them to choose from a range of different courting partners—North African states often preferred doing business with a range of smaller Eastern European states who would bid against each other.

The People's Republic of China had its own vision of interconnectedness. Following the Sino-Soviet split of 1960, it questioned the Eastern Bloc's rhetorical division of the world into the anti-imperialist socialist camp on one hand, and the imperialist-capitalist on the other. Péter Vámos here details the alternative global view that China's Three Worlds Theory propagated: the Soviets became the aggressive superpower alongside the United States in the "First World"; Western Europe, Eastern Europe, and Japan became the developed but colonized regions of the "Second World"; and the rest, including China, were the "Third World." A politics pursued through such an imaginary aimed to isolate the Soviets from both Eastern Europe and the Afro-Asian bloc and to undermine Moscow's conception of a unified anti-imperialist world under its own leadership. Indeed, the Chinese equated the Soviet invasion of Czechoslovakia in 1968 with the American intervention in Vietnam and hence positioned the Eastern Bloc as one of those many "intermediate zones" to be understood primarily as victims of big-power imperialism. By 1970 it was anti-Sovietism, not anti-Westernism, which dominated Chinese conceptions of the world. Unlike the Eastern Bloc attempts to construct the idea of a new socialist world bound by a common anti-imperialism, the Chinese vision played down the differences between social systems—instead considering the level of development of countries as the basic classification. Such a scheme would position China as the emerging leader of less economically developed regions of the world. Thenceforth the Soviets and Eastern Europeans had to promote their visions not only against the West but also against the Chinese. This forced the Soviet Union to focus more on anti-imperial revolution—as they came to embrace the New International Economic Order (NIEO) by 1976 following a period of initial skepticism—even to the detriment of the class struggle it supported in Europe.[30] As Jeremy Friedman argued, "Soviet policy in effect now supported a view of the world in which workers in the First World and workers in the Third World were enemies."[31] The Sino-Soviet split, in other words, led to a further pluralization of socialist globalizations.

Alternative and Entangled Globalizations?

Given this background, does it make sense to invoke the existence of "one" alternative socialist world apart from a capitalist world order?[32] Certainly Eastern Bloc states deployed a rhetoric that suggested they were contributing to the construction of an alternative world, asserting that their approach to development was both distinct and superior to that offered in the West—claims that, at least until the 1970s, were often received positively in the decolonizing world.

Yet most authors in this volume place their histories in the context of what has been called a *geteilte Globalisierung*—a term developed to describe a globalization that consists of competing but unequal projects in an interconnected but still politically divided world. Similarly, many contributions illustrate that numerous actors in the socialist camp believed that they were providing an alternative to a capitalist-led globalization, while also being closely related and connected to it.[33] Using Soviet archival documents, Oscar Sanchez-Sibony engages with the idea of socialist globalization but argues that the dialectical relationship between capitalism and decolonization drew the Soviets into the widening gyre of an expanding international politics. Global capitalism, as shaped by Western financial and commercial institutions and practices, constrained and enabled Soviet relationships in the Global South, imparting its rhythms to them and dictating their rate of progress. Decolonization, meanwhile, drew the Soviets into regional politics they could do little to control or influence.

Others argue that socialist actors in Eastern Europe aimed to offer an alternative project of interconnectedness, which often became powerful precisely because its ideological roots lay in transnational, trans-systemic postwar attempts to create a new "progressive" world. These ideas not only stemmed from the regional experiences of peripheralization under nineteenth-century empires and from the experience of suffering under fascism but also drew on globally resonant progressive ideas collectively forged at international organizations prior to and after the Second World War.[34] For Hanna Jansen and Maxim Matusevich, the Soviets drew on such debates regarding cultural and racial equality that were commonly held at major international organizations such as UNESCO and did not map clearly onto the ideological boundaries of the Cold War. When we investigate Soviet or Eastern European experiences in the Third World, we thus need to bear in mind that their influence might be as much the result of their effective advocacy of progressive ideas of cultural or economic development that existed across blocs rather than accept the socialist states' own rhetorical claims that they provided clear alternatives in a politically divided world.

In fact, the postcolonial moment in many ways also increased contact between the Eastern Bloc with Western Europe and North America. Experts from the bloc worked internationally, staffed centers, and took up postings in which they were not shut off from the capitalist world: many traveled, worked for UN organizations and alongside Western colleagues, and engaged in broader debates around, for example, underdevelopment, inequality, culture, and heritage.[35] In this regard Eastern European experts reconnected with the internationalism of the interwar period and before; Soviet experts, by contrast, after a much longer experience of Stalinism and socialism in one country, often had to forge such connections anew and were less adept at it.[36] Łukasz Stanek shows how, once "on the ground," Eastern European architects saw themselves not as representatives of a Socialist Bloc, but rather as part of the "one world" of the international culture of modern architecture. Even if socialist experts articulated a belief in welfare, equality, and respect for tradition that distinguished their form of development from that of their capitalist counterparts, there were nevertheless important similarities in their offer to the South[37]—both promoted urbanization; Fordist production; technological development (and environmental damage); an appreciation of science and higher education; the merits of hygiene and medicine; mass mobilization; the spread of bureaucracy; and efforts to control and manage populations.[38]

Others maintain that attempts at a specifically socialist globalization in the 1960s laid the foundation for a "transideological" integrative globalization in the 1970s.[39] During détente in the mid-1970s, as Mark and Feygin argue, so-called tripartite industrial projects brought together Western and Eastern European firms in development projects in Africa and elsewhere, moving beyond the bilateral schemes that had dominated a decade previously.[40] From this perspective, European cooperation was discovered in the Third World. Additionally, some socialist states gave up on exporting a specific socialist industrial modernity to the Global South, simply viewing less developed countries as a source of raw materials, just as their Western counterparts did.[41] Massimiliano Trentin explores how, from the mid-1970s, Berlin tried to adapt its practice of cooperation to the standards of the international markets to reap more profits and moderated its anti-imperialist, militant stance in the region to preserve its positions in a Middle East in which conservative, anticommunist forces were back on the offensive.

By the 1970s some partners of the Eastern Bloc questioned whether the socialist states were still committed to a new world in which the continuing struggle against the legacies of imperialism would be prioritized. Moscow often faced resistance from those it wished to assist, especially in circumstances in which its domestic economic goals did not always sit easily with its ideological commitments. From the 1960s Comecon countries tried to establish more economically advantageous forms of trade with the developing world as part of an "international socialist division of labor." Since that meant that agricultural economies would continue to be commodity producers rather than developing industries, critics rightly asked whether socialist globalization was all that different from the capitalist variety. This opened the Eastern Bloc up to further Chinese criticism: Soviet aid was presented as paternalistic and encouraging dependency, whereas Beijing's assistance, or so it was claimed, relied on principles such as equality and mutual benefit and promoted self-reliance.[42] By the 1970s many socialist states from Africa and Asia began to take this view too: in 1976 their representatives at UNCTAD popularized the term *Global North*—a notion that served to lump developed capitalist and socialist states together, hence implying that there was an increasingly less real distinction between the modernizing globalization projects pursued by both the Soviet Bloc and the West.

Alternative Globalizations and Domestic Socialist Culture

Socialist globalization was a state-initiated project, and one socialist leaders presumed they could control. Yet the consequences of the processes it unleashed were unpredictable, especially when we consider its impact on domestic culture. From the late 1950s socialist states in the Eastern Bloc also chose to use these internationalist engagements "at home." Through solidarity movements, commemorations, educational initiatives, and mass media coverage, citizens of socialist states were socialized to identify their own national projects with progressive anti-imperialist struggles around the world.[43] Some authors suggest that it is far too simple to see such internationalism as an artificial solidarity imposed from above with little societal resonance or longer-term legacies.[44] Rather, they explore how internationalism was built on a variety of intellectual and cultural traditions and had an appeal across a wide range of political currents. For Adam Kola and Łukasz Stanek, the breadth of Polish sympathy for anti-imperialist movements was a result of a widely held memory of their own national experience as a partitioned colony kept as an economic hinterland serving the needs of other parts of Europe. Such engagements also had appeal in that they could make citizens feel important in the world—as Maxim Matusevich's exploration of the 1957 International Youth Festival in the Soviet Union shows.[45] In the case of Romania, as Bogdan Iacob argues, engagement with anticolonial struggles elsewhere could provide a language of resistance to one's subaltern status, even within the bloc. An anti-imperialist internationalism in an age of decolonization provided a new language of political expression that leaders could put to many uses—both orthodox and oppositional.

Such internationalist outreach also brought students, exiles, and labor migrants into societies that had previously experienced low levels of migration from the extra-European world. As Alena K. Alamgir and Christina Schwenkel, as well as Maxim Matusevich argue, the arrival of these newcomers was often due not to the needs of the host society—as was the case with migrant labor in the Western world at this time—but rather to their having been pushed out by their home countries, which lacked capacity in technical education or sought to export laborers for whom they had no jobs.[46] Until the mid-1970s the hosting of such communities was publicly presented as a token of fraternal aid by more developed Eastern European countries. The experiences of such incomers were mixed: some endured racism, although incidents in this period appear to have been infrequent. Still, with authorities reluctant to accept that racism could be a feature of the socialist system, the state repeatedly failed to deal with those episodes that did occur.[47] Maxim Matusevich examines another aspect of this interaction by focusing on the experience of African students in the Soviet Union. He asks whether, despite its avowed commitment to antiracism, the USSR was actually prepared to deal with the racial politics that decolonization brought to the fore. A regime that had made antiracism and anticolonialism the centerpieces of its Cold War stance vis-à-vis the West often found itself unprepared to deal with the complexities of race relations—in the United States, in Europe, in former colonies, and eventually even within its own borders.

Nevertheless, many others came away with positive impressions of their stays. Although few returned as communists, many nursed a sense of gratitude and respect toward their host countries.[48] For citizens of the socialist world, the presence of foreign students confirmed a somewhat paternalistic sense of the economic and cultural superiority of their own societies: it was the rest of the world, after all, that came to learn from them. Although student and migrant numbers remained high until the end of state socialism, attitudes toward outsiders changed dramatically in the 1980s.[49] Schemes that had begun as training programs and as part of technical aid became vehicles to mitigate labor shortages. No longer seen as evidence of the Eastern Bloc's confident entry on to the global scene, migrants, now framed as economically necessary rather that the object of political solidarity, came to be demonized as competitors for scarce resources—and faced heightened levels of racism.[50]

Many contributors chart how this global engagement could disrupt the order of socialist societies in Eastern Europe. The socialist world's outreach involved often incompatible understandings of culture, sometimes with colonialist overtones; it raised uncomfortable questions for Soviets about how authentic their version of culture truly was. Central Asians who traveled to other Muslim countries as representatives of the Soviet state were frequently challenged on the degree of religious freedom or the ability to publish in their own language back home. The language of uplift or liberation that communist countries used abroad could be used by groups at home in their claims for rights or recognition. Hanna Jansen's contribution highlights how Khrushchev's pitch to the Third World embraced the ideas of a spiritual humanism and cultural equality between East and West—for instance, parading the freedom of Muslims or Buddhists to worship as evidence of the Soviet Union's respect for its minority non-European cultures. Although these were often misleading exaggerations, religious leaders at home could use the rhetoric to argue greater freedom for cultural expression.[51] The presence of others who came from fraternal socialist nations could be disturbing too. African students were far readier to challenge authority in public spaces—whether in Moscow, Leningrad, Minsk, or Baku. Moreover, their relative wealth and ability to travel marked them as fascinating cosmopolitans with links to the alien and exotic, whose freedom could undermine Soviet citizens' faith in their system's rhetoric. Labor migrants, concentrated in certain areas and unable to send convertible currency home, would often buy goods to send—causing shortages of consumer products and resentment in local populations.[52]

Alternative Globalizations and the End of State Socialism

The study of state socialism's fall in Eastern Europe remains rather parochial. Most of the literature focuses on the collapse either as a regional story or as one of rejoining the West. Little work considers how relationships with the Global South were part of the story of state socialism's decline. There has been scant interest in exploring the importance of the connections between these regions in explaining the decline of alternative forms of global interconnectedness or the relationship between the collapse of Western European empires across the twentieth century and the fall of their Soviet counterpart at its end.[53]

The fall of state socialism needs to be written into the history of multiple attempts to fashion a global economy. As James Mark and Yakov Feygin argue, it was not that the socialist world rejected a more economically interconnected world; it was rather that their versions of connectivity failed to retain the power to shape the global economy. From the late 1970s, the power to set the terms of the global economy had moved to international institutions such as the International Monetary Fund (IMF) and World Bank, where such countries held little sway. The debt crisis of the 1980s was the final nail in the coffin of this "alternative globalization": it undermined the growing alternative forms of economic cooperation and trade of the 1970s, as countries in both the Eastern Bloc and Global South prioritized the repayment of loans to Western institutions over their debts to each other and, through their reliance on Western institutions of debt, became gradually absorbed into the capitalist financial system—often long before 1989. As Alamgir and Schwenkel argue, the 1980s also witnessed the decline in the concept of political solidarity that had held socialist countries together; instead, trade relationships were more often exclusively based around economic self-interest, and labor migrants from socialist countries such as Cuba and Vietnam were viewed as commodities, commonly treated in racialized terms or seen as unwelcome competitors for scarce goods.

Connections between Eastern Europe and what was becoming known as the Global South also played a role in explaining the wider global trend away from central planning and toward a reduction in size of the welfare state. China's embrace of entrepreneurship, marketization, and openness to world trade was a key moment in the erosion of faith in the Soviet model of planning.[54] Middle Eastern regimes increasingly found the statist GDR model unattractive, while some liberal GDR economists promoted the liberalization of the Syrian economy from the mid-1970s. Steffi Marung argues that the failures of Soviet-style agricultural modernization in Africa found their way into Soviet journals and expert debates and added to dissatisfaction with Khrushchev's modernization project, opening the way for the reorganization of farming under Leonid Brezhnev.

Nevertheless, there were alternative models of transformation in the 1980s. Growing interconnectedness or globalization was not necessarily the same as Westernization, and scholars have too often fallen into the trap of a retroactive teleology, in which all worldwide entanglements were predestined to merge into free markets and liberal democracies. Socialist states were in fact still providing alternative models for global economic engagement in the 1980s. And for some, integration into a more connected global economy seemed for a time to be compatible with state socialism: James Mark and Yakov Feygin, for instance, note in their chapter the attractiveness of authoritarian transitions to an open, globalized economy—akin to Chile's or Spain's experiments in the 1970s—for Eastern European elites in the 1980s.[55] In such accounts, the democratic explosion of 1989 becomes only one of many routes through which socialist-era interconnectedness might have developed.

The growth of opposition to state socialism can also be viewed in the long-term context of the collapse of European empires, decolonization, and the powerful political and cultural forces these processes unleashed. Despite the fact that the end of state socialism from Berlin to Vladivostok was accompanied by, and entangled with, the collapse of the Soviet "empire," this process has seldom been compared with the collapse of other European empires. Adam Kola, for instance, highlights that, although postcolonial thinking has been used to compare Eastern Europe's postcommunist identity struggles with other regions that have thrown off empires, there has been until recently little attempt to make sense of the period 1989–91 as one in a longer, linked chain of "end of empire" stories.[56]

The interconnectedness of socialist culture—at the level of everyday interactions and elite contacts—deepened as a response to the global processes of decolonization that followed the Second World War.[57] These interactions occurred in particular on peripheries of the Soviet-dominated bloc—in Eastern

Europe and Central Asia. Yet this played out differently in the two regions. In the 1960s a language of anticolonialism was used effectively by Soviet elites and experts to bring the experiences of the "Soviet South" (i.e., Central Asia and the Caucasus) into a closer relationship with the Global South. The former was used by the Soviet authorities to show how their cultural and economic model could provide meaningful development to areas formerly marginalized within empires—wherever they may be in the world. Yet by the 1980s, as the promises of development for the Soviet Union's southern periphery faded, the same anticolonial language that had been popularized in the 1960s could be turned against the Soviet state by more assertive Central Asian elites. Many now characterized the Soviet Union as an imperial power that had confined Central Asia to the periphery, rendering it akin to the Third World in the global system.

On the western edge of the European socialist camp, the oppositional use of anticolonialism was at its height in the 1960s: left-wing Polish "68ers" such as Jacek Kuroń or Karol Modzelewski decried the bureaucratic turn in Polish socialism by invoking the commonalities with their radical compatriots in the South, whereas conservative exile groups and oppositionists hoped that the collapse of European empires in Africa would act as a prelude to the end of the Soviet control of Eastern Europe.[58] The differences in the two cases had much to do with the proximity of the region to Western Europe: a younger European generation forged cultural ties across the Iron Curtain despite limited mobility and utilized anticolonial ways of thinking to express dissatisfaction with the political status quo—whether that be the colonization of Europe by either the United States or USSR or the excessive centralization of power.[59]

The global anticolonial explosion of the 1950s also contributed to the articulation of more self-assertive national and regional identities in the bloc. Iacob's chapter examines the role of the United Nations Educational, Scientific, and Cultural Organization (UNESCO) as a space of intellectual and cultural transmission between Southeast European countries and the Global South. He argues that the encounter with newly self-confident regions whose histories and values had been sidelined under European empires encouraged academics and politicians in Southeastern Europe to rethink their own place in Europe and the world. Drawing on newly assertive anticolonial discourses, leaders began to assert the notion of a Balkan identity more forcefully, to challenge the region's marginalization as a "periphery" in the world system, and to assert their own importance as contributors to a broader European culture. Such discourses enabled these intellectual cultures not only to challenge their marginalization within their own region but also to discover a broader European identity.[60] Such ideological shifts played a role in the collapse of communism and the so-called return to the West.

Yet unlike their Central Asian counterparts in the 1980s, Eastern European dissidents did not consider themselves part of a broader anticolonial movement beyond the Soviet Bloc. Certainly, the young 1960s oppositional figures and groups, many of whom would develop into dissidents in the 1970s and 1980s, had their initial experience of opposition molded by this leftist internationalism. By the 1980s an increasingly assertive nationalism, devoid of socialist anti-imperialist rhetoric, and often explicitly antisocialist in tone, predominated—and called for a recreation of national culture and a "return to Europe." As Kim Christiaens and Idesbald Goddeeris argue, the international imagination of the Polish sixties generation—who had been socialized in the age of the Cuban Revolution and the Vietnamese War—was significant in so far as it engendered an internationalism that contributed to the outward-facing nature of the struggle of the largest opposition movement in the history of the Eastern Bloc—the trade union Solidarność (Solidarity) in Poland. Nevertheless, the Polish opposition did not make use of analogies with the fight against other empires because—even if they had sympathies with such struggles—any anticolonial language was vitiated by its associations with a Marxist lexicon that they rejected out of hand. Solidarność was therefore not able to lend full-throated support to the anti-apartheid struggle of the African National Congress, despite the commonalities in their struggles as trade unions fighting for workers' rights—both because the later struggles of decolonization in Africa were supported by the Warsaw communists and because right-wing Poles in exile in South Africa gave generously to support Solidarność's anticommunism. Only the struggle of the mujahideen in Afghanistan—interpreted as a parallel national struggle against Soviet domination—caught the eye of Solidarność's leaders. Yet if anti-imperialism might no longer unite, a newly dominant antitotalitarian paradigm could: connections between Latin America and Eastern Europe emerged out of a shared political identity that prized the common democratic struggle against centralized authoritarian power over older Cold War divisions between right and leftist movements. It was for this reason that anticommunist Solidarność could find common cause with the leftists who resisted Pinochet in Chile.

Yet the internationalism that had been cultivated since the 1950s continued to shape opposition in the last years of state socialism in important ways. As Quinn Slobodian argues, the GDR had socialized its citizens to think internationally, to claim the right to criticize ethical infractions, and to conceive of themselves as a part of a civilized world community that transcended their immediate national borders. This, Slobodian explains, was one reason why the violence that followed the Tiananmen Square protests had such an impact: GDR citizens reclaimed the meaning of solidarity, protesting against their own regime for betraying its values by supporting the repressive forces of the Chinese state. Such lessons were eventually absorbed by communists across the whole of Eastern Europe: elites in Hungary, Poland, and the GDR, having witnessed the "Chinese solution" to protest, lost their appetite for similar repressive measures in the bloc and, with the exception of Romania, did not resort to force in the defense of their respective regimes.[61]

Elites in the Eastern Bloc were turning away from the Global South too, long before the final collapse of their systems. In many of the smaller countries of Eastern Europe, the more global geography of socialist expert cultures of the 1950s and 1960s began to shrivel in the context of the Helsinki Process, through which the reorientation toward Europe and the West became slowly institutionalized. With this re-Europeanization, socialist internationalism reverted to the geographies of the nineteenth century, a return serving as a prelude to the reperipheralization of the region in the context of European Union (EU) enlargement.[62] The shift in the Soviet Union came slightly later; yet, already in the early 1980s, scholars specializing in the "socialist world system," such as philosophers Iuriy Novopashin and Anatoliy Butenko, were arguing that "contradictions" in the socialist camp could become "antagonistic"—which ran counter to the orthodox view.[63] Mikhail Gorbachev translated this line of thinking into his political doctrine. The new Communist Party of the Soviet Union (CPSU) program passed by the Twenty-Seventh Party Congress in 1985 spoke only of "sympathies" for the aspirations of postcolonial countries and called for socialist-oriented states to develop their economies "mainly through their own efforts."[64] This would then lead to a precipitous decline in development aid for the countries in the Global South in general, and Africa in particular. Gorbachev's "new thinking" in foreign policy, which expressed reservations toward military support and asserted the need for a reduction of "ideological fervor" in relations with Asia and Africa, was a reaction both to a broader disillusionment in the Soviet partnership with the Global South and to the challenges posed by the crisis at home.[65]

Contradictory Legacies

The wave of economic, cultural, and political globalizations that took off in the 1950s included the socialist world. The Somali-Italian writer Igiaba Scego recalled how in the 1970s she could easily travel between Mogadishu, Rome, and Prague, where her brother studied and how this compared favorably with the restriction of movement she and her Somali family faced after 1989. From her perspective, the world of the Cold War, which Europeans associate with barbwire borders, was in some ways more interconnected than the contemporary world.[66] The European, Asian, African, and Latin American parts of the socialist world had increasingly integrated among themselves. If it was not for socialist globalization, there would have been no Mozambican and Angolan contract workers in Saxony, no Chinese development aid workers in Tirana, no Soviet-Cuban encounters in Addis Ababa, no Cuban female factory workers in Hungary, and no Polish engineers in Ghana. North Koreans would not have shared their preferred architectural styles with colleagues in Bucharest, their expertise in stadium choreography with Ethiopians, and their military strategies with Mexican and Namibian guerrillas. Southern Yemenis would not have studied alongside Sri Lankans at universities in Ukraine, and Vietnamese and Cuban doctors would not have worked in the Congo and Angola. These multiple connections and encounters had an impact on the political economies of postcolonial states, shaped new patterns of social and economic mobility transregionally, and still inform new modes of political opposition in the Global South.[67]

For Russia and Eastern Europe, it is tempting to see this story of alternative globalizations as a relic of a lost world: the product of a particular moment bookended by the acceleration of decolonization after the Second World War and the collapse of state socialism and socialist movements in Europe, Africa, and some parts of Asia in the 1980s and 1990s. In Eastern Europe in particular, the end of Communist regimes seemed to promise a final wrenching away of the region from the temptation of socialist internationalism and toward a European identity and Western integration.[68] In Romania, which clung to its extra-European relationships with greater steadfastness than any other of its socialist neighbors, those who opposed Nicolae Ceauşescu certainly saw it this way. In the well-known "Letter of Six," composed by disgruntled members of the politburo in 1989, it was precisely this tearing away of Romania from Europe that had to be ended: "Romania is and remains a European country and as such must advance along with the Helsinki process and not turn against it. You [Nicolae Ceauşescu] . . . cannot remove Romania to Africa."[69] As state socialism collapsed, so an earlier anti-imperialist socialist internationalism was vilified. In one extreme example, in 1992 former Bulgarian leaders Todor Zhivkov and Andrey Lukanov (a former prime minister) and twenty Communist Party officials were accused of economic sabotage, because between 1986 and 1989 they had approved financial aid and loans to Communist parties in countries such as Cuba, Nicaragua, and Laos. International solidarity was now recast as a source of incapacitating increases in foreign debt, and hence a criminal activity. The Eastern European left did not draw on the legacies of the anticolonial internationalism of the Cold War period either, as their counterparts in the West and South more commonly did. This was a legacy of both the instrumentalization of such internationalism by former communist regimes and their effective re-Europeanization under late and postsocialism.

Certainly, "the fall" in 1989–91 meant the demonization and effective silencing of these earlier multiple, alternative socialist-led global projects. In most accounts this moment represented the victory of capitalist globalization—which exerted a powerful influence over both history and popular memory. In the case of Poland, for example, a new, self-confident global positioning was legitimated both by the country's successful accession to the European Union and by its historical experience in the nonimperial, multinational

Polish-Lithuanian Commonwealth since the ourteenth century. Their national narrative simply jumped over the twentieth century to explain why Poland could provide a model for development and democratization for the Global South.[70] Such triumphalism usually obscured the more complex range of legacies of socialist-era trade and geopolitical imaginaries and alliances.

Yet this story has not lost its relevance—and nor has its influence entirely gone away. First, we can ask how these alternative globalizations helped to shape the forms of capitalism and global integration that came to dominate after 1989. A Western-led financialized globalization, which developed powerfully in the 1970s, did not grow in a vacuum but was shaped through interaction with the socialist-led forms of interconnectivity. There is much to be said for the view that the integration of the socialist world into a globalized economy cannot be viewed simply as a story of defeat, but one of common contributions to the creation of modern globalized economic forms from the 1970s. Leslie Sklair and others have explored the rise of "socialist multinationals" in the late 1970s, which were "more active in the rest of the world than TNCs [transnational corporations] from capitalist countries were in Comecon countries."[71] The Soviet Union's desire to protect their dollar reserves was instrumental in the late 1950s in the creation of the so-called Eurodollar market, which was to become by some distance the largest source of global finance in the late twentieth century.[72] The threat of socialist globalization helped to shape the forms of capitalist globalization as we see them today: US elites, for instance, enabled the consolidation of the power of their oil multinationals in the 1960s—against campaigns to break them up as excessive monopolies—in order to counter the Soviet challenge.[73] The United States was also prepared to let Japanese and Korean economies grow without the interference of American corporations and guaranteed access to its large home market, rather than let them become peripheries open to other ideological influences.[74] Indeed, the rise of neoliberalism and the Washington consensus has been understood as a reaction to the power of the challenge from a new alternative world order in the 1970s.[75]

Second, we can consider whether the interconnections created in this period have actually disappeared or if these encounters still have political, cultural, and economic ramifications all over the world. In those countries where Communist regimes survived the upheavals of the early 1990s, the influences are certainly easy to discern. Following the Western backlash against China after Tiananmen and the collapse of Communist regimes across Eurasia, China looked to reinvigorate its connections with Africa, drawing on earlier internationalist rhetoric of the common cause against a paternalistic West.[76] The development of Cuba's post–Cold War "professionalized" internationalism—which mainly focused on medical aid and generated significant hard currency for the country—was rooted in the experience they gained in their delivering of military and civilian aid during the conflict in Angola (1975–91).[77] Even where Socialist regimes did collapse, legacies of such travel and exchange remained. Susan Bayly coined the term *socialist ecumene* to describe the endurance of socialist-era values in forms of trade and assistance to other parts of the world in a similar peripheral position in the neoliberal globalized order.[78] Socialist-era trading networks and labor migration from Eastern Europe to the Far East still survive, while patterns of migration established across the Comecon states now shape patterns of transnational religious evangelism.[79] The hundreds of thousands of alumni from "socialist" universities work in almost all the states of the Global South. Vietnamese restaurants are legion in Berlin, as are North Korean statues all over Africa. The small shops of former Vietnamese guest workers (derogatively called *Fidschis*) became an indispensable part of the consumer infrastructure in most cities in Eastern Germany.[80] There continued to be a substantial presence of Russian tourists, artists, and freelance online workers in Southeast Asia. Even NATO and the United States have drawn on some of the connections of the socialist world: in 2003, former Yugoslav engineers were enlisted in the search for Saddam Hussein, as they had built many of the dictator's underground bunkers. In the War in Afghanistan, Czech army pilots, who had been trained with Soviet technology during the Cold War, instructed both Afghans and Americans to fly Russian helicopters—better suited to local conditions than US-made machines.[81] Scholarly literature does not often consider the amount of socialist content left in these connections, but certainly the roots of these contacts go back to entanglements within the socialist world during the Cold War.

The idea of alternative globalizations also retains its relevance if we consider this postwar moment of socialist-led globalization as part of a longer story of searching for political and economic alternatives in what has been called the global "peripheries" or "semi-peripheries." Indeed, the current popular and academic reawakening of interest in "entanglements" within the socialist world does result from a political context. The Western triumphalist vision of the 1990s has given way to an acknowledgment that large parts of the former socialist world do not follow the path of Western modernization without question. China resisted the "liberal" in liberal capitalism and became a successful global player in Asia and Africa, and reached out to reestablish links with Eastern Europe with its 16+1 strategy. After the shock waves of the Boris Yeltsin years, Russia under Vladimir Putin redefined its global role, pursuing its ideas of a polycentric world, often in explicitly anti-Western alliances, which tended to be built on connections of Cold War Soviet internationalism, albeit stripped of the earlier socialist content. The secular dictators of Syria and Egypt enjoyed military support from the Kremlin, just as they had done fifty years ago. Vietnam, following the Chinese path of Communist rule combined with economic liberalism, remained a strategic partner for Russia in the area of military-technical cooperation. Both Egypt and Vietnam signed free trade agreements with the Eurasian Customs Union, Russia's great "alternative" geopolitical project under Putin. Cuba, Venezuela, and Nicaragua, the latter again ruled by the former socialist Daniel Ortega, supported—at least rhetorically—Russia's neoimperialism in the South Caucasus and Ukraine.

This also has been true for the smaller states of Eastern Europe. A turn toward Europe and Western integration that began long before 1989—but was confirmed by the changes of that year—is now under question. In Viktor Orbán's Hungary, for instance, political figures have rediscovered links with Moscow and a shared contempt for Western liberalism. From 2010 the conservative and anticommunist Hungarian FIDESZ administration adopted a policy of "global opening" (*globális nyitás*). To balance a declining economic growth within Europe and a perceived Western liberal cultural imperialism from the European Union, it promoted the intensification of educational and economic links between Hungary, East Asia, and Africa—and with it the relationships that had been forged in the late socialist period were rediscovered.[82] The study of socialist globalization is not a matter of nostalgia. It enlightens not only the forms of the second wave of modern globalization from the 1950s but also the behavior of world regions and many shifts in contemporary geopolitics.

Notes

1. For globalization as a form of Western imperialism, see Andreas Eckert and Shalini Randeria, *Vom Imperialismus zum Empire: Nicht-westliche Perspektiven auf Globalisierung* (Frankfurt: Suhrkamp, 2009).

2. Contemporary political science took the claim of an expanding Soviet-dominated world seriously indeed. See, e.g., Raymond L. Garthoff, *Détente and Confrontation: American-Soviet Relations from Nixon to Reagan* (Washington: Brookings Institution, 1985).

3. See, e.g., Johanna Bockman, "Socialist Globalization and Capitalist Neocolonialism: The Economic Ideas behind the New International Economic Order," *Humanity* 6, no. 1 (2015): 109–128; Steven L. B. Jensen, *The Making of International Human Rights: The 1960s, Decolonization, and the Reconstruction of Global Values* (New York: Cambridge University Press, 2016).

4. For an account along these lines, see André Steiner, "The Globalization Process and the Eastern Bloc Countries in the 1970s and 1980s," *European Review of History* 2 (2014): 165–181.

5. Michael Geyer and Charles Bright, "World History in a Global Age," *The American Historical Review* 100, no. 4 (1995): 1042.

6. Ibid., 1049.

7. See, e.g., Christopher Bayly, *The Birth of the Modern World 1780–1914* (Oxford: Wiley, 2004); Jürgen Osterhammel, *The Transformation of the World: A Global History of the Nineteenth Century* (Princeton, NJ: Princeton University Press, 2015); Jürgen Osterhammel

and Akira Iriye, eds., *Global Interdependence: The World after 1945* (Cambridge: Harvard University Press, 2014).

8. In this regard Asia has received increasing attention, see, e.g., Andre Gunder Frank, *ReOrient: Global Economy in the Asian Age* (Berkeley: University of California Press, 1998); Kenneth Pomeranz, *The Great Divergence: China, Europe, and the Making of the Modern World Economy* (Princeton: Princeton University Press, 2000).

9. Jane Burbank and Frederick Cooper, *Empires in World History: Power and the Politics of Difference* (Princeton, NJ: Princeton University Press, 2010); Martin Thomas and Andrew Thompson, "Empire and Globalization: From 'High Imperialism' to Decolonisation," *The International History Review* 36, no. 1 (2014): 142–170; Anthony G. Hopkins, "Rethinking Decolonization," *Past & Present* 200 (2008): 211–247.

10. On this divide, see Sharad Chari and Katherine Verdery, "Thinking between the Posts: Postcolonialism, Postsocialism, and Ethnography after the Cold War," *Comparative Studies in Society and History* 1 (2009): 16. Countering this, see David Chioni Moore, "Is the Post- in Postcolonial the Post- in Post-Soviet? Toward a Global Postcolonial Critique," *PMLA* 116, no. 1 (2001): 111–128; Nikolay R. Karkova and Zhivka Valiavicharska, "Rethinking East-European Socialism: Notes toward an Anticapitalist Decolonial Methodology," *Interventions*, 20 no. 6 (2018): 785–813.

11. Histories of globalization in Eastern Europe usually start in 1989. See, e.g., Katalin Fábián, ed., *Globalization: Perspectives from Central and Eastern Europe* (Bingley, UK: Emerald, 2007). For a challenge, see Besnik Pula, *Globalization Under and After Socialism: The Evolution of Transnational Capital in Central and Eastern Europe* (Stanford, CA: Stanford University Press, 2018).

12. David Engerman, "The Second World's Third World," *Kritika* 12, no. 1 (2011): 183–211; Odd Arne Westad, *The Global Cold War: Third World Intervention and the Making of Our Time* (Cambridge: Cambridge University Press, 2007).

13. Matthew Connelly, "Rethinking the Cold War and Decolonization: The Grand Strategy of the Algerian War for Independence," *International Journal of Middle East Studies* 33, no. 2 (2001): 221–245.

14. For the growing literature, see, e.g., Engerman, "Second World's Third World"; Philip Muehlenbeck, *Czechoslovakia in Africa, 1945–1968* (Basingstoke: Palgrave, 2016); Jeremy Friedman, *Shadow Cold War: The Sino-Soviet Competition for the Third World* (Chapel Hill: University of North Carolina Press, 2015); Tobias Rupprecht, *Soviet Internationalism after Stalin: Interaction and Exchange between the USSR and Latin America during the Cold War* (Cambridge: Cambridge University Press, 2015); Artemy Kalinovsky and Sergey Radchenko, eds., *The End of the Cold War and the Third World: New Perspectives on Regional Conflict* (New York: Routledge, 2011); Ragna Boden, *Die Grenzen der Weltmacht: Sowjetische Indonesienpolitik von Stalin bis Brežnev* (Stuttgart: Franz Steiner Verlag, 2006); Andreas Hilger, ed., *Die Sowjetunion und die Dritte Welt: UdSSR, Staatssozialismus und Antikolonialismus im Kalten Krieg 1945–1991* (Munich: De Gruyter Oldenbourg, 2009); Sergey Mazov, *A Distant Front in the Cold War: The USSR in West Africa and the Congo, 1956–1964* (Stanford: Stanford University Press, 2010); Christine Phillou, "Introduction: USSR South: Postcolonial Worlds in the Soviet Imaginary," *Comparative Studies of South Asia, Africa and the Middle East* 33 (2013): 197–200; Nataša Miškovič, Harald Fischer-Tiné, and Nada Boskovska, eds., *The Non-Alignment Movement and the Cold War: Delhi–Bandung–Belgrade* (London: Routledge, 2014); Petr Zidek, *Československo a francouzská Afrika 1948–1968* (Prague: Libri, 2006);

and for the effort of bringing into communication Eastern European history and global history, see, e.g., Martin Aust, ed., *Globalisierung imperial und sozialistisch: Russland und die Sowjetunion in der Globalgeschichte 1851–1991* (Frankfurt am Main and New York: Campus, 2013).

15. Arguments about the specificity of the mid-nineteenth century transformations can be found also in the major overviews, such as Bayly, *Birth of the Modern World* and Osterhammel, *Transformation of the World*; Geyer and Bright, "World History in a Global Age"; Frederick Cooper, "What Is the Concept of Globalization Good For? An African Historian's Perspective," *African Affairs* 100 (2001): 189–213.

16. Susan Zimmermann, *GrenzÜberschreitungen: Internationale Netzwerke, Organisationen, Bewegungen und die Politik der globalen Ungleichheit vom 17. bis zum 21. Jahrhundert* (Vienna: Mandelbaum-Verlag, 2010).

17. Kevin Callahan, "'Performing Inter-Nationalism' in Stuttgart in 1907: French and German Socialist Nationalism and the Political Culture of an International Socialist Congress," *International Review of Social History* 45, no. 1 (2000): 51–87; Christine Collette, "Friendly Spirit, Comradeship, and Good-Natured Fun: Adventures in Socialist Internationalism," *International Review of Social History* 48, no. 2 (2003): 225–244; Robert Service, "Russian Marxism and Its London Colony before the October 1917 Revolution," *SEER (The Slavonic and East European Review)* 88, nos. 1–2 (2010): 359–376.

18. Austin Jersild, "The Soviet State as Imperial Scavenger: 'Catch Up and Surpass' in the Transnational Socialist Bloc, 1950–1960," *The American Historical Review* 116, no. 1 (2011): 109–132.

19. Hakim Adi, *Pan-Africanism and Communism: The Communist International, Africa and the Diaspora, 1919–1939* (Trenton, NJ: Africa World Press, 2013); Holger Weiss, *Framing a Radical African Atlantic: African American Agency, West African Intellectuals, and the International Trade Union Committee of Negro Workers* (Leiden: Brill, 2014).

20. On various bloc countries in China, see Austin Jersild, *The Sino-Soviet Alliance: An International History* (Chapel Hill: University of North Carolina Press, 2014).

21. Odd Arne Westad, *Restless Empire: China and the World since 1750* (London: Vintage/Random House, 2013), 304.

22. For an overview of the field, see Engerman, "The Second World's Third World"; Tobias Rupprecht, "Die Sowjetunion und die Welt im Kalten Krieg: Neue Forschungsperspektiven auf eine vermeintlich hermetisch abgeschlossene Gesellschaft," *Jahrbücher für Geschichte Osteuropas* 3 (2010): 381–399; William S. Logan, *Hanoi: Biography of a City* (Seattle, WA: University of Washington Press, 2000); Westad, *The Global Cold War*; Muehlenbeck, *Czechoslovakia in Africa*; Oscar Sanchez-Sibony, *Red Globalization: The Political Economy of the Soviet Cold War from Stalin to Khrushchev* (New York: Cambridge University Press, 2014), chapter 5.

23. Francis Fukuyama, *Political Order and Political Decay: From the Industrialization to the Globalization of Democracy* (London: Profile Books, 2014), 328–334.

24. David C. Engerman, "Learning from the East: Soviet Experts and India in the Era of Competitive Coexistence," *Comparative Studies in South Asia, Africa, and the Middle East* 33, no. 2 (2013): 230; David C. Engerman, *The Price of Aid: The Economic Cold War in India* (Cambridge, MA: Harvard University Press, 2018).

25. On the competition with the United States over whose technology and know-how could best feed people—and how that led the United States to invest in aid to India in the

1950s, see Nick Cullather, *The Hungry World: America's Cold War Battle against Poverty in Asia* (Cambridge, MA: Harvard University Press, 2010).

26. On failing development and cooperation schemes, see also Alessandro Iandolo, "The Rise and Fall of the 'Soviet Model of Development' in West Africa, 1957–64," *Cold War History* 12, no. 4 (2012): 683–704.

27. James Mark and Péter Apor, "Socialism Goes Global: Decolonization and the Making of a New Culture of Internationalism in Socialist Hungary, 1956–1989," *Journal of Modern History* 87, no. 4 (2015): 852–891; Paul Betts, "Humanity's New Heritage: UNESCO and the Rewriting of World History," *Past and Present* 228 (2015): 249–285.

28. Also note that by the 1980s, according to Victor Petrov, Bulgaria had developed a highly advanced computing industry directed at a market outside Europe.

29. Łukasz Stanek, "Socialist Networks and the Internationalization of Building Culture after 1945," *ABE Journal* 6 (2004), http://abe.revues.org/1266.

30. Friedman, *Shadow Cold War*, 207–208.

31. Ibid., 213.

32. Zsuzsa Gille, "Is There a Global Postsocialist Condition?" *Global Society* 24 (2010): 1–12.

33. On "shared and fragmented globalization," see Eckert and Randeria, *Vom Imperialismus Zum Empire*; Osterhammel and Iriye, *Global Interdependence*.

34. On Eastern European actors in international organizations before and after the First World War, see Katja Naumann, "Verflechtung durch Internationalisierung," in *Handbuch einer transnationalen Geschichte Ostmitteleuropas, Vol. 1: Von der Mitte des 19. Jahrhunderts bis zum Ersten Weltkrieg*, eds. Frank Hadler and Matthias Middell (Göttingen: Vandenhoeck & Rupprecht, 2017), 325–402.

35. Still little is written on the exchange of Eastern and Western experts. For a few exceptions, see Paul Betts, "The Warden of World Heritage: UNESCO and the Rescue of the Nubian Monuments," *Past and Present* 226 (2015): 100–125; Sandrine Kott, "Cold War Internationalism" in *Internationalisms: A Twentieth Century History*, eds. Glenda Sluga and Patricia Clavin (Cambridge: Cambridge University Press, 2016), 340–362; Sandrine Kott, "Par-delà la guerre froide: Les organisations internationales et les circulations Est-Ouest (1947–1973)," *Vingtième Siècle: Revue d'histoire* 109 (2011): 143–154.

36. Naumann, "Verflechtung durch Internationalisierung."

37. Berthold Unfried and Eva Himmelstoss, *Die eine Welt schaffen: Praktiken von "Internationaler Solidarität" und "Internationaler Entwicklung"* (Vienna: Akademische Verlagsanstalt, 2012); Hubertus Büschel, *Hilfe zur Selbsthilfe: Deutsche Entwicklungsarbeit in Afrika 1960–1975* (Frankfurt: Campus, 2014); Antonio Giustozzi and Artemy Kalinovsky, *Missionaries of Modernity: Advisory Missions and the Struggle for Hegemony in Afghanistan and Beyond* (London: Hurst, 2016).

38. This began with the literature on "convergence" that emerged from the European New Left and Marxist revisionists in the late 1960s. Contemporary views often hold that Soviet and Western concepts were both variants of an enlightenment legacy; see Westad, *The Global Cold War*; Engerman, "The Second World's Third World."

39. For Eastern Europe's role in this, see André Gunder Frank, "Long Live Transideological Enterprise! The Socialist Economies in the Capitalist International Division of Labor," *Review (Fernand Braudel Center)* 1, no. 1 (Summer 1977), 91–140.

40. Patrick Gutman, "West-östliche Wirtschaftskooperationen in der Dritten Welt" in *Ökonomie im Kalten Krieg*, eds. Bernd Greiner, Christian Müller, and Claudia Weber (Hamburg: Hamburger Edition, 2010), 395–414.

41. Sara Lorenzini, "Comecon and the Global South in the Years of Détente," *European Review of History* 21 (2014): 188.

42. See also G. Thomas Burgess, "Mao in Zanzibar: Nationalism, Discipline, and the (De) Construction of Afro-Asian Solidarities," in *Making a World after Empire: The Bandung Moment and Its Political Afterlives*, ed. Christopher J. Lee (Athens, OH: Ohio University Press, 2010), 196–234.

43. Mark and Apor, "Socialism Goes Global." See also Jeremiah Wishon, "Peace and Progress: Building Indo-Soviet Friendship"; and David Tompkins, "Red China in Central Europe: Creating and Deploying Representations of an Ally in Poland and the GDR," both in *Socialist Internationalism in the Cold War: Exploring the Second World*, eds. Patryk Babiracki and Austin Jersild (London: Palgrave, 2016).

44. Toni Weis, "The Politics Machine: On the Concept of 'Solidarity' in East German Support for SWAPO," *Journal of Southern African Studies* 37, no. 2 (June 2011): 351–367.

45. See also Kristin Roth-Ey, "'Loose Girls' on the Loose?': Sex, Propaganda and the 1957 Youth Festival," in *Women in the Khrushchev Era*, eds. Melanie Reid, Susan E. Reid, and Lynne Atwood (New York: Palgrave, 2004), 86.

46. Constantin Katsakioris, "Soviet Lessons for Arab Modernization: Soviet Educational Aid towards Arab Countries after 1956," *Journal of Modern European History* 8 (2010): 85–106.

47. Abigail Judge Kret, "'We Unite with Knowledge': The Peoples' Friendship University and Soviet Education for the Third World," *Comparative Studies of South Asia, Africa and the Middle East* 33, no. 2 (2013): 248.

48. Rupprecht, *Soviet Internationalism*, 191–228. Tanja Müller, *Legacies of Socialist Solidarity: East Germany in Mozambique* (Lanham, MD: Lexington Books, 2014).

49. As late as 1990, 23,809 African students came to study in the Soviet Union. This was the highest number of any year in Soviet history: Constantin Katsakioris, "Creating a Socialist Intelligentsia: Soviet Educational Aid and Its Impact on Africa (1960–1991)," *Cahiers d'études Africaines* 226, no. 2 (2017): 277.

50. Jonathan R. Zatlin, "Scarcity and Resentment: Economic Sources of Xenophobia in the GDR, 1971–1989," *Central European History* 40, no. 4 (2007): 697. Maxim Matusevich, "Probing the Limits of Internationalism: African Students Confront Soviet Ritual," *Anthropology of East Europe Review* 27, no. 2 (Fall 2009): 28–30; Maxim Matusevich, "Testing the Limits of Soviet Internationalism: African Students in the Soviet Union," in *Race, Ethnicity and the Cold War*, ed. Philip E. Muehlenbeck (Nashville: Vanderbilt University Press, 2012), 155–159; Weis, "The Politics Machine," 366. On skinhead attacks on Cubans in Hungary, see James Mark and Bálint Tolmár, "Encountering Cuba in Socialist Hungary," (forthcoming).

51. See a similar phenomenon for Soviet Buddhists in Ivan Sablin, "Illusive Tolerance: Buddhism in the Late Soviet State," Conference "Human Rights after 1945 in the Socialist and Post-Socialist World," German Historical Institute, Warsaw, March 3–5, 2016; and for Muslims in Yugoslavia, see Brenna Miller, "Faith and Nation: Politicians, Intellectuals and the Official Recognition of a Muslim Nation in Tito's Yugoslavia," in *Beyond Mosque, Church, and State: Alternative Narratives of the Nation*, eds. Theodora Dragostinova and Yana Hashamova (Budapest and New York: CEU Press, 2016), 133.

52. See also Alena Alamgir, "The Moped Diaries: Remittances in the Czechoslovak-Vietnamese Labor Migration Scheme," in *New Directions in Labour and Migration: Historical Legacies, Present Predicaments and Futures Trends*, ed. Mahua Sarkar (De Gruyter Oldenbourg, forthcoming); Zatlin, "Scarcity and Resentment," 708.

53. For an exception, see Artemy Kalinovsky and Sergey Radchenko, eds., *The End of the Cold War and the Third World: New Perspectives on Regional Conflict* (New York: Routledge, 2011). On 1989 as a global moment, see, e.g., Ulf Engel, Frank Hadler, and Matthias Middell, eds., *1989 in a Global Perspective* (Leipzig: Leipziger University Press, 2015).

54. Ibid., 48, 51; Odd Arne Westad, conclusion, in *The Global 1989: Continuity and Change in World Politics*, ed. George Lawson et al. (Cambridge: Cambridge University Press, 2010), 273.

55. Johanna Bockman claims that Eastern European socialist economists were co-contributors to the neoliberal economic consensus of the late twentieth century: "The Long Road to 1989: Neoclassical Economics, Alternative Socialisms, and the Advent of Neoliberalism," *Radical History Review* 112 (2012): 9–42; Johanna Bockman, "Scientific Community in a Divided World: Economists, Planning, and Research Priority during the Cold War," *Comparative Studies in Society and History* 50 (2008): 581–613; Tobias Rupprecht, "Formula Pinochet: Chilean Lessons for Russian Liberal Reformers during the Soviet Collapse, 1970–2000," *Journal of Contemporary History* 51, no. 1 (2016): 165–186.

56. For some attempts, see James Mark et al., *1989: A Global History of Eastern Europe* (Cambridge: Cambridge University Press, 2019), 173–218; James Mark and Quinn Slobodian, "Eastern Europe in the Global History of Decolonization," in *The Oxford Handbook of the Ends of Empire*, eds. Martin Thomas and Andrew Thompson (Oxford: Oxford University Press, 2018), 351–372; Johannes Feichtinger, Ursula Prutsch, and Moritz Csáky, eds., *Habsburg (post-colonial): Anmerkungen zur inneren Kolonisierung in Zentraleuropa* (Innsbruck: Studienverlag, 2003).

57. See also Mark and Apor, "Socialism Goes Global."

58. James Mark, Péter Apor, Radina Vučetić, and Piotr Osęka, "'We Are with You, Vietnam': Transnational Solidarities in Socialist Hungary, Poland and Yugoslavia," *Journal of Contemporary History* 50, no. 3 (2015): 459.

59. James Mark and Anna von der Goltz, "Encounters," in *Europe's 1968: Voices of Revolt*, eds. Robert Gildea, James Mark, and Anette Warring (Oxford: Oxford University Press, 2013), 131–163.

60. See also Samuel J. Hirst, "European Periphery: The Meaning of Soviet-Turkish Convergence in the 1930s," *Slavic Review* 72, no. 1 (2013): 32–53.

61. Péter Vámos, "The Tiananmen Square 'Incident' in China and the East Central European Revolutions," in *The Revolutions of 1989: A Handbook*, ed. Wolfgang Mueller et al. (Vienna: Austrian Academy of Sciences Press, 2014), 106–111.

62. József Böröcz and Melinda Kovács, *Empire's New Clothes: Unveiling EU Enlargement* (Telford: Central European Review, 2001).

63. I͡uriĭ Novopashin, "Vozdeĭstvie real'nogo sot͡sialisma na mirovoĭ revolyut͡sionnyĭ prot͡sess: metodologicheskie aspekty," *Voprosy filosofii* 36, no. 8 (1982): 3–16; Jonathan C. Valdez, *Internationalism and the Ideology of Soviet Influence in Eastern Europe* (Cambridge: Cambridge University Press, 1993), 22–25; Melvin A Goodman, *Gorbachev's Retreat: The Third World* (New York: Praeger, 1991), 158–159.

64. Francis Fukuyama, "Gorbachev and the Third World," *Foreign Relations* 64, no. 4 (1986): 715.

65. Goodman, *Gorbachev's Retreat.*

66. Igiaba Scego, "At Sea, Devoured by Our Indifference," *Massachusetts Review*, accessed June 16, 2015, https://www.massreview.org/node/443. On the freedoms of the "red passport," see Stef Jansen, "The Afterlives of the Yugoslav Red Passport," *Citizenship in Southeast Europe* (October 2012).

67. See Marcia Catherine Schenck, "Socialist Solidarities and Their Afterlives: Histories and Memories of Angolan and Mozambican Migrants in the German Democratic Republic, 1975–2015" (PhD diss., Princeton University, 2017).

68. Gurminder K. Bhambra and John Narayan, eds., introduction, in *European Cosmopolitanism: Colonial Histories and Postcolonial Societies* (Abingdon: Routledge, 2017).

69. This was an open letter sent to Ceaușescu by six party veterans who denounced his excesses, economic policies, and the deterioration of Romania's international status. For details see Vladimir Tismaneanu, *Stalinism for all Seasons: A Political History of Romanian Communism* (Berkeley, CA: University of California Press, 2003), 227–229.

70. Steffi Marung, *Die wandernde Grenze: Die EU, Polen und der Wandel politischer Räume, 1990–2010* (Göttingen: Vandenhoeck & Ruprecht 2013), 241ff.

71. Leftist scholars such as Leslie Sklair have explored the rise of "socialist multinationals" in the late 1970s in *Globalization: Capitalism and Its Alternatives* (Oxford: Oxford University Press, 2002), 224.

72. Chris O'Malley, *Bonds without Borders: A History of the Eurobond Market* (Chichester: Wiley, 2015), 13.

73. Douglas Rogers, "Petrobarter: Oil, Inequality, and the Political Imagination in and after the Cold War," *Current Anthropology* 55 (2014): 137–138.

74. Christopher Chase-Dunn, "Globalization: A World-Systems Perspective," *Journal of World-Systems Research* 2 (1999): 187–216.

75. Mark Mazower, *Governing the World: The History of an Idea* (New York: Penguin Press, 2012), chapter 12. Nils Gilman, "The New International Economic Order: A Reintroduction," *Humanity* 6, no. 1 (2015): 6–8.

76. Denis M. Tull, "China's Engagement with Africa: Scope, Significance, and Consequences," in *Making a World after Empire: The Bandung Moment and Its Political Afterlives*, ed. Christopher Lee (Athens: Ohio University Press, 2010), 290–292. Ian Taylor, "China's Foreign Policy towards Africa in the 1990s," *The Journal of Modern African Studies* 36, no. 3 (1998): 443–460.

77. Christine Hatzky, *Cubans in Angola: South-South Cooperation and Transfer of Knowledge, 1976–1991* (Madison: University of Wisconsin Press, 2015), 290–292; Piero Gleijeses, *Conflicting Missions Havana, Washington, and Africa, 1959–1976* (Chapel Hill, NC and London: University of North Carolina Press, 2002), 392–393; John Kirk, "Cuba's Medical Internationalism: Development and Rationale," *Bulletin of Latin American Research* 28, no. 4 (2009): 497–511.

78. Susan Bayly, "Vietnamese Narratives of Tradition, Exchange and Friendship in the Worlds of the Global Socialist Ecumene," in *Enduring Socialism: Explorations of Revolution and Transformation, Restoration and Continuation*, eds. Harry West and Parvathi Raman (New York/Oxford: Berghahn, 2008), 125–147.

79. Christina Schwenkel, "Affective Solidarities and East German Reconstruction of Postwar Vietnam," in *Comrades of Colour: East Germany in the Cold War World*, ed. Quinn Slobodian (New York/Oxford: Berghahn, 2015), 267–292; Gertrud Hüwelmeier, "Postsocialist Bazaars: Diversity, Solidarity, and Conflict in the Marketplace," *Laboratorium: Russian Review of Social Research* 1 (2013): 52–72; Pal Nyíri, *Chinese in Russia and Eastern Europe: A Middleman Minority in a Transnational Era* (London: Routledge, 2007).

80. Nadja Laske, "Die nächste Generation," in *Sächische Zeitung*, July 14, 2018, https://www.sz-online.de/nachrichten/die-naechste-generation-3975462.html.

81. "S vrtulníky to umíte, chválí Čechy NATO" [You sure know how to fly helicopters, NATO, praises Czechs], in *Hospodářské Noviny*, June 12, 2012.

82. István Tarrósy and Péter Morenth, "Hungarian Africa Policy," *African Studies Quarterly* 14, nos. 1–2 (2013): 89; Chris Moreh, "The Asianization of National Fantasies in Hungary: A Critical Analysis of Political Discourse," *International Journal of Cultural Studies* 19, no. 3 (2016): 341–353.

JAMES MARK is Professor of History at the University of Exeter. He is author of *The Unfinished Revolution: Making Sense of the Communist Past in Central-Eastern Europe* and coauthor of *Europe's 1968: Voices of Revolt* and *1989: A Global History of Eastern Europe*.

ARTEMY M. KALINOVSKY is Senior Lecturer in East European Studies at the University of Amsterdam. He is author of *Laboratory of Socialist Development: Cold War Politics and Decolonization in Soviet Tajikistan* and *A Long Goodbye: The Soviet Withdrawal from Afghanistan*.

STEFFI MARUNG is Senior Researcher at the Centre for Area Studies at the University of Leipzig. She is author of *Die wandernde Grenze: Die EU, Polen und der Wandel politischer Räume, 1990–2010* and coauthor of *Spatial Formats under the Global Condition* and *In Search of Other Worlds: Essays Towards a Global Historical Reading of Area Studies*.

PART I
RED GLOBALIZATION?

1 The Soviet Union, Eastern Europe, and Alternative Visions of a Global Economy 1950s–1980s*

James Mark and Yakov Feygin

In both scholarly and popular literature, the United States and other advanced industrialized capitalist countries are often assumed to be the primary agents of what from the early 1990s became popularly known as "globalization."[1] In such accounts, "real" postwar globalization begins with the growth of Western-led financialized capitalism in the early 1970s.[2] The perceived winners in this process framed forms of global integration and interconnectedness developed by socialist states as blind alleys, as oddities outstripped by history. Scholarly study of attempts to contest neoliberal globalization has mainly been restricted to accounts of the antiglobalization movements from the 1990s onward, as documented by sociologists and political scientists.[3]

Such accounts not only start too late, they leave out alternative forms of global economic integration pursued by non-Western actors during earlier decades of the Cold War. The so-called reglobalization of the world economy in fact began in the 1950s as a rejection of the nationalistic, autarkic economics that had dominated the world since the Great Depression. This ambition was not limited to European integration and the American attempt to create a free trade order but included the aspirations of a socialist world connected to the "anti-imperialist" developing states. Indeed, in often incongruous ways, both Eastern European socialist states and the Soviet Union challenged the terms under which postwar interconnectedness was being reconstructed. However, despite the increasing prevalence in the work of scholars of the region of theoretical frameworks invoking "globalization," such a term was not used by socialist actors at the time to signify their own projects of economic and social integration.[4] Indeed, repeated use of the term *globalization* threatens to marginalize the manner in which the socialist world did contribute to this interconnectedness by judging its success according to criteria set by another, wholly different ideological project. Nevertheless, the vocabulary that Eastern Bloc states employed betrayed their global ambition, albeit in different terms: theirs was a world of international development and solidarity, the "socialist division of labor," anti-imperialist trade and economics, interdependence, and the world scientific-technical revolution.

Yet, language aside, to what extent and in what manner were such states both interested in and able to construct an alternative vision for globalization or a global economy? Some of the most stimulating literature on globalization addresses the role of human agency in constructing the new institutional, legal, and financial arrangements needed to underpin new forms of global interconnectedness and understands such processes as a battle between different agents to promote and control various types of economic flows, information, and institutions.[5] Drawing inspiration from such work, this chapter will explore the participation and commitment of the Soviet Union and Eastern European countries and their experts to "globalize" through the anti-imperialist free trade initiatives within the United Nations in the 1960s; in the proposals for a "New International Economic Order" in the 1970s; and in the region's own attempts to reshape a global order through international investment banks and through the expansion beyond Europe of their own economic organization—Comecon (the Council for Mutual Economic Assistance).

The Rise of an Alternative World Order?

From the mid-1950s until the late 1960s, anti-imperialist visions were the order of the day: how could the world overcome the massive imbalances of wealth and the restricted nature of trade that the currently collapsing European colonial empires had bequeathed to it? In the late 1950s the Soviet Union under Nikita Khrushchev and its Eastern European allies slowly abandoned economic isolationism and considered the roles they might play in a world in which empires appeared ripe to be politically and economically remade. Joseph Stalin's focus on autarkic development and "socialism in one country" was gone. A plethora of newly constituted states in the Global South, many of which were adopting progressive programs, offered the possibility of new alliances that could potentially mount a serious challenge to an older imperial world economy.[6] Khrushchev offered a fresh and compelling vision—of a growing, interconnected progressive movement encompassing socialist states, national liberation movements, and democratic revolutionaries—all elements that might merge into "a single revolutionary world process undermining and destroying capitalism."[7]

Free Trade

The power of this vision was first tested on an international stage at the United Nations Conference on Trade and Development (UNCTAD), established in 1963 to promote free trade in the name of reshaping a global economy that still bore the marks of disintegrating European empires. Over the 1960s and 1970s, the UNCTAD was one of the most important sites at which ideas for a progressive recasting of the global economy were articulated. Its inaugural meeting brought together over 4,000 representatives in Geneva, Switzerland. Among them were representatives of various socialist states and movements, including Che Guevara, the president of the National Bank of Cuba and the Cuban minister of industry. Free trade would no longer be a servant of empire, the socialists claimed; rather, it could be harnessed to a new anti-imperialist vision of the global economy.[8] Through regional cooperation between Eastern Europe, Asia, Africa, and Latin America, new patterns of global trade could be established that might break the stranglehold of imperial networks. Participants at the UNCTAD agreed on fifteen "General Principles to govern international trade relations and trade policies conducive to development," including the notion that each nation should have the right to trade freely with all others and that the system of global trade should be aimed at a division of labor consonant with the needs of developing countries.[9] It is important to note that the UNCTAD's founding principles established at Geneva did not insist on a connection between the domestic economic system and free trade abroad: it was supposed that socialist-planned economies could successfully engage in trade with countries with very different systems of ownership and production. Every socialist country voted in favor of these principles, while the United States voted against or abstained on nearly every point. A more global economy—conceptualized by the UNCTAD's leaders in terms of an openness to multidirectional, multilateral trade across regions—was seen as the cause of a progressive world.

Most of the socialist states of Eastern Europe were represented at the first UNCTAD meetings and, at least in public, professed enthusiastic support for its goals. Indeed, Soviet newspapers made the unwarranted claim that Khrushchev had inspired the conference's foundation.[10] It was certainly the case that the Soviets, following Stalin's death, had pushed for new international agreements on trade following the failure of the international community to establish an international trade organization; this concern had become all the more pressing after the foundation of the European Economic Community in 1958, given the concomitant fear that world trade rules would be set by Western, developed countries.[11] Yet by the early 1960s, another alliance played a more significant role: emerging as a follow-up to the Belgrade Summit of 1961, the 1962 Cairo Conference on the Problems of Developing Countries brought together key players from nonaligned and developing countries, who called for an international economic conference to be established. The eventual decision to convene the UNCTAD was taken by the UN Economic and Social Council (ECOSOC) in 1962 after Brazil, Ethiopia, India, Senegal, and Yugoslavia submitted a draft resolution.[12]

Although they had not been directly involved in the foundation of the UNCTAD, Eastern Bloc states were initially in favor, judging it an institution that might provide them with greater bargaining power in the world economy. They did not have the economic influence of the Western powers, and Cold War economic blockades, embargoes, and sanctions had restricted their participation in international trade. In 1947 the United States had imposed new controls on socialist Eastern European states. In 1950 all NATO countries except Iceland imposed similar restrictions: the CoCom (Coordinating Committee for Multilateral Export Controls) list. By 1951 the US Mutual Defense Assistance Control Act "forbad all economic, financial, and military assistance to countries that exported strategic material to the East."[13] As part of their strategy to access strategically important Western resources and advanced technology, Eastern European states embraced a variety of approaches, pursuing bilateral, most favored nation statuses and supporting multilateral free trade initiatives, such as the UNCTAD.

Yet from the start, Eastern Bloc states were often not as enthusiastic about the use of free trade to build an alternative global economic order as the UNCTAD's nonaligned founders. The new conference was attractive in part because it offered the future possibility of trade with Western European markets across the Iron Curtain. While supporting the UNCTAD, several Eastern European socialist states were simultaneously trying to join the General Agreement on Tariffs and Trade (GATT)—viewed by the Soviets and UNCTAD supporters as a club of rich capitalist countries. Poland joined in 1967, Romania in 1971, and Hungary in 1973.[14] Moreover, a commitment to a new type of anti-imperialist alliance was not always so rapturously received: at the first UNCTAD conference in 1964, the USSR, Hungary, Poland, and Bulgaria expressed their concern that there was too great a focus on the developing world. While new trade links were welcome, they suggested that an overemphasis on a new anti-imperialist axis risked undermining attempts to open up trade with Western Europe.

The obtainment of Western technology—to promote more efficient industrial production—was crucial for economic development in the Second World and the Third World alike. In this sense, some Eastern socialist countries used a forum created mainly by actors from the Global South to compensate for their weaker position vis à vis the West. Chinese antirevisionist propaganda from the early 1960s made much of this: Beijing claimed that Eastern Europe's seemingly all too easy accommodation of the capitalist world for the sake of technology imports could only be at the expense of commitment to an alternative world order. Thus it was only the Chinese, the propagandists argued, who could claim global leadership in the developing world. This challenge pressured the Soviets to continue their public declarations of support for the UNCTAD as a symbol of commitment to an internationalist progressive cause in the face of Chinese claims to the contrary.[15]

Eastern Bloc states were often uncomfortable with the UNCTAD's regional approach. The structure of the UNCTAD encouraged its members to put aside national interests in favor of a regionalist "country group" system. Countries joined one of four regional groupings—Group A for African and Asian countries; Group B for advanced capitalist countries; Group C for Latin America; and Group D for Eastern European socialist countries—in which they negotiated common positions. (Group A included socialist Yugoslavia.)[16] This structure was designed to give collective bargaining power to weaker players in the global economy. It also expressed the UNCTAD leadership's faith in new intraregional trading systems: by creating value chains—from the production of raw materials to high-level industrial production—within regions, wealth would not escape so easily from the formerly colonized to their former political colonizers.[17]

Such a multilateral framework sat uncomfortably with the Eastern Bloc's emphasis on national sovereignty as the organizing principle for international relations. Despite perennial discussions of the "socialist international division of labor"—launched by Khrushchev in a 1962 statement of principles that lasted until 1989—Eastern European countries did not, by and large, embrace regional economic integration. Raúl Prebisch, the intellectual driving force behind the UNCTAD, often complained of "Second World bilateralism" in the organization of trade.[18] Reasons for this varied across the bloc. The more conservative Soviet trade institutions, in a hangover from the Stalinist era, were reluctant to embrace those initiatives that threatened their economic independence. They usually sought to limit engagement with a capitalist world economy to the import of (often-advanced) capital goods necessary for the growth of the national economy.[19] Even after 1956 grave doubts remained as to whether multilateral trade was possible under a world economy still dominated by capitalism, with many wondering how it would be possible to integrate foreign products and even foreign persons into an autarkic Soviet legal and economic order.[20] Many Eastern European leaders feared that, with weak export industries, opening up to multilateral trade might lead to severe indebtedness. This created structural impediments to integration into any grouping that threatened national sovereignty. In later decades, only those Eastern European countries, such as Hungary, that had undergone significant domestic economic reform and had a higher quality of export remained open to the West and countenanced a more liberalized, multilateral system.[21]

Other Eastern European states rejected a regional grouping, implying as it did Soviet hegemony: Romania and Yugoslavia, for example, preferred bilateral trade agreements as a means to integrate the economic activities of small- and medium-sized states to the mutual benefit of both, rendering them freer from the influence of the world's superpowers, including the Soviets. From early in the UNCTAD's existence, Eastern European states criticized its lack of realism, put their own national interest before solidarity, and preferred individual trade agreements with nations of the Global South based on their own mercantilist needs.[22] Eastern European states thus initially embraced the UNCTAD as a venue to negotiate bilateral agreements with developing states to gain access to their natural resources.[23]

Eastern Bloc states often preferred working with the United Nations Industrial Development Organization (UNIDO) rather than the UNCTAD, due to the former's emphasis on bilateral technology exchange and industrialization as a development strategy. The UNIDO was the perfect venue for propagating the Soviet developmental model because it allowed the USSR and its allies to leverage their expertise in planning to compensate for their inability to establish an efficient multilateral trading system. A Soviet report from 1968 concluded that it could not compete with American private finance capital in offering material support to developing countries in UNIDO meetings, it could help the organization "retain its progressive character" by offering borrower countries expertise in how to best control Western investments with a view to retaining their economic sovereignty. "This way," the report concluded, the USSR could "propagandize" its ideas of development without having to compete with the West's superior resources.[24]

Expertise and the Establishment of Bilateral Developmentalism

The Eastern European commitment to trade as a tool to build an anti-imperialist socialist world was partial at best; nevertheless, in order to understand the specificity of the Eastern European (socialist) "globalization" project, analyzing trade and capital flows is not enough. As the facilitator and exporter of a specifically socialist form of development, regional actors played major roles in building new forms of global economic interconnectedness. The export of Soviet and Eastern European planning and industrialization was one of the main "globalizing" forces of the mid- to late twentieth century. Eastern European and Soviet involvement with the developing world emphasized a transfer of knowledge as much as a transfer of resources. The Socialist Bloc's belief in the priority of domestic, heavy industrial development meant that its efforts to expand the planning model often directly contradicted the expansion of multilateral trade with Comecon and between Eastern Europe and the developing world.

From the late 1950s, most Eastern European states saw it as their duty to help build the economies of newly independent states through long-term credits, technological transfer, and professional training that would assist rapid industrialization free from the assistance of the capitalist world.[25] Such development, leaders hoped, would create an indigenous working class that would lead their newly decolonized countries to socialism. Many postcolonial states from Indonesia to Ghana built their new countries with inspiration from the authoritarian socialism of the Eastern Bloc.[26]

These initiatives were often grafted onto local intellectual traditions. Eastern Europe had served as a model for overcoming underdevelopment—programs to address the region's economic backwardness in the interwar period became templates for projects in "underdeveloped regions" in the postwar period across Europe and the world.[27] As Paul Rosenstein-Rodan put it in 1944: the "international development of Eastern and South-Eastern Europe [. . .] provides a model presenting all the problems which are relevant to the reconstruction and development of backward areas [i.e., across the world]."[28] World-renowned economists such as Poland's Oskar Lange and Michał Kalecki drew on their own nation's experience of building economic sovereignty after gaining nationhood and of dealing with problems of rural overpopulation as they directed their expertise to similar issues found in the new nation-states that emerged from European colonial empires. Poland in particular became a favored destination for economists from developing countries: in the 1960s, the UN Economic Commission for Europe organized educational exchange programs to Warsaw every summer for economists from Africa and Latin America working on development issues.[29]

The Eastern European export of developmental expertise and the financing of large industrial projects was never effectively coordinated across the whole bloc. Comecon—through its Commission for Technical Assistance—tried to coordinate technical assistance and present a united front to the decolonizing world;[30] however, such initiatives were in practice ignored. Eastern European states often advocated contrasting industrialization strategies and developed institutes to propagate these, such as the Center of Research on Underdeveloped Economies (CRUE), founded in Poland in 1962, the Afro-Asian Research Center in Hungary (1963), or the Soviet Institute of World Economy and International Relations (IMEMO), founded in 1956.[31] As Eastern European socialist economic models began to drift apart—with countries such as Hungary embracing greater economic liberalization and Yugoslavia abandoning the last vestiges of the Soviet model—so did the economic advice they proffered. By the mid-1960s, bloc countries began to compete over the provision of assistance to Third World projects—a phenomenon that has been described as "proxy wars in expertise exports to the 'Third World.'"[32]

However, Eastern Bloc export of developmental assistance was significant across many sectors—energy, transport, agriculture, pharmaceuticals, chemical industry, and so on—in part because it was organized without Soviet influence or an enforced regionalism. For the most part, such initiatives stemmed from national elites' recognition of the possible advantages that would be afforded to their own countries by investing abroad and from pride that their own traditions of expertise could now be showcased on the world stage. Moreover, the autarkic national models of development that had dominated in Eastern Europe long before the Communist takeovers—the same traditions that had proved so much of an obstacle to the creation of regional cooperation in Eastern Europe in the postwar period—were in fact attractive to newly decolonized nations looking to ensure their own economic sovereignty and political independence. Bilateral developmental agreements with politically sympathetic states were also popular, as multilateral arrangements were thought by some postcolonial leaders to render their states vulnerable to the demands of Western foreign capital looking to "open doors" to their economies.[33]

Rethinking the Alliance 1968–1989

In the last decades of the Cold War, the economic relationship between the Eastern Bloc and a developing world expanded in many different ways. Trade grew significantly between Eastern Europe and Africa from the 1970s: commerce between the Soviet Union and the developing world expanded almost tenfold based on energy and weapons supply.[34] The integration of non-European countries into Comecon offered new opportunities for deeper forms of developmental cooperation. Yet Eastern Bloc countries nevertheless found themselves increasingly unable to influence the terms of debate over the global economy. By the end of the 1970s, ideas of planning and development that had emerged from UN institutions played less of a role. Increasingly, the Bretton Woods Institutions—the World Bank and the International Monetary Fund (IMF)—gained much greater influence. The first signs of change were visible early in that same decade. The combination of the collapse of Bretton Woods' capital controls, the emergence of the Eurodollar market, and the need for oil-rich states to recycle their surpluses shattered the previous consensus. The 1970s saw a spectacular rise in acceptance of the flow of capital across borders. A hybrid system emerged in which states and private interests met in the market for foreign exchange funds. This meant that instead of direct lending to specific development projects, mediated by international organizations such as the United Nations, the funding of projects in developing nations was arranged on the bond markets through portfolio investment.[35]

This gave experts from socialist Eastern Europe, who often had less expertise in these areas, far less influence.[36] The increasing powerlessness felt in the Soviet expert community was reflected in a 1979 conference on international monetary policy run by the Soviet Union's Institute of World Economy and International Relations (IMEMO), the country's preeminent think tank on global economics. In a report to the Central Committee, the institute explained that there was no consensus in the expert community about how to deal with the emerging reorganization of the financial system. Some delegates to the conference advocated that the Soviets follow the example of Hungary and Romania and join the Bretton Woods institutions to influence them from within, while others cautioned against such a move. The overriding conclusion was that the USSR had no influence over these changes to the global economic system.[37]

In the early 1980s Margaret Thatcher and Ronald Reagan resisted any attempts to bring the World Bank or the IMF under the control of the United Nations—fearing that the debtor countries in the East and South would take advantage in an institution in which they had greater leverage.[38] As cross-border capital flows and debt began to overtake industrialization as the main concern of global development, the USSR's lack of hard currency meant that it had lost the leverage that its export of expertise once gave it. This was a sea in which the socialist states of the "Second World" could no longer navigate, thereby losing their position as models for development in the "Third World."[39]

At the same time, many Eastern Bloc countries refused to commit themselves to the assertive models of global economic redistribution that were emerging from the developing world. In June 1964 seventy-seven states from the South formed an intergovernmental organization known as the "Group of 77" (G77). In the mid-1970s, this new grouping conceptualized what became known as the New International Economic Order (NIEO), a program which asserted a right to development, advocated regulating capital flows to prevent the reproduction of the injustices of colonialism, and urged international institutions to engineer a global redistribution of wealth from North to South.[40] Among Eastern European nations, only Romania and Yugoslavia—one a renegade member of the Eastern Bloc and the other a nonaligned state outside the Soviet sphere of influence—were members. Indeed, as one of the least developed countries of the Eastern Bloc, Romania presented itself as part of this peripheralized world of the South. Indeed, its delegation at UNCTAD III (the third session of the conference) defined Romania as a "developing Latin American country" and called for the creation of a mechanism enabling it to be reimbursed for losses incurred due to changes in capitalist countries' currency exchange rates.[41]

Many experts in the Soviet Union, Hungary, Czechoslovakia, and Poland, by contrast, saw the NIEO as a parochial and excessively utopian response to the difficulties of building a new world economy and were more critical of plans to redistribute global wealth.[42] In response, many from the developing world discarded earlier ideological claims that had drawn them into natural solidarity with the Eastern Bloc. Thus, at UNCTAD IV in 1976, the states of the South decided to stop differentiating between the socialist and capitalist states of the Northern Hemisphere; rather, the fundamental division in the world was now between an underdeveloped Global South and an industrialized Global North that clung to its structural advantages in the world economy. Bloc experts were not impressed by this argument: their representatives at UNCTAD stressed that this was a massive oversimplification.[43] O. T. Bogomolov, the director of the Institute for the Study of the Socialist World System (IMESS) and a well-connected reformist scholar, considered it an error to gather "developed" states into one category: this artificial merging obscured "the ideological differences" between socialist states and developed capitalist countries. "No one," he explained, "could accuse the socialist countries of exploiting the developing world and contributing to the misdistribution of global profits."[44]

The Soviets advocated an alternative. During the 1970s and 1980s, they presented Comecon as a model of equitable international economic integration that could reshape the world order in a manner superior to that of the NIEO.[45] They claimed the addition of Cuba, Mongolia, and Vietnam demonstrated its appeal and feasibility.[46] It could indeed enable more complex forms of developmental cooperation. For instance, Cuba joined Comecon in 1972 and used its structures to ensure the successful and rapid expansion of its citrus fruits industry, built with machinery from the GDR, irrigation from the Soviets and Hungarians, and packaging from Poland.[47]

Nevertheless, major schemes designed to integrate Eastern Bloc states and the developing world failed. One of the main aims of Comecon's International Investment Bank (IIB), founded in January 1971, was to finance energy infrastructure that would tie the Eastern Bloc to Third World oil suppliers. One of these was the Adria pipeline, which would link Central Europe to the Middle East. This initiative arose from fears that the Soviets were in danger of running out of energy and that the smaller bloc countries were overly reliant on cheap subsidized oil to pay for advanced manufacturing of products that they alone profited from through export to the West. Soviet experts feared, if such arrangements were to continue, their country would be confined to the role of a primary extraction economy, losing the value-added production industries that Marxist-Leninist theory argued would be the "base of Communism."[48] Such a shift, it was thought, would redress these imbalances and reduce the reliance of East Europeans on the Soviet Union. There was some readjustment: the GDR, for example, made efforts through bartering to increase oil imports from Angola, Libya, and Iran and coal from Mozambique as a response to the reduction of Soviet subsidies.[49] Yet, more broadly, this new initiative only helped the people's democracies increase their borrowing from Western money markets by enabling fund managers to assume that the full faith and credit of the Soviet Union was behind the bank. The IIB also financed the Soyuz pipeline, which delivered gas from the Soviet fields at Orenburg to Czechoslovakia, East Germany, Hungary, and Poland—exactly the kind of energy project the IIB's founders had hoped to avoid.[50]

The Failures of Multilateralism and Specialization

From the late 1960s, experts across the bloc began to ponder how they might overcome the limits of the Eastern Bloc's engagement with the world economy. They wondered whether their region could learn to specialize in high-quality goods in sectors in which they might hold a comparative advantage. This was unlikely from the start: even schemes that attempted to develop specialization within Comecon met with limited success. Since the Comecon's meetings were regularized in 1958 schemes of integration had been proposed, and in 1962 the Soviet Union had even floated a plan for a socialist division of labor that would see individual countries within the bloc specialize in specific forms of production. Yet Soviet leaders argued that many enterprises would fail to reach a level of productivity and technological development at which exposure to free trade would strengthen them through competition. Such a move contained a profound risk to growth and to levels of domestic consumption. This was especially important in the late 1960s when reformism and "socialism with a human face" had been crushed, and economic arguments for the legitimacy of socialism were becoming ever more important.[51] A more serious set of proposals came in 1971 when a Comprehensive Program for Socialist Economic Integration was adopted by Comecon to replace the dominance of ad hoc bilateral agreements with a system that coordinated planning and created connections between enterprises across borders on a multilateral basis.[52] Yet this program and those that followed mainly supported joint investment in large specific developmental projects rather than market-making or integrative programs based on freer trade across bloc borders. For Soviet and Eastern Bloc leaders of that generation, the national economy was still privileged as *the* site of production. Despite its aspirational rhetoric, Comecon never operated as a multilateral institution, and most trade between Eastern Bloc states was conducted on a bilateral basis, often motivated by political rather than economic factors.[53]

The structural biases against trade were also evident in the attempts made to integrate the monetary systems of Eastern Bloc economies and to use them to develop trade relationships in the Global South. From the mid-1960s, Soviet experts discussed increasing the use of the "transferable rouble," a convertible currency that might enable developing countries to sell to one Eastern Bloc country and buy from another—incentivizing different socialist countries to specialize. To this end, the Comecon's investment bank lent transferable roubles to projects in the bloc that had potential for greater integration. This scheme faltered because the transferable rouble could not be converted into any other hard currency and could not in practice be used to purchase many types of goods even from within the bloc. This was in large part because it was not easy to move the transferable rouble into domestic currency accounts—meaning that Soviet and Eastern European enterprises and production ministries had no incentive to conduct trade in it, as their plans prioritized the marketing of goods in domestic currency. As a result, those goods that could be paid for by transferable rouble were made only in the USSR—making any multilateral clearing to facilitate multilateral trade worthless as goods could not generally be purchased from elsewhere in the bloc.[54]

Rather, commerce was still primarily conducted through bilateral relationships and through barter or so-called counter-trade—in which the seller accepted goods and services and repaid partially or fully in other goods or services.[55] In such conditions, even if trade with the developing world did take off by volume, it was not conducive to developing specializations in high-quality goods for the longer term. Rather, Eastern Bloc states continued to export weapons, lower quality industrial products, or turnkey projects—especially when they could undercut the West. Bulgarians were successful in selling computers to India, and the GDR exported major factories to East Africa and the Middle East well into the 1980s. Nevertheless, such projects were reliant on the exclusion of higher quality Western competitors or on countries of the South embracing simpler industrial goods. Some African states, for example, saw an advantage in obtaining machinery that was not only cheap but of a lower technological level: it was thus labor intensive and could soak up the growing (and potentially threatening) numbers of urban unemployed.[56]

The crux of the problems of socialist cooperation with the developing world lay on the fact that both sides of the exchange prioritized the cultivation of economic independence. As soon as one partner in these bilateral exchanges sought to pressure the other to specialize, whatever advantages that accrued from the Soviet development model disappeared. Thus, while trade and exchange were supposed to be central to Eastern Bloc aid to the developing world, these relationships were envisioned between self-contained states rather than between sectors within economies. Economic bargaining between bloc countries was not for the development of joint advantage but was usually an attempt by smaller bloc countries to gain subsidies for raw materials they needed from the Soviets.[57] Despite rhetoric to the contrary, Comecon continued to rely on bilateral ties or collaboration among multiple partners around specific developmental projects—rather than building a "free trade zone" with regional specializations based on comparative advantage.[58]

Nor were domestic enterprises—with a few exceptions—sufficiently rewarded for foreign trade sales to incentivize them to create products of a quality that could stand up to competitors on the world market. Some dissenting voices from the late 1960s had argued for this: in 1971 the economist Yu. S. Shiraev proposed that the USSR open its industry to international competition to force domestic producers out of low productivity activities and channel resources into more efficient branches of industry, only to see his recommendations rejected by the Academy of Sciences despite the backing of some of its more progressive leaders.[59] Socialist enterprises, burdened with often contradictory incentives, prioritized the fulfillment of targets set by their superiors in production ministries rather than initiatives that emerged from foreign trade ministries. Moreover, even as socialist systems took steps to increase the role of profits and monetary gains to incentivize enterprises, the inability of firms to directly access and convert profits made from foreign trade into local currency lowered incentives to increase the quality of exports.[60] And even where potentially competitive sectors did develop—such as clothing and textiles in Hungary—exporters were heavily taxed to subsidize basic goods for the population at home.[61] Whatever the intentions of small reform-minded segments of the elite may have been, the system could not handle the fundamental reforms required to develop the specialization needed to integrate effectively with goods of enhanced quality into the world economy.

Debt Crisis

The sovereign debt crisis of the late 1970s, which hit countries in both the Second and the Third World simultaneously, confirmed that their power to shape the terms of global economy was in serious decline as state-led globalization was replaced by a new hybrid private-public system of international exchange.

From 1981 increasing numbers of countries across Eastern Europe, Africa, and Latin America announced their difficulties—and in some cases their inability—to pay back the external debt they had incurred throughout the 1970s. The centrality of debt in the 1980s confirmed a shift in management of the world economy that had been discernible from the early 1970s—away from those UN bodies that had focused on managing economic development through heavy capital construction to those institutions that managed the financial side of the economy, such as debt repayment. During this time the IMF and World Bank became the important centers of management for the world economy.

These newly influential institutions held sway over countries in both the Second and the Third Worlds that had borrowed too much. This had been the result of "cheap money" in the 1970s, made available through the massively expanding Eurodollar market (which the Soviets helped to create as a means to keep the dollars they earned from energy exports outside the control of the US Treasury) and financed through so-called petrodollars that flowed out of energy-producing states as a result of the sudden rise in oil prices in 1973.[62] Countries such as Hungary and Poland bet on a future that never came: through spending borrowed money on Western technology, they had hoped to increase productivity and eventually repay the loans.[63] However, faced with only low rises in productivity and coupled with the failures of the Eastern Bloc to create a convertible currency that would have allowed them to gain hard currency by selling to their neighbors, these countries became reliant on the favors of other export markets in the West and South, and on Western finance.[64] With the spiraling costs of raw materials and rising interest rates in the late 1970s and then the so-called Volcker Shock of 1981 (huge rises in interest rates on US loans), these and other debtor countries, particularly in Latin America, were forced to implement austerity measures to deal with their liabilities. This recast both the Eastern Bloc and Global South as the objects of, rather than producers of, a new economic order.

This debt crisis of the 1980s drove a wedge between the Second World and the Third World. While it was well-known that many bloc states owed significant sums to Western creditors, the fact that many Eastern European countries were owed huge sums by Middle Eastern and African states is often omitted in standard accounts.[65] Even those bloc states that were far less indebted to Western financial institutions were nonetheless affected—the Soviet Union alone was owed USD 150–160 billion by sixty-one countries.[66] Its largest debtors were Cuba, Mongolia, Vietnam, India, Syria, Afghanistan, Yemen, Iraq, Ethiopia, North Korea, Algeria, Angola, Egypt, Libya, and Nicaragua. The debt crisis interrupted these repayments, as debtor countries outside Europe were more concerned in paying back those creditors that issued hard currency. Priority was often given to settling with the Paris Club—an informal group of (mainly Western) major creditor countries that worked together to negotiate conditions for bilateral claims. Since these countries had greater amounts of credit available, debtors preferred to remain in good standing with them, and Paris Club creditors required that debtors not be in arrears with the IMF and often worked together to force repayment or deny new loans.[67] Debt had thus expanded the reliance on Western creditors for both Eastern European countries and the developing world.[68]

Debt also undermined trade ties between the Eastern Bloc and developing countries. Through the 1970s the tenfold expansion in commerce between the Soviet Union and the developing world had been facilitated in part by the absence of convertible currency in these transactions. Developing countries were paid in roubles for (in many cases) primary products that had to be spent on Soviet goods—in the absence of free convertibility to other currencies. Nonaligned and socialist countries also used countertrade, a form of barter, in which the seller accepted goods and services and repaid partially or fully in other goods or services.[69] Yet as states' debts to their Western creditors increased, so the need for convertible currencies to pay them back rose too.[70] For example, in 1979 India and Bulgaria ceased to conduct trade in rupees and began denominating their transactions in convertible currencies.[71]

The shift to convertible currencies had a corrosive effect on the Second-Third World relationship: first, it gradually undermined the importance of the type of transactions that had tied these worlds' trade together. Second, it increased tensions between the two worlds as Eastern European states were reluctant to hand over the hard currency that they needed to pay to the West. The opportunity costs of convertible export credits were far higher for Eastern European countries than for their Western competitors. For example, Yugoslavia, which had relied on nonconvertibility to finance the rapid international expansion of its multinational companies, faced a severe decline in its current account.

Changing Values in the Second-Third World Relationship

Already in the late 1960s, many Comecon countries had decided together to abandon solidarity-based loans to "progressive" regimes across Africa, Asia, and Latin America—and henceforth only to offer them with an assessment of economic advantage. Recipient states found themselves less often viewed as the object of their solidarity-based developmental largesse.[72] Earlier conceptions of solidarity-based development and trade founded on anti-imperialism were now complemented, or in some cases replaced, by visions that, although still ostensibly committed to building a progressive world, now subordinated political solidarity to questions of economic efficiency and "mutual advantage." Moreover, with a relaxation of tensions in Europe, new forms of economic cooperation were taking off: Eastern Bloc and Western European enterprises undertook 226 so-called tripartite projects targeting developing world markets between 1965 and 1979.[73] Western companies could both leverage the benefit of a socialist partner to undermine ideological reservations of Third World partners and lower the cost of bids using Eastern Bloc labor. Often accepting their role in a newly emerging international division of labor, socialist transnational enterprises took the lead, sometimes supported by the UNCTAD.[74] The first tentative steps were made by Czechoslovak and Romanian firms, which collaborated with their West German counterparts in the Middle East and Africa.[75] The commitment to assisting in development outside Europe became less tied to a rigid anti-Western ideology.[76] From the early 1970s Czechoslovak enterprises used Belgian companies to sell their products to consumers in Central Africa.[77] In 1977 Hungary officially abandoned the prioritization of collaboration with socialist-oriented countries through Comecon;[78] in the early 1980s, the Hungarian enterprise Vegyépszer helped the United States construct Pepsi plants in Baghdad.[79]

The USSR, by contrast, was far less inclined to experiment with westward integration. Soviet elites saw economic interaction with capitalist countries as a way to acquire new technology: its enterprises were still primarily governed by state directives designed to maximize gross domestic output and had little interest in developing markets elsewhere. Proposals by IMESS to establish Comecon-operated joint enterprises in the developing world that would take the pressure off Soviet primary resource supplies to Eastern Europe faltered under bureaucratic inertia.[80] Moreover, the collapse of Soviet-American détente in the late 1970s and the passage of the Jackson-Vanik Amendment, which tied most favored nation status to the right of minorities to immigrate, further lowered Soviet appetites for expanded trade relations with the West.[81]

The economics of the debt crisis would further subordinate the political to the economic. This shift was spearheaded in the mid-1970s by some of the smaller bloc countries that exported arms, particularly to Africa, partly to pay off their debts to the West.[82] The Czechoslovak government, for instance, reconceptualized military hardware as an ideologically neutral industrial project in the mid-1960s and enormously expanded trade with both socialist and nonsocialist countries.[83] From the mid-1970s, the country made substantial hard-currency earnings by selling weapons and other military equipment in the wars in southern Africa.[84] Yet these shifts did not occur everywhere at the same pace: in the Soviet Union "old party bosses" successfully lobbied against this prioritization of economic criteria. Under pressure from Chinese criticisms that the Soviets had surrendered to imperialism, forces in the Central Committee, the intelligence services, and the military industrial complex continued to see the postcolonial world as a site for the future of the revolution. Policy toward Africa was left in the hands of the Central Committee's International Department and the KGB, which prioritized supporting "national liberation" movements rather than the more conservative, détente-focused policies emanating from the foreign ministry.[85] Nevertheless, by 1989 even the Soviet Union, which supplied a staggering 46 percent of all weapons delivered to the Global South, succumbed to this logic: faced with a sovereign debt crisis in Africa that had reduced demand for its products and its own rising indebtedness due to falling energy revenues from the mid-1980s, the USSR formalized hard currency, rather than ideology, as the determining factor in its arms trade.[86]

New pressures to develop other export industries to obtain hard currency and pay off debts also played a role in Eastern Bloc states' use of Third World labor. Workers from Vietnam, Cuba, Mozambique, and elsewhere began arriving in Eastern Europe at the behest of their own states, which wished to "export unemployment" and to gain high-quality training for parts of their labor force. Initially these schemes had been supported by Eastern Bloc states keen to express their solidarity-based generosity. By the 1980s, however, this intersocialist labor migration began to be used by receiving countries to address labor shortages and to develop profitable hard-currency earning export sectors by using migrant laborers who were cheaper to employ.[87] Some bloc states also began to examine the experiences of formerly developing countries outside Europe. In the late 1980s dynamic East Asian "tiger states," which appeared to have overcome their formerly peripheral economic conditions and to have integrated successfully into the world economy, became objects of fascination across the bloc. Looking to develop the competitiveness of their export industries, reform-minded economists and political elites looked to Augusto Pinochet's Chile and to South Korea as models for authoritarian-led development in which a one-party system had been maintained.[88] In 1987 and 1988, free trade zones were created to encourage higher quality exports, and the right of enterprises to access international markets or establish joint enterprises expanded.[89] The UNCTAD began to support East Asian regional trade initiatives to open up East European markets to their direct investment—a process that was to lead to significant investment by South Korea in Central Europe after the collapse of state socialism.[90]

Conclusion

The idea of Western capitalism as the only engine of globalization has left us with a distorted view of socialist and Third World states as entirely inward-looking and isolated from global trends until the capitalist takeover in the 1980s and 1990s.[91] Growing interconnectedness was not the same as Westernization. Eastern European states adopted a variety of approaches to engagement with the global economy from the 1950s, which shifted over time. A strong belief in the possibility of a broader anti-imperialist refashioning of the world economy in the 1960s brought together Eastern Europeans with the Third World. This relationship was also responsible for one of the largest transfers of technical expertise and investment in history.

Yet this project was riddled with contradictions: globalizing the socialist economy meant dealing with the tension between the socialist development model's emphasis on mobilizing domestic resources and the sacrifices and trade-offs needed for integration. From the late 1950s Eastern Europe's nationally focused development and preference for bilateral exchange proved popular to newly decolonized states seeking to consolidate their own economic sovereignty, yet in the 1970s such a model had a limited shelf life given the acceleration of economic interdependence. These states' continued obsession with the defense of economic sovereignty, their reluctance to collaborate regionally, and their avowed bilateralism meant that they were never able to develop an effective system of multilateral free trade that could shepherd industries into the world economy and allow them to develop comparative advantage. Moreover, Eastern Bloc states' commitment to alternative forms of globalization were often no more than half-hearted: even in the 1960s most countries' engagement with "progressive" internationalist projects such as those undertaken at the UNCTAD was as much about securing Western markets and technology as it was concerned with building a global economy based on anti-imperialist values. Connections were further reshaped by the requirements of loan repayment during the parallel crises that hit both the Eastern Bloc and large swathes of the Global South from the late 1970s: these pressures helped forge a new political language around debt that undermined earlier forms of political solidarity. The conflicts became more pronounced with these countries' increasing powerlessness to shape globalization in the face of new forms of economic flows. As the intellectual production of global economic norms shifted to ideologically unfamiliar institutions, the domestic institutions of socialist states were incapable of responding effectively, and they lost any authority to forge a language of economic interconnectedness.

However, the weaknesses and contradictions inherent in these "alternative globalizations" do not mean that they are unworthy of study. The fate of these initiatives not only may serve to shed light on the internal contradictions of the state-socialist development model that ultimately led to its demise but also may clarify the contours of our own global capitalism. Indeed, the rise of so-called neoliberalism and the Washington consensus has been understood by some as a reaction to the challenge from the alternative world order that these exchanges had promised.[92] This account also counters the notion that Eastern Europe only became globalized economically after 1989; rather, one form of international engagement eroded as another took its place. Trade and development in fact grew between Eastern Europe and the Third World in the late socialist period—with, for instance, Soviet trade, Yugoslav multinationals, and Central European joint enterprises successfully expanding into Africa and the Middle East. We must consider a more multidirectional approach to the knitting together of the global economy in the postwar period.[93] Without this approach, we also miss the more complex range of legacies of socialist-era trade and connection that survived its demise.[94]

Notes

* James Mark would like to acknowledge the support of the Arts and Humanities Research Council (UK)–supported project "Socialism Goes Global: Cold War Connections between the 'Second' and 'Third Worlds'." Thanks to those who read and commented, including Ljubica Spaskovska, András Pinkász, and Steffi Marung.

1. The term *globalization* had restricted usage until the late 1980s, being understood in the late 1950s and 1960s as universalization or shared rules. From then onward, globalization was understood to mean a Western-led, corporate-led capitalist interconnectedness.

2. Mark Mazower, *Governing the World: The History of an Idea* (New York: Penguin, 2013), especially the chapter on "The Real New International Economic Order."

3. Nick Bisley, *Rethinking Globalization* (New York: Palgrave MacMillan, 2007); Elisabeth Mudimbe Boyi, *Beyond Dichotomies: Histories, Identities, Cultures, and the Challenge of Globalization* (New York: State University Press, 2002).

4. See Oscar Sanchez-Sibony, *Red Globalization: The Political Economy of the Soviet Cold War from Stalin to Khrushchev* (New York: Cambridge University Press, 2014).

5. Kevin H. O'Rourke and Jeffrey G. Williamson, *Globalization and History: The Evolution of a Nineteenth-Century Atlantic Economy* (Cambridge: MIT Press, 2001); Katharina Pistor, "A Legal Theory of Finance," *Journal of Comparative Economics*, Law in Finance 41, no. 2 (May 2013): 315–330; Geoffrey M. Hodgson, *Conceptualizing Capitalism: Institutions, Evolution, Future* (Chicago and London: University of Chicago Press, 2015).

6. Professor Orlov, "West Hinders Solving World Trade Problems," *Izvestiya*, February 1, 1968, 2.

7. Quoted in Alfred B. Evans, *Soviet Marxism-Leninism: The Decline of an Ideology* (Westport, CT: Praeger, 1993), 73.

8. There had been a tradition of "free trade thinking" as an anti-imperialist cause of the left since the late nineteenth century; see Johanna Bockman, "The Long Road to 1989: Neoclassical Economics, Alternative Socialisms, and the Advent of Neoliberalism," *Radical History Review* 112 (2012): 9–42.

9. Final Act and Report of the First United Nations Conference on Trade and Development—UNCTAD I (March 23–June 16, 1964), (E/CONF.46/141, Vol. I)—6/16/1964, 10.

10. Telegraph Agency of the Soviet Union (TASS) International Service, March 24, 1964. On the Hungarian commitment to support free trade advantageous to Africa, see "Afrika a mai világban—kapcsolataink Afrikával," *Nemzetközi Szemle* (1966): 86.

11. John Toye, *Unctad at 50: A Short History* (Geneva: United Nations, 2014), 7.

12. In the region, nonaligned Yugoslavia played a larger role in its establishment in the early 1960s; Diego Cordovez, "The Making of UNCTAD," *Journal of World Trade* 1, no. 3 (1967): 258–260.

13. Paul Luif, "Embargoes in East-West Trade and the European Neutrals: The Case of Austria," *Current Research on Peace and Violence* 7, no. 4 (1984): 221–222.

14. "East-West Trade, the General Agreement on Tariffs and Trade (GATT) and the Cold War: Poland's Accession to GATT (1957–1967)," in *East-West Trade and the Cold War*, eds. Jari Eloranta and Jari Ojala (Jyväskylä: University of Jyväskylä Press, 2005), 77–93.

15. Jeremy Friedman, *Shadow Cold War: The Sino-Soviet Competition for the Third World* (Chapel Hill, NC: UNC Press, 2015), 205–210. On this battle of perceptions, see James Jeffrey Byrne, "Beyond Continents, Colours, and the Cold War: Yugoslavia, Algeria, and the Struggle for Non-Alignment," *The International History Review* 37, no. 5 (2015): 912–932.

16. Branislav Gosovic, *UNCTAD: Conflict and Compromise* (Leiden: A. W. Sijthoff, 1972), 46.

17. Johanna Bockman, "Socialist Globalization and Capitalist Neocolonialism: The Economic Ideas behind the New International Economic Order," *Humanity* 6, no. 1 (2015): 114–116.

18. Raúl Prebisch, "Statement at Informal Meeting of the Second Committee" (1963) Report. Myrdal Papers–General Files–UNCTAD 1963–4, GF 93 95 (UN Archive, Geneva).

19. Some Soviet experts might have seen the UNCTAD's regionalism as a means to encourage Comecon integration—so that the Eastern Bloc as a whole could envisage a role within a broader socialist world economy. Nevertheless, these initiatives met with resistance in other bloc countries and from within its own government.

20. This problem is outlined in Michael Ellman, *Socialist Planning* (Cambridge: Cambridge University Press, 2014), 329–361; and Per Högselius, *Red Gas: Russia and the Origins of European Energy Dependence* (New York: Palgrave Macmillan, 2013), which describes the "neomercantilist" motivations for Soviet natural gas export to Western Europe.

21. By 1973 this included trade with Ghana, Switzerland, Israel, and Spain. Letter of Permanent Hungarian Mission to the UN, to the Secretary General of UNCTAD, April 16, 1973, 2: ARR 40 1929 064 Box 548.

22. In its preparations for UNCTAD II (February–March 1968), the Hungarian Ministry for External Trade was critical of developing countries' "lack of realism" (Report to Government from Foreign Trade and Foreign Ministry, April 1968).

23. TASS International Service, March 24, 1964.

24. RGAE F. 9480 O. 9 D. 489 L. (1968), 102–109.

25. Early European Commission (EC) initiatives, such as the Yaoundé Convention, did indeed aim to keep Africa as a raw materials producer to Western European economies. See Veronique Dimier, *The Invention of a European Development Aid Bureaucracy: Recycling Empire* (New York: Palgrave Macmillan, 2014).

26. Massimiliano Trentin, "Modernization as State Building: The Two Germanies in Syria, 1963–1972," *Diplomatic History* 33, no. 3 (2009): 487–505. Alessandro Iandolo, "The Rise and Fall of the 'Soviet Model of Development' in West Africa, 1957–64," *Cold War History* 12, no. 4 (2012): 683–704; Friedman, *Shadow Cold War*, 29–31. See the useful discussion in David Engerman, "The Second World's Third World," *Kritika* 12, no. 1 (2011): 198–202. Francis Fukuyama, *Political Order and Political Decay: From the Industrialization to the Globalization of Democracy* (London: Profile Books, 2014), 328–334.

27. Michele Alacevich, "Planning Peace: Development Policies in Postwar Europe," paper at Development and Underdevelopment in Postwar Europe workshop, Columbia University, October 2014.

28. P. N. Rosenstein-Rodan, "The International Development of Economically Backward Areas," *International Affairs* 20, no. 2 (April 1944): 164.

29. European Commission for Europe In-Service Stipend Scheme, Reports, 1961–2, GX 22/46 (Geneva UN archive).

30. Sara Lorenzini, "Comecon and the South in the Years of Détente: A Study on East–South Economic Relations," *European Review of History* 21, no. 2 (2014): 185.

31. This was founded by József Bognár, who worked on Ghana's first Seven-Year Plan with Kwame Nkrumah. József Bognár, "Összefoglaló jelentés Ghanában végzett munkámról és ennek során szerzett tapasztalataimról." 1962. MNL OL XIX-A-90-c box 153.

32. Łukasz Stanek, "Socialist Networks and the Internationalization of Building Culture after 1945," *ABE Journal* 6 (2004).

33. See, for example, the Sri Lankan and Jamaican resistance to GATT membership as claimed by the Soviet TASS agency. See "Developing Countries Victory," *Moscow TASS*, April 9, 1964.

34. Mark Kramer, "The Decline in Soviet Arms Transfers to the Third World, 1986–1991," in *The End of the Cold War and the Third World: New Perspectives on Regional Conflict*, eds. Artemy Kalinovsky and Sergey Radchenko (Abingdon: Routledge, 2011), 56–57. On East Germany, see Klaus Storkmann, *Geheime Solidarität: Militärbeziehungen und Militärhilfen der DDR in die "Dritte Welt"* (Berlin: Christoph Links, 2012); Ruben Berrios, "The Political Economy of East-South Relations," *Journal of Peace Research* 20, no. 3 (1983): 240–241.

35. Michael Pettis, *The Volatility Machine: Emerging Economies and the Threat of Economic Collapse* (Oxford: Oxford University Press, 2001).

36. Eric Helleiner, *States and the Re-Emergence of Global Finance: From Bretton Woods to the 1990s* (Ithaca, NY: Cornell University Press, 1996); Perry Mehrling, "Essential Hybridity: A Money View of FX," *Journal of Comparative Economics* 41, no. 2 (May 2013): 355–363.

37. RGANI, f. 5, op. 76 d. 246 ll. 5–20.

38. *UNCTAD at 50*, 63.

39. Similar observations about Soviet power in a specifically Latin American context are made by Duccio Basosi, "The 'Missing Cold War' Reflections on the Latin American Debt Crisis 1979–1989," in *The End of the Cold War*, eds. Kalinovsky and Radchenko, 208–228.

40. For an excellent summary, see Nils Gilman, "The New International Economic Order: A Reintroduction," *Humanity* 6, no. 1 (Spring 2015): 2–4.

41. "Directives for the Romanian Delegation at UNCTAD III," ANIC, CC al PCR, *Cancelarie* 24, 1972, 22–23. Thanks to Bogdan Iacob for this reference.

42. Elizabeth Kridl Valkenier, "Revolutionary Change in the Third World: Recent Soviet Assessments," *World Politics* 38, no. 3 (1986): 423–424.

43. *Proceedings of the United Nations Conference on Trade and Development Fourth Session*, Nairobi, May 5–31, 1976, volume 1 report and annexes, 72.

44. O. T. Bogomolov, *Sotsialism i perestroika mezhdunarodnykh ekonomicheskikh otnosheniĭ* (Moscow: Mezhndunarodnaya Otnoshenia, 1982), 140–141.

45. At UNCTAD IV they offered the UNCTAD greater assistance from Comecon to assist developing regions with economic integration. Proceedings UNCTAD 1976, annex C, 150.

46. Lorenzini, "Comecon and the South," 189. It should be noted that many Eastern Bloc specialists were skeptical.

47. The level of Cuban citrus production almost doubled in value between 1981 and 1985. Anne Dietrich, "Bartering within and outside the CMEA: The GDR's Import of Cuban Fruits and Ethiopian Coffee," in *Between East and South Spaces of Interaction in the Globalizing Economy of the Cold War*, eds., Anna Calori, Anne-Kristin Hartmetz, Bence Kocsev, James Mark and Jan Zofka (Berlin: de Gruyter Oldenbourg, 2019).

48. This was initially signaled in a 1965 executive report produced for Alexei Kosygin by the Academy of Sciences in the wake of Khrushchev's ouster. It noted that the USSR would soon be a net importer of commodities and advocated the expansion of trade ties with developing countries to satisfy the USSR's growing needs. ARAN f. 1849 op. 1 d. 51 ll. 82–84. For later developments, see research delivered by IMESS in 1972 in ARAN f. 1933 op. 1 d. 88 ll. 52–59.

49. Hans-Joachim Döring, *Es geht um unsere Existenz: Die Politik der DDR gegenüber der Dritten Welt am Beispiel von Mosambik und Äthiopien* (Berlin: Links, 1999). On the attraction of Eastern Europe as a market for Iranian oil in the 1980s, see "Iran-Iraq Seeking to Expand Barter Trade with Eastern Europe," B-Wire, September 20, 1984, HU OSA 300-40-1- Box 717 (OSA Archive, Budapest). The Iranians valued Eastern Europe's willingness to engage in barter trade (against OPEC rules), as hard currency reserves had been drained by the war with Iraq.

50. David R. Stone, "CMEA's International Investment Bank and the Crisis of Developed Socialism," *Journal of Cold War Studies* 10, no. 3 (Summer 2008): 48–77.

51. Conversations between Leonid Brezhnev and the GDR leader Walter Ulbricht (1969): APRF f. 80 op. 1. d. 981 ll. 64 ob. - 7 ob. republished in *Leonid Brezhnev rabochie i denvnikovye zapisi 1964–1982*, eds. A. N. Artizov et al. (Moscow: Istlit, 2016), 354–355.

52. Randall W. Stone, *Satellites and Commissars: Strategy and Conflict in the Politics of Soviet-Bloc Trade* (Princeton: Princeton University Press, 1996), 115–202.

53. Stone, *Satellites and Commissars*, 3–14.

54. Stone, "CMEA's International Investment Bank," 48–77.

55. Karl Wohlmuth, "Structural Adjustment and East-West-South Economic Cooperation: Key Issues," *Structural Adjustment in the World Economy and East-West-South Economic Cooperation* (Bremen: Institute for World Economics and International Management, University of Bremen, 1989), 26.

56. Dietrich, "Bartering"; Victor Petrov, "The Rose and the Lotus: Bulgarian Electronic Entanglements in India (1967–1990)," paper presented at Spaces of Interaction between the Socialist Camp and the Global South: Knowledge Production, Trade, and Scientific-Technical Cooperation in the Cold War Era, November 2017, Leipzig.

57. Stone, *Satellites and Commissars*, 27–39.

58. Elena Dragomir, "The Formation of the Soviet Bloc's Council for Mutual Economic Assistance: Romania's Involvement," *Journal of Cold War Studies* 14, no. 1 (2012): 34–47.

59. Nikolai Fedorenko, *Vospaminau proshloe, zagliadyvau v budushie* (Moscow: Nauka, 1999), 376–377.

60. Stone, *Satellites and Commissars*, 246–248.

61. In South Korea, by contrast, taxes on exports were used to further support exporting companies.

62. Chris O'Malley, *Bonds without Borders: A History of the Eurobond Market* (Chichester: Wiley, 2015), 13.

63. Stephen Kotkin, *The Kiss of Debt: The East Bloc Goes Borrowing*, in *Shock of the Global: The 1970s in Perspective*, eds. Niall Ferguson et al. (Cambridge, MA: Harvard University Press, 2010), 80–96.

64. Tamás Gerőcs and András Pinkasz, "Debt-Ridden Development on Europe's Eastern Periphery," in *Global Inequalities in World-Systems Perspective: Theoretical Debates and Methodological Innovations Series*, eds. Manuela Boatcă, Andrea Komlosy, and Hans-Heinrich Nolte (London: Routledge, 2017).

65. Postwar surveys of Iraqi debt found that approximately two-thirds of its 130 billion in foreign debt was owed to non–Paris Club states, including former Comecon members such as Poland, the Czech Republic, and Bulgaria. Martin Weiss, *Congressional Research Survey*, "Iraq's Debt Relief: Procedure and Implications for International Debt Relief," Washington, DC, Congressional Research Service, 2011, https://fas.org/sgp/crs/mideast/RL33376.pdf.

66. At the same time the Soviet Union owed approximately 75 billion dollars, or half of the amount owed to it. "To whom did we give 85,800,000 rubles 'in loans'," *Chas Pik* 1 (Feb. 26, 1990), 2. Thanks to Johanna Bockman for sharing this.

67. Paris Club, "The Five Key Principles." Thanks to Johanna Bockman for this information.

68. On this parallel crisis, we are grateful to Johanna Bockman, who shared her manuscript, "The 1980s Debt Crisis Revisited: The Second and Third Worlds as Creditors."

69. Wohlmuth, "Structural Adjustment," 26.

70. Berrios, "The Political Economy," 243.

71. S. D. Muni, "Major Developments in India's Foreign Policy and Relations, July–December 1978," *International Studies* 19, no. 1 (1980): 71–85. A 1987 UNCTAD report on trade between the Eastern Bloc with Cuba and Vietnam noted that the Soviet Union was insisting that loans no longer be paid back in commodities but in convertible currency. "Project Buy Back Arrangements," 1. UNCTAD archive (Geneva): ARR 40 1929 064 Box 548.

72. For an early account of this shift, see László Csaba, *Eastern Europe in the World Economy* (Cambridge: Cambridge University Press, 1990), 127–129. Pál Germuska, "Failed Eastern Integration and a Partly Successful Opening Up to the West: The Economic Reorientation of Hungary during the 1970s," *European Review of History* 21, no. 2 (2014): 278. Two hundred and twenty-six Hungarian firms had arranged joint ventures across the Iron Curtain by 1976 but only 7 percent in third markets. HU OSA 300-2-5-Box 49 (Open Society Archive, Budapest).

73. Patrick Gutman, "Tripartite Industrial Cooperation and Third Countries," in *East-West-South: Economic Interactions Between Three Worlds*, ed. Christopher T. Saunders (London: Macmillan, 1981), 337.

74. UNCTAD archive (Geneva): ARR 40/1929/ 549 (Tripartite Industrial Cooperation folder).

75. Lorenzini, "Comecon and the South," 187. The leftist Friedrich Ebert Foundation was at the forefront of this. Sara Lorenzini, "Globalising Ostpolitik," *Cold War History* 9, no. 2 (2009): 223–242.

76. Johnathan Zatlin, *The Currency of Socialism: Money and Political Culture in East Germany* (Cambridge: Cambridge University Press, 2008), 93–139; Vladislav Zubok, *A Failed Empire: The Soviet Union in the Cold War from Khrushchev to Gorbachev* (Raleigh, NC: University of North Carolina Press, 2007), 201–226.

77. Jan Záhořík, "Czechoslovakia and Congo/Zaire under Mobutu, 1965–1980," *Canadian Journal of History* 52, no. 2 (2017): 311.

78. Germuska, "Failed Eastern Integration," 278.

79. *Hungarian Exporter*, March 3, 1983.

80. See, for example, ARAN f. 1933 op. 1 d. 110 ll. 232–238.

81. Zubok, *Failed Empire*, 227–277.

82. An estimated 20 percent of hard currency earnings for the Soviet Union came from arms sales in the 1970s. Laure Despres, "Third World Arms Trade of the Soviet Union and Eastern Europe," in *East-South Relations in the World Economy*, ed. Marie Lavigne (Westview: Boulder and London, 1988), 58.

83. "Report about the Principles for Realization of Special Material Trade and for Discussion about and Affirmation of Business Negotiations and Supplies," Central Military Archive (Vojenský Ústřední Archiv), Czech Republic, series Ministry of National Defense (Ministerstvo Národní Obrany), 1970, box 254.

84. Petr Zídek and Karel Sieber, *Československo a Blízký východ v letech 1948–1989* (Ústav mezinárodních vztahů: Prague, 2009), 19–49.

85. It did not hurt that touting the dubious successes of these operations to the increasingly ailing Brezhnev boosted the prestige of these factions at home. Yuval Weber, "Petropolitics and Foreign Policy: The Fiscal and Institutional Origins of Russian Foreign Policy 1964–2012," PhD diss., University of Texas at Austin, 2014, 64–71; Odd Arne Westad, *The Global Cold War: Third World Interventions and the Making of Our Times* (Cambridge: Cambridge University Press, 2011), 194–249; Christopher Andrews, *The World Was Going Our Way: The KGB and the Battle for the Third World* (New York: Basic Books, 2006), 29–36.

86. Mark Kramer, "The Decline of Soviet Arms Transfers to the Third World, 1986–1991," in *The End of the Cold War*, eds. Kalinovsky and Radchenko, 46–100. This compared to 16 percent of the market supplied from the United States.

87. See the chapter in this volume by Alena K. Alamgir and Christina Schwenkel, "From Socialist Assistance to National Self-Interest: Vietnamese Labor Migration into CMEA Countries."

88. James Mark and Tobias Rupprecht, "Europe's 1989 in Global Context," in *History of Communism*, *vol. 3*, eds. Silvio Pons, Juliane Furst, and Mark Selden (Cambridge: Cambridge University Press, 2017), 227; Tobias Rupprecht, "Formula Pinochet: Chilean Lessons for Russian Liberal Reformers during the Soviet Collapse, 1970–2000," *Journal of Contemporary History* 51, no. 1 (January 2016): 165–186. Chris Miller, *The Struggle to Save the Soviet Economy: Mikhail Gorbachev and the Collapse of the USSR* (Chapel Hill: University of North Carolina Press, 2016), 25–30.

89. The UNCTAD Division for Trade with Socialist Countries, "Developments in Economic and Foreign Trade Management Systems in the Socialist Countries of Eastern Europe," December 9, 1987. ARR40 1929 065 Box 546.

90. UNCTAD Report from the second Asian Regional State Trading Organizations Meeting, Manila, Philippines, September 1988. ARR 40/1929/070.

91. For an account along these lines, see André Steiner, "The Globalisation Process and the Eastern Bloc Countries in the 1970s and 1980s," *European Review of History* 20, no. 2 (June 2014): 165–181.

92. Mazower, *Governing the World*, chapter 12. Gilman, "The New International Economic Order," 6–8. Elites in the United States enabled the consolidation of the power of their oil multinationals in the 1960s—against campaigns to break them up as excessive monopolies—in order to counter the Soviet challenge. Douglas Rogers, "Petrobarter: Oil, Inequality, and the Political Imagination in and after the Cold War," *Current Anthropology* 55, no. 2 (April 2014): 137–138. The United States was also prepared to let Japanese and Korean economies grow by guaranteeing access to their large home markets rather than let them become peripheries open to other ideological influences. Christopher Chase-Dunn, "Globalization: A World-Systems Perspective," *Journal of World-Systems Research* 5, no. 2 (August 1999): 187–216.

93. Andreas Eckert and Shalini Randeria, *Vom Imperialismus zum Empire: Nicht-westliche Perspektiven auf Globalisierung* (Frankfurt-on-Main: Suhrkamp Verlag, 2009); Leslie Sklair, "A Transnational Framework for Theory and Research in the Study of Globalization," in *Frontiers of Globalization Research: Theoretical and Methodological Approaches*, ed. Ino Rossi (Berlin: Springer, 2007), 93–108.

94. Susan Bayly coined the term *socialist ecumene* to describe the endurance of socialist-era values in forms of trade and assistance to other parts of the world in a similar peripheral position in the neoliberal globalized order. Susan Bayly, "Vietnamese Narratives of Tradition, Exchange and Friendship in the Worlds of the Global Socialist Ecumene," in *Enduring Socialism: Explorations of Revolution and Transformation, Restoration and Continuation*, eds. Harry West and Parvathi Raman (Oxford: Berghahn, 2008), 125–147.

JAMES MARK is Professor of History at the University of Exeter. He is author of *The Unfinished Revolution: Making Sense of the Communist Past in Central-Eastern Europe* and coauthor of *Europe's 1968: Voices of Revolt* and *1989: A Global History of Eastern Europe*.

YAKOV FEYGIN is History and Policy Fellow at the Harvard Kennedy School of Government at Harvard University.

2 The Cold War in the Margins of Capital: The Soviet Union's Introduction to the Decolonized World, 1955–1961

Oscar Sanchez-Sibony

Even as the geographical contours of Cold War narratives expand to encompass global politics, the assumptions underpinning the Cold War paradigm have remained Eurocentric: the Cold War meant a division of Europe, and therefore, it was supposed, there had to be a division of the world along similar lines. The language used to describe this division has changed. The war that was once imagined as one between capitalism and communism, or between totalitarianism and the free world, is now examined as a conflict between two contesting projects of modernity.[1] But while changing the terms may bring a number of subtleties to historical analysis, it does little to elucidate what the Cold War was. The problem lies in the failure to interrogate the problematic nature of capitalism, and by extension communism. With a wink and a yawn, author and reader agree on a set of crude economic notions about liberal capitalism, an understanding that communism was its opposite (often simply anticapitalism), and finally a complete separation between the two systems that is understood to be a core feature of "communist ideology." Existing liberal capitalism is understood, against much evidence, to stand for free trade as a matter of principle, so that its opposite must stand for, well, the opposite.[2] This notion of socialist autarky does the intellectual work of expunging the Soviet Union from the liberal world order so it can be imagined as a camp at war defined by its will to oppose.[3]

It is within this epistemological context that the search for a specifically socialist world system makes sense, that is, only within the wider discursive structure of the Cold War as envisioned by academics who are reluctant to question capitalism as a historical category.[4] There is, in this rendering, no political logic to the organization of finance and trade flows, no colonial-built environments shaping postcolonial worldviews. What is proposed, instead, are two powerful states with sharply differing visions of modernity acting in a Hobbesian international political arena. Power is interpreted as having an ideational source that leaves little room for the vastly differing levels of material and institutional command the United States and the Soviet Union could bring to bear internationally. This chapter originates in work that, like this volume, inscribes the Communist Bloc into the globalizing impulses of the postwar world, both passively and actively. However it insists on seeing these impulses as something more than the realization of ideological projects (whether socialist, capitalist, or neoliberal). It instead attempts to explore the ideas that guided Soviet aid and trade politics in the Global South within the material possibilities and realities that constrained and generated their field of vision. The documentary evidence is clear: the Soviets felt the force of the capitalist world economy in their bones—as did their partners in the South. They wrote about it to each other endlessly and explicitly forged and recast their policies in the Global South within the gravitational field of relation to the West, though not as an antithesis to it in practice. One of the most significant built environments within which the Soviets were introduced to the decolonized world was the Bretton Woods system, or more accurately its failure in the 1950s.[5] The initial decline of the Bretton Woods project was, however, no less decisive, perpetuating a general autarky the Soviets and the Global South sought to escape through a series of second-best arrangements on the margins of capital.[6]

Bearing material differences in mind, the view from the Soviet side of the superpower equation becomes decidedly more equivocal. Although a wide range of different thematic and geographical approaches can be employed to interrogate the narrative framework of Cold War bipolarity, this chapter will scrutinize Soviet economic relations with the Global South, which conventional wisdom represents almost exclusively as an arena of bipolar competition, an area of geostrategic expansionism contested by the two superpowers in the wake of imperial obsolescence. If scholars in the past discerned a coherent Soviet foreign policy strategy, today descendant narratives speak of "socialist projects" and models of "socialist forms of development" that in circular reasoning often turn out to be socialist merely because of where they originated. Is a steel mill socialist when provided by a socialist country or owned by a state, and capitalist otherwise? Are categories of motivation and action such as "solidarity" and "planning" exclusively or even primarily socialist? Given the restructuring power that material and financial flows ultimately had on the world in the 1970s and 1980s, is it wise to disentangle this sociopolitical force from Soviet purpose in the world?[7] Might the use of such terms as *project* and *model* lend an unearned coherence to Soviet international action?

This kind of perceived coherence in Soviet foreign economic relations so prevalent in Cold War–era narratives of Soviet foreign policy was the first casualty of the archival revolution.[8] There was no great communist crusade. Indeed, the choice of countries on which the USSR lavished goodwill, such as India, Egypt, and Indonesia, were often much too large and politically pluralist to be easily influenced, as the West had known for some time—and conveniently forgot when talk turned toward communist subversion. The closest thing to a strategy was the view that Soviet economic relations should generally foster the growth of the public sector and that economic decision making should be centralized. This was not so different from then-prevailing liberal development thought or the development thinking of the Global South; with respect to Africa, Daniel Speich has shown that "capitalism and socialism were taken up as complementary sources of developmental knowledge rather than as mutually exclusive ethics of distribution."[9] The belief in the transformational power of the state to foster economic development was widespread—even in the rich, liberal countries that practiced economic aid to poorer countries in ways that benefited urban elites and state power.[10]

In the mid-1950s poor countries, particularly former colonies, which did not have diversified trade, started knocking at the Soviets' door to initiate new trade channels. When Nikita Khrushchev went on his boisterous first trip to Southeast Asia in 1955 to speak on the successes of the Soviet Union and its commitment to the principle of peaceful coexistence, Prime Minister U Nu of Burma wanted to know only one thing: what could the Soviet Union offer in terms of trade, and how quickly could it be developed between the two countries?[11] The same went for Indonesia, which in 1954 entrusted its ambassador with the task of developing direct trade with the Soviet Union to lessen dependence on the Dutch for international commercial needs.[12] This was also the reason the Moroccans approached the Soviet trade representative in Paris in 1957 with a plan to obviate French intermediation and establish direct trade between the two countries.[13] These countries were not joining the socialist camp. Their attraction to socialist ideals was real, hybridized, and sociopolitically consequential, and that created the multiplicity of exchanges documented in this volume. More immediately, however, what they sought in the Soviet Union was something concrete: a mediator that could weaken the rigors of a taxing world economy still dominated by the preponderance of the West and the logics of a capitalist system. The West continued to be the fulcrum that prized open and regulated the USSR's relations with the Global South. The Soviets did not abandon the rhetoric of developing an alternative "socialist world market." But this never took any discernible institutional form, in contrast to the powerful impulses emanating from the liberal institutions of Western pedigree (IMF, GATT, World Bank, BIS, etc.). Meaningful economic possibilities and their attendant political imaginaries permeated the liberal institutions around which the world orbited and found anchor in the international monetary sovereignty of the US dollar, leaving the Soviet Union and its partners in the Global South to improvise on the margins of capital. Marginality in the inchoate capitalist globalization of the 1950s and early 1960s, rather than a positive alternative vision of economic organization, was the context within which the Soviet Union first encountered the Global South.

Soviet Aid at Inception in the Late 1950s

Semyon Skachkov was the longtime head of the State Committee for Foreign Economic Relations (Gosudarstvennyi komitet po vneshnim ekonomicheskim sviaziam, henceforth GKĖS), the Soviet aid agency. This is what he wrote in a 1959 report to the Central Committee by way of justifying his agency's work: "Foreign economic relations, if built on the foundation of equality and mutual benefit, promote economic progress and lead to a mutual understanding among states and peoples, advance the weakening of international pressure and improve relations among governments."[14] The historical experience of many governments, the report continued, "convincingly proves that this task of progress cannot be achieved without the construction of domestic industry and the development of a diverse economy."[15] To this end the Soviet Union was also willing to shoulder its share of the white man's burden and refashion the poor countries of the world in its industrial image.

The parallels in the philosophy of aid between the liberal West and the communist East were striking.[16] They were also, of course, not acknowledged; as in almost everything else, the Soviets represented themselves as the antithesis of capitalism. Their worldview was one dependency theorists would recognize. In their own self-representation, the "goal and terms of Soviet help to underdeveloped countries differs favorably from the help of capitalist countries. Our goal is clear: we strive to help underdeveloped countries ensure their economic independence, more quickly stand on their own two feet, create a modern national industry, more fully utilize their natural resources, lift agricultural production and so contribute to improving the lives of the people of these countries."[17] This, they argued, stood in sharp contrast to the position of capitalist countries, which were interested only in stimulating raw material production for export and reinforcing their monopolistic position to draw these economies to theirs in an exploitative embrace.[18]

And yet when put into practice, the policies were the same as those of the West. They both focused on the "hardware" of developing economies through large-scale infrastructure and industrial projects—a far cry from the microlending and educational "software" approach that is in fashion today. Although both countries tended to emphasize large, engineering projects, the Soviet Union supported import substitution much more self-consciously than the United States. As Skachkov's report envisaged, Soviet credits, to be repaid in twelve years from the moment of the project's completion at 2.5 percent interest, were directed to the construction of enterprises that would not only pay off the debt in that time frame but also create capital for the further development of the economy.[19] Most damningly, as with their rich, liberal counterparts, the Soviets insisted on their aid credits being spent on Soviet industrial products, thus stimulating Soviet domestic production rather than production and employment in recipient countries.

But despite the similarities in worldview, in what they understood to be the role of economic relations in world politics, and in practice, there were several differences between Soviet aid and that of the West. One immediate difference was in the role of recipient governments in economic relations. In extending aid to poor countries, the Soviets sought to strengthen the public sector of the target country, whereas Western countries insisted on strengthening the private sector, even as they often followed a more confused policy.[20] India is the most famous case in point. Aid from the West was usually channeled through the Aid-India Consortium, which included eleven countries and the World Bank and which disbursed aid to a mix of public and private-sector projects.[21] The Soviets, however, liked to support large—and conspicuous—industrial projects, sometimes muscling out private Indian consultants and subcontractors that the Indian government sought to involve.[22]

Most often, however, Soviet aid-giving idiosyncrasies arose from a lack of a capability to project power and an absence of clearly articulated material interests. A lack of defined purpose lay behind a real and important difference between East and West, one that the Soviets liked to advertise: communist investments did not entail ownership of the enterprises they built in poor countries; this meant no repatriated profits and no enduring foreign presence.[23] The utility of such a no-strings-attached approach to aid would be reconsidered early in the 1960s. Furthermore, as Khrushchev pointed out in his memoirs about aid projects approved during his rule, the Soviets were also weary of having locals work under Soviet management. Direct Soviet management of aid projects might lead to unwelcome conflicts with the recipient country's workers, which would reflect badly on the first proletariat state on earth.[24] So rather than build on a contract basis, acting as employers as other aid donors did, the Soviet leadership often sent technicians, engineers, and administrators to give technical direction and manage equipment deliveries; the plans were, of course, also Soviet. The only profit they derived, besides the export of goods and services, was the 2.5 percent interest on the money they lent to build the various factories and projects.

On one issue, at least, Soviet avowed motives had a salutary tinge of self-interest. The GKĖS laid out a set of public relations recommendations for the expansion of economic relations with developing countries given to the Central Committee in December 1958. Not only was profit making in poor countries against the principles of the Soviet Union, GKĖS argued, it could disorient progressive circles within these same countries and could furnish arguments against the growth of economic cooperation with the Soviet Bloc.[25] That rationale illustrated a modicum of strategic thinking but also a telling anxiety: Soviet policy makers had a deeply ingrained sense of inferiority when it came to power politics. And why should they not? They were, after all, fundamentally of less consequence than the United States, with an economy perhaps equivalent to, or at most slightly bigger than, that of Great Britain or France in GDP terms. The 1958 GKĖS recommendations bespoke an implicit sense of weakness and lack of standing: "In relation to [developing] countries," it noted, "the most important task at the moment is the punctual fulfillment of the Soviet Union's responsibilities according to our concluded agreements."[26] Fear of breaking promises and agreements made with developing countries would become an important theme in prioritizing production for aid, a task domestic industry preferred to shun.

The 1958 GKĖS warning on the punctual fulfillment of responsibilities reflected no idle fear. The disorganization of aid exports paralleled the endemic disorganization in the Soviet domestic economy; inefficiencies were rife, and the power relations at play in domestic inter-industry exchange that often managed inefficiencies nationally had little purchase when international credibility was on the line. Rather than making use of the typically Soviet supply expediter (the famous *tolkach*), GKĖS—or whichever other ministry was being inconvenienced by the incompetence of others—could appeal directly to the top to get the issue resolved, usually to Gosplan (the State Planning Committee), the Council of Ministers, or the powerful Presidium member Anastas Mikoyan directly. While the United States and the European powers could afford to dally and politicize their aid as a tool of coercion and discipline, the Soviet Union fretted over delays, disorganization, and general ineptitude, which, as every Soviet official trying to get something done was quick to point out, might harm the Soviet Union's image in the eyes of the aid recipients.[27]

To be sure, not all Soviet aid was incompetently delivered. In his memoirs Khrushchev recalls the construction of the Bhilai Steel Plant in India, of all Soviet aid projects second in fame and prestige only to the Aswan Dam. The Indians had asked the (West) Germans and the British along with the Soviets for help in building three different steel mills, and even had them check each other's plans and blueprints before starting on them.[28] Khrushchev was determined that the Soviet steel mill should begin producing steel and iron before that of the Germans, and, as he reports it, it did in October 1959. Furthermore, production went smoothly, and the Indians soon asked to have its capacity increased, a service the Soviets again provided competently.

Nevertheless the Bhilai Steel Plant was an exceptional case. Khrushchev followed this particular project personally and assigned as its manager a renowned

Soviet engineer, V. E. Dymshitz, who had played a prominent role in the construction of such important projects as the Kuznetsk and Magnitogorsk metallurgical plants in the 1930s and went on to retire as a deputy chairman of the Council of Ministers in 1985 after passing through high-level posts at Gosplan and other state committees. Dymshitz reported directly to the Indian prime minister Jawaharlal Nehru on the progress of the plant, and the competitive context of the project, an atypical circumstance, virtually guaranteed the Indians a high level of involvement on the part of the Soviets.[29]

But issues of competence are auxiliary to a more important detail: Soviet aid, although generous for a financially humble nation, was never extensive. It is estimated that from the end of the Second World War until its fall, the Soviet Union offered a total of $68 billion in economic aid, of which about $41 billion had been delivered; this is about the same as the United States provided Israel alone during a similar period.[30] Again India serves as an example. It is often asserted that India leaned toward the Soviet camp during the Cold War, and Soviet aid was alternatively seen as a reason and an outcome of that close relationship.[31] Diplomatic statements by Khrushchev and Nehru, as well as a high-profile aid project or two, are often held as proof. This speaks only to the remarkable propagandistic success of Soviet aid, which convinced the academic establishment—and the impressionable CIA. Actual figures, as the graphs below illustrate, make it difficult to sustain the material correlation so often implied between aid and political allegiance.

On the question of aid and the political loyalty of India, the grand framework of superpower confrontation once again leads us astray.[32] Both with respect to India and the countries of the Global South more broadly, a far more important determinant in Soviet undertakings in the world economic and political arena was the former colonies' inherently weak position in the world economy. The Soviet Union did not and could not hope to replace the West as an aid provider and general economic partner in exchange for a geopolitical alliance; Soviet leaders thought this a presumptuous and ludicrous notion. And neither did leaders in the South anticipate such a change in economic orientation, aware as they quickly became of the limits of Soviet power. Moreover, this would have been anathema to their ambition for full independence. Only the feverish imaginings of American policy makers kept this idea alive—armed as American policy makers were with the lurid estimates of Soviet economic might imagined by the CIA.

Too much has been made of the Soviet "aid offensive" that Khrushchev initiated in the mid-1950s, commentators ascribing to it more weight than seems appropriate considering its absolute volume as well as its volume vis-à-vis Western aid. West German aid to India alone surpassed Soviet aid all the way to 1965 in aggregate terms and every individual year thereafter to the 1980s;[33] where are all the studies

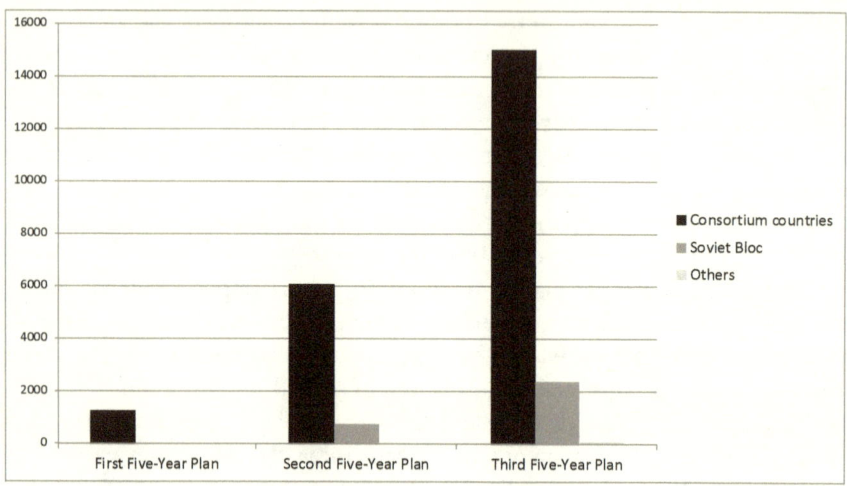

Fig. 2.1. Utilized Soviet loans to India, 1951–1966 (in millions of Rupees). (Economic Survey 1966–67, Government of India).

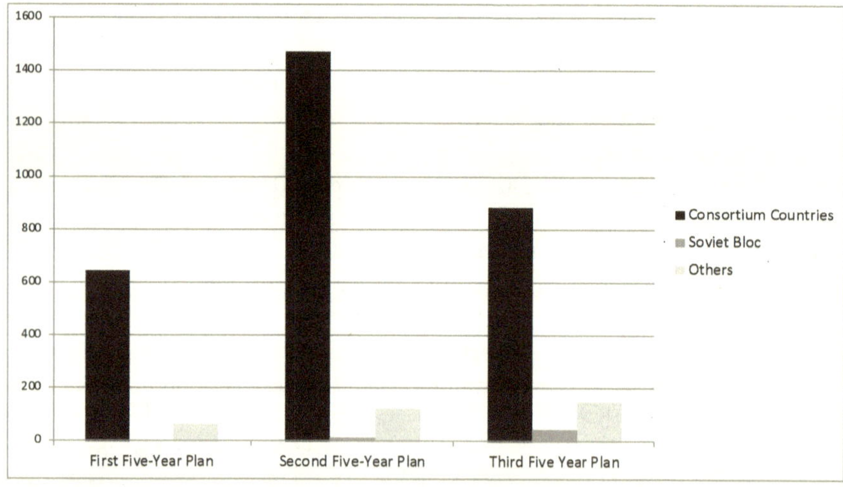

Fig. 2.2. Utilized Soviet grants to India, 1951–1966 (in millions of Rupees). (Economic Survey 1966–67, Government of India).

on the West German aid offensive? Soviet aid is better understood as a component of the Soviet Union's main strategic priority: its entrance into the world economy as a major trade partner, particularly in the Global South. The idea was not to subvert countries through lavish gifts but to become a presence and to help dependent economies achieve greater autonomy. In this sense, Soviet officials hoped Soviet aid would complement trade to work in tandem toward the same goal.

"The granting of technical and economic aid to underdeveloped countries," argued Skachkov in a December 1958 set of recommendations to the Central Committee, "must necessarily be supplemented and strengthened with the development of extensive trade relations, as only a regulated exchange of goods can serve a stable and fundamental development of economic cooperation between the Soviet Union and the countries of the East. Trade based on the principles of equality and mutual benefit serves as a form of aid from the Soviet Union to the countries of the East, easing for the latter the fight in strengthening their positions in the economic relations with the developed, imperialist governments."[34] Like aid, Skachkov continued, trade should support the growth of the public sector, although it should also be used to fortify nationalist elements in the private sector, inasmuch as their strength would lead to the weakening of foreign capital. All these developments would improve the economic position of the Soviet Union, as it would give the Soviets the chance to obtain products they had heretofore been buying in international markets directly from the producing countries, particularly raw materials and foodstuffs such as rubber, cocoa, and leather goods.[35]

Neither to the East nor to the West, the South Looks to the South

Apparent Soviet success in establishing aid and trade networks is not the only proof historians routinely produce to establish the Soviet Union as a conspiratorial superpower on the march in the Third World. The proof also lies, we are told, in its power to inspire imitation. The progress of the state sector in many former colonies, the inward redirection of their industrial production, and the outright appropriation of typically Soviet institutions such as collectivization in Tanzania or Five-Year Plans in India constitutes incontrovertible evidence of Soviet influence and its power to inspire revolution against the West. Melvyn Leffler's book on the bipolar confrontation, for example, proposes a narrative of such equivalence between the two sides, one so strictly bipolar, that the Soviet Union cannot but be the great inspiration for Third World leaders. "From Cuba to Algeria to Ghana to Egypt to India and to Indonesia, new nationalist leaders voiced their support for planning," Leffler writes. "Most of them were not communists, indeed they sometimes repressed and imprisoned communists. But *planning* was their common vocabulary."[36] The list of countries is always the same when historians want to invoke Soviet "advances" in the Third World. In fact, where planning was concerned, Leffler might have added Spain and South Korea to the list; after all, India's indicative, largely market-based Five-Year Plans had much more in common with the Five-Year Plans that guided the economy of those two staunch enemies of the Soviet Union than with the strictly mobilizational Five-Year Plans drawn up at Gosplan headquarters. But then the point is to posit the Soviet Union as a pole of attraction and inspiration. The equation is:

planning + economic engagement with the USSR = advance of the Soviet world order. But planning was too universal to belong solely to that equation, and economic engagement with the USSR was radical only because American hostility to it made it so. The fact is that many postcolonial governments assumed the tasks of planning from their colonial predecessors, and for many of them American (or Western) aggression determined their economic engagement with the Communist Bloc much more decisively than anything the communists did or stood for.

A narrative not so steeped in the determinism of bipolarity affords a more illuminating perspective. Political economist Jeffry Frieden offers a different point of departure.[37] Rather than looking East, Frieden has the newly independent countries looking toward the southern cone of the Western Hemisphere. South America led the postwar world in experimenting with import-substitution industrialization (ISI), and the reasons for this can readily be found in the economic crucible of the 1930s.[38]

The 1930s had been a time of economic isolation for Latin America—as in the Soviet Union and everywhere else. Production until then had been centered to a large degree on commodity exports such as coffee and copper, and these commodities had seen their markets dry up during the worldwide turn to autarky of the interwar years and the Second World War. This in turn reduced imports of manufactured products from Europe and the United States, which fostered local industry in Latin America in order to meet demand formerly satisfied by the industrialized nations.[39] "Urban classes and masses expanded to fill the economic, social, and political vacuum left by the disintegration of the traditional open economies," Frieden explains. "Latin America was transformed from a bastion of open-economy traditionalism to a stronghold of economic nationalism, developmentalism, and populism."[40] At this point the region developed in a similar pattern to that of the United States, where the rise of industry that overtook the cotton and tobacco export farmers in the second half of the nineteenth century was accompanied by protectionist measures. Latin America was merely half a century behind. By the time international trade was revived once again under the auspices of the Bretton Woods system, the social and political context in Latin America had turned decisively against export farmers and miners (the latter in many cases now nationalized) and in favor of domestic industrialists and powerful labor movements that called for protection. As a corollary, much of the communications and energy infrastructure passed into state control, as did many steel mills and other industrial assets. These were often too large for local capitalists to finance, and the Great Depression and Second World War had starved them of capital and brought many to bankruptcy. Their production would now work to further national industrial development.[41]

Developments in the colonial world followed a similar path and were compounded by developments in the metropoles.[42] The interwar period and then the Second World War left a legacy of strengthened urban and local business interests in the colonies. Despite an initial intensification of imperial efforts in the immediate postwar period, by the early 1950s the overwhelming success of the Marshall Plan and the general effort on the part of the United States to tear down political and economic barriers among European countries created conditions that increasingly underscored the economic irrelevance of empire. With Western Europe under American military protection and given the rapid expansion of intra-European and transatlantic trade, the geopolitical justification for empire also weakened.

It waned in the face of the increasing difficulties the Europeans found in their colonies. But what is important to note here is that these soon-to-be-independent countries were not a tabula rasa on the lookout for ideological direction.[43] With the Europeans and their local allies dominating the agricultural and primary export sectors of the colonial economies, the urban capitalist and working classes, which agitated for independence and which were often close to the military, were far from confused about the national development strategy they would support after empire's end. Import substitution industrialization (ISI), Frieden concludes, "was the universal postcolonial solvent."[44]

Of course, this impressionistic generalization masks a broad plurality of experiences in the former colonial world that also depended on domestic contingencies and the rise of idiosyncratic leaders. Furthermore, the colonial experience of different regions diverged widely one from another, which in turn helped set different developmental paths. South Korea and Taiwan, for example, opted for a developmental state that replicated their colonial political economy and the export-led success of their late-developing former colonial master, Japan.[45] In contrast, empire on the cheap in West Africa left woefully underdeveloped state institutions, some of which, such as Nigeria, went on to become rapacious and self-serving.[46] Importantly, however, imperial rule had left newly independent countries an authoritarian legacy and a hegemonic belief—shared by many in Western Europe, for that matter—in the transformative powers of the state.

Despite these differences, the analogous consequences of the disintegration of the world economy in the 1930s are nevertheless striking. Indeed, the most meaningful development in the newly independent countries after the liberal world's meltdown was not their position in a left-right spectrum that belied their allegiances in a bipolar world. As Frieden points out, the Global South opted out of a liberal system en masse—inasmuch as they reasonably could—and yet did not favor a Soviet-style economy. Broadly, the majority of these countries followed South America's lead in establishing ISI as their preferred economic strategy.

They also looked to enter into commercial relations with the Soviet Union. Essentially, Third World ISI policies dovetailed quite well with the Soviet Union's foreign trade strategy to end the isolation it had lived through. That complementarity of interests led to a convergence of ideas—a rather different starting point for analysis than the ideological capture implicitly invoked in the bipolar framework. Both parties agreed that import substitution freed former colonies from dependence on Western markets and products, thus weakening international pressure. It also strengthened the role of the state in its economic functions, another desirable outcome that would facilitate further trade expansion with the Soviet Union, as Skachkov had explained in his report to the Central Committee. This was a position that had already been well staked out academically in the Soviet Union by the late 1950s.[47]

This point of departure may have been lost on Western analysts, but Soviet analysts were not so ideologically blinkered; moreover, when it came to matters of planning and state-led development, rather than instinctively lumping everything into one sinister category of analysis, the Soviets understood differences in degree and kind and felt the sting of competition. This was brought to Gosplan's attention—in case it had been missed—in an appeal by A. Efimov, the director of the Economic Research Institute (the Nauchno-Issledovatel'skij Ekonomicheskij Insitut, or NIEI). The director explained that from the mid-1950s the majority of the developing countries in Africa, Asia, and Latin America had been trying to organize a planned economy, or at least a plan to develop their economy. Many had come to the Soviet Union asking for specialists who would speak their language, but the Soviets were not able to supply enough specialists to meet the demand.[48] There might have been a shortage of specialists with language skills in the Soviet Union, but not at the United Nations. In that bastion of centralized development planning, these countries found eager bourgeois economists ready to help them, Efimov warned his superiors. There was also a lack of Soviet academic textbooks on how to plan an economy, so the leaders of these countries turned again to the works of bourgeois economists.[49]

Some Soviet Conclusions, 1961

The 1960s witnessed a consolidation of sorts in the Soviet relationship with the Global South. This was not so much in the character of the relationship; economic relations with the Third World were as disparate as the members of that sweeping category themselves. It was its value in the structure of Soviet economic relations that mattered. Historians of the Cold War make the clever observation that once the bipolar enmity froze in place in Europe, a process that found its culmination in the Berlin Wall, the rivalry pivoted out of its European origins and into the international arena. But economically this narrative does not make any sense. The alleged political freeze in Europe was actually the beginning of a

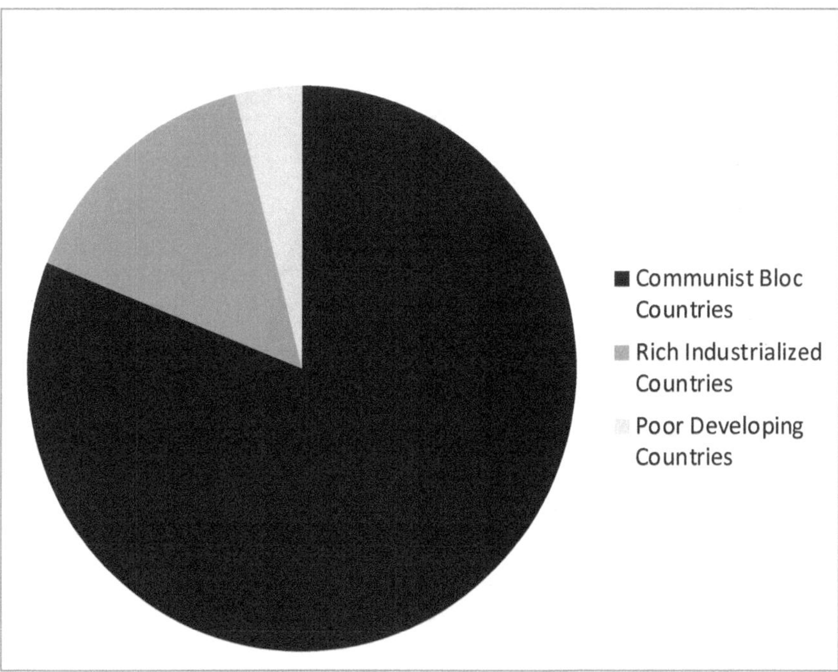

Fig. 2.3. Regional weight of Soviet foreign trade, 1950. (Calculated from Ministerstvo vneshniĭ torgovli, *Vneshniaia torgovlia SSSR, 1922–81. Iubileinyĭ statisticheskiĭ obzor.*) (Moscow: Izdatel'stvo financy i statistika, 1982, 26–27.)

continental economic integration that saw a continuous increase in trade with the West, while the economic pivot to the Global South had little to do with a positive development of purposeful Soviet policy. The ambitions that drove that shift are more fruitfully sought in the Global South than in the halls of the Kremlin. What the Soviets lacked in strategic vision for the South, they counterpoised in their obsession with normalizing relations with the West.

Trade with what the Soviets called the economically developing capitalist countries did not stagnate in absolute terms (each succeeding pie in the figures above is substantially greater than the one before), but as the figures show, it did stagnate relative to overall trade. This meant that trade continued to grow—after all, the Kremlin remained committed to commercial growth—but it did so less rapidly than trade with developed capitalist countries. It could not be otherwise; the problem was structural. Underdeveloped economies have by definition a limited foundation on which to develop a robust economic relationship.

Soviet approach to foreign aid had a marked lack of staying power and lasting influence in underdeveloped regions of the world. The problem was analyzed

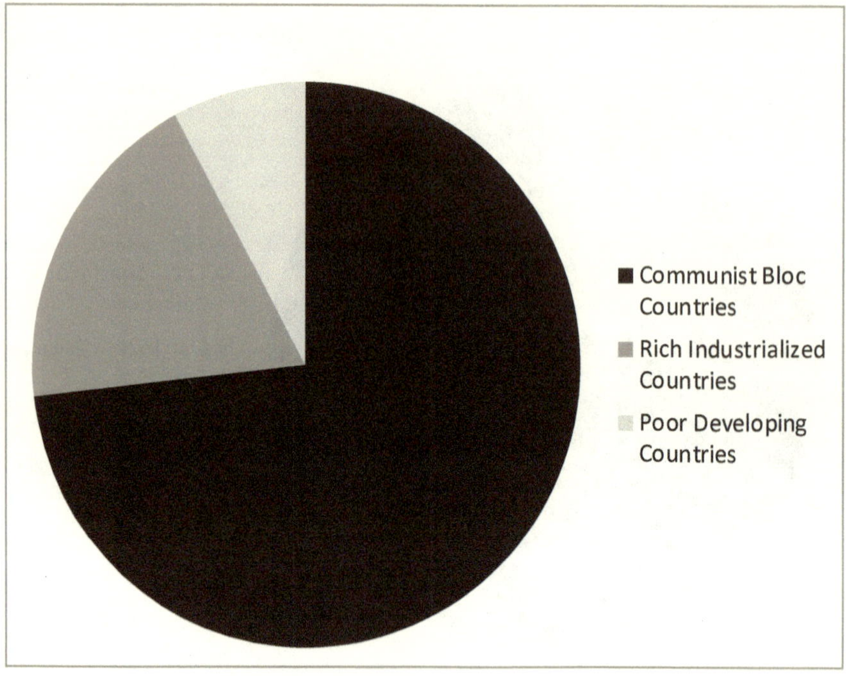

Fig. 2.4. Regional weight of Soviet foreign trade, 1960. (Calculated from Ministerstvo vneshniĭ torgovli, *Vneshniaia torgovlia SSSR, 1922–81. Iubileinyĭ statisticheskiĭ obzor.*) (Moscow: Izdatel'stvo financy i statistika, 1982, 26–27.)

by GKĖS as early as 1961, but short of a complete overhaul, there was little to be done that could fix it. The report noted certain trends that had become visible that undermined the political effectiveness of Soviet aid, which held back profitable development of trade with the Third World. Most markedly, Western companies were taking advantage of Soviet-financed projects, often a result of the fact that the norm throughout the Global South was the mixed economy. The report was armed with examples of wasted opportunities arising from a lack of strategic planning in Soviet foreign trade. A Soviet built auto repair shop in Afghanistan that quickly proved unprofitable was managed by (West) Germans. A hotel in Burma built through Soviet grants was handed over to a consortium of Western companies.[50] Future aid, the report suggested, should be given only after careful consideration of the profitability of the project and the quality of the end product, or it would continue to be under threat of co-option by Western companies.

At other times, the execution of projects had little to do with the economic needs of the target country, creating debt rather than economic development.

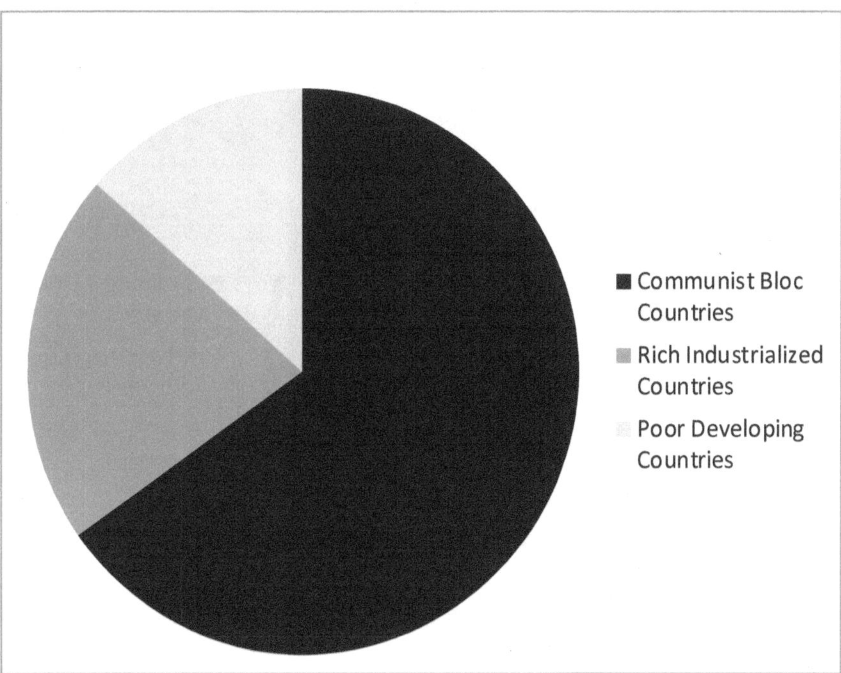

Fig. 2.5. Regional weight of Soviet foreign trade, 1970. (Calculated from Ministerstvo vneshniĭ torgovli, *Vneshniaia torgovlia SSSR, 1922–81. Iubileinyĭ statisticheskiĭ obzor.*) (Moscow: Izdatel'stvo financy i statistika, 1982, 26–27.)

In Laos and Cambodia the Soviets had carried out expensive oil prospecting, likely because those states were in search of easy profits. The reality was that these countries had little use for oil and none of the auxiliary industry and infrastructure to build an economically viable oil industry.[51] Soviet aid had left these countries with significant debts for no results, at a generous interest rate of 2.5 percent.

A more important problem, in GKĖS's reckoning, was the shortage of local specialists trained in the technical expertise necessary to take advantage of Soviet aid, which often left countries vulnerable to the "predations" of Western business.[52] Many of these countries, GKĖS noted, were weary of cooperating with the Soviet Union in the training of technical cadres, fearing they might become ideologically compromised. The agency suggested doing its utmost to extinguish these fears of subversion or risk losing projects to Western governments, as was happening in Iraq.[53]

Several scholars have noted a tightening of criteria in the Soviet Union's rendering of aid. Historian Elizabeth Valkenier dated this development to around 1964, but before Khrushchev's fall. Mikoyan had already hinted at a reevaluation

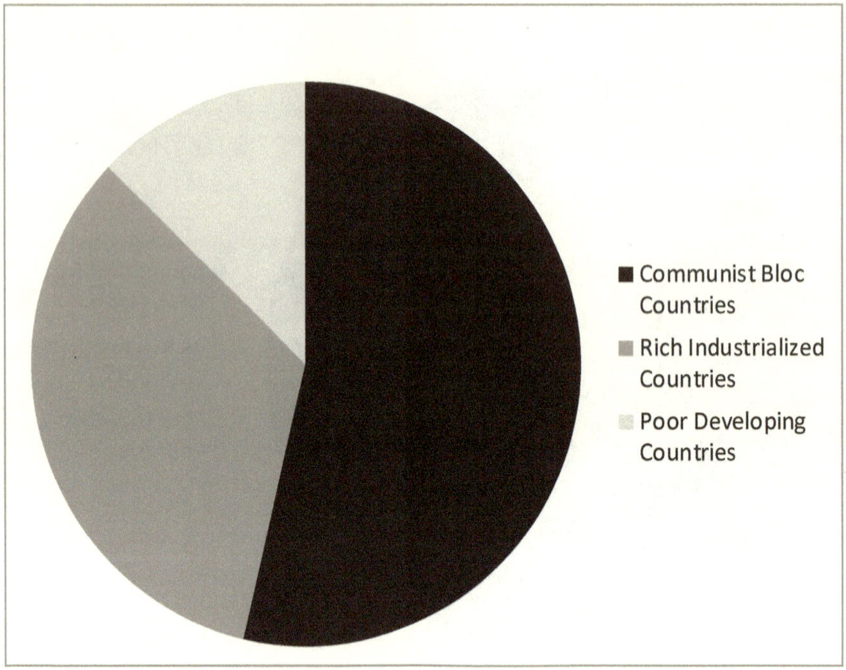

Fig. 2.6. Regional weight of Soviet foreign trade, 1980. (Calculated from Ministerstvo vneshniĭ torgovli, *Vneshniaia torgovlia SSSR, 1922–81. Iubileinyĭ statisticheskiĭ obzor.*) (Moscow: Izdatel'stvo financy i statistika, 1982, 26–27.)

of aid practices at the Twenty-Second Party Congress in October 1961, and soon academic institutions were called on to analyze the effectiveness of Soviet aid. This development, according to Valkenier, was cemented after Khrushchev's overthrow, when "the pursuit of economic advantage became an important criterion."[54] The economist Franklyn Holzman was likely closer to the mark in suggesting that profit calculation had always been an important criterion in Soviet aid and trade, albeit one that became more pronounced during the Brezhnev era.[55]

In fact, in 1961 GKĖS was already having second thoughts about the Soviet Union's simple aid policies. There was no consideration, for example, of providing aid that would encourage an intensification of trade between the USSR and the target country. In India the Soviets were building oil refineries without stipulating increased crude deliveries to that country, and their management was being passed over to Royal Dutch Shell. In Turkey a glass factory built by the Soviets was being supplied by Americans. In Cambodia, Indonesia, and Burma, the Soviets built hospitals without insisting that they supply the medicines as well.[56] Furthermore, barter lists were not given due consideration and were often left vague, so that the Soviets ended up accepting products they had little use for, as happened when the Egyptians insisted that they clear their debts to the Soviets with vegetables. "In the determination of projects in which the USSR is going to cooperate with developing countries, it is necessary not only to take into account their requests, but also our interest in obtaining products from those countries necessary to our economy," the report suggested.[57] With respect to Indonesia, for example, the Soviets were interested in rubber and tin, and yet they had not rendered any aid that would increase the output of those products. Indeed by 1961, there seemed to be little thought given to Marxist reservations on exploitative trade at the offices of the GKĖS.

Sovietologists have long discussed Soviet trade and aid within a false binary: the political versus the economic. The political took into consideration communist political subversion; the economic was strict profit calculation. These considerations were not the ones under debate at the Kremlin. At issue was the economic dependence of the former colonies, and it was thought that as long as that dependence existed, the Soviet Union would not enjoy the fair and mutually beneficial trade they hoped to carry out with developing countries. The outcome would be the perpetuation of a commercial subsistence for both Soviets and partners under the unrelenting pressure of a hostile and economically overwhelming West. Commercial attitudes did not exist outside political aims in a constant balancing act that was Soviet foreign policy. Commerce was foreign policy; economic exchange, with all its attendant issues of debt, development, independence, and interdependence, *was* the politics, rooted in an ideology that stressed the desirability of material exchange rather than the autarkic refusal to be integrated into the global capitalist economy that has formed the core of historiographical assumptions on Soviet foreign policy.[58]

Most of the economies of the Third World remained stubbornly mixed. Furthermore, the Soviets were well aware of the inadequacies of their products in these places, where demand for them decreased a decade after the Soviets had broken into those markets for the first time.[59] By the mid-1960s the share of trade with the Third World as a percentage of total Soviet foreign trade stabilized around 10 to 13 percent, even as the share of trade with Europe, Japan, and the United States continued to grow. In contrast to Cold War historical metanarratives, it was a Ricardian ideology of international exchange, not a conflict over forms of modernity, that most decisively informed the Soviet Union's insertion into the Global South. Our categories for understanding the Soviet Union and our epistemology of capitalism and socialism must change to accommodate the variety of ideas that comprise Soviet Cold War policy. In searching for specifically socialist forms of exchange between South and East, we will do well to analyze and disentangle capitalism, not frivolously as a model of modernity, but as a powerful, pervading force for organizing international economic life, thought, and politics.

Notes

1. The formulation was popularized by Odd Arne Westad, *The Global Cold War: Third World Interventions and the Making of Our Times* (Cambridge: Cambridge University Press, 2005).

2. On the interesting proposition that the United States and former colonial powers were antiliberal obstacles to globalization, see Johanna Bockman, "Socialist Globalization against Capitalist Neocolonialism: The Economic Ideas behind the New International Economic Order," *Humanity: An International Journal of Human Rights, Humanitarianism, and Development* 6, no. 1 (2015): 109–128.

3. This chapter thus positions itself within the recent historiographical challenge to the bipolar paradigm of works such as Sari Autio-Sarasmo and Katalin Miklóssy, eds., *Reassessing Cold War Europe* (London: Routledge, 2011); and Johanna Bockman, *Markets in the Name of Socialism: The Left-Wing Origins of Neoliberalism* (Stanford: Stanford University Press, 2011). Literature in the adjacent fields of science, technology, and environmental history have likewise blurred Cold War binaries, such as Jenny Leigh Smith, *Works in Progress: Plans and Realities on Soviet Farms, 1930–1963* (New Haven, CT: Yale University Press, 2014); Benjamin Peters, *How Not to Network a Nation: The Uneasy History of the Soviet Internet* (Cambridge: MIT Press, 2016); and Eglė Rindzevičiūtė, *The Power of Systems: How Policy Sciences Opened Up the Cold War World* (Ithaca, NY: Cornell University Press, 2016).

4. Cold War history is not yet following the trend in the field of American history of reintroducing capitalism (and by extension communism) as a category of analysis.

5. Oscar Sanchez-Sibony, "Capitalism's Fellow Traveler: The Soviet Union, Bretton Woods, and the Cold War," *Comparative Studies in Society and History* 56, no. 2 (2014): 290–319.

6. Inasmuch as setting up the Bretton Woods system was a single-minded, collaborative effort with clear objectives that formed a set of fixed and purposeful institutions, I use the term *project* advisedly.

7. In order to allow an interpretation that makes ideas the ultimate motor of history, Odd Arne Westad performs a disentangling operation of precisely this kind, arguing that "even though Soviet capabilities overall were more on the scale of Britain and France than on those of the United States, the militarization of the Soviet economy and its society made it a formidable opponent in international affairs. First and foremost it constituted the other superpower as a result of its oppositional ideology," in "The Cold War and the International History of the Twentieth Century," in Melvyn P. Leffler and Odd Arne Westad, eds., *The Cambridge History of the Cold War*, vol. 1 (Cambridge: Cambridge University Press, 2010), 11. In a narrative arc echoed in chapter 1 in this volume, trade and finance are first depreciated only to come back as central to the denouement of the Cold War and the Soviet project, explained by the seemingly impersonal, deus ex machina economic restructurings of the 1970s. Others have also noted Westad's timidity in analyses of political economy, for example Perry Anderson, *American Foreign Policy and Its Thinkers* (New York: Verso, 2015), 48.

8. Ragna Boden, "Cold War Economics: Soviet Aid to Indonesia," *Journal of Cold War Studies* 10, no. 3 (2008): 110–128; Vojtech Mastny, "The Soviet Union's Partnership with India," *Journal of Cold War Studies* 12, no. 3 (2010).

9. Daniel Speich, "The Kenyan Style of 'African Socialism': Developmental Knowledge Claims and the Explanatory Limits of the Cold War," *Diplomatic History* 33, no. 3 (2009): 451.

10. A classic example is Walt Whitman Rostow, *The Stages of Economic Growth: A Non-Communist Manifesto* (Cambridge: Cambridge University Press, 1960). A useful retelling of the origins of modernization theory in the United States is David Ekbladh, *The Great American Mission: Modernization and the Construction of an American World Order* (Princeton, NJ: Princeton University Press, 2010).

11. RGANI, f. 5, op. 30, d. 116, ll. 228–234.

12. RGANI, f. 5, op. 30, d. 71, ll. 61–62.

13. RGANI, f. 5, op. 30, d. 224, ll. 54–58.

14. RGANI, f. 5, op. 30, d. 305, l. 117.

15. Ibid.

16. A quick rundown of this position can be read in Westad, *The Global Cold War*, 31–35.

17. RGANI, f. 5, op. 30, d. 305, l. 120.

18. Ibid.

19. Ibid., l. 121.

20. RGANI, f. 5, op. 30, d. 272, l. 177. This report also makes clear that in particular circumstances the Soviets would also provide aid to private enterprises, as long as they belonged to representatives of "progressive circles" within the country.

21. Jagdish Bhagwati and Padma Desai, *India Planning for Industrialization: Industrialization and Trade Policies since 1951* (London: Oxford University Press, 1970), 185.

22. Padma Desai, *The Bokaro Steel Plant: A Study of Soviet Economic Assistance* (Amsterdam: North-Holland Publishing Company, 1972). An abiding lack of concern for local agency and local consequences in favor of grand visions was shared by the United States, see Nick Cullather, *The Hungry World: America's Cold War Battle against Poverty in Asia* (Cambridge: Harvard University Press, 2010).

23. RGANI, f. 5, op. 30, d. 305, l. 122.

24. Khrushchev mentions this concern throughout his memoirs but particularly in relation to the Bhilai Steel Plant and the Aswan High Dam in Egypt, both major projects in which the Indians and Egyptians respectively asked that they be done on a contractual basis. See Sergei Khrushchev, ed., *Memoirs of Nikita Khrushchev: Statesman*, vol. 3 (University Park: Pennsylvania State University Press, 2007), 772 and 827.

25. RGANI, f. 5, op. 30, d. 272, l. 178.

26. Ibid.

27. For examples of inefficiencies and aid delays, see GARF, f. 5446, op. 95, d. 1031, ll. 103–104, 114–115; this makes up the bulk of GKÈS's correspondence with the Council of Ministers.

28. Khrushchev, *Memoirs of Nikita Khrushchev*, 769–770.

29. Ibid., 771.

30. Both are estimates for economic aid, as distinct from military aid. Quintin V. S. Bach, *Soviet Aid to the Third World: The Facts and Figures* (Sussex: Book Guild, 2003), 79; and Clyde R. Mark, "Israel: US Foreign Assistance," Issue Brief for Congress, April 2005: http://www.fas.org/sgp/crs/mideast/IB85066.pdf. Aid to Israel has constituted about one-sixth of all US aid.

31. See, for example, Jeffry Frieden's casual description of India as a Soviet ally in *Global Capitalism: Its Fall and Rise in the Twentieth Century* (New York: W. W. Norton & Company,

2006), 322; or Vladislav Zubok and Constantine Pleshakov, *Inside the Kremlin's Cold War: From Stalin to Khrushchev* (Cambridge: Harvard University Press, 1996), 231, in which Nehru is the "leader of the Non-Aligned movement and a new geopolitical ally of the USSR."

32. Matthew Connelly, "Taking off the Cold War Lens: Visions of North-South Conflict during the Algerian War of Independence," *American Historical Review* 105, no. 3 (2000): 739–769.

33. Santosh Mehrotra, *India and the Soviet Union: Trade and Technology Transfer* (Cambridge: Cambridge University Press, 1990), 65, as shown in table 4.2. West German aid to the end of the Third Five-Year Plan (that is, to 1965) amounted to 3.4 billion rupees, while Soviet aid was 2.9 billion rupees.

34. RGANI, f. 5, op. 30, d. 272, l. 187.

35. Ibid., ll. 187–188.

36. Melvyn Leffler, *For the Soul of Mankind: The United States, the Soviet Union, and the Cold War* (New York: Hill & Wang, 2007), 171.

37. In Frieden, *Global Capitalism*, especially chapter 13.

38. In fact, one could go further back in time and build a genealogy for the Third World's anti–free market stance that begins with examples of late-industrializing—relative to Great Britain—countries such as the United States and Germany, which successfully deployed ISI-type policies that catapulted their economies to the forefront of economic development.

39. Frieden, *Global Capitalism*, 302–303.

40. Ibid.

41. Ibid., 304–305.

42. See also William Martin, "The Making of an Industrial South Africa: Trade and Tariffs in the Interwar Period," *International Journal of African Historical Affairs* 23, no. 1 (1990): 59–85.

43. Speich, "The Kenyan Style of 'African Socialism.'" Speich sees no structural difference in the aid practices of East and West and positions those practices within an "emerging global knowledge society," a far more fruitful basis for investigation than Cold War paradigms.

44. Frieden, *Global Capitalism*, 312.

45. See Bruce Cumings, "The Origins of the Development of the Northeast Asian Political Economy: Industrial Sectors, Product Cycles, and Political Consequences," *International Organization* 38, no. 1 (1984): 1–40, which places the origins of that development squarely in the colonial period. A wide-ranging discussion of the "developmental state" can be found in Meredith Woo-Cumings, ed., *The Developmental State* (Ithaca, NY: Cornell University Press, 1999).

46. Atul Kohli, *State-Directed Development: Political Power and Industrialization in the Global Periphery* (Cambridge: Cambridge University Press, 2004) analyzes state intervention in the domestic economies of Brazil, Korea, India, and Nigeria and generally finds the origins of future state economic behavior in the latter half of the twentieth century in those countries' colonial experience, particularly during the 1930s.

47. See Elizabeth Kridl Valkenier, *The Soviet Union and the Third World: An Economic Bind* (New York: Praeger, 1983), especially chapter 3 on development theory.

48. RGAE, f. 99, op. 1, d. 125, ll. 67–71.

49. Ibid.

50. RGANI, f. 5, op. 30, d. 371, l. 228.

51. Ibid., l. 229.

52. See also RGAE, f. 4372, op. 66, d. 439, ll. 23–30.
53. RGANI, f. 5, op. 30, d. 371, ll. 230–231.
54. Valkenier, *The Soviet Union and the Third World*, 12.
55. Franklyn Holzman, *Foreign Trade under Central Planning* (Cambridge: Harvard University Press, 1974), see chapter 16.
56. RGANI, f. 5, op. 30, d. 371, l. 235.
57. Ibid., l. 236.
58. Arne Westad, "The Cold War and the International History of the Twentieth Century," in *The Cambridge History of the Cold War*, vol. 1, eds. Melvyn P. Leffler and Odd Arne Westad (Cambridge: Cambridge University Press, 2010), 11. "By [this refusal]," Westad mistakenly continues, "[the Soviet Union] carved out a primary role for itself in international affairs, at great expense to its own development over time."
59. RGANI, f. 5, op. 30, d. 371, ll. 233–234.

OSCAR SANCHEZ-SIBONY is Assistant Professor of History at the University of Hong Kong. He is author of *Red Globalization: The Political Economy of the Soviet Cold War from Stalin to Khrushchev.*

3 The Soviet Bloc and China's Global Opening-Up Policy during the Last Years of Mao Zedong

Péter Vámos

On July 1, 1949, three months before the founding of the People's Republic of China (PRC), Mao Zedong published an article in *Renmin Ribao* (People's daily) "On the People's Democratic Dictatorship," in which he announced that China would "lean to one side," the side of socialism.[1] Mao and his fellow leaders hoped that after a century of imperialist humiliation, their country, with Soviet military and economic support, might recover its former greatness and centrality in international affairs. By the mid-1950s, however, Chinese leaders made it increasingly clear that China was unwilling to be the subordinate member of an alliance led by the USSR. At first, China's cultivation of an independent stance manifested itself in ideological debates, but by the mid-1960s an open power struggle erupted. In the wake of the Sino-Soviet split, the PRC wished to garner support for its struggle against a "hegemonism" exercised by both superpowers. By 1969 Chinese strategic goals changed once again. Instead of confrontation with the world's two most powerful countries, Beijing decided to improve relations with its archenemy, the United States, to bolster its position in relation to its former ally, the Soviet Union.

In the course of the 1970s, anti-Sovietism became the center of Chinese foreign policy. Although official Chinese propaganda never ceased to attack American imperialism, China's main foreign policy goal was to forge a worldwide anti-Soviet coalition. The "Global South" (Mao Zedong preferred the term "Third World") played a key role in Beijing's global policy.[2] Mao portrayed his country as an integral part and a natural ally of the Third World. Drawing on its own experience, China was destined, Mao believed, to lead the oppressed nations irrespective of their particular social system or ideology. Presenting the Chinese road of development as a model, Beijing spared no efforts to limit Soviet influence over the Third World, using propaganda and deploying economic and military aid on highly advantageous terms. Chinese propaganda suggested that the Soviet Union had become an imperialist power and that the PRC was under an obligation to engage in a worldwide struggle against every kind of imperialism. As we shall see, the Soviets and their closest allies examined China's international political activities through the prism of anti-Sovietism. The Soviet debate on China's international relations focused entirely on the anti-Soviet line of Chinese foreign policy. No other motives behind Beijing's initiatives were judged to be relevant.

The forging of the Sino-Soviet partnership and the subsequent split—occasioned by the conflict of interests inherent in that relationship—has been the subject of a growing number of recent studies.[3] Jeremy Friedman in his groundbreaking book *Shadow Cold War* shows how the Chinese and the Soviets attempted to garner support from the Third World by promoting their respective models of revolution. He argues that the Soviet promotion of anticapitalist revolution and the Chinese push for anti-imperialist revolution resulted in a "socialist competition" in the developing world.[4] Relying primarily on Hungarian archival evidence, this chapter investigates how this competition was driven by mutual obsessions. The Chinese intended to gain influence in the Third World at the expense of the Soviet Union. At the same time, the Soviets were obsessed with the anti-Soviet nature of China's international activism, and this obsession provided the framework for the Soviet Bloc's own assessment and condemnation of the PRC's policies toward the Third World. Moreover, Hungarian documents show that this mutual obsession was not only observed but also exacerbated within the wider socialist camp and that the Soviet Union cultivated the support of the socialist states to bolster its international standing.

Soviet Bloc diplomats carefully scrutinized, assessed, and shared information about China's activities in the Third World. In Moscow, the International Department of the Central Committee of the Communist Party of the Soviet Union (hereafter: CPSU CC) and the Soviet Ministry of Foreign Affairs were responsible for gathering information as well as shaping and sustaining the unanimity of the official viewpoint on China within the Soviet Bloc. Through a complete system ensuring the close coordination of policies on China, the Soviets sought to control all spheres of cooperation between their satellites and China. The political mechanism of control proved highly effective, to judge by the uniformity of opinion between the Soviets and their closest allies prevailing throughout the 1970s. The Central Party and Foreign Ministry documents from the Eastern European socialist countries (in this case the Hungarian archives), are reliable primary sources that may serve to introduce and substantiate the Soviet stance in relation to China.

The first part of this chapter presents an overview of Sino-Soviet relations during the first two decades of the PRC. It is followed by an outline of the evolution of China's foreign policy doctrine toward the Third World and a summary of China's goals and anti-Soviet strategies in its relations with the developing countries, with a special focus on Africa. The third section highlights Soviet Bloc perceptions and assessments of China's policies toward the Third World during the last years of Mao Zedong's life.

China: A Part of the Soviet Bloc or a Third Great Power?

Ever since the founding of the PRC, Beijing's main preoccupation had been its relationship with Moscow. China was eager to learn from the Soviet Union and emulate the Soviet model of economic and social development. Having China as an ally was likewise of especial importance to the Soviet Union in its fight for the worldwide victory of socialism. In the summer of 1949, Joseph Stalin and Liu Shaoqi, the Chinese Communist Party's (CCP) second-in-command, agreed in Moscow that while the USSR would remain the center of the international communist movement, it would be the task of the CCP to lead the world revolution in Asia. Moscow provided political and economic assistance for this cause. Hundreds of major investment projects were initiated, designed to serve the development of China's heavy and chemical industries. With the free transfer of manufacturing expertise becoming regular practice, Chinese factories and workshops based on Soviet blueprints were built. Thousands of Soviet experts—political and military advisers as well as technical and technological specialists—worked in China, while tens of thousands of Chinese engineers and students were trained in the Soviet Union. Friendship societies were formed and exhibitions and arts festivals were held to promote Russian culture and to popularize the Soviet experience of socialist construction.[5]

China's new leadership imagined that the Middle Kingdom had become an autonomous, sovereign member of the Soviet-led international alliance of socialist countries and approached international politics accordingly. The CCP's ideological foundation, Marxism-Leninism supplemented by Mao Zedong Thought, drew a clear distinction between China and the "imperialist" powers and fostered a community of socialist "fraternal countries." Meanwhile, the emphasis on China's developmental peculiarities—indigenous leadership and self-reliance, whereby China could achieve significant social and economic development within a short period of time and the importance of rural society in the process of modernization—also provided an appropriate framework for a pragmatic foreign policy that took China's own interests into account.

Mao Zedong and his comrades wanted to restore China to its rightful place in the international community as one of the great powers, a place they believed China well deserved. Mao did not accept the bipolar power structure of the Cold War. In 1946 he set forth his theory of the "intermediate zone," in which he argued that the American imperialists and the Soviet Union were separated "by a vast zone which includes many capitalist, colonial and semi-colonial countries in Europe, Asia and Africa." Furthermore, he claimed that the Americans' real intention was to subjugate these countries, as an attack on the Soviet Union before the intermediate zone came under US control was "out of the question."[6] Mao and the Chinese leaders asserted that China not only belonged to the intermediate zone but occupied a central position within it. They were convinced that, to judge by the experience of the CCP, China was destined to play a leading role in the worldwide revolutionary struggle of the oppressed peoples for decolonization and national independence. In December 1949 Liu Shaoqi contended that the victory of the Chinese revolution served as a convincing model for other national liberation movements. Liu concluded that the path of the Chinese revolution was "the path that the people in many colonial and semi-colonial countries must adopt in order to pursue national independence and people's democracy."[7]

The Afro-Asian Conference at the Indonesian city of Bandung in April 1955 was the first major event in the relationship between China and the newly independent countries (in Indonesian president Sukarno's words: "Newly Emerging Forces") in Asia and Africa. Bandung provided the Chinese leadership with the first opportunity to present their country as a responsible major power independent of the Soviet Union. Beijing wished to sustain momentum and become leader of the Afro-Asian movement, but the disaster of the Great Leap Forward and the emerging ideological debate with the Soviet Union and its allies delayed the process until the early 1960s. With the revival of Maoist radicalism in the fall of 1962, China tried to break out of its international isolation by organizing a second Afro-Asian Conference. As part of the preparatory campaign, at the turn of 1963–64, prime minister Zhou Enlai embarked on a tour of ten different African countries to rally support for Beijing's position and promote China's anti-Soviet revolutionary ideology. When the Egyptian leader Gamal Abdel Nasser issued an invitation to the representatives of the Soviet Union and the majority of African states came out in favor of Soviet participation, Beijing's leaders dropped the whole idea of a second Bandung.[8]

In 1963 Mao refined his theory, differentiating between two distinct intermediate zones. He argued that the developing countries of Asia, Africa, and Latin America belonged to the first intermediate zone, while the developed countries of Europe, Japan, Australia, and Canada formed the second intermediate zone.[9] In Mao's opinion, China, which was part of the first intermediate zone, needed to oppose both superpowers and present itself as the true representative and supporter of national liberation movements.

Mao's ardent supporter, minister of defense Lin Biao, drew up the global strategic outlook of the radicalized Chinese leadership in his article "Long Live the Victory of People's War!" In a similar vein to Liu Shaoqi in 1949, Lin Biao referred to the Chinese experience of the people's war as a model for revolutionary movements worldwide. Lin's starting point was that Mao's theory of people's war had not only brought success for the Chinese revolution but also was "a great contribution to the revolutionary struggles of oppressed nations and peoples throughout the world." He evoked Mao Zedong's thesis that "political power grows out of the barrel of a gun" and emphasized that Mao's theory of the establishment of rural revolutionary base areas and the encirclement of the cities from the countryside was "of outstanding and universal practical importance for the present revolutionary struggles of all the oppressed nations and peoples, and particularly for the revolutionary struggles of the oppressed nations and peoples in Asia, Africa and Latin America." Lin Biao likened these three regions to the "global countryside" and North America and Western Europe to the "global city," therefore calling on the global countryside to encircle the global city.[10] In Mao's view, just as the Chinese people had set an example for all oppressed nations by relying on themselves in their fight for independence and national sovereignty, so too was it China's "internationalist duty" to assist others in their struggle for liberation.[11]

This theoretical innovation was followed by a revolutionary foreign policy offensive. During the 1960s the PRC's activities focused on the propagation of Mao Zedong Thought and the organization of a worldwide coalition of oppressed nations. By the end of 1967, Mao's writings had been published in twenty-five languages with more than 4.6 million copies in 148 countries.[12] Apart from the propaganda campaign, Beijing also stepped up its efforts to provide material aid to countries that, according to Chinese hopes, might become allies of the internationally isolated Communist China. In January 1964 in the Ghanaian capital Accra, Zhou Enlai laid out eight guiding principles of China's foreign aid policy. As an explicit challenge to both American and Soviet ways of providing development aid, these included equality and mutual benefit; respect for sovereignty with no conditions attached; interest-free or low-interest loans; promotion of self-reliance, not dependency; quick results; use of best-quality equipment of Chinese manufacture; technology transfer through technical assistance; and the expectation that the living standards of Chinese experts would not exceed those of local workers.[13]

The Role of the Third World in Mao's Struggle against the Soviet Union

In the aftermath of the deterioration of Sino-Soviet relations in the early 1960s, Mao set out to prove that the Soviet Union neither deserved nor was suited to assuming the leadership of the international communist movement. Indeed, the Soviet Union in his judgment had become ideologically revisionist; having left the Leninist road of building socialism, it was now working to restore capitalism. He argued that Moscow's leaders followed the path of peaceful reform, relied on material incentives, and abandoned class struggle, turning instead to capitalist restoration.[14]

During the first decade of the PRC's existence, Chinese material aid for foreign countries was more symbolic than substantial—North Korea, backed by immense Chinese military support during and after the war, being an exception. Beijing launched its foreign aid program to nonsocialist states in the aftermath of the Bandung Conference, with the allocation of USD 5 million to Egypt after the Suez Crisis. According to Soviet estimates, between 1956 and 1960 Chinese foreign aid totaled USD 70.6 million, which Beijing channeled to six countries, Egypt, Yemen, Guinea, Nepal, Cambodia, and Indonesia.[15] In the 1960s the Chinese leadership persevered with this program and even enhanced its foreign aid policy despite the grave economic difficulties that the country had to face in the wake of the devastating Great Leap Forward. The vast majority of Chinese material aid was granted to socialist states (Albania in Europe and North Vietnam and North Korea in Asia), and only about 20 percent was channeled to nonsocialist developing countries. According to Soviet sources the total sum of Chinese aid provided to Third World countries between 1961 and 1965 amounted to USD 793 million. Even during the first years of the Cultural Revolution, China continued to fulfill its "international obligations" toward the Third World by providing USD 760 million of economic aid.[16]

The intervention of Warsaw Pact military forces in Czechoslovakia in August 1968 marked a nadir in Sino-Soviet relations. The Chinese compared the intervention to Hitler's invasion of Poland, to the US aggression in Vietnam, and to Japanese imperialism in China thirty years earlier. Two days after the Czechoslovak invasion, Premier Zhou Enlai delivered a speech at Romania's National Day reception in Beijing during which he declared that "Soviet revisionism [has] degenerated into social-imperialism and social-fascism."[17] A week later *Renmin Ribao* published an article on socialist imperialism and explained that the Soviet's foreign policy was "imperialism under the banner of socialism." The article contended that "the armed occupation of Czechoslovakia is the most characteristic and most prominent expression of the ugly face of [the Soviet Union's] social imperialism."[18] For the next two years, "social-imperialist" became the epithet of choice for the Soviet Union in the Chinese press and in Chinese leaders' speeches. This verbal onslaught reflected their fears that the Soviets might apply the Brezhnev doctrine to China as well. Chinese leadership began to consider a military assault from the North as the greatest threat to the country's national security. In an attempt to forge national unity and rally support for their anti-Soviet policies, they launched a concerted propaganda campaign against Soviet neocolonialism in Southeast Asia and Eastern Europe, drawing a parallel between tsarist imperialism and Soviet social imperialism and stressing that the Soviets had turned Mongolia into their colony, "robbed Eastern Europe and occupied Czechoslovakia."[19]

In a reaction to the intervention in Czechoslovakia and to the Soviet militarization of the Chinese border, Mao even went so far as to precipitate a limited foreign policy crisis. Verbal attacks were followed on March 2, 1969, by a military provocation near the uninhabited Zhenbao Island on the Ussuri River.[20] This carefully controlled and limited preemptive strike was part of a deterrence strategy against an enemy that Beijing's leaders feared was heading toward a major military confrontation with the PRC. The purpose of the Zhenbao clash was to highlight for the domestic audience the overriding danger from the USSR, to foster a crisis atmosphere and the necessary anti-Soviet hysteria needed to mobilize the Chinese party and people, and to justify the fundamental reorientation of China's foreign policy on the eve of the Ninth CCP Congress.[21] The true purpose of the Chinese provocation is illustrated in Lin Biao's report to the congress, roughly two weeks after the massive Soviet counterattack on March 15. Mao's designated successor drew a parallel between the Soviet Union's "dispatch of hundreds of thousands of troops to occupy Czechoslovakia and its armed provocations against China on our territory Zhenbao Island." He continued:

> In order to justify its aggression and plunder, the Soviet revisionist renegade clique trumpets the so-called theory of "limited sovereignty," the theory of "international dictatorship" and the theory of "socialist community." What does all this stuff mean? It means that your sovereignty is "limited," while his is unlimited. You won't obey him? He will exercise "international dictatorship" over you—dictatorship over the people of other countries, in order to form the "socialist community" ruled by the new tsars, that is, colonies of social-imperialism, just like the "New Order of Europe" of Hitler, the "Greater East Asia Co-prosperity Sphere" of Japanese militarism and the "Free World Community" of the United States.[22]

As well as asserting the social-imperialist nature of Moscow's foreign policy, the Ninth CCP Congress also denied the socialist character of the Soviet Union and its closest allies. In his report to the congress, Lin Biao portrayed China as the true leader of the international revolutionary movement.

After 1968 a strategic shift occurred in Chinese foreign policy. On the surface, nothing appeared to have changed. The propaganda machinery praised the results of socialist construction, trumpeted the necessity of class struggle, and launched renewed attacks against revisionists and US imperialists and their lackeys. Mao reiterated his thesis of the 1940s that globally the principal contradiction was between the peoples of the intermediate zone and the two superpowers. *Renmin Ribao* described the struggle of the nations of the world against the two superpowers as an "irresistible historical trend" and predicted the victory of small- and medium-sized countries. However, by the early 1970s the PRC had switched sides.[23] Whereas in the 1940s Mao presented the United States as the dominant imperialist power and tended to lean toward the Soviet Union, after Czechoslovakia he established closer relations with the United States and did his utmost to discredit the Soviet Union and present it as the more dangerous superpower.

Soviet Bloc diplomats closely observed these developments and referred to them as proof of China's anti-Soviet great power politics. According to Hungarian diplomatic sources, Beijing was particularly active in those Middle Eastern countries that had established close relations with the Soviet Union in the past but, for one reason or another, had now loosened ties. In Egypt, China intensified its relations with the post-Nasser leadership and aimed to improve Sino-Egyptian relations in the wake of Anwar Sadat's decision to ask Soviet military advisors to leave. On the other hand, the Hungarians accounted for China's low profile in Middle Eastern countries in terms of their failure to regard China as a plausible alternative to the Soviet Union and the Socialist Bloc. In the case of Iraq in the early 1970s, Chinese propaganda focused on Kurdish separatists and Palestinian organizations based in the Iraqi capital. According to the Hungarian embassy in Baghdad, these organizations were made to believe that "it was the Soviet Union that China regarded as its main enemy, and not the United States."[24]

As an increase in the Soviet Union's power anywhere in the world was viewed as a potential threat, China embarked on a new policy of building a global coalition against the USSR. The Chinese leadership fostered ties with any country that showed the slightest signs of willingness to form part of that coalition. China moved simultaneously on all fronts, and on all continents. The Chinese opened up to the United States and the developed part of the intermediate zone, including Japan and Western Europe—which also served as China's major sources of advanced technology—and emphasized their shared interests with the Third World as an independent political and economic force prepared to defy both superpowers.

Relations with African countries both individually and collectively were of particular importance. The Sino-Soviet split, which led to China's isolation within the Internationalist Communist movement, coincided with the independence of twenty-nine African colonies between 1960 and 1965. The fact that by the mid-1960s fifteen new African states had established official relations with China indicates the success of the campaign to win international recognition. The support of African states—of which twenty-six had recognized the PRC by 1971—led inevitably to a majority of votes being cast at the UN General Assembly for the resolution, passed on October 25, 1971, which recognized the PRC as the only lawful representative of China to the United Nations.

The Chinese viewed Africa as a field to launch campaigns for particular objectives and against perceived enemies and to present China as part of the accepted common ground. The aim of these "camouflage operations" was to persuade African governments and liberation movements to support China's strategic and political designs.[25] One of the main aims was to challenge Soviet influence and subvert Soviet revolutionary credibility. On the surface, China showed generosity in providing aid and at the same time refrained from interference in the internal affairs of African countries. However, in exchange for offering assistance to Moscow-backed liberation movements such as the Mozambique Liberation Front (FRELIMO) and the SWAPO Party in Namibia, Beijing expected these movements to condemn both Western imperialism and Soviet revisionism. However, the propagation of revolutionary people's war proved to be a failure. As a fair indication of the fiasco of Maoist propaganda, *Peking Review*, the PRC's weekly journal, listed seventy-five foreign communist, Marxist-Leninist parties whose representatives paid tribute or expressed their condolences in September 1976 at the mourning ceremony in Mao Zedong's honor, but not one of them was from Africa.[26]

Whereas during the 1960s the PRC exported Maoism and used aid to support resistance against colonial powers, by the 1970s it had developed more sophisticated strategies. China intended to promote itself as a benign, cooperative ally, a more accommodating external power than the superpowers, and a nation that posed no threat to the region either economically or militarily.[27] Beijing's leaders maintained that China was not a donor but an equal partner, allowing countries to develop infrastructure and invest in productive activities. In fact, the methods used to enhance China's international image were similar to those applied by the Soviets in China twenty years earlier. Beijing provided grants and long-term, low-interest, or interest-free loans with a grace period; financed infrastructural construction and industrial projects; organized friendship societies; published information bulletins; and dispatched experts. As a specifically Chinese way to win the sympathy of local peoples, Beijing also launched its global ping-pong diplomacy. Building on the success of the visit of the US table tennis team to the PRC in April 1971, Chinese players and trainers were sent to developing countries, and foreign players were invited to China.[28] Chinese activities were closely observed throughout the socialist camp. A Hungarian diplomatic report regarded these tournaments with Chinese participation as the most spectacular part of China's bilateral relations in the Third World.[29]

Financial assistance proved to be the most successful tool to gain international support and recognition. China provided credits and other forms of material aid to countries willing to recognize the PRC. The major recipients of Chinese aid were Tanzania, Zambia, and Mali in Africa and Pakistan and Nepal in Asia. Other major recipient countries included Sudan, Somalia, and Mauritania in Africa, South Yemen and Iraq in the Middle East, and Guyana, Chile, and Peru in Latin America. The Chinese focused on turnkey infrastructure projects, including the construction of railways and auto routes, bridges, light industrial plants, farms, hospitals, health centers, irrigation plants, and some prestige projects, such as sports stadiums or conference centers. In accordance with Chinese aid principles, the PRC emphasized that equipment of Chinese manufacture and Chinese experts were to be sent to the recipient countries for the construction.

The bulk of China's economic aid went to Africa, thus highlighting China's aspirations to become the leading power in the region.[30] Tanzania was the single most important recipient of Chinese economic aid during this period. Having won their independence in the early 1960s, even before their union in 1964, Tanganyika and Zanzibar were receptive to Chinese overtures. Thomas Burgess demonstrates that, in Zanzibar, China was regarded as *the* model for the island's future development.[31] The Sino-Tanzanian Treaty of Friendship was signed in 1965, during President Julius Nyerere's first visit to Beijing. Nyerere, who visited China thirteen times, was inspired by Chinese collective farming and modeled his project of socialist cooperatives on China's experience.[32] By the early 1970s around 30,000 Chinese experts were working in Tanzania, about half of them on the construction of the single most important Chinese construction project in Africa: the Tan-Zam Railway. The 1,860-kilometer railway line, connecting Tanzania's major seaport of Dar es Salaam and Zambia's capital Lusaka, was built between 1970 and 1976 and financed by Chinese loans totaling USD 400 million. It was designed to prove to the world that the construction and financing of such huge projects were not the privilege of superpowers.[33] Indeed, during his 1974 visit to Beijing, Nyerere treated the PRC as a socialist great power and an inspiration for Africa: "Two things convince me that socialism can be built in Africa and that it is not a Utopian vision. For Capitalism is ultimately incompatible with the real independence of African states. The second thing which encourages me is China." The Tanzanian president referred to China as a country that is "providing encouragement and an inspiration for younger and smaller nations which seek to build socialist societies."[34]

Nevertheless, African leaders repeatedly assured the Soviets and their closest allies that their relations with China were strictly based on shared economic interests, not emotion.[35] During this period, members of the socialist countries' diplomatic corps were commissioned to regularly report to their capitals and to share information with other fraternal countries on China's activities in the Third World. In 1974 Hungarian diplomats in Beijing were invited to the Tanzanian embassy, where the ambassador made it clear that although his country considered China to be a part of the developing world, "the PRC was not destined to [play] a leading role and was not entitled to enforce its will and ideology on other countries."[36] This critique was echoed by Gabon's newly appointed ambassador in Beijing. He had been sent to Beijing to study Chinese socialism, he told the Soviets, but during the six months that he spent in Beijing, he learned little about the country, and what he did learn did not match his expectations of socialism.[37] All these comments served as proof for Soviet Bloc diplomats that even though China was doing its level best to gain influence in the Third World at the expense of the Soviet Union, its efforts were not successful.

By the early 1970s it became widely known in the Soviet Bloc that China's main goals in the Third World were more politically driven than economically motivated. In line with Soviet views, a score of Hungarian diplomatic reports claimed that influencing and "winning over" Afro-Asian and Latin American developing countries was a crucial element in China's great power politics.[38] Moreover, it was also widely known within socialist diplomatic circles that the main thrust of China's foreign aid policy in Africa was to promote Beijing's anti-Soviet policy.[39] The East Europeans reinforced the Soviet view that the PRC's international activities could only result in the weakening of progressive movements worldwide. In 1972, referring to the Soviet argument, a Hungarian Foreign Ministry analysis concluded that under such circumstances the task for socialist countries was to provide as much economic assistance to the developing countries as possible and to intensify their propaganda work in order to "acquaint the developing countries with China's real political goals."[40]

The Three Worlds Theory and the Soviet Struggle against Maoism

In February 1974 Mao elaborated further on the intermediate zones theory and introduced his Three Worlds thesis. During his meeting with Zambian president Kenneth Kaunda, Mao explained that the United States and the Soviet Union belonged to the First World; the developed countries in Europe, Japan, Australia, and Canada made up the Second World; and the developing countries in Asia, Africa, and Latin America, including China, belonged to the Third World.[41] Two months later, Vice-Premier Deng Xiaoping delivered a speech at the UN General Assembly elaborating on the essence of the theory publicly for the first time. He contended that China was a socialist country and a developing country, which would never become a superpower. He also provided a definition of a superpower: "A superpower is an imperialist country which everywhere subjects other countries to its aggression, interference, control, subversion or plunder and strives for world hegemony." Referring to the Soviet Union, he added, "If capitalism is restored in a big socialist country, it will inevitably become a superpower."[42] There was a major difference between Mao's conceptual framework and the class-based Soviet formula of the antagonistic opposition of socialism and imperialism. In fact, Mao ignored the differences between social systems and considered the level of development of countries as the basic feature of classification. This apostasy caused outrage and was greeted with heavy criticism in the Soviet capital.

In Moscow a handful of specialists on China played a preeminent role in assessing changes in China's domestic politics and international activities as well as shaping and exercising monolithic control over policy in relation to the Soviet Bloc and China. Within the Communist Party of the Soviet Union (CPSU), the key figure was Oleg B. Rakhmanin, the first deputy director of the International Department for Relations with Fraternal Parties of the CPSU CC, who dealt with ruling Communist parties in Asia and was also in charge of policy coordination within the Soviet Bloc. Mikhail S. Kapitsa, the chief of the Foreign Ministry's Far East Department, was responsible for conducting state-to-state relations with China and supervised the Soviet satellites' diplomatic contacts with China. Together with Mikhail I. Sladkovskii, who headed the Institute of Far Eastern Studies at the Soviet Academy of Sciences, the main center of contemporary research on China, and Sergei L. Tikhvinskii, advisor of foreign minister Andrei Gromyko and later president of the Diplomatic Academy of the Ministry, these specialists on China could call on extensive networks of experts and observers providing information about Chinese activities.

The Soviet approach to China was entirely self-centered. According to the basic principle of Soviet foreign policy, the national interests of the Soviet Union were consonant with the interests of the international communist movement. It was generally accepted in the socialist camp that the national interests of the Soviet Union as a socialist great power—and the international interests of the socialist countries that had forged an alliance with the Soviet Union—were manifested primarily within international relations in their entirety. It was therefore the whole sweep of Chinese policy, and not only Sino-Soviet bilateral relations, that affected the Soviet Union's foreign policy interests.[43] Rakhmanin liked to quote Hungarian leader János Kádár's speech at the Twenty-Third CPSU Congress in 1966, which clearly expressed this attitude: "Hungarian communists have always believed that the touchstone of internationalism was always and still is today the comradely principled relationship with the Soviet Union. There is no anti-Soviet communism and never will be."[44]

In the second half of the 1960s, Rakhmanin and his comrades initiated the coordination of policies concerning China within the Soviet Bloc. The general term used for the coordination process was *Interkit* (China international). The phrase is derived from the Russian word for China, *Kitai*, and refers to a series of meetings on China held by turns in the different capitals of the Soviet Bloc between 1969 and 1984. Participants were representatives from the party central committee international departments of fraternal parties, of the USSR and its Warsaw Pact allies—Bulgaria, Czechoslovakia, East Germany, Hungary, but not Romania—and other nations aligned with the Kremlin: Mongolia from the beginning, Cuba starting from the mid-seventies, Vietnam from the late seventies, and Laos in the early eighties. But broadly speaking, the phrase also covers the whole coordination process of policies of the Soviet Bloc during the second half of the Cold War, including economic and trade relations, cultural contacts, and propaganda in relation to China. In the case of Hungary, Interkit boosted China-related research, especially the study of China's foreign policy. On the one hand, this kind of research was facilitated by the fact that the Hungarian leadership firmly believed that it was of vital interest for Hungary to gain insight into the domestic and foreign political developments in China. However, the initial impetus for this research activity had been provided by the Soviets. Consequently, the critical tone of the Hungarian publications on China reflected not only the analysts' own convictions but also the intense political pressure exerted by the Soviet Union.

The Soviet specialists on China set the tone at the Interkit meetings by precirculating their main points, which were then discussed and ratified by the participants. The Soviet analysis prepared for the Warsaw Interkit, held in 1970, stated that the Communist movement's program "offered the peoples of liberated countries a realistic perspective to eliminate underdevelopment and achieve rapid social progress by means of anti-imperialist struggle and cooperation with the socialist world." The Maoists, on the other hand, "presented a program which was nationalistic, which on the surface speculated on the real interests of the peoples of the Third World, but in reality was intended to serve their subordination to Chinese influence and as a basis for China's transformation into a superpower."[45]

On the theoretical foundations of Maoism, the Soviets argued, the Chinese leadership had refused community and unity of action with the Soviet Union and the socialist countries in its political practice; therefore, it was fundamentally antisocialist. The Soviet leadership concluded that mutually exclusive global strategic objectives made the normalization of relations between the two parties and the two countries impossible. Under such circumstances, the CPSU Politburo set itself three tasks: first, to continue the principled struggle against the CCP's ideological and political line; second, to unmask Beijing's hostile propaganda; and third, to defend the national interests of the Soviet state.[46]

Soviet authorities stressed the need for a new Third World strategy, arguing that Maoism was exerting an ideological influence on the unstable petty bourgeois elements in the world revolutionary movement. They further argued that the workers' consciousness of their own interests remained weak and distorted; they were therefore incapable of seeing through the Maoist plot. Reporting on a symposium on China's foreign policy held in Berlin in April 1973 with the participation of experts on China from Soviet satellites, Barna Tálas, a Hungarian specialist on China summarized the Soviet views as follows: "Whereas the Soviet Union proposes a longer and harder way to socialism, many are deceived by the Chinese proposal of a quick, radical solution. The task of the communists is to free those deceived from China's influence."[47] The Soviets argued that the real strategic aim of Maoist leadership was to establish hegemony, the domination of China, first in East Asia, then in the whole of the Third World, and finally across the globe. They also contended that world imperialism was a de facto ally of Beijing in its fight against the international revolutionary forces. The Maoists' involvement with the United States was emphasized, along with the attempts by China to woo Western Europe, Canada, Australia, and the Third World.

G. V. Astafiev, deputy director of the Institute of Far Eastern Studies, equated China's anti-Soviet activities to hegemonism. Outlining the chronology of China's "hegemonic aspirations," the Soviet analyst identified three distinct phases. He dated the first phase between 1958 and 1962, when China had pursued hegemony within the socialist camp. From 1963 to 1968, according to Astafiev, China strove to gain hegemony within liberation movements and the international workers' movement, primarily by undermining the Soviet Union and the CPSU. He characterized the third phase, which he dated from 1969, in terms of China's unrelenting attempts to split the international workers' movement along "a sharp and open anti-socialist and anti-Soviet line" and to form a bloc against socialism with the imperialist forces. Astafiev argued that the Maoists applied different tactics to achieve their strategic goal of hegemony: until 1965 they took into account class considerations, but after 1969 they openly cast aside class principles and deserted the anti-imperialist cause. Assessing the Chinese theory of the two superpowers, he was convinced that China's ultimate aim was to isolate both the United States and the USSR and to become a "hyper-superpower" (*supersverchderzhava*) with the help of the Third World. "This is where China arrived ten years after it allegedly had gone into battle for the 'purity of Marxism-Leninism,'" Astafiev lamented.[48]

For Moscow, October 1971 marked the beginning of a new phase for China's anti-Soviet policy. The PRC's UN membership meant that Beijing had finally broken out of its isolation and created a new forum for the articulation of its policy line. In response, the hard-line guardians of Soviet propaganda conveyed their message through Soviet and Eastern Bloc diplomats worldwide that Maoism was an unrepentant enemy of Communism and that Moscow had to prepare for a protracted struggle against it. The Soviet position was well summarized by a diplomat in West Germany. The Soviet press attaché summoned the attachés of socialist embassies and familiarized them with the new Soviet theoretical approach to Maoism. His conclusion was that "Maoism is not a paper tiger. It poses a great threat to us. It is an enemy similar to imperialism. It is particularly dangerous in underdeveloped countries and in the workers' movement."[49] Under the new circumstances, Soviet Bloc countries felt obliged to play their part in Soviet resistance to Chinese expansion. An analysis drafted by the Hungarian embassy in Beijing—dated October 25, 1971, the day of the PRC's admission to the United Nations—concluded that China's policy of building new relationships and gaining influence in the Third World had been successful and that coordinated efforts were needed to counter China's advance.[50]

The Soviets considered joint action with their satellites an issue of vital importance and stepped up their efforts at coordination. Scholarly symposiums were organized, and joint publications were launched. The book *Maoism: An Ideological and Political Opponent of Marxism* was nicknamed as "anti-Mao" and was used for direct propaganda purposes to provide a "scientifically established" element for the Kremlin's anti-Chinese campaign. At a meeting with representatives of fraternal parties in 1974, Rakhmanin remarked, "It is desirable to give maximum publicity to the publication of the book."[51] An agreement was reached that the analyses by the socialist specialists on China "may be extensively used by every country for publication purposes and in the most varied forms, either in the field of party education or that of mass propaganda." As a result of the increasingly hard-line Soviet attitude, genuine debates among East European scholars on China were quickly suppressed. In 1975 a book entitled *Criticism of Maoism, I-II*, was published by the Institute of International Affairs but only for restricted use—copies of the book were not available in bookstores.[52] The Hungarian leadership fulfilled all Soviet expectations but at the same time subtly expressed its reservations regarding the coordination of policies concerning China.

Conclusion

During Mao's last years in power, Chinese and Soviet Third World policies were driven by a mutual obsession and struggle over which power would lay claim to the dominant theory of revolution and socialist transformation. The Chinese concepts of Third World politics mirrored Mao Zedong's intention to regain China's great power status after a century of humiliation under imperialist domination. During the first decade of the PRC, Mao's China was a loyal disciple of the Soviet Union and accepted the leading role of the CPSU within the international communist movement. However, the emergence of the intermediate zone theory in the wake of the Second World War signified that Mao did not accept the Cold War dyad and battled hard to restore China's rightful place in the world. Although China lagged far behind the two superpowers in terms of military technology and economy, Mao's theory, which by the 1960s had evolved into the theory of the two intermediate zones and assumed its final form in 1974 as the theory of the Three Worlds, described an alternative world order and consequently portrayed China as leader of the developing world. Armed with this original theory, Beijing's leaders attempted to establish a new sphere of influence and an alliance system that would undermine Soviet global positions.

The Soviets condemned Maoism and labeled it "an unforgiving enemy and antipode of socialism."[53] In the Soviet opinion, China's independent foreign policy strategy lacked a class basis and represented a repudiation of Marxism-Leninism—according to which the main contradiction lay between the socialist and the capitalist world systems. Moreover, China's foreign policy practice was driven by the conviction that China's main enemy was the Soviet Union, not only ideologically, because it had become revisionist, but also because it constituted the main threat to China's national security as a social-imperialist power. In sum, China's global outreach was largely motivated by the leadership's desire to limit Soviet influence on all continents and to build a global coalition against the Soviet Union. In the Soviet opinion, this was the main goal of China's Africa policy as well.

The Soviet Union continued to deal with China from a position of strength. By the late 1960s the Soviet Union had boosted its military presence along the Sino-Soviet and Sino-Mongolian borders, augmented its military capabilities along the periphery of China, and expanded its naval presence on the Pacific and Indian Oceans. Aiming at the military, political, diplomatic, economic, and ideological isolation and neutralization of China, the Soviet leadership also pursued aspects of its policy on China through multilateral diplomacy and propaganda. As a result, the Eastern European socialist states not only observed but also took an active part in the protracted war against Maoism. The official interpretation within the Soviet Bloc of developments in China's domestic policy and its international activities was based on the view from Moscow, which focused on the sharp antagonism between the Soviet Union and China and did not acknowledge the legitimacy of different perspectives.[54]

However, Moscow's leaders believed that one day China would return to the fold and that the relationship would revert to its original form after the establishment of the PRC under Soviet leadership. In 1974 the CPSU CC prepared an analysis of the prospects for China's foreign policy to be discussed by the closely cooperating fraternal parties in which they declared, "We firmly believe that the long-term interests of the Soviet and Chinese people are compatible and that at the end China would join the Soviet Union and the other socialist countries and march on the path of socialism."[55]

In the wake of Mao's death, Deng Xiaoping became China's paramount leader. Deng implemented his reform and opening-up policy to facilitate economic development and promote China's integration into the global market. This reform program resulted in the replacement of Maoist radicalism by pragmatic moderation, the corresponding shift from the primacy of ideology to that of economics, and China's recent global activism. In the twenty-first century, although China continues to have a mixed global image, it has become a global power, not least because of the credibility that the Chinese have gained during several decades of constant presence in Asia, Africa, and Latin America.

Notes

1. Mao Zedong, "On the People's Democratic Dictatorship." *Renmin Ribao*, July 1, 1949, 1.
2. As we shall see, Mao used the term *Third World* in a different way from the Western concept. The idea of a third world, distinct from the worlds of Western-style capitalism and

Soviet-style socialism, emerged during the early period of the Cold War. See B. R. Tomlinson, "What Was the Third World?," *Journal of Contemporary History* 38, no. 2 (April 2003): 307–321.

3. Lorenz M. Lüthi, *The Sino-Soviet Split: Cold War in the Communist World* (Princeton, NJ: Princeton University Press, 2008); Sergey Radchenko, *Two Suns in the Heavens: The Sino-Soviet Struggle for Supremacy, 1962–1967* (Washington, DC: Woodrow Wilson Center Press/ Stanford University Press, 2009); Austin Jersild, *The Sino-Soviet Alliance: An International History* (Chapel Hill: University of North Carolina Press, 2014).

4. Jeremy Friedman, *Shadow Cold War* (Chapel Hill: University of North Carolina Press, 2015).

5. On the Sino-Soviet alliance and the Soviet experts' experience in China, see Shen Zhihua, *Sulian zhuanjia zai Zhongguo (1948–1960)* [Soviet experts in China: 1948–1960] (Beijing: Zhongguo guoji chubanshe, 2003); and Shen Zhihua, Li Bin (Douglas A. Stiffler), eds., *Cuiruode lianmeng: lengzhan yu ZhongSu guanxi* [Frail alliance: The Cold War and Sino-Soviet relations] (Beijing: Shehui kexue wenxian chubanshe, 2010).

6. "Talk with the American Correspondent Anna Louise Strong," *Selected Works of Mao Tse-tung Volume IV* (Peking: Foreign Languages Press, 1961), 97–101.

7. "Speech by Liu Shaoqi," *Pravda*, January 4, 1950, 3.

8. See Lorenz M. Lüthi, "The Sino-Soviet Split and Its Consequences," in *The Routledge Handbook of the Cold War*, eds. Artemy M. Kalinovsky and Craig Daigle (New York: Routledge, 2014), 81–83.

9. "There Are Two Intermediate Zones," *Mao Zedong on Diplomacy* (Beijing: Foreign Languages Press, 1998), 387–389.

10. Lin Biao, *Long Live the Victory of the People's War!* (Beijing: Foreign Language Press, 1965), 42–58.

11. "Talk with African Friends," *Quotations from Chairman Mao Tse-tung*, August 8, 1963. This book is also known as the Little Red Book.

12. Wang Taiping, ed., *Zhonghua Renmin Gongheguo waijiaoshi, 1957–1969, Vol. 2* [Diplomatic history of the PRC] (Beijing: Shijie Zhishi Chubanshe, 1998), 11.

13. *Renmin Ribao*, January 18, 1964, 4.

14. Joseph W. Esherick, "On the 'Restoration of Capitalism': Mao and Marxist Theory," *Modern China* 5, no. 1 (January 1979): 41–77.

15. Hungarian MFA Department of Studies and Analyses and 8th Territorial Department, report by Levente Lénárt: "Main Tendencies of PRC Foreign Policy in the Third World," Budapest, July 20, 1972. Hungarian National Archives (hereafter: HNA) XIX-J-1-j-Kína-78-10 -001076/3-1972. The main source for the Hungarian analysis was a "Soviet book, for internal use only, 1971."

16. Ibid.

17. "Telegrams from the Romanian Embassy, Beijing, to the Romanian Ministry of Foreign Affairs, 22–24 August 1968," August 24, 1968, History and Public Policy Program Digital Archive, Romanian Foreign Ministry Archives (AMAE), fond Telegrams, Pekin 1968, vol. 2, 272–274. Republished in Romulus Ioan Budura (coordinator), *Relațiile Româno-Chineze 1880–1974: Documente*, Arhivele Naționale [National archives], 2005, 901–902.

18. "Shenme shi shehui diguozhuyi?" [What is social imperialism?] *Renmin Ribao*, August 30, 1968, 4.

19. Hungarian MFA 4th Territorial Department, China Desk, Note by Ottó Juhász: "Anti-Soviet Campaign in China (Provocation on the Soviet-Chinese Border)," Budapest, March 5, 1969. HNA XIX- J-1-j-Kína-1-001539-1969.

20. Zhenbao, the Chinese name of the small island, means "treasure." The Russian name of the island is Damanskii.

21. Kenneth G. Lieberthal, *Sino-Soviet Conflict in the 1970s: Its Evolution and Implications for the Strategic Triangle* (RAND: July 1978), 6; Yang Kuisong, "The Sino-Soviet Border Clash of 1969: From Zhenbao Island to Sino-American Rapprochement," *Cold War History* 1, no. 1 (August 2000): 31, 41–44.

22. Lin Biao, "Report to the Ninth National Congress of the Communist Party of China," delivered April 1 and adopted April 14, 1969 (Beijing: Foreign Languages Press, 1969).

23. Chen Jian, "The Sino-American Rapprochement, 1969–1972," *Mao's China and the Cold War* (Chapel Hill and London: University of North Carolina Press, 2001), 238–276.

24. Ambassador József Ferró's report (reporter: László Fehérvári): "Chinese Diplomatic Activity in the Middle-East and Iraq," Baghdad, December 7, 1972. HNA XIX-J-1-j-Kína-78-10-00699/4-1972.

25. Philip Snow, "China and Africa: Consensus and Camouflage," in *Chinese Foreign Policy: Theory and Practice*, eds. Thomas W. Robinson and David Shambaugh (Oxford: Clarendon Press, 1994), 283–321.

26. "Eternal Glory to Chairman Mao, the Greatest Marxist of the Contemporary Era: Comrades of Foreign Marxist-Leninist Parties and Organizations, Foreign Friends and Experts Attend the Mourning Ceremony," *Peking Review* 39, September 24, 1976, 31–33.

27. On the positive African reception, see G. Thomas Burgess, "Mao in Zanzibar: Nationalism, Discipline, and the (De)Construction of Afro-Asian Solidarities," in *Making a World after Empire: The Bandung Moment and Its Political Afterlives*, ed. Christopher Lee (Athens, OH: Ohio University Press, 2010), 196–234.

28. On China's ping-pong diplomacy, see Guanhua Wang, "'Friendship First': China's Sports Diplomacy during the Cold War," *Journal of American-East Asian Relations* 12, no. 3/4 (Fall–Winter 2003): 133–153.

29. Ambassador József Ferró's report (reporter: László Fehérvári): "Chinese Diplomatic Activity in the Middle-East and Iraq," Baghdad, December 7, 1972. HNA XIX-J-1-j-Kína-78-10-00699/4-1972.

30. On Chinese aid policy in Africa, see Deborah Brautigam, *The Dragon's Gift* (Oxford: Oxford University Press, 2009).

31. Burgess, "Mao in Zanzibar."

32. Brautigam, *Dragon's Gift*, 39.

33. On the construction of the Tan-Zam Railway, see Jamie Monson, *Africa's Freedom Railway* (Bloomington and Indianapolis: Indiana University Press, 2009).

34. "President Nyerere Ends Visit to China," *Peking Review* 17, no. 14, April 5, 1974, 7.

35. Ambassador Miklós Bárd's report: "Recent Developments in the PRC's Activities in Tanzania," Dar Es Salaam, January 25, 1972. HNA XIX-J-1-j-Kína-78-10-00698/1-1972.

36. Ambassador Ferenc Gódor's report (reporter: József Tóth): "Visit to Tanzania's Second Secretary L. L. Ngatwika," Beijing, February 5, 1974. HNA XIX-J-1-j-Kína-78-146-001731/1974.

37. Ambassador Ferenc Gódor's report: "The Problematics of the Relations between China and the 'Third World.'" Beijing, January 15, 1975. HNA XIX-J-1-j-Kína-78-105-001312/1975.

38. See, e.g., Ambassador Ferenc Gódor's report (reporter: László Bihari): "The PRC's Economic Activities in the Developing and Certain Latin American Countries," Beijing, October 25, 1971. HNA XIX-J-1-j-Kína-78-50-003083/1971.

39. Ambassador Dr. Zoltán Gyenge's report (reporter: József Györke): "The PRC's Activities in Africa," Addis Ababa, January 26, 1972. HNA XIX-J-1-j-Kína-78-10-00698-1972.

40. Hungarian MFA Department of Studies and Analyses and Eighth Territorial Department, report by Levente Lénárt: "Main Tendencies of PRC Foreign Policy in the Third World," Budapest, July 20, 1972. HNA XIX-J-1-j-Kína-78-10-001076/3-1972.

41. "On the Question of the Differentiation of the Three Worlds," February 22, 1974, in Mao Zedong, *On Diplomacy* (Beijing: Foreign Language Press, 1998), 454.

42. Speech by chairman of the delegation of the People's Republic of China, Teng Hsiao-Ping, at the Special Session of the UN General Assembly (Beijing: Foreign Languages Press, 1974), 20–21.

43. Hungarian MFA First Territorial Department. Note by Dr. András Köves: "Some Actual Questions of Soviet-Chinese Relations," Budapest, November 18, 1971. HNA XIX-J-1-j-Kína-78-10-558/8/1971.

44. Speech by János Kádár, "A kommunizmus újabb győzelme felé." Az SZKP XXIII. kongresszusa, 1966. március 29.–április 8." [Toward a newer victory of communism: The Twenty-Third CPSU Congress, March 29–April 8, 1966] (Budapest: Kossuth, 1966), 117.

45. "The China Problem Following the Ninth CCP Congress: Theses of the Warsaw Meeting of Representatives of the International Departments of Central Committees of the Ruling Parties of Seven Closely Coordinating 'Fraternal' Countries." Warsaw, March 10–14, 1970. On the Soviet Bloc policy coordination process, see James G. Hershberg, Sergey Radchenko, Péter Vámos, and David Wolff, *The Interkit Story: A Window into the Final Decades of the Sino-Soviet Relationship* (Washington, DC: Woodrow Wilson International Center for Scholars, Cold War International History Project, 2011), working paper no. 63.

46. "Speech by CPSU Politburo Member Viktor V. Grishin at the Festive Meeting Held in the Kremlin in Commemoration of the 54th Anniversary of the Great October Revolution," *Pravda*, November 7, 1971, 1–2.

47. Note by Barna Tálas: "(Confidential) Symposium on China's Foreign Policy: Berlin, April 10–16, 1973," Budapest, June 15, 1973. HNA XIX-J-1-j-Kína-78-10-00619/8/1973.

48. Ibid.

49. Ambassador László Hamburger's report (Reporter: J. Szimon): "Assessment of Maoism," Cologne, November 6, 1971. HNA XIX-J-1-j Kína 78–10 002523/2/1971.

50. Ambassador Ferenc Gódor's report: "The PRC's Economic Activities in the Developing and Certain Latin American Countries," Beijing, October 25, 1971. HNA XIX-J-1-j-Kína-78-50-003083/1971.

51. International Department of the HSWP CC. "Memorandum of Tamás Pálos and Mátyás Szűrös for Comrades Árpád Pullai and Imre Győri on the Planned Publication of the Documents about China." Budapest, June 18, 1974. HNA M-KS 288. f., 32/b/1974, 100. ő.e. In Hungary the book was published in 1975. See *A maoizmus: a marxizmus-leninizmus eszmei és politikai ellenfele* (Budapest: Kossuth, 1975).

52. *A maoizmus kritikája I-II: Szocialista országok Kína-kutatóinak 1974-ben készült tanulmányaiból* (Budapest: Institute of International Affairs, 1975).

53. Hershberg et al., *The Interkit Story*; Document no. 13, "East German Report on the Interkit Meeting in Moscow, May 1973," SAPMO-BA Berlin, DY 30, IV B 2/20/583.

54. On the Soviet debate on Chinese socialism, see Gilbert Rozman, *A Mirror for Socialism: Soviet Criticisms of China* (Princeton, NJ: Princeton University Press, 1985).

55. "Soviet-Chinese Relations: Confidential Information" (Prepared by the CPSU CC International Department for the Budapest Interkit), Budapest, March 25–26, 1974.

PÉTER VÁMOS is Senior Research Fellow at the Institute of History at the Hungarian Academy of Sciences and Associate Professor at the Károli Gáspár University in Budapest. He is the coeditor of *Beyond the Kremlin's reach? Eastern Europe and China in the Cold War era.*

4 From Socialist Assistance to National Self-Interest: Vietnamese Labor Migration into CMEA Countries

Alena K. Alamgir and Christina Schwenkel

Despite the emergence of a large literature on labor mobility in the late twentieth and early twenty-first century, there has still been remarkably little attention paid to the phenomenon of overseas labor exchange schemes that emerged within the socialist world. The literature that does exist often simply reels off a list of dismal features, pitched in altogether negative terms that mobilize ghastly images of "slavery" and "captivity." This nascent literature tends to agree with *The Economist*'s assessment, arguing that these programs "bore [a] striking resemblance to those of its capitalist rivals"[1] and that socialist internationalism, which provided the ideological framing for the programs, was a mere "fig leaf," that is, economic exploitation masquerading as economic aid.[2] The situation was far more complex, shaped by key changes as socialist globalization gathered pace, particularly in the shift from an emphasis on development assistance toward new mobilities that were motivated by national self-interest and rested on asymmetrical labor hierarchies. Programs in the four countries (Soviet Union, East Germany, known as the GDR, Czechoslovakia, and Bulgaria) with which Vietnam maintained a series of training and labor exchange schemes from the late 1960s through to the end of the 1980s passed through three distinct phases, which unfolded in similar though not identical ways in each of the receiving countries. These phases were set in motion by specific intergovernmental treaties that organized, structured, and conceptualized the project somewhat differently. In other words, while the successive treaties built on their predecessors (and in the case of the earliest ones, from 1966 to 1967, on agreements regarding the training of university students), they each introduced institutional innovations that shaped the program and the lives of migrant Vietnamese workers differently. What began as a history of technology transfers (conceptualized as assistance to a decolonizing country with the goal of developing socialist infrastructure) changed, in part because of the deepening of the economic crisis in industrialized socialist countries, into a venture in which self-interest played an ever-increasing role. Eventually, the aspiration to train new socialist persons as a means of building global socialism was replaced by the need to recruit a large number of (Third World) laboring bodies to cope with the difficulties produced by the shortcomings of planned economies in the industrialized state-socialist countries. And unlike the West, these were, especially at the outset, initiated and managed primarily by the state—though this, too, changed somewhat in the mid-late 1980s. This intense state involvement not only significantly shaped the form of the program but also influenced the repertoires available to, and indeed used by, migrant workers to push for their interests and rights.[3]

In what follows we draw on ethnographic material, documents from Czech, German, and Vietnamese archives and secondary literature to provide the first comprehensive, comparative account of Vietnamese labor migration into Eastern Europe during the state-socialist era. According to a Vietnamese author writing in Russian, Vietnam sent 244,186 contract workers and 23,713 trainee-workers for work in Eastern Europe during this period (roughly 1967–90).[4] Vietnam signed training and labor agreements with four primary countries: the Soviet Union, the German Democratic Republic, Czechoslovakia, and Bulgaria. We argue that while a comparison of capitalist and socialist forms of labor migration can be fruitful, the comparison is only meaningful if we avoid positing the former as the yardstick against which the latter is measured; instead, state-socialist training and labor exchange programs must be understood on their own social and historical terms.

State-Sponsored Labor Migration in Western Europe

Although the use of temporary labor in Europe has its roots in colonial projects, such as the reliance on "coolies" in the Dutch East Indies,[5] the organized recruitment systems deployed roughly between 1870 and 1920 by Germany, France, and Switzerland are the more immediate predecessors of the state-sponsored labor migration schemes later found across Western Europe.[6] However, it was reconstruction efforts after the Second World War and the accompanying economic boom that ushered in modern guest worker programs, characterized by a significant involvement of the state, primarily through bilateral agreements, in the recruitment and regulation of foreign labor imports. The program put in place by the German Federal Republic is today perhaps best known. Indeed the generic label applied to these programs comes from it—"guest worker" is the translation of German *Gastarbeiter*.[7] West Germany, however, was actually one of the last among the Western European states to launch this type of program. Its program followed those of France, Switzerland, Britain, Holland, and Belgium, which started recruitments as early as 1945;[8] the Federal Republic of Germany initiated its first labor recruitment treaty in 1955. In contrast to forced labor during the Second World War, these programs emphasized labor migration as desirable and voluntary. The early recruits came from the Mediterranean (Italy, Spain, Greece, and Portugal) and were later joined by Yugoslavs and Turks.[9] By 1975 foreign workers constituted 10 percent of the labor force in Western Europe.[10] Though these programs were by no means identical and the role and extent of state involvement differed in each case,[11] they all tended to channel foreign workers into particular industrial sectors.

Because labor programs in Western Europe served as a strategy of national economic growth for the receiving states, it was these states, and not the poorer sending states, that initiated the schemes.[12] Though originally conceived mainly as a means of addressing labor market shortages, it would be a mistake to see these programs exclusively as mechanisms through which badly needed workers were supplied to booming industries. The supply of low-paid manual labor also served to depress wages "by enlarging the workforce available to certain target industries,"[13] thus increasing profit levels and fueling postwar Western Europe's "economic miracle." The temporary nature of the foreign workers' presence was ensured through the application of the "rotation principle," in which workers would return to their home countries on the completion of their contracts.[14] Following the economic stagnation precipitated by the oil crisis, most Western European countries halted their labor recruitment programs in the mid-1970s. However, because of family reunification laws, the numbers of migrants in these countries actually continued to climb even after the formal cessation of recruitment programs, and the guest worker programs began to lean toward permanent immigration. These processes aroused concerns about immigrants' ability to integrate into the majority society and about the strain they allegedly put on state budgets in the receiving states and their citizens, which, in turn, often led to discrimination against the migrants and to racialization.[15]

State-Sponsored Labor Migration in East-Central Europe

It was roughly when guest worker programs were halting recruitment that labor migration schemes in the socialist East began to increase, despite the fact that these countries, too, were affected by the oil crisis. In contrast to the West, these programs were not originally envisioned or articulated as a strategy for economic growth in the receiving countries. Rather, they were—as the GDR's prime minister Otto Grotewohl put it in his telegram to President Ho Chi Minh on July 22, 1954—framed as acts of solidarity [*Solidarität*] and fraternal aid [*brüderliche Hilfe*].[16] If labor schemes in Western Europe were conceived as a means of rebuilding postwar Europe and the *receiving* countries, labor migration schemes in Eastern Europe revolved around the training of labor and thus the means of rebuilding the *sending* country—a newly reunified Vietnam emerging from the

French (1946–54) and American (1955–75) wars. They were also seen as a means of ensuring the growth of socialism globally. Technological transfer became a priority of the socialist "civilizing mission," which included an effort to populate newly independent socialist countries with skilled workers and thus usher in socialist modernity.[17] This effort started first through the training of university students in the early 1950s, following the establishment of diplomatic ties between Vietnam and the Soviet Union and, in short order, its European allies, and then developed in the late 1960s into a vocationally oriented training of technicians and blue-collar workers. The latter is of key importance for this chapter. Since the training either took place in factories or was followed by "practice labor" in local enterprises during which the trainee workers received regular wages and were incorporated into standard production processes, we argue that it constitutes the earliest form of state-sponsored labor migration between Vietnam and the Council for Mutual Economic Assistance (CMEA) countries.[18]

During the early stages, training-cum-labor programs provided the Eastern European states with an opportunity to display their technical superiority. Assistance based on this technological prowess was conceptualized as help to "kin."[19] This is evident from Vietnamese language that maintained hierarchies of unequal power relations. When talking about their relationship with European socialist states, the Vietnamese often referred to these countries as "big brothers" (*anh*) and to themselves as their needy younger "siblings" (*em*).[20] Czechoslovak administrators of the program built on the same conceptual hierarchies when they conveyed to their higher-ups that Vietnamese representatives had every confidence in the program because of "the high level of [the Czechoslovak] economy and technology."[21] When asked about the things they found most striking when they first arrived in Czechoslovakia, migrants' most frequent answers included: "a very modern country," "industrial products of high quality," "social order," "high standards of living," and "modern transport."[22] Vietnamese workers in the GDR expressed similar sentiments, commenting on the country's wealth compared with Vietnam, its advanced and well-functioning infrastructure, its high standard of living, and its clean and orderly streets.[23] This framing, which relied on emphasizing the difference between "modern" advanced socialist countries and a modernizing Vietnam is, on the one hand, a reminder of the global inequalities that underpinned such "altruistic" assistance. On the other hand, the foregrounding of Vietnam's relative economic weakness helped the representatives of the Vietnamese state to add urgency to the demands they made on the receiving European countries. This would often boost Vietnam's negotiating position: the framing of the exchanges as instances of socialist assistance meant that the receiving states had a political and moral *obligation* to accommodate Vietnamese requests.[24] Vietnamese officials employed this rhetorical technique as late as the 1980s, when the structure of the program was veering off its original socialist, internationalist, and altruistic path and inching closer to a self-interest-based, quasi-market model.

Prelude: Student Migration

Socialist labor programs emerged from a history of comprehensive development aid, in which technology and knowledge transfer were strategies for supporting politically aligned countries, especially in their anticolonial struggles, and for furthering the socialist cause globally. The programs were based on the recognition that, in Marxist terminology, the "material base" had to be developed to avert the danger of newly independent nations becoming ensnarled in neocolonial economic relationships with their former colonizers. Thus, starting in the 1950s, the Soviet Union and the state-socialist European states provided extensive material and technical aid to Vietnam during the war against the French. This aid included the training of Vietnamese secret service and police (by the GDR) and instrumental military aid,[25] as well as everything from machine tools, compressors, tractors, equipment for hydroelectric power stations, all the way down to sewing needles and condensed milk.[26]

Over time, technical training emerged as central to the building of a postcolonial nation-state, since, at the end of the French colonial period, Vietnam was faced with a dearth of trained professional and skilled workers at all levels. The sending of university and vocational students overseas was seen as instrumental to ameliorating the situation. Even before Vietnam's victory over France at Điện Biên Phủ in 1954, ministerial officials in Hanoi dispatched the first cohorts of Vietnamese students overseas to train in technical fields considered critical to the development of a modern, independent nation-state. China (in the early years) and the Soviet Union received the largest numbers of students, who remained abroad for up to seven years (one year of language training and six years of study). The first group of twenty-one students and trainee-interns (*stazhër praktikant*) arrived in Moscow in the fall of 1951 to pursue higher education in chemistry, mechanics, metallurgy, agriculture, jurisprudence, and architecture, followed by forty-nine more students in 1953. The numbers continued to climb so that in 1981–82, for instance, 1,027 Vietnamese citizens were enrolled at various Soviet universities, of whom 694 were bachelor-to-master level students, 99 graduate students (*aspirant*), and 209 postgraduate interns (*stazhër*).[27] According to the Vietnamese Ministry of Education and Training, between 1955 and 1990, the Soviet Union educated more than 3,400 Vietnamese research students, 4,800 trainees, 20,700 university (MA) students, and 2,000 advanced research students.[28] By 1988 an estimated 30 percent of professors at the three largest universities in Hanoi had been trained in the Soviet Union.[29]

Similarly, in October 1953 the first cohort of four Vietnamese students arrived in the GDR, followed by another fifteen in September 1954.[30] The number of students increased following the ratification of the 1956 Agreement on Scientific and Technical Cooperation. By 1967 there were 445 Vietnamese students in the GDR registered in technical colleges, a number that would rise to 680 following a new agreement in 1973. In total, more than 4,000 students went on to receive their degrees in East Germany. Czechoslovak-Vietnamese relations followed a similar course. Czechoslovakia began by awarding university degrees to 30 Vietnamese citizens annually. The number increased to 100 in the 1965–66 school year, and 200 in the following year.[31] Thereafter, the number settled at about 150 people a year. In 1979, for instance, there were some 600 Vietnamese citizens receiving university education in Czechoslovakia, and Vietnamese students comprised the largest contingent of foreign students at Czechoslovak universities.[32] It should be noted that, with the collapse of state-socialist regimes, many graduates found themselves unemployed as their knowledge and technical training in highly specialized fields came to be seen as outdated almost overnight.[33]

Such technology transfers were often multisited and multidirectional. Concerning the former, cadres and technical workers were not only trained in Europe but also in Vietnam: Between 1965 and 1973—the years of the US air war—337 German experts traveled to Vietnam to train 2,694 cadres and technical workers. This number increased to more than 3,000 between 1973 and 1975 and continued to climb during postwar rehabilitation with the construction of vocational schools that would establish a technical and pedagogical infrastructure for training a larger population over the long term.[34] Perhaps even more interesting is the multidirectionality of the migratory paths: Vietnam sent its students and workers to be trained in East-Central Europe but also sent thousands of its own experts to train technicians and scientists in Africa.[35]

Phase 1: Labor Migration as Socialist Assistance

In the late 1960s support for the economic and technological development of Vietnam coalesced in a series of diplomatic initiatives aimed at training a highly skilled, professional labor force that would lay the foundations for the scientific and economic development of state socialism. As the war with the United States escalated, Vietnam signed a number of key cooperation agreements that aimed at securing training for relatively modest numbers (compared to the numbers in the 1970s and 1980s) of Vietnamese citizens in the GDR, Czechoslovakia, Bulgaria, and the Soviet Union. While the emphasis of these early projects was on training, after the initial period the trainee workers joined local enterprises and became de facto short-term labor migrants. Based on an amendment to the 1956 Agreement on Scientific and Technical Cooperation, signed in March 1966, the GDR agreed to accept 2,700 Vietnamese citizens for vocational training.[36] In the Soviet Union, the number exceeded 6,000.[37] In a treaty from August 1967, Bulgaria agreed to provide training and work for 500 Vietnamese "engineers, technicians and workers."[38] Depending on the source, between 2,146[39] and 2,400[40] Vietnamese citizens arrived in Czechoslovakia between 1967 and 1972 in five separate batches for training and work. In all four countries, Vietnamese trainee workers were channeled primarily into technical fields, including chemistry, engineering, optics, the food industry, construction and mechanics, and other heavy industry, consistent with Vietnam's First Five-Year Plan for economic development (1960–65). It is worth noting, however, that the Czechoslovak program also included the training of fifty-six people in companies under the purview of the Central Headquarters of Czechoslovak Film. This, arguably, reflected the unique nature of the state-socialist understanding of economic and developmental aid and labor migration.

During the initial phase, enterprises typically paid the trainees untaxed monthly stipends—six-month subsidies to unskilled workers and three-month subsidies to the skilled; technicians and engineers were to be subsidized for a whole year. The idea was that after these variously calibrated training periods, the trainees would become integrated into regular production and receive regular wages. However, in Czechoslovakia, only about 30 percent of the trainees were able to transition to the status of regular workers by the second year of their stays,[41] which meant that the remaining 70 percent continued to receive stipends rather than earn wages. As a result, the costs to the Czechoslovak state were greater than anticipated, and the officials decided to treat these costs as an "irrecoverable loan" (*nenávratný úvěr*). This willingness to absorb higher costs and, concomitantly, to accept the postponement of the moment when the Vietnamese workers would contribute, through their productive labor, to the Czechoslovak economy indicates that the framing of the project as socialist assistance significantly shaped the scheme. This was evident in all four countries. The first paragraph of the Bulgarian-Vietnamese agreement, for instance, stated that the treaty was drafted with "the needs of the DRV for technical cadres and skilled workers (*rabotnit͡si-spet͡sialisti*)" in mind. The Bulgarian, Czechoslovak, and GDR[42] treaties all contained a contingent stipulation for cases in which workers failed to earn wages at least equal to the amount of the initial stipend—in these cases, the receiving states' governments supplied the difference.

Thus, in contrast to the government-sponsored labor migration schemes in Western Europe, these Socialist Bloc projects were built on and embedded in a framework of economic and development aid provided by the receiving countries chiefly for the purpose of rebuilding Vietnam. Since after the initial training periods the workers were incorporated into regular production processes in the receiving countries, we classify these initiatives under the rubric of labor migration, seeing them as an early iteration of such labor exchange programs.

Phase 2: Labor Migration Embedded in Vocational Training

The second phase of labor migration and training programs followed the signing of the Paris Peace Accords in January 1973. During this stage, the training and labor migration programs expanded considerably in all four countries. For example, the Soviet Union signed an agreement through which 8,000 Vietnamese citizens were trained and worked in the country.[43] A similar treaty, signed in April 1974, brought some 5,500 Vietnamese citizens to Czechoslovakia over the course of the 1970s. A treaty between Vietnam and the GDR in 1973 meant that, by 1980, an estimated 10,000 Vietnamese apprentices had enrolled in East German vocational schools,[44] and on the eve of reunification, the GDR had provided more than 20,000 Vietnamese citizens with vocational and technical training in the fields of engineering (industrial, mechanical, and electrical), chemistry, physics, architecture, construction, mathematics, medicine, and printing.[45]

The 1973–74 treaties brought to the fore a model applied to the last batch of the trainees brought in to Czechoslovakia through the 1967 treaty. This consisted of Vietnamese first attending vocational schools for two and a half to three years—following largely the same curriculum as local students—and only then starting to work as skilled workers in local enterprises, for roughly two to three years.[46] These apprentice workers were between seventeen and twenty-five years old when they arrived and had completed at least seven years of education in Vietnam. The receiving states again covered all the costs (with the exception of the initial train journey to the destination countries), including the substantial living and educational expenses incurred during the period of training in vocational schools. However, concerns over costs of the program, which seemed absent during the first phase, surfaced in the 1970s, as documents from Czechoslovakia and the GDR reflect. From 1983 on, the state Solidarity Committee (Solidaritätskomitee), funded by public donations, shouldered the costs for the education and training of Vietnamese students and apprentices in the GDR, as per the decision of the Socialist Unity Party of Germany's (SED) Central Committee in November 1982.[47] This move effectively transferred the burden of international training from a strained state budget onto private citizens, who had already provided much of the material and financial support for Vietnam during and after the war.

Nonetheless, in the 1970s, the programs were still conceptualized as an essentially internationalist project, in which the Vietnamese state's needs ultimately trumped the concerns over the costs incurred by the receiving country's economy.[48] As Raia Apostolova has argued, the programs at this point were not envisaged as a means of importing "labour solely for the purpose of the extraction of surplus value." Although the Bulgarian government wanted to import workers, the Vietnamese government was insistent that it secure vocational training for its citizens and call them trainees. The Vietnamese officials pushed until they forced their Bulgarian counterparts to accede to their request.[49] Oral history interviews reveal that this phase was seen by both the Vietnamese and the Czechoslovak officials as something of a "golden age" and the most successful form of the program—the Vietnamese received solid language training and quality technical training during the first half of their stay and worked productively in Czechoslovak companies during the second half (or longer, as many asked to have their contracts extended), thus benefitting both states.

Phase 3: Labor Migration Based on Self-Interest

While the apprenticeship-to-factory work model remained in use and thousands of Vietnamese citizens continued to arrive under its auspices, in the 1980s, a new model became dominant. This model was connected with the economic slump in the bloc starting in the late 1970s and throughout the 1980s. Although the slowdowns in the average national income growth rates varied—Czechoslovakia's dropped down to 1.5 percent between 1981 and 1984 from 5.7 percent ten years earlier, whereas GDR's loss was less severe at 4.3 percent versus 5.4 percent during the same period[50]—the general downward trend was unmistakable. In this context, a new model grew out of a new set of treaties, in which the guiding principle was not that of socialist assistance but rather "mutual interest" and "economic acceptability." Because of this model, between 1981 and 1989, tens of thousands of Vietnamese citizens arrived in the GDR, Czechoslovakia, Bulgaria, and the Soviet Union for work. While the treaties still included references to training, it was now to take place exclusively on the job (rather than in vocational schools) and sometimes fell by the wayside. Between 1981 and 1991, more than 103,000 Vietnamese citizens worked in Soviet enterprises. Remarkably, they reportedly comprised 10–15 percent of the total number of workers in the enterprises employing them.[51] This exemplifies a crucial feature of the schemes during the 1980s: Vietnamese labor came to be used in increasing numbers by the CMEA countries to address the dual problems of low productivity and mounting labor shortages.

The 1980s phase meant a dramatic increase in the numbers of arriving Vietnamese workers, although exact statistics are difficult to compile as sources, even primary ones, often contradict each other. As best as we are able to tell, in 1981, the number of Vietnamese workers in Czechoslovakia reached 11,543. To appreciate what a dramatic increase this represented, consider that twice as many people arrived in a single year as had come from Vietnam to Czechoslovakia during the whole of the previous thirteen years. Throughout the decade, the numbers climbed still higher:[52]

Table 4.1. Total number of Vietnamese workers in Czechoslovakia, 1980–1989.

	Total number of Vietnamese workers in Czechoslovakia in given year
1980	3,529
1981	11,543
1982	21,314
1983	22,446
1984	*
1985	15,300
1986	11,400**
1987	18,900
1988	28,955
1989	35,609

*missing data
**expected number (actual numbers unknown)

Table 4.2. Total number of arrivals of Vietnamese workers to the GDR, 1980 to 1990.

Year	**Number of new arrivals**
1980	1,534
1981	4,027
1982	4,740
1983	644
1984	668
1985	248
1986	135
1987	20,448
1988	30,567
1989	8,881
1990	53
Total	**71,965**

Table 4.3. Total number of arrivals of Vietnamese workers and interns in four CMEA countries between 1966 and 1981.

	Wave 1		**Wave 2**		**Wave 3**	
	Treaty signed	**# of workers**	**Treaty date**	**# of workers**	**Treaty date**	**# of workers**
GDR	Mar 1966	2,700	1973	≈10,000	Apr 1980	≈72,000
Czechoslovakia	Feb 1967	2,400	Apr 1974	≈5,500	Nov 1980	≈50,000
Bulgaria	Aug 1967	500	Jul 1973	3,000*	1980	≈17,000
USSR	Jul 1967	6,000	Jul 1973	8,000*	Apr 1981	≈103,000

The 1980s thus saw an important shift from an emphasis on the *quality* of labor (acquisition of technical skills and their global transfer from an industrialized country to a decolonizing one) to the *quantity* of workers in terms of the sheer numbers of Third World laboring bodies summoned to rescue beleaguered socialist economies in state-socialist Europe.

During this period, foreign labor was increasingly used to extract surplus value, not unlike *Gastarbeiter* schemes in Western Europe. However, in the context of planned economies, the ability to deploy foreign labor to mitigate endemic labor shortages continued to be at least as important as the newly found desire for the extraction of surplus value. This was because the labor shortages were reflected in the unsatisfactory situation in the consumer goods market, which began to be viewed by Eastern European political elites as a threat to their legitimacy.[53] Accordingly, in 1987 GDR foreign minister Oskar Fischer directly tied the decision to increase employment of Vietnamese workers to efforts to expand the production of consumer goods in light manufacturing industries.[54] The decision to channel migrant workers to these types of enterprises was often due to wages in these industries being relatively low, which made attracting and keeping a local workforce difficult. For instance, as James Mark and Bálint Tolmár[55] report in the case of Hungary (which did not have a labor agreement with Vietnam), almost 60 percent of Cuban workers employed by state enterprises in the 1980s were women, precisely because the Hungarian state needed workers for textile manufacturing, which historically had been a low-paying industry employing primarily female laborers. The same was true in the USSR, where in April 1981 Vietnam and the Soviet Union also signed a new agreement "on the sending and receiving of Vietnamese citizens for professional training and work in the enterprises and organizations of the USSR."[56] Vietnamese labor was no longer channeled primarily into heavy and machinery industries but instead used to supply the consumer goods market: 60 percent of Vietnamese workers in the USSR were now placed in light and textile industries the majority of whom were women.[57]

The GDR and Vietnam signed a labor agreement in Berlin on April 11, 1980.[58] The treaty generated two waves of Vietnamese labor migration: the first, between 1981 and 1983, represented a smaller number of approximately ten thousand more highly skilled workers, which included apprentices who had been trained in East German vocational schools.[59] There was still concern with technology transfers: Vietnamese workers were to receive on-the-job training as *Facharbeiter* (skilled worker), with a view to returning home to apply their new technical knowledge and skills to advance socialist industrialization.[60] In contrast with the university students and apprentice workers, however, contract workers received only three months of job and language training. This was insufficient for a deeper integration into German society but consistent with the growing emphasis on labor (and surplus value for East Germany), rather than the training of new, skilled persons.

During the second wave between 1987 and 1989, a revised protocol, signed on January 27, 1987, effectively shifted the focus from result-oriented, occupational training to a larger and lower skilled production-oriented labor force. Indicating a profound change in the character of the program, a new paragraph was appended to article 1. The paragraph stipulated that between 20,000 and 25,000 workers would be assigned positions in GDR firms *according to the opportunities and interests of the GDR*. Henceforth, Berlin abandoned its emphasis on the quality (and applicability) of its technical-scientific training and channeled its efforts into recruiting as large a number of Vietnamese workers as it could. An additional 60,000 workers would arrive by the time the Wall came down—more than double the original predictions. These workers, often mistakenly identified in academic and public discourse as *Gastarbeiter*, were referred to in the agreement as *Werktätiger*—a broad socialist term applied to workers or those involved in productive labor activities. In everyday vernacular, they were referred to as *Vertragsarbeiter*, or contract workers, people whose social identities were constructed in relation to their laboring bodies, in contrast to the *Lehrlinge*, or apprentices, whose labor was made largely invisible through the focus on skill acquisition.

In Czechoslovakia the new treaty was signed in November 1980,[61] and it stipulated that the workers be between eighteen and forty years of age, that they be physically capable of performing assigned jobs, and that they be *already skilled*. While the first two conditions were met, the last one often was not. From the 5,000 new arrivals in 1989, almost half (2,170) were directed into companies under the purview of the Federal Ministry of Metallurgy, Mechanical, and Electrical Engineering. Another 1,775 were dispatched to enterprises under the purview of the Czech and Slovak ministries of industry. The remaining fifth were distributed among companies administered by the ministries of building and construction, agriculture and nutrition, and wood and water management.[62] While this latest iteration of the program, in which blue-collar workers arrived on four-year contracts, was still formally presented as an act of socialist internationalism, the needs of the receiving states now took precedence when it came to the industrial areas into which the workers were channeled. The program also started to become decentralized from 1987, with ministries and even individual companies forging direct ties with their Vietnamese counterparts.[63] During this phase, both the Czechoslovak state and enterprises came out ahead in financial terms. There were not years of vocational school expenses to cover, only a three-month language course, an initial clothing donation, and a modest annual per-worker fee that the Czechoslovak state paid to its Vietnamese counterpart.[64] In the context of endemic labor shortages, this seemed like a bargain—until it prompted industrial unrest. As the Czechoslovak state started to commodify Vietnamese workers, that is, to treat them primarily as a convenient source of "fully mobile" labor power, the workers responded with resistance, not infrequently in the form of strikes, usually protesting their wages and compulsory monetary transfer. Czechoslovak archival documents contain evidence of at least twenty-two strikes, lasting anywhere from a day to a couple of weeks, carried out by Vietnamese workers in Czechoslovak enterprises in the early 1980s. It bears mentioning that the Czechoslovak officials administering the program often felt that their Vietnamese counterparts tolerated, if not directly encouraged, workers' resistance.[65] It is further significant that both the strikes and the interventions by Vietnamese officials often led to concessions from the Czechoslovak state and enterprises, though not systemic policy changes.

The 1980 Bulgaria-Vietnam negotiations, Apostolova argues, unfolded in a markedly different context and were conducted in a noticeably different tone. The 1980 bilateral agreement stipulated that 17,000 Vietnamese citizens would travel to Bulgaria for work between 1981 and 1985 for stays of "no fewer than five years." Of these, 10,000 were to work in construction, 4,000 in agriculture, 1,000 in engineering, 500 in metallurgy, transportation, and forestry each, and 500 in various other sectors. While, as in other countries, the workers continued to enjoy the staples of state-socialist welfare—a paid vacation, free health care, cheap transport, and subsidized housing—there were also changes that affected their wellbeing and place in society, including the reduction of language training to three months, as in the GDR and Czechoslovakia. As in the other cases, Vietnamese workers in Bulgaria were to help "recover the costs incurred" to employ them,[66] while creating revenue for both the sending and receiving countries.

Labor migration schemes were nevertheless still propagated as "mutually beneficial." On the one hand, they were to benefit the CMEA countries, as a Czechoslovak document put it, by providing them with a "fully mobile" (*plně mobilní*) labor force[67] that could be channeled to whatever production lines were deemed important for the development of their economies, thus alleviating the ever-present labor shortage problem. In addition, the receiving states kept much of the surplus value generated by the workers in the form of the taxes they paid. While part of those taxes covered the health care that the workers were provided with on the same basis as citizens of the receiving countries, Vietnamese workers were not eligible to draw pensions from the countries for which they worked. The sending country, Vietnam, benefited in multiple ways. In addition to receiving a trained workforce, it also benefited from the payments that it received for its contract workers (discussed below). Further, workers who went abroad provided

Vietnam with relief from high levels of unemployment and supplied their families with much-needed material aid.

Reactions and Responses: Agency and Xenophobia

The Cold War framework in the West informed dominant understandings of socialist labor migrations. And yet in the ethnographic research we conducted, including oral history interviews, not a single informant described their participation in the program in terms of slavery or captivity. Instead, most recalled their time in East-Central Europe with fondness, even nostalgia. A former participant in the Vietnamese-Czechoslovak program said that "should another country attack the Czech Republic, [he] would not hesitate to defend it with a weapon."[68] To be sure, we need to exercise caution when interpreting such statements; people are often wistful when recalling their past. There was also more to overseas labor contracts than "money, alcohol, parties [and] freedom."[69] There was long-term separation from families, including young children left in the care of relatives; drastic differences in climate and diet (although most gradually adjusted); mounting xenophobia; hard and—for women particularly—low-paid work; and after 1989 abruptly canceled contracts and blatant racism, including physical attacks. Still, discounting the workers' positive recollections amounts to stripping them of agency, silencing their voices, and distorting the historical record.

Income was an area in which both Vietnamese workers and the government exhibited their agency and ability to shape the social and economic terms of the labor contracts. In the GDR treaty in 1980, as per article 4 of the labor agreement, Vietnamese migrants were to be given "the same rights and responsibilities as East German workers," including equal pay, medical care, and an allowance for children back home. This was the same in Bulgaria and Czechoslovakia. Nonetheless, wages were a point of contention among workers and the Vietnamese government, which viewed GDR labor practices as discriminatory. Gross monthly wages averaged 800 to 900 East marks, though this amount varied with hours of overtime work and productivity levels. Such pay fluctuations led to confusion and cynicism among Vietnamese workers. Though these figures did not diverge markedly from the earnings of East Germans (who also complained of large discrepancies between male and female pay), Vietnamese officials recognized that their workers—especially women—were frequently assigned to perform less complex tasks and compensated at a lower wage level. A Vietnamese document on the revised protocol in 1987 condemned the salary difference between GDR and Vietnamese workers, which also meant less money transferred to the Vietnamese state.[70]

In the 1980s in Czechoslovakia, Vietnamese workers were often dissatisfied with their wages as well, and at times they expressed this dissatisfaction through strikes that lasted anywhere from a day to a couple of weeks.[71] However, as in the GDR, the problem was not the average wage, or even low wages across the board, but rather the dramatic differences in wage levels in the different industrial areas in which the workers were employed. Expressions of dissatisfaction, including strikes, tended to appear in specific sectors, primarily the textile industry, agriculture, and construction.[72]

The 1980s were also marked by a rise in xenophobia and racism directed at foreign workers. In part, the racially tinged hostility was a ripple effect of planned economies. In lieu of remittances, Vietnamese migrants used their savings to buy certain types of goods, including bicycles, motorbikes, sewing machines, cameras, foodstuffs, clothing, and other smaller items. A 1989 GDR report described Vietnamese workers' hostels as "veritable warehouses." Owing to an illicit trade in desired commodities—purchasing "scarce" stock to sell back to eager consumers (both local and foreign)—it did not take much for local stores to run out of these favored items. The practice of sending care parcels home, usually once every three months, also prompted shortages, as sudden increases in demand by large numbers of foreign workers posed a problem for planned economies. A tendency emerged in the majority societies to misdirect their anger at the Vietnamese, whom the locals saw as buying up goods that did not belong to them, thus bypassing the actual cause of their frustration: the shortcomings of the regimes' economic policies.[73]

Distinctiveness of State-Socialist Labor Migration Schemes

Although the migrant labor programs that Vietnam maintained with four of its allies increasingly came to resemble labor programs in the capitalist West, there are particular qualities that set them apart. Aside from the obvious temporal disjuncture—with socialist programs gathering pace after the end of the US air strikes in 1973, whereas capitalist programs were winding down in the face of the oil crisis—one important distinction was in the objectives of the socialist programs: assistance and training. In the early stages, socialist labor programs were not conceived of as a means of economic development for the receiving countries but rather as solidarity with the sending country. By using such language the Vietnamese government was able to exercise a significant degree of control over the fate of its workers overseas, becoming involved at times in disputes that arose between workers and local enterprises, holding officials who administered the programs accountable, and pushing for workers' rights. The ideology and vernacular of socialist internationalism, even if often trampled on in practice, thus remained a moral and political resource available to leverage the Vietnamese state's involvement in the affairs of its workers overseas.

Another important distinction concerned remittances.[74] In capitalist labor migration schemes, these usually took the form of currency sent home to families. Because socialist currencies were not easily convertible, workers used their savings to purchase goods and send those home. Although the treaties included stipulations that purchased goods should be for individual use only, this was elastically defined and difficult to control. Bikes and motorbikes were not only bought to cover personal transportation needs but also for resale or as investments—one of our informants saved enough to buy three Czechoslovak-made Babetta (JAWA) mopeds, which, on return, he sold and used the money to purchase a house in which his relatives live to this day in Vietnam. East German–made Simson motorbikes (three also equaled one house) and Soviet-made Minsks—which can still be found on the streets in Hanoi—played a similar role. In an effort to mitigate the impact that such consumption practices had on the local population struggling with shortages, receiving countries established purchase limits and tariffs on hard-to-acquire goods, which the Vietnamese government considered to be discriminatory[75] and consequently protested.[76] In contrast to the West, where xenophobia focused on foreigners as competitors for *jobs*, in the East, hostility toward foreigners revolved around competition for scarce *goods*.[77]

Another critical difference concerned the issue of compulsory monetary withholdings. With the 1980s agreements, the Vietnamese state put in place a system of compulsory remittances in all four partner countries. In the Czechoslovak context, it was called *transfer*, which meant that, originally 15 percent, later 10 percent, of workers' wages were withheld by the enterprises employing them and sent to an account administered by the Vietnamese state.[78] This money was withheld in addition to the taxes that the receiving states collected from migrant workers' wages. As in the case of Bulgaria, where the withholdings began at 20 percent and were eventually lowered to 10 percent, transfer payments were described in the documents as being applied toward "the costs of [workers'] recruitment and preparation for [their] trip to Czechoslovakia and deposited into the fund for the defense and construction of the homeland."[79] A similar terminology of "national reconstruction" was used in the other treaties to justify obligatory withholdings, though the tax rates varied according to the country. In the Soviet Union, this amount was also first set at 20 percent before it was lowered to 10 percent in 1986. In the case of Bulgaria and Czechoslovakia, proceeds were also slated to pay off Vietnam's foreign debts with the host country.[80] Notably, the requirement applied only to contract workers, not apprentice workers. In the GDR, the Vietnamese government had 12 percent of the wages its workers garnered by employers. By way of comparison, the Cuban government withheld a full 25 percent from the paychecks of their workforce in the GDR. These numbers would become critical points at issue between the governments, as well as workers. In 1987 Vietnamese officials, for example, debated increasing the rate to 18–20 percent, using the Cuban rate as an argument. As the numbers of workers that Vietnam sent to East-Central Europe increased, the resources flowing into Vietnam from these compulsory remittances became considerable—in 1987, for example, the Vietnamese state collected 43.6 million marks from its workers in East Germany alone.[81]

On the one hand, this obligation put the two sides—the workers and the Vietnamese state officials—at odds as it reduced workers' take-home wages, leading to strikes or, more often, to complaints to Vietnamese supervisors. However, the obligation also led to the opposite: It *aligned* the workers' and the state's financial interests since the amount of money that the Vietnamese state was able to collect hinged on both the size of the earnings and the sheer number of its overseas workers. As a result, it was in the Vietnamese state's interest to fight for wage increases for its workers. In an internal document, the Vietnamese ambassador proposed an increase in wages of 500 marks for its workers in the GDR.[82] Likewise, Vietnamese officials in Prague and Hanoi put sustained pressure on their Czechoslovak counterparts, through formal and informal channels, to increase their workers' incomes.[83] Their pressure was often effective, and changes were implemented—at times in an ad hoc fashion and at other times through the rewriting of bilateral agreements, such as the 1987 revised protocol between Vietnam and the GDR.

The final feature that made these programs distinctive was their origin as work *and* training programs. While the treaties signed in 1980–81 meant that the training element was gradually pushed into the background (though it did not disappear: the apprentice worker model continued alongside the contract worker model), there were some continuities. The 1980s model differed by virtue of the states pursuing their self-interest and increasingly commodifying workers in the process. Nonetheless, this model incorporated a number of structural features from earlier programs, including the principle of group (not individual) migration and benefits such as health care, initial clothing donations, and paid local and Vietnamese holidays. In both the GDR and Czechoslovakia, workers were allowed extra paid vacation days on the two most important Vietnamese state holidays (Independence Day and the Lunar New Year) as per negotiation on the part of the Vietnamese government, which continued to advocate for its workers.

Explaining the Turn to National Self-Interest

By way of conclusion, an accurate reading and understanding of these programs requires attending to both the changes *and* continuities as they developed over time. The question, however, begs to be answered as to why these changes happened in the first place, and more especially what accounts for the shift from a project guided mainly by internationalist imperatives, ideological impulses whose net effect was altruistic, to one foregrounding the receiving states' economic self-interest.

We propose that the shift was connected to critical social, economic, and political changes that socialist states in East-Central Europe were undergoing. For example, Katherine Verdery points to internal forms of resistance and covert acts of sabotage that contributed to a crisis of legitimacy.[84] Labor shortages that produced the need for foreign workers were compounded by an "oppositional cult of non-work," which significantly reduced productivity, adversely affecting the economy to the point of crisis.[85] These perspectives are important in that they emphasize the role of people, particularly workers but also elites and officials engaged in their own forms of opposition, as active participants in such a process.

Socialism's articulation with flexible global capitalism was also crucial to the change we outline above.[86] Such an interface between competing systems was already under way in Asian socialist countries. Beijing's "socialism with Chinese characteristics" and the implementation in rural areas of "reforms from below" (in contrast to the Soviet Union's more hierarchical, state-guided approach) generated unprecedented growth in agriculture and industry alike.[87] Reeling from conflicts with Cambodia and China and a longstanding US-led embargo that further impoverished a population still recovering from war, Vietnam cautiously began to open its economy to Western capitalism in 1986 in a series of reforms called *Đổi mới*. The Vietnamese government's complicity to some degree (though with some protest, as noted above) in the exploitation of its workforce overseas speaks to the growing desperation that gripped the nation during the "subsidy years" (*thời bao cấp*).

In Eastern Europe, on the other hand, reviewing various economic and statistical indicators, Ivan Szelenyi and Balazs Szelenyi[88] argue that "on the whole, there is solid evidence that until the mid-1970s socialist societies were competitive with the West." But "between 1975 and 1989 their growth slowed and the gap between capitalist and socialist countries at a similar level of economic development began to widen again and eventually their socioeconomic and even ecological and demographic system began to decay." One of the major exogenous factors is the world economy, specifically four aspects of it: the steep rise in oil prices, the concomitant cheap credit offered by Arab countries, the revolution in information technology, and the opening of some East-Central European countries to world markets. The various structural changes they started implementing in the economic, social, and political realms, including more self-interested labor training and import programs, were part of this effort to adjust.

Conclusion: Global Pasts in the Present

As we have argued above, state-socialist labor migrations were part of "the oft-overlooked circulation of people, goods, knowledge and capital"[89] that took place among the Socialist Bloc countries that formed an alternative global world of interconnections. In an earlier work, challenging the assumed view of state socialism as a form of *immobility*, Christina Schwenkel referred to these circulations as "socialist mobilities," drawing attention to the fact that the movement of people was essential to socialism both as an ideology and as a set of political institutions and economic practices.[90] These mobilities did not just create a sui generis, state-socialist alternative globalization that rivaled other forms of global capitalist interconnection. Rather, these transnational mobilities have become an integral part of global processes as they unfold today. Socialist mobilities transformed Vietnamese university and vocational students, as well as low-skilled workers, into world citizens, or "socialist cosmopolitans," with new forms of sociability and new economic ties that have proven useful to integration in a world market economy, suggesting that these competing systems were more symbiotic and interdependent than previously recognized.[91] There are a number of contemporary initiatives and joint ventures that continue to exist and thrive owing to the linkages forged through such mobilities. Former labor migrants have returned to found new companies, such as Việt Đức Xúc Xích (Vietnam Germany sausages) or Hoa Viên Bräuhaus, a chain of Czech breweries. Two towers of a high-rise shopping mall, Vincom Center, were built with investment from a Ukrainian company owned by a Vietnamese-born entrepreneur.[92] The Vietnamese-Czech Friendship Hospital in the city of Haiphong, built with Czechoslovak funds and expertise in the 1950s[93] remains in operation to this day, as does the Vietnam-German Friendship Hospital in Hanoi (both of which began as colonial infirmaries), while both the Czech Republic and Germany continue to extend material and financial support to these hospitals: socialist assistance has morphed into postsocialist development aid.

We see these continuities also in the realm of human resources. At least six current and past members of the Vietnamese cabinet obtained their university degrees in state-socialist Czechoslovakia and have occupied such high-profile posts as deputy prime minister, foreign affairs minister, and finance minister. Numerous senior government officials were likewise awarded their degrees in East Germany, including a former deputy prime minister and a minister of education. Those trained in the GDR often returned to midlevel cadre positions in government offices, though their acquired foreign knowledge was often viewed with suspicion or regarded as inapplicable.[94] Nonetheless, these powerful people not only form a direct link between the socialist past and a market socialist present but also contribute in important ways to shaping Vietnam's current global geopolitical engagements. Former contract workers have also made important contributions to Vietnam's economy. Thus, the economic, social, and human capital that people accumulated through socialist pathways of migration has enabled them to actively participate in, even if not always to benefit from, contemporary capitalist globalization. Just as colonial power once shaped the infrastructure landscape for the socialist regime that followed it, so has socialist power shaped the landscape in which state capitalism operates in Vietnam today.

Notes

1. Jude Howell, "The End of an Era: The Rise and Fall of GDR Aid," *The Journal of Modern African Studies* 32, no. 2 (1994): 305–328.
2. Konrad H. Jarausch, "Beyond Uniformity: The Challenge of Historicizing the GDR," in *Dictatorship as Experience: Towards a Socio-Cultural History of the GDR* (New York: Berghahn Books, 1999).
3. See Alena Alamgir, "'Inappropriate Behavior': Labor Control and the Polish, Cuban and Vietnamese Workers in Czechoslovakia," in *Labor in State Socialist Europe after 1945: Contributions to Global Labor History*, eds. Marsha Seifert and Susan Zimmermann (Central European University Press, forthcoming); Alena Alamgir, "From the Field to the Factory Floor: Vietnamese Government's Defense of Migrant Workers' Interests in State-Socialist Czechoslovakia," *Journal of Vietnamese Studies* 12, no. 1 (2017), 10–41; and Alena Alamgir, "The Moped Diaries: Remittances in the Czechoslovak-Vietnamese Labor Migration Scheme," in *Work out of Place*, edited by Mahua Sarkar (De Gruyter Oldenbourg, 2017).
4. Nguen An Kha, "Trudovoe sotrudnichestvo mezhdu V'etnamom i Rossiey v nachale XXI veka: vozmozhnosti i problemy," in *Rossiysko_v'etnamskie otnosheniya: sovremennost' i istoriya: Vzglyad dvukh storon*, eds. Yevgeniy Kobelev and A. A. Kozlov (Institut Dal'nego Vostoka, 2013).
5. Vincent Houben and Thomas Lindblad, *Coolie Labor in Colonial Indonesia: A Study of Labor Relations in the Outer Islands, c. 1900–1940* (Wiesbaden: Harrassowitz, 1999).
6. Stephen Castles, "The Guest-Worker in Western Europe—An Obituary," *International Migration Review* 20, no. 4 (1986): 761–778. See also Ulrich Herbert, *A History of Foreign Labor in Germany, 1880–1980: Seasonal Workers, Forced Laborers, Guest Workers* (Ann Arbor, MI: University of Michigan Press, 1990); Robert E. Rhoades, "Foreign Labor and German Industrial Capitalism 1871–1978: The Evolution of a Migratory System," *American Ethnologist* 5, no. 3 (1978): 553–573.
7. This label replaced *Arbeitgäste*, a word discredited by Nazi labor import schemes; Rhoades, "Foreign Labor and German Industrial Capitalism."
8. Such as the Belgian *contingentensystem* and the French labor program under the *Office National d'Immigration* (ONI). Castles, "The Guest-Worker in Western Europe."
9. Stephen Castles and Godula Kosack, *Immigrant Workers and Class Structure in Western Europe* (Oxford: Oxford University Press, 1985).
10. Michael J. Piore, *Birds of Passage: Migrant Labor and Industrial Societies* (Cambridge: Cambridge University Press, 1979).
11. For example, while Swiss employers recruited their workers directly (per regulations by the state), in Germany the control over recruitment remained with the Federal Labor Office. Philip L. Martin and Mark J. Miller, "Guestworkers: Lessons from Western Europe," *Industrial and Labor Relations Review* 33, no. 3 (1980): 315–330.
12. Piore, *Birds of Passage*.

13. Cindy Hahamovitch, "Creating Perfect Immigrants: Guestworkers of the World in Historical Perspective," *Labor History* 44, no. 1 (2003): 69–94.

14. See, e.g., Castles and Kosack, *Immigrant Workers and Class Structure*; Rita Chin, *The Guest Worker Question in Postwar Germany* (Cambridge: Cambridge University Press, 2007).

15. Thomas F. Pettigrew, "Reactions toward the New Minorities of Western Europe," *Annual Review of Sociology* 24 (1998): 77–103.

16. Joachim Krüger, "Die Anfänge der Beziehungen zwischen der DDR und der DR Vietnam," *Asien, Afrika, Lateinamerika* 19, no. 5 (1991): 815–826.

17. See Katherine Pence and Paul Betts, eds., *Socialist Modern: East German Everyday Culture and Politics* (Ann Arbor: University of Michigan Press, 2008).

18. Also known as Comecon, an organization for economic and trade cooperation among the Soviet Union and its allies, founded in 1949 and disbanded in 1991.

19. Christina Schwenkel, "Socialist Mobilities: Crossing New Terrains in Vietnamese Migration Histories," *Central and Eastern European Migration Review* 4, no. 1 (2015): 13–25.

20. Christina Schwenkel, "Rethinking Asian Mobilities: Socialist Migration and Postsocialist Repatriation of Vietnamese Contract Workers in East Germany," *Critical Asian Studies* 46, no. 2 (2014): 235–258.

21. Czech National Archive (NA), uncatalogued source, "Zpráva o jednání federálního ministerstva práce a sociálních věcí s vládní delegací Vietnamské demokratické republiky o odborné přípravě občanů VDR v Československé socialistické republice," June 1973.

22. Tereza Kušníráková, "Vztah vietnamských navrátilců předlistopadové imigrace k československému státu a jeho společnosti," *Český lid* 99, no. 1 (2012).

23. Based on interviews carried out in Hanoi and Hai Phong, June–September 2007.

24. On the Vietnamese government's request that pregnant Vietnamese workers be able to give birth in Czechoslovakia, see Alena K. Alamgir, "Recalcitrant Women: Internationalism and the Redefinition of Welfare Limits in the Czechoslovak-Vietnamese Labor Exchange Program, 1967–1989," *Slavic Review* 73, no. 1 (2014): 133–155.

25. Vietnam National Archives III, File 7409, Văn Phòng Chính Phủ 1957–1995.

26. NA, F. 02/1, s. 11, a.j. 12.

27. Mikhail Petrovich Isaev and Al'bert Sergeevich Chernyshev, *Istoriya sovetsko-v'etnamskikh otnosheniy: 1917–1985* (Mezhdunarodnye otnosheniya, 1986).

28. *Quân hệ Hữu nghị và Hợp tác Toàn diễn Việt Nam—Liên Xô*, Hà nội: NXB Sự Thật, 1988, cited in Buu Hoan, "Soviet Economic Aid to Vietnam," *Contemporary Southeast Asia* 12, no. 4 (March 1991): 360–376, here, 367.

29. *Quân hệ Hữu nghị*, cited in Buu Hoan, 367–368.

30. Krüger, "Die Anfänge der Beziehungen," 823. In 1955 approximately 350 pupils between the ages of nine and fifteen were sent to school in the GDR. Many of these children, who became known as the "Moritzburger," would eventually return as young adults to learn a profession.

31. "Dary a ostatní formy pomoci Československé socialistické republiky Vietnamské demokratické republice; K bodu: Návrh ÚV MSDS na koordinaci vojenské pomoci Vietnamu," August 19, 1967. Fond: KSČ-ÚV-02/1, KSČ—Ústřední výbor 1945–1989, Praha—předsednictvo 1966–1971, svazek 42, archivní jednotka 43.

32. Fond ÚV KSČ, "Informace o současném stavu československo-vietnamských vztahů a plnění přijatých dokumentů," report drafted by the Federal Ministry of Foreign Affairs, presented at the ÚV KSČ meeting on September 28, 1979.

33. Christina Schwenkel, "The Soviet-Trained Scientist," in *Figures of Southeast Asian Modernity*, eds. Joshua Barker, Erik Harms, and Johan Lindquist (Honolulu: University of Hawai'i Press, 2013), 59–61.

34. Vietnam National Archives III, File 9132, Văn Phòng Phủ Thủ Tướng 1954–1985.

35. Susan Bayly, "Vietnamese Intellectuals in Revolutionary and Postcolonial Times," *Critique of Anthropology* 24, no. 3 (2004): 320–344.

36. Dieter Knöfel, "Hilfe und Zusammenarbeit: Die Wirtschaftsbeziehungen zwischen der DDR und Vietnam," *Die DDR und Vietnam, Teil 2*. Verband für Internationale Politik, 2011, 20–38, here, 37.

37. Исаев and Чернышев, Isaev and Chernyshev, *Istoriya sovetsko-v'etnamskikh otnosheniy.*

38. Central State Archives (CSA), Sofia, 136.44.344 (fond 136, inventory number 44, archival unit 344).

39. MZV: 145/112, 1973–74.

40. Ibid.

41. Ibid.

42. Odds are, this was true of the USSR-Vietnamese agreement as well, but, at the time of this writing, the authors are unable to verify the supposition.

43. Isaev and Chernyshev, *Istoriya sovetsko-v'etnamskikh otnosheniy.*

44. Oliver Raendchen, *Vietnamesen in der DDR: Ein Rückblick* (Berlin: SEACOM, 2000), 3.

45. From this number, Lulei estimates that 4,562 Vietnamese received their university diplomas (other estimates go as high as 5,435), one-third of all foreign students who received degrees in the GDR. Wilfried Lulei, "Die DDR-Solidarität für Vietnam auf dem Gebiet der Wissenschaft und Bildung," *Die DDR und Vietnam, Teil 2* (Verband für Internationale Politik, 2011), 62–69, here, 63.

46. "Dohoda mezi vládou Československé socialistické republiky a vládou Vietnamské demokratické republiky o odborné přípravě občanů Vietnamské demokratické republiky v československých organizacích," signed in Hanoi on April 8, 1974.

47. Wilfried Lulei and Ilona Schleicher, "Die DDR-Solidarität mit Vietnam: Erbe für die deutsch-vietnamesischen Beziehungen," *Die DDR und Vietnam, Teil 1* (Verband für Internationale Politik, 2011), 98–99.

48. "Zpráva o stavu zabezpečení odborné přípravy občanů Vietnamské demokratické republiky v československých organizacích a k návrhu příslušné mezivládní Dohody," September 1973.

49. Raia Apostolova, "From Real Socialism to Real Capitalism: The Making and Dismantling of the Vietnamese Worker in Bulgaria," in *Situating Migration in Transition: Temporal, Structural and Conceptual Transformations of Migrations, Sketches from Bulgaria*, eds. Raia Apostolova, Neda Deneva, and Tsvetelina Hristova (Sofia: Collective for Social Interventions, 2014), 29.

50. Martin Myant, *The Czechoslovak Economy 1948–1988: The Battle for Economic Reform* (Cambridge, UK: Cambridge University Press, 1989), 223.

51. Anatoliy Sokolov, "V'yetnamtsy v Rossii: istoriya, kul'tura, integratsiya," *Diaspory: nezavisimyy nauchnyy zhurnal* no. 1, 2011: 219–244.

52. Data compiled from various reports prepared by the Czech Labor Ministry (i.e., republic-level, not federal Czechoslovak), usually entitled "*Přehled o počtech zahraničních pracovníků k 31. prosinci [rok] podle resortů a jednotlivých zahraničních partnerů.*"

53. Eszter Bartha, "Welfare Dictatorship, the Working Class and the Change of Regimes in East Germany and Hungary," *Europe-Asia Studies* 63, no. 9 (2011): 1591–1610.

54. Mike Dennis, "Working under Hammer and Sickle: Vietnamese Workers in the German Democratic Republic, 1980–89," *German Politics* 16, no. 3 (2007): 339–357. We reproduce the article's figures, but note that they in fact total 71,945.

55. James Mark and Bálint Tolmár, "From Heroes Square to the Textile Factory: Encountering Cuba in Socialist Hungary 1959–1990," forthcoming.

56. "Soglashenie mezhdu Pravitel'stvom SSSR i Pravitel'stvom Sotsialisticheskoy Respubliki V'etnam o napravlenii i prieme v'etnamskikh grazhdan na professional'noe obuchenie i rabotu na predpriyatiyakh i v organizatsiyakh SSSR," (Zakoncheno v g. Moskve 02.04.1981), available at http://www.lawrussia.ru/texts/legal_530/doc530a274x543.htm.

57. Din' Kha Mi, "Migratsiya iz V'etnama v Rossiyu - problema nezashchishchennosti immigrantov," a presentation at the conference "VII Vserossiyskoy konferentsiiin" in Tomsk, April 23–25, 2014.

58. In Vietnamese: Hiệp định giữa 2 chính phủ về việc người lao động Việt Nam làm việc có thời hạn và bởi dưỡng nghiệp vụ tài các xí nghiệp CHDC Đức [Bilateral agreement on the temporary employment and training of Vietnam workers in GDR enterprises]; and in German: Abkommen zwischen der Regierung der Deutschen Demokratischen Republik und der Regierung der Sozialistischen Republik Vietnam über die zeitweilige Beschäftigung und Qualifizierung vietnamesischen Werktätiger in Betrieben der Deutschen Demokratischen Republik.

59. Knöfel, "Hilfe und Zusammenarbeit," 37. Others report this number closer to twelve thousand.

60. National Archives, Berlin, File DQ3 2143.

61. Uncatalogued archival documents obtained at the Czech Ministry of Labor and Social Affairs, henceforth "MPSV": "Dohoda mezi vládou Československé socialistické republiky a vládou Vietnamské socialistické republiky o dočasném zaměstnávání kvalifikovaných pracovníků Vietnamské socialistické republiky spojeném s další odbornou přípravou v československých organizacích."

62. MPSV, appendix to "Prováděcí protokol o spolupráci mezi Československou socialistickou republikou a Vietnamskou sociliastickou republikou v oblasti dočasného zaměstnávání kvalifikovaných pracovníků Vietnamské sociliastické republiky spojeného s další odbornou přípravou v československých organizacích v roce 1989," signed in Hanoi on April 6, 1989.

63. MPSV, letter from the federal deputy labor minister, Milan Kyselý, to the Czech deputy labor minister, Václav Karas, dated February 5, 1987.

64. MPSV, "Zpráva ke sjednání Dohody mezi vládou Československé socialistické republiky a vládou Vietnamské socialistické republiky o dočasném zaměstnávání kvalifikovaných pracovníků Vietnamské socialistické republiky spojeném s další odbornou přípravou v československých organizacích."

65. See, e.g., "Odborné školení vietnamských pracovníků v MZVž [Ministerstvo zemědělství a výživy] (výňatky z komentářů podniků ke statistice)."

66. Ibid.

67. "Informace o možnostech zaměstnávání vietnamských občanů v ČSSR a návrh dalšího postupu," received by the Presidium of the Government (*Úřad předsednictva vlády*) on April 7, 1976.

68. Kušníráková, "Vztah vietnamských navrátilců předlistopadové imigrace k československému státu a jeho společnosti," 62.

69. Ronen Steinke, "Wir waren jung und schön," *Süddeutsche Zeitung*, Juli 30, 2014, 3. "Nichts war toller als der DDR," Ulrich van der Heyden et. al., eds. Mosambikanische Vertragsarbeiter in der DDR-Wirtschaft: Hintergrund, Verlauf, Folgen, Münster: LIT Verlag, 2014.

70. Vietnam National Archives III, File 4409, Văn Phòng Chính Phủ 1957–1995.

71. See Alena K. Alamgir, "Socialist Internationalism at Work: Changes in the Czechoslovak-Vietnamese Labor Exchange Program, 1967–1989" (PhD diss., Rutgers University, 2014), ch. 5.

72. Alamgir, "Socialist Internationalism."

73. See Jonathan Zatlin, "Scarcity and Resentment: Economic Sources of Xenophobia in the GDR, 1971–1989," in *Central European History* 40 (2007), 683–720, as well as Alamgir, "Moped Diaries"; Alena Alamgir, "Race Is Elsewhere: State-Socialist Ideology and the Racialisation of Vietnamese Workers in Czechoslovakia," *Race & Class* 54, no. 4 (2013): 67–85; and Raia Apostolova, "Duty and Debt under the Ethos of Internationalism: The Case of the Vietnamese Workers in Bulgaria," *Journal of Vietnamese Studies* 12, no. 1 (2017): 101–125; "Socialist Mobilities," 245–246.

74. For a detailed analysis of the politics of remittances in the Czechoslovak-Vietnamese program, see Alamgir, "Moped Diaries."

75. MPSV, "Informace pro jednání s delegací Státního sekretariátu pro práci a mzdy NDR o zaměstnávání zahraničních pracovníků dne 29.8.1989," dated August 25, 1989.

76. National Archives, Berlin, Files DY30 6494 and DY 30 6547.

77. Zatlin, "Scarcity and Resentment," 679. Note that hostility was also generated in Vietnam as families with relatives overseas were able to secure a higher standard of living. Schwenkel, "Rethinking Asian Mobilities."

78. MPSV, Zápis z jednání mezi ministrem práce a sociálních věcí Československé socialistické republiky s. Michalem Štanclem a ministrem práce Vietnamské socialistické republiky s. Dao Tien Thi v Hanoji ve dnech 9.-13. března 1981.

79. Ibid.

80. Vietnam National Archives III, File 4501, Văn Phòng Chính Phủ 1957–1995.

81. Vietnam National Archives III, File 4409, Văn Phòng Chính Phủ 1957–1995.

82. Ibid.

83. See Alamgir, "Socialist Internationalism at Work."

84. Katherine Verdery, *What Was Socialism and What Comes Next?* (Princeton, NJ: Princeton University Press, 1996), 20.

85. "Socialist Internationalism," 23.

86. Ibid., 33.

87. Yia-Ling Liu, "Reform from Below: The Private Economy and Local Politics in the Rural Industrialization of Wenzhou," *The China Quarterly* 130 (1992): 293–316.

88. Ivan Szelenyi and Balazs Szelenyi, "Why Socialism Failed: Toward a Theory of System Breakdown—Causes of Disintegration of East European State Socialism," *Theory and Society* 23, no. 2 (1994).

89. "Rethinking Asian Mobilities," 236.

90. Ibid.

91. Gertrud Hüwelmeier, "Socialist Cosmopolitanism Meets Global Pentecostalism: Charismatic Christianity among Vietnamese Migrants after the Fall of the Berlin Wall," *Ethnic and Racial Studies* 34, no. 3 (2011): 436–453, here, 440.

92. Ola Söderström, "What Traveling Urban Types Do: Postcolonial Modernization in Two Globalizing Cities," in *Critical Mobilities*, eds. Ola Söderström et al. (Lausanne: EPFL Press/Routledge, 2013), 29–57, here, 45.

93. Archive of the Czech Ministry of Foreign Affairs (MZV), "Informace o vztazích mezi ČSSR a VDR" part of "Informační materiál k přijetí delegace NS VDR v ČSSR," dated May 7, 1974, third territorial department, 1970–74, Vietnam T, 2, 145/112, 1973–1974.

94. Schwenkel, "Socialist Mobilities," 8.

ALENA K. ALAMGIR is Instructor of Sociology at Emory University. She is editor of *Labor and Labor Migration in State Socialism*.

CHRISTINA SCHWENKEL is Associate Professor of Anthropology and Director of the Program in Southeast Asian Studies at the University of California, Riverside. She is author of *The American War in Contemporary Vietnam: Transnational Remembrance and Representation* (Bloomington: Indiana University Press, 2009).

Part II

A Socialist Age of Development?

5 "Socialist Development" and East Germany in the Arab Middle East

Massimiliano Trentin

Most of the scholarly literature on the German Democratic Republic (GDR) has focused on the domestic workings of the regime; study of the GDR's international relations has been limited to its role as a subordinate partner of the USSR or, at best, to the part it played in the struggle against the containment doctrine of the Federal Republic of Germany (FRG). Recent research, however, has analyzed how the GDR engaged with postcolonial countries and highlighted the relevance of the connections between its stance on the Cold War and the topic of development. According to this line of argument, Berlin delivered its own variant of socialist development as a model for rapid state-led industrialization under the aegis of a hegemonic party, support for mobilization, and the control of society through mass organizations.[1] Though such elements were present in other socialist states, they played a more prominent role in the GDR because their reception by progressive forces in postcolonial countries would help to legitimize Berlin's claim to statehood and sovereignty against its Western "imperialist" rival in Bonn. Quite limited in its diplomatic, military, and economic standing, the GDR had thus to invest considerable material and ideational energies in forging political ties with progressive movements. If we compare the situation of the GDR to that of its comrades in Europe, we find a stronger emphasis on the suitability of socialist patterns of development for modernization, which would constitute the ultimate basis for the viability of socialist internationalism. Once the GDR had gained full, international recognition from the late 1960s, Berlin shifted toward a more routine intergovernmental politics and raison d'état, but ideology and militant internationalism remained a constant, original feature of the GDR stance in the postcolonial world. The salience of the GDR in shaping a kind of "socialist globalization" thus lay on the comparatively high relevance it attached to ideas like internationalism, anti-imperialism, and development; and how sincere commitment served the interests of a regime whose domestic legitimacy was intimately connected to the fortunes of socialist movements in international politics.

The GDR faced huge challenges in its attempts to create a new global socialist community. Efforts by GDR leaders proved successful in the 1960s, as long as their economic and institutional approaches converged with the politics of the postcolonial Middle East. Yet there were difficulties from the start: inter-German competition placed a heavy burden on GDR economic cooperation and "solidarity," which already suffered from logistical problems; their patterns of institution building turned out to be of only limited relevance to local patterns of social allegiance and mobilization; and their own more radical partners in the region often risked jeopardizing the GDR's overall regional strategy. Moreover, the GDR was faced with local leaderships who preferred not to align with a single ideological camp and were prepared to exploit Cold War rivalry for their purposes. From the 1970s it increasingly appeared that some of the fundamental ideological identifications that had underpinned these (albeit fragile) relationships were being seriously undermined. The GDR's aging industrial model set the country at odds with ongoing trends in the Middle East. The politics and economics of the oil shocks and debt crisis (see also chapter 1 in this volume) favored links to Western and capitalist countries; these same problems led to the crisis of state-centered, secular regimes in the Middle East, which the GDR had previously been keen to support.

The International Relations of the GDR

As both Germanies were created by the Cold War partitioning of Europe, the FRG became a showcase for free market capitalism, whereas the GDR became a vanguard model for orthodox Marxist-Leninism in politics and economics. Even compared to the USSR and other East European socialist countries, GDR state and official institutions attached particular importance to concepts like internationalism (both proletarian and socialist) and anti-imperialism.[2] These concepts were "realist" in so far as the Socialist Unity Party of Germany (Sozialistische Einheitspartei Deutschlands, or SED) leaders needed legitimacy abroad for the GDR to be recognized as a full-fledged sovereign nation. Yet viewed in another light, these concepts were also genuine and had grassroots support because many East German citizens believed in constructing a new democratic regime that would break with the recent past of Germany and support peace and progress worldwide.[3] The GDR leadership fully embraced Marxist-Leninist ideology to frame their analysis of world events and set their own policy accordingly. They believed their country was part of the world revolutionary movement "and thus ipso facto a global revolutionary force."[4]

Three pillars guided the GDR's theory in foreign policy: first of all, GDR officials subscribed to the doctrine of "peaceful coexistence" toward capitalist states, which was established at the Twentieth Congress of the Communist Party of the Soviet Union (CPSU) in 1956: this would avoid any direct confrontation between the superpowers in Europe, and consequently on German soil.[5] Second, "socialist internationalism" was the approach adopted toward socialist countries and movements in the late 1960s. Third, there was "proletarian internationalism," which dated back to Karl Marx and Friedrich Engels's 1848 *Communist Manifesto* and had been mainly aimed at the industrial proletariat but was then used to make sense of the predicament of postcolonial countries and of the role of national liberation movements as a "new working class" in the global system. Proletarian internationalism provided the basis for socialist "solidarity": though not fully sharing common socialist credentials, postcolonial countries and forces were deemed important allies because they could limit both imperialist aggression and capitalist expansion, the GDR being believed to be at the forefront of the struggle to contain the West. "Anti-imperialist solidarity" ranked high among GDR official principles and was even included in article 6, paragraph 3 of the 1974 constitution, to stress once again the difference with the supposed "imperialism" of West Germany, despite the fact that the two countries had normalized relations in 1972. As such, postcolonial forces had to be supported and trained to discover and strengthen "objective," if not "natural," common interests with the socialist camp.[6] Proletarian internationalism and anti-imperialist solidarity challenged the requirements of raison d'état once socialist and communist forces had grasped state power and jealously upheld respect for national sovereignty. Indeed, GDR scholars and officials were eager to assure their nationalist partners that their solidarity did not mean interference in the domestic affairs of other nations.[7]

Fully aware of the heterogeneity of the postcolonial world, the GDR selected political movements and postcolonial countries according to their (expected) contribution to the world revolutionary movement and, above all, to the socialist camp's own viability: the more they leaned toward *real existierender Sozialismus* (really existing socialism), the more they were granted solidarity and cooperation. To navigate the complexity of the postcolonial world and to match political and economic convenience, the GDR leadership adopted the theory of the non-capitalist road (NCR) to development, promoted by Moscow from 1961.[8] The NCR model was conceived as a road map first to national independence, second to "national democracy," and finally to socialism for those progressive forces of national liberation movements (NLMs) that had seized power. The overtures to noncommunist movements constituted a major breakthrough as they represented the abandonment of the strict norms established by Joseph Stalin in the Communist Information Bureau (Cominform) in 1947.[9]

Above all, the noncapitalist road asserted the primacy of politics over economics, categorizing postcolonial countries according to the degree of class differentiation, the imperialist presence, and the strength of revolutionary forces. Once NLMs had seized control of the state, they would centralize the administrative and coercive apparatus to consolidate their hegemony over society and thus to overcome "conservative" opponents. The latter had to be marginalized because their ties to Western imperialism would thwart social reforms as well as act as a drain on national resources. East German scholars focused on the category of national democracy that "would make the transition to non-capitalist development easier":[10] though not of a socialist type, the state would have to be strengthened to become the main agent for domestic capital accumulation and industrialization; the centralized, bureaucratic state was conceived as the best engine to match the efficient use of scarce resources with equitable patterns of wealth redistribution. Private entrepreneurship had to survive, but as subservient to the public sector rather than as the driving force for growth. The state should first protect domestic industry, for example, by nationalizing the property of foreign monopolies, and only at a later stage could the country integrate into world markets: that is, only when their bargaining power was strong enough to face foreign competition. The NCR approach recognized that the capitalist camp retained much of the world's resources in terms of finance and technology, and, under certain conditions, developing countries could still take advantage of capital flows and technology transfer.[11] What also made the NCR so attractive to postcolonial leaders was that it legitimized the "strong state" and gave them a road map for strengthening their political autonomy. As far as the Arab world was concerned, the NCR was well suited to the political tradition of regimes and governance that had been legitimized by quietist or conservative Islam as well.[12]

To enhance the chances of the NCR, East Germany and the socialist states could grant bilateral cooperation through a variety of policies and instruments. These were diplomatic, political, and even military support in international arenas; long-term credits; and technological transfer and professional training, mostly based on buyback and clearing agreements. These latter policies marked a fundamental difference with Western capitalist countries: to confront the shortages of hard currency in transactions, they forestalled a partial or total repayment both in the form of the exchange of goods on a barter basis and through the resultant products stemming from the "complete plants" that had been installed with the related credits.[13]

"Solidarity" and Cooperation, Not Aid

The German Democratic Republic rejected the notion of development aid because in its judgment it still bore the hallmarks of imperialist encroachment on the peoples and territories of former colonies. Development aid as practiced by First World countries led to the diversion abroad of value generated by labor and to the exploitation of natural resources; as such, it perpetuated the dependence of the "peripheries." Instead, East Germany provided socialist "solidarity," the breadth and depth of which depended in the main on political and economic convergence with the local recipients.

The principal institutions involved in the decision-making process of GDR state solidarity were the Ministry of Foreign Affairs (Ministerium für Auswärtige Angelegenheiten, MfAA), the Ministry of Foreign Trade (Ministerium für Aussen- und Innerdeutschen Handel, MAI), and the Commission for Economic Planning (Staatliche Plankommission). Since the mid-1960s, the Council of Ministers (Ministerrat) had increasingly centralized control. However, the final decision rested with the party: first, in the Department for International Relations (Abteilung Internationale Verbindungen) of the Central Committee, which oversaw the international relations of the party and of the whole country as a consequence of its hegemonic role; and second, in the Politburo of the Central Committee, which held ultimate responsibility.[14] These institutions were supplemented by other actors, such as the Free German Workers' Union (Freier Deutscher Gewerkschaftsbund, FDGB), the Free German Youth Organization (Freie Deutsche Jugend, FDJ), the friendship brigades (Freundschaftsbrigaden), and by a vast range of solidarity committees, such as the Afro-Asian Solidarity Committee (Afro-Asiatisches Solidaritätskomittee), which operated in postcolonial countries within the framework of official state policies.[15]

In the economic realm the GDR structured its "solidarity" on foreign trade (Außenhandel) and on Economic and Technical Cooperation (Wirtschaftliche und Technische Zusammenarbeit, WTZ). The latter, in particular, was intended to highlight the equal and cooperative relationship between Berlin and the recipient partner. The official aim was to support the recipient partner's independence and to relieve it of the burden of international asymmetry in economics and politics. The WTZ's work was based on the transfer of scientific and technical expertise through the development of joint research programs, the provision of vocational training courses, and the enrolling of large numbers of foreign students in GDR schools and universities. A great deal of importance was attached to health programs through education, training, and technology transfer.[16] As in West Germany, higher technical education was a priority for the GDR: on the one side, it complemented the export of industrial plants and the knowledge to run such complexes once installed; on the other side, it was explicitly aimed at training the future national elites while at the same time instilling common habits, shared languages, and rational thinking. *Erziehung zur Arbeit* (training for work), with an ethic based on discipline, punctuality, and productivity, was conceived as a major pillar for efforts to develop the productive forces of any industrial society—progressive and socialist ones included.[17] This emphasis on discipline, responsibility, and training found a receptive audience among ruling elites in the Arab world who, from Mehmet Ali in Egypt in the first part of the nineteenth century to progressive modernizers in the early 1960s, held labor training as a key factor in the struggle for modern development. The social disciplinary features of the "politics of productivity" were far from an issue confined to the Western world.[18]

The boundaries between foreign trade and WTZ were never clearly defined and increasingly overlapped to serve the political and economic interests of the GDR. Four main periods can be observed in this respect. The first ran from the 1950s to the mid-1960s, when the GDR leadership gave priority to political and diplomatic goals in its activities in the postcolonial world.[19] International diplomatic recognition constituted the highest priority in Berlin's agenda, and international solidarity was used as a tool to gain political legitimacy: small credits were granted to a wide range of countries, and intense contacts were developed with the national liberation movements at the levels of government, party, and mass organizations. Such networks would help the GDR in standing against West Germany and the Hallstein Doctrine at the United Nations, as well as in Afro-Asian conferences. East Germany's engagement also accelerated as the country's agricultural and industrial growth picked up after 1963: economic cooperation with developing states would foster further technological specialization, as had been planned in the New Economic System (Neues ökonomisches System der Planung und Leitung, or NÖSPL) of 1963 and 1964, and the now-growing needs for raw material imports and industrial product exports would be guaranteed.[20] There were, however, significant obstacles to this acceleration. Support from nationalist elites could not be suitably rewarded, and local rulers were not inclined to challenge the FRG and the entire Western camp directly. Moreover, the GDR was wholly dependent on Soviet international policies, which did not necessarily put GDR diplomatic issues at the forefront of their agenda. Help from the Council for Mutual Economic Assistance (CMEA) proved disappointing too, because of the lack of cooperation and integration among members.[21]

In line with the further economic specialization of the Ökonomisches System des Sozialismus (Economic System of Socialism) in 1967, East Germany became more selective in its solidarity with the Third World, and especially the Middle East. From 1969 Berlin focused on those postcolonial regimes labeled as having a "socialist orientation" (*Sozialistische Orientierung*) that actually provided more opportunities for a diplomatic breakthrough as well as domestic development.[22] These strategic countries (*Schwerpunktländer*) were targeted with more substantial credits for larger industrial projects, usually connected with ambitious infrastructure built by the USSR, such as the Tabqa Dam on the Euphrates River in Syria (started in 1966).[23] Foreign trade was conducted through state enterprises and agencies, so that the expansion of the state sector in the recipient, postcolonial country matched the GDR's preference for long-term agreements, avoidance of financial transactions in hard currency, and stability of prices. Broadly following the Soviet model, the GDR offered its partners long-term, governmental agreements, which comprised soft loans for buying industrial plants and machinery in exchange for raw materials, foodstuff, textiles, or typical products. Despite rhetoric on the differences from their Western rivals, such patterns did not deviate much from the standard, capitalist patterns of international trade: at best, the GDR's approach helped to expand domestic production and consumption, consistent with the goals of international institutions such as the United Nations Conference on Trade and Development (UNCTAD), which promoted a "trade not aid" policy.

Once Arab countries had granted the GDR diplomatic recognition in 1969 and the GDR had signed the Basic Treaty with the Federal Republic of Germany in 1972, a new phase in economic relations began. Officials in the Ministry of Foreign Trade (MAI) endeavored to conduct foreign trade according to more sound financial criteria. The GDR offered governmental credits (*Regierungskrediten*) to "strategic countries" that were to be paid back in eight to ten years at low interest rates, usually 2.5 to 3 percent. For other countries, commercial credits (*kommerzielle Kredite*) lasted five to seven years, with an interest rate of 4 to 5 percent, which were quite similar to the average conditions set by Western states.[24] Facing harsher competition from the West, the GDR strongly pushed the export of industrial technology, especially in the form of complete plants (*fertige* or *komplette Anlagen*), to all developing countries, irrespective of the recipients' political orientation. Hard currency and trade surpluses with the postcolonial countries were needed to offset the GDR's fast-growing deficits with the Soviet Union and Western Europe. However, the attempt to accumulate surpluses in trade suffered from the impact of the oil shocks, which reversed Berlin's trade balance with Arab countries. Thus, Berlin looked to the African continent and its privileged contacts with left-leaning national liberation movements, whereas it tried to enforce financial discipline (Ökonomisierung) and realpolitik with Arab partners.

It was only in the mid-1980s that the relationship between economics and diplomacy underwent a serious reversal, and political solidarities established in earlier decades had to serve first and foremost the grave financial needs of the GDR.[25] Here again, however, hopes were dashed because the oil counter-shocks in 1986 led most of the GDR's Arab partners to the verge of bankruptcy: the lack of hard currency to fund trade led East Germany and its Southern partners to resort once more to buy-back, clearing, and barter-based deals.[26] On the one hand, such scarcity revived traditional markets and solidarities, as for example with Syria, but, on the other hand, it did not provide any significant contribution to counter the overall decline of productive forces in the GDR.

GDR Solidarity in the Arab Middle East

As a junior partner of the USSR, Berlin framed its Middle East policy along the strategic lines set by Moscow and, like its Western rival, gave absolute priority first to the Cold War dynamics in Europe and the German Question (*Deutschlandfrage*): the Middle East was thus perceived by the East German leaders as a central arena but of secondary importance in international relations. Despite the "coordinated foreign policy" (*Koordinierte Aussenpolitik*) or strategic linkage to the USSR, the GDR policy in the Middle East featured a number of peculiarities, which were evidence of a wish to assert its political autonomy within a system of alliances.[27] For example, Berlin was skeptical about Moscow's plans for the deployment of the Soviet fleet in the eastern Mediterranean from the late 1960s because it feared this would spark confrontation between NATO and the Warsaw Pact, which would have a direct impact on German territory.[28] The GDR never sent "boots on the ground" in the various armed conflicts affecting the Middle East, and, deprived of any viable military industry that would support major exports, Berlin focused instead on training military cadres at home.[29] Of all the socialist countries, East Germany was perhaps one of the staunchest supporters of Palestinian rights to self-determination. Indeed, it established close, preferential relations with leftist forces like the Palestinian Democratic Liberation Front or the Palestinian Popular Liberation Front compared to the nationalist Al-Fatah. The GDR provided training and intelligence for their middle- and high-ranking officers, who would be the security pillars of a future Palestinian "statehood." However, frictions emerged regarding the GDR–Palestine Liberation Organization (PLO) relationship. Already in 1956 Berlin had diverged from its Arab partners when it argued for the right to self-determination of the Palestinian people to be matched with the recognition of Israel's sovereignty, which the PLO officially resisted until the late 1980s. In fact, the so-called two-states solution would fit well with the GDR defense of its own sovereignty against its Western rival.[30]

The most important peculiarity concerned the so-called German cold war in the Middle East. Since it had resumed formal sovereignty from the Soviet Union in 1954, the GDR engaged in a worldwide struggle against the FRG to obtain diplomatic recognition, which was countered by the West German Hallstein Doctrine. The rise to power of Arab nationalist forces in key states including Egypt, Iraq, Syria, Algeria, and later Libya opened up a wide range of opportunities.[31] The GDR banked on anti-Western sentiment—both because of the experience of Western colonialism in the region and on account of the failed attempts of NATO members to extend containment through political-military alliances such as the Baghdad Pact in 1955 or by overturning progressive governments in Syria in 1956 and 1957. Drawing the parallel between the GDR and Arab resistance to Western imperialism, Berlin championed its claims to diplomatic recognition as a gesture of solidarity.

The GDR had seen some early success in the mid-1950s, when the state opened consulates in several Arab capitals, but this fell short of the major breakthrough of full diplomatic recognition.[32] Nevertheless, it was the actions of the FRG that did most to advance Berlin's cause: with the revelations of the secret delivery of West German tanks and weaponry to Israel in 1964—swiftly followed by the establishment of full formal ties between the FRG and Israel the following May—most Arab capitals broke off relations with Bonn.[33] Among the retaliatory measures, radical Arab states upgraded the diplomatic status of the GDR from consulates to general consulates (General-Konsulat). The GDR rewarded this gesture with generous credits to its Arab partners: USD 92 million to Egypt and USD 25 million to Syria, for example, putting additional stress on GDR finances.[34] Later, attempts at full recognition were complicated by hard Arab bargaining over credits, as well as demands for support against Israel. Central Committee member Gerhard Weiss expressed his anger at his Syrian partners' approach in 1966: "How high should the economic price for the recognition of the GDR be?"[35]

The supposed objective linkage between the GDR and Arab countries against imperialism did not prevent diplomatic recognition from being treated as a political commodity. If in 1965 East German success was dependent on the crisis between West Germany and Arab countries, the wave of diplomatic recognitions in 1969 were instrumental first to Soviet-Arab relations and second to inter-Arab rivalry. Iraq moved first because it needed political and material support from the socialist camp and Moscow in its dispute with Western-backed Iran.[36] The recognition of the GDR was designed to appease the socialist camp, and Sudan, South Yemen, Syria, Egypt, and Algeria moved soon after because they feared being overshadowed by Baghdad as they fought for privileged partnerships with the socialist countries. The relaxation of the Hallstein Doctrine by the coalition government of Willy Brandt was also a decisive factor in easing the fears of an economic boycott in Arab capitals: the recognitions in 1969 were rightly perceived in Bonn as not a direct challenge to the FRG, whose inaction proved how much West German politics was changing.[37] Once again, substantial credits, usually double those provided in 1965, were granted to Arab partners, and in the early 1970s, five out of the ten main recipients of GDR capital investments in the Third World were Arab states. Egypt, Algeria, Syria, and Iraq received 92 percent of all solidarity aid to the Arab world, and 69 percent of all the aid given by the GDR to developing countries.[38]

Mutual Advantage as Raison d'état

After having exchanged diplomatic recognition with most Arab states between 1969 and 1972, GDR finances were under strain because the economic agreements contained favorable conditions for Arab partners. Officials in the GDR had already begun planning the "rationalization" of Berlin's economic policies in the Middle East in the late 1960s; yet economics had to be in tune with the struggle for recognition. Now, the financial discipline (Ökonomisierung) faced the negative consequences unleashed by the energy shocks in 1973 and 1979: the bill for oil and Western imports pushed officials to consider a readjustment in the South along the lines of "mutual advantage."[39] In 1974–75 for the first time, the GDR suffered a deficit in its balance of trade with developing countries because of the rise in commodity prices; Berlin therefore focused on oil-producing, friendly states such as Iraq and Libya. Up to the 1970s, East Germany imported 80 percent of its oil from the USSR but from 1975 the amount of OPEC-Middle Eastern oil imported steadily rose to 30 percent. From the late 1970s, the Middle East was among the most important trade partners of the GDR: it accounted for almost 60 percent of GDR foreign trade outside the CMEA. The most important partners in the region were Iraq, Egypt, Syria, Libya, and Algeria.

The GDR also planned to conduct trade according to international standards, namely by resorting to convertible currencies for payments and granting shorter and higher interest loans:[40] the hard currency it hoped to gain through the export of industrial complexes, technological products, and machinery would be exchanged for expensive oil imports or reinvested to balance the trade deficit with Western countries throughout the late 1970s and 1980s. However, these plans were not successful for two basic reasons: the GDR shortage in hard currency prevented the granting of credits attached to major investments (*Kapitalhilfe*), and it faced the fierce resistance of Arab negotiators who, once flush with so-called petrodollars, prioritized trade with Western markets over exchange with their socialist allies. The fact that armaments and military training in the GDR had to be paid for in hard currency was a bone of contention, both for "rich" states such as Libya, which then turned to Western Europe, and for standing allies such as Syria or South Yemen, which, short of funds, engaged Berlin in long, "tough negotiations" for discounted prices.[41] Not least, Berlin's efforts to expand economic relations to every country in the Middle East, even conservative ones, met with little success: in the Gulf region, the GDR could only strike an agreement with Kuwait, which proved short-lived when the Arab monarchy pressured the GDR to liberalize its economy in the 1980s.[42] Eventually, the mid-1980s witnessed a financial crisis for both East Germany and its Arab partners. As soon as the tide of oil prices fell back in 1986, scarcity forced Arab states to revert to the GDR and socialist solidarity to circumvent financial transactions. The position occupied by the GDR and the socialist camp in Arab countries proved meaningful mostly in times of nationalization as well as of crisis and recession.

As for international politics, matching up socialist internationalism with realism proved controversial. The GDR faced the dilemma of supporting civilian leaderships that coupled non-capitalist road development with radicalism in foreign policy, in particular in the Arab-Israeli conflict during the 1960s. Thus the

GDR's partners clashed with Berlin on the stability it promoted in international politics. Ultimately, along with the Soviet Union in the late 1960s, the preferences of the SED increasingly tilted toward moderate, if not conservative, leaders with roots in the military establishment.[43] The party leadership was greatly concerned by the possible escalation of regional conflicts into superpower confrontation: they feared the Arab-Israeli conflict would derail détente in Europe. Hence, despite its ongoing political and military support for the Arab Steadfastness Front, namely those countries and Arab forces that refused "to capitulate" to Israel and the United States, the GDR continued to advocate for the responsible economic and social consolidation of those regimes with "Sozialistischer Orientierung" (socialist orientation), such as in Syria, Iraq, Algeria, or South Yemen. However, from the mid-1970s Berlin's proletarian or socialist solidarity in the Middle East faced an increasingly unfavorable context: the consolidation of the so-called opportunistic or bureaucratic bourgeoisie led to the marginalization of communist forces in Egypt, Syria, Iraq, and later on within the PLO and South Yemen, thus dealing a major blow to Berlin's hopes of tilting the balance of forces in Arab states toward socialism.[44] The GDR to some degree supported legal opposition forces where political liberalization occurred, while at the same time preserving official state-to-state relations.

In the case of Syria, relations showed considerable consistency from the mid-1970s. Mild criticism was offered when Hafez al-Assad intervened in Lebanon against Palestinian and leftists forces in 1976, and Berlin cooled down cooperation in 1979 at the time of the Islamist insurgency against al-Assad. Conversely, it could not help but welcome the friendship treaty with Moscow in 1982: cooperation expanded from economic matters to diplomacy and security.[45] Yet trade and cooperation continued to be based on barter and clearing procedures due to lack of financial resources. Furthermore, the fact that Syrian leaders first paid their debts for military imports to their socialist allies, and only later civilian imports, for which the GDR was credited, did not help to adjust Berlin's finances.[46] Consistent with its preference for stability and state-centered partnerships, the GDR continued to support the Syrian Communist Party attached to the National Progressive Front (NPF) in Damascus, while distancing itself from the more radical, revolutionary forces that opposed the Baath Party. As for the Syrian radical left, which had opened up to the Islamist opposition during the armed rebellion between 1979 and 1982, the GDR openly accused it of "radicalism" and "adventurism."[47] Where cooperation between intelligence and security services was concerned, Berlin refused to engage fully, despite constant requests by Damascus. Mindful of events in neighboring Iraq, the SED leadership feared their techniques of control and repression of political dissent would be used against their Syrian comrades; that their techniques might be handed over to Western intelligence services by "reactionary" elements within the Syrian leadership; or the Baathist regime might be undone in the struggle with the Islamist insurgency in the late 1970s.[48]

Relations with Iraq proved more difficult. During the 1970s Iraq's oil wealth fueled imports from both East and West, and the GDR was paid in cash and oil for its technology: Berlin congratulated Baghdad on being the first Arab country to grant diplomatic recognition to the GDR in 1969, thus unleashing a wave of similar recognitions in the region. East German experts had already established a firm foothold in the Iraqi oil market, having trained and supported the expansion of the Iraq National Oil Company (INOC) during the 1960s; they were consequently rewarded after its takeover of foreign companies in 1972.[49] East Germany welcomed the decision of the Baathist regime in Iraq to sign the Friendship and Cooperation Agreement with the Soviet Union in 1972, the establishment of the National Progressive Front with the Iraqi Communist Party in 1973, as well as negotiations with the Kurdish nationalists of the Kurdish Democratic Party. Though Berlin recognized that such moves were a consequence of the partnership with the socialist camp and of the consolidation of power in the south and center of the country, it hoped that the Iraqi Baathists would eventually embark on state-led development leading to socialism.[50]

However, from the beginning, GDR officials had their suspicions about the contradictions in the Iraqi Baathist-styled pattern of development.[51] Recent archival research has found the Ministry for State Security (Staatssicherheit) and SED leadership withholding support for information exchange or transfer of surveillance techniques and equipment because they knew these were used against their communist comrades in Iraq as well as abroad. In fact, once the Baathist Saddam Hussein seized full power in 1978, he wiped out the large Iraqi Communist Party and all domestic opposition and later waged a devastating war against the Islamic Republic of Iran in 1980. Like the Soviet Union, the GDR generally supported a political solution to the conflict but leaned toward Baghdad by supplying the Iraqis with arms and signing new economic and technical cooperation agreements.[52] Berlin began to distance itself from Baghdad, however, once Iraq improved its relations with the United States, France, and the Federal Republic of Germany between 1982 and 1984. Fearing Western espionage through the "unreliable" Iraqi intelligence service and angered by the latter's assassinations of communist exiles in socialist countries, the SED authorities restricted partnership to economic exchanges. Here too, however, the GDR faced difficulties because Iraqi finances were further depleted by military expenditure and by the oil counter-shock of 1986: Iraq was no longer a reliable financial partner, and Baghdad now had to ask for credits to support its foreign trade.[53]

The systematic repression of communist forces by nationalists proved a major point of contention in mutual discussions. GDR officials pressed both

Arab comrades and nationalists for moderation and cooperation: the establishment of the NPF in Syria in 1972 and in Iraq in 1973 was a sincere as well as a realistic attempt to match internationalism with raison d'état.[54] The fronts would preserve the political and organizational autonomy of communist parties, a cornerstone of Leninism, but they also confirmed their marginal status in institutional systems based on dominant, if not hegemonic, one-party rule. Since the state was deemed the axis of development, Berlin encouraged progressive partners to work in public institutions, where they might be the recipients of GDR training. A few, albeit patchy achievements were recorded in Syria, Egypt, and Iraq. Here, disputes arose over the selection of students and officials to be sent to the GDR for further study or training: Berlin favored communist or left-leaning individuals alongside the far greater numbers of nationalists or not-engaged students. Beyond the regular faculty syllabuses, special courses on politics and Marxism-Leninism were scheduled, but only for the comrades.[55] In fact, most Arab students and officials retained much of what they had learned technically and in vocational training in the GDR with no compelling influence or direct impact of socialist indoctrination once they had returned home.

For example, GDR-trained economists supported *infitah* (liberalization) policies in the 1970s; others opposed it, deeming it a favor paid to Western imperialism and its domestic agents by crony capitalism.[56] The former argued in favor of liberalization not because they considered it to be intrinsically beneficial but because it might serve to remedy the shortcomings of the public sector and the shortages of the national market. Faced with a wide range of problems from the late 1960s, including the decline of production and productivity of the public sector as well as the managerial incompetence of politically appointed officials, those economists resorted to private forces to enlarge the supply of industrial and consumption products; liberalization would contain black market and smuggling too and provide the state with a larger tax base. However, the state would retain its monopoly over the "commanding heights" of the economy, such as energy or cement production and finances, while private entrepreneurs, old and new, would focus more on consumption goods.[57] Ultimately, this acknowledgment of the public sectors' limited local capacities and capability to deliver a wide range of goods led socialist-leaning cadres toward pragmatism.

Preliminary Conclusions

Due to its status as one of the most economically advanced members of the socialist camp, the GDR focused on the transfer of technology and expertise, vocational training, or, in a few cases, partnership in institution-building. As such, patterns of GDR solidarity did not deviate greatly from the standards of

North-South trade or aid to development between industrial and postcolonial developing countries.[58] However, the GDR garnered widespread sympathy in many Arab countries because of its massive resort to nonfinancial transactions, its refusal to apply major economic or political conditionality, and the disciplined loyalty of its personnel to the principle of international solidarity.

The gradual prioritization of raison d'état and pragmatism over proletarian and socialist solidarity in the 1970s, and yet more forcefully in the 1980s, was the consequence of two processes in particular: a growing skepticism as to whether GDR- or Soviet-styled socialism would ever take root in the postcolonial world and a political adaptation to an unfavorable context in the Middle East, for which Berlin was not actually responsible. Indeed, Berlin's pragmatism appeared to develop in parallel with the crisis and decline of leftist forces in the Middle East during the 1970s, and then adjusted to the conservative backlash during the following decade.

Notes

1. For a review of the growing literature on the GDR foreign policy toward postcolonial countries, see also, e.g., Joachim Scholtyseck, *Die Außenpolitik der DDR* (Munich: Oldenbourg Verlag, 2003), 65; Klaus Storkmann, *Geheime Solidarität. Militärbeziehungen und Militärhilfe der DDR in die "Dritte Welt,"* (Berlin: Ch. Links Verlag, 2012); Miriam Müller, *A Spectre Is Haunting Arabia: How the German Brought Their Communism to Yemen* (Bielefeld, Transcript, Political Science, 2015); Young-Sun Hong, *Cold War Germany, the Third World, and the Global Humanitarian Regime* (New York: Cambridge University Press, 2015).

2. On Marxism-Leninism as a fluid mix strand of theories and policies, see Brigitte Schulz, *Development Policy in the Cold War Era: The Two Germanys and Sub-Saharan Africa, 1960–1985* (Münster: LIT Verlag, 1995), 12.

3. See also Berthold Unfried, "Instrumente und Praktiken von '*Solidarität' Ost und 'Entwicklungshilfe' West: Blickpunkt auf das entsandte Personal*," in *Die eine Welt schaffen. Praktiken von "Internationaler Solidarität" und "Internationaler Entwicklung,"* eds. Berthold Unfried and Eva Himmelstoss (Vienna: Akademischer Verlagsanstalt, 2012), 73–98.

4. Schulz, *Development Policy in the Cold War Era*, 12; Silvio Pons, *La rivoluzione globale: Storia del comunismo internazionale, 1917–1991* (Turin: Einaudi), 236, 248.

5. Roger E. Kanet, "The Superpower Quest for Empire: The Cold War and Soviet Support for 'Wars of National Liberation,'" *Cold War History* 6, no. 3 (2006): 331–352.

6. In this respect, the GDR's proletarian and anti-imperialist solidarity was believed to match the category of "group-based solidarity" that stems "from the common social position" and "interests" of workers in the past and in current revolutionary movements or states. See Kössler, "Development and Solidarity. Conceptual Perspectives" in Unfried, Himmelstoss, *Die eine Welt schaffen*, 29–35; Ingrid Muth, *Die DDR-Außenpolitik 1949–1972: Inhalte, Strukturen, Mechanismen*, Ch. Links Verlag, Berlin, 2001, 36–46; Schulz, *Development Policy in the Cold War Era*, 17–26.

7. Authorenkollektiv, *Die Leninsche Prinzipen des Sowjetischen Außenpolitik* (Moscow, 1970), 190; Yevgeny Primakov, *Russia and the Arabs: Behind the Scenes in the Middle East from the Cold War to the Present* (New York: Basic Books, 2009), 75.

8. See Kai Hafez, "Von der nationalen Frage zur Systempolitik: Perioden der DDR-Nahostpolitik, 1949–1989," *Orient* 36, no. 1 (1995): 78–99; Scholtyseck, *Die Außenpolitik der DDR*, 76, 80.

9. See also William D. Graf, "The Theory of the Non-Capitalist Road," in *The Soviet Bloc and the Third World*, eds. Brigitte Schulz and William W. Hansen (Boulder: Westview Press, 1989), 27–52; David C. Engerman, "Ideology and the Origins of the Cold War, 1917–1962," in *The Cambridge History of the Cold War*, eds. Melvyn Leffler and Odd Arne Westad, vol. 1 (Cambridge: Cambridge University Press, 2010), 20–43.

10. Gustav Hertzfeld and Jochen Rodde, "Nationale Demokratie. Objektiver Inhalt des gegenwärtigen nationales Befreiungsbewegung," *Einheit* no. 11, December 1961: 1757.

11. The conditions for trading with the capitalist world included the following: absence of any political condition undermining sovereignty; use of foreign funds to correct deformed sectors; greater efficiency of the financed operations over their costs; preference for bilateral government credits over foreign direct investment (FDI), the latter being more difficult to take under control; establishment of joint ventures controlled by the recipient state; tax breaks with well-defined time limits; and labor training attached to all investments. Graf, "The Theory of the Non-Capitalist Road," 34–37.

12. Nazih N. Ayubi, *Overstating the Arab State: Politics and Society in the Middle East* (London: I. B. Tauris, 2006), 21, 82, 196.

13. Graf, "The Theory of the Non-Capitalist Road," 48–52. See also János Kornai, *The Socialist System: The Political Economy of Communism* (Oxford: Clarendon Press, 1992), 341–344, 351–354; Adam Zwass, *Money, Banking and Credit in the Soviet Union and Eastern Europe* (London: McMillan, 1979), 215; Oscar Sanchez-Sibony, *Red Globalization: The Political Economy of Soviet Cold War from Stalin to Khrushchev* (Cambridge: Cambridge University Press, 2014), 125.

14. Muth, *Die DDR-Außenpolitik 1949–1972*, 54–86; Scholtyseck, *Die Außenpolitik der DDR*, 69–75; Müller, *A Spectre Is Haunting Arabia*, 125–150.

15. Sara Lorenzini, *Le due Germanie in Africa: La cooperazione allo sviluppo e la competizione per i mercati di materie prime e tecnologia* (Florence: Polistampa, 2003), 98–102.

16. Sara Lorenzini, "The Dilemmas of Solidarity: East German Policies in Africa in the Age of Modernization," in *Die eine Welt schaffen*, eds. Unfried and Himmelstoss, 59, 61.

17. Corinna R. Unger, "Industrialization vs. Agrarian Reform: West German Modernization Policies in India in the 1950s and 1960s," *Journal of Modern European History* 8, no. 1 (2010): 47–65.

18. See Michel Seurat, "Etat et industrialisation dans l'Orient Arabe: les fondements socio-historiques," in *Industrialisation et changements sociaux dans l'Orient Arabe*, ed. André Bourgey (Beirut: Cermoc, 1982), 37; Charles S. Maier, "The Politics of Productivity: Foundations of American Economic Policy after World War II," in *Between Power and Plenty: Foreign Economic Policies of Advanced Industrial States*, ed. P. Katzenstein (Madison: University of Wisconsin Press, 1978), 23–51.

19. Steffen Wippel, *Die Außenwirtschaftsbeziehungen der DDR zum Nahen Osten, Einfluss und Abhängigkeit der DDR und das Verhältnis von Außenwirtschaft zu Außenpolitik* (Berlin: Klaus Schwarz Verlab, 1996), 10–16.

20. Sapmo-Bundesarchiv, DE1 VA 45390, *Richtlinien für Leitung und Koordinierung der wirtschaftlichen und wissenschaftlich-technischen Beziehungen zu Entwicklungsländern*, 1964, cited in Lorenzini, *Due Germanie in Africa*, 118, 128; André Steiner, *Die DDR-Wirtschaftsreform der sechziger Jahre: Konflikt zwischen Effizienz und Machtkalkül* (Berlin: Akademie Verlag), 38–48.

21. See Ivan T. Berend, *An Economic History of Twentieth-Century Europe* (Cambridge: Cambridge University Press, 2006), 166; Adam Zwass, *Economies of Eastern Europe in a Time of Change* (New York: Routledge, 2015), ch. 2.

22. *Internationale Beratung der kommunistischen und Arbeiterparteien in Moskau, 1969* (Berlin, 1969), 33; Storkmann, *Geheime Solidarität*, 55.

23. Wippel, *Die Außenwirtschaftsbeziehungen der DDR zum Nahen Osten*, 19; Hans Siegfried Lamm and Siegfried Kupper, *DDR und Dritte Welt* (Munich/Vienna, 1976), 122; Steiner, *Die DDR-Wirtschaftsreform der sechziger Jahre*, 78.

24. Lorenzini, "The Dilemmas of Solidarity," 64.

25. Berend, *An Economic History of Twentieth-Century Europe*, 172–189; Kornai, *The Socialist System*, 552. See also Stephen Kotkin, "The Kiss of Debt: The East Bloc Goes Borrowing," in *The Shock of the Global : The 1970s in Perspective*, eds. Ferguson Niall, Maier Charles S., and Manela Erez (Cambridge, MA: Belknap Press, 2010), 80–96.

26. Wippel, *Die Außenwirtschaftsbeziehungen der DDR zum Nahen Osten*, 41–43.

27. Heinz-Dieter Winter, *Konfliktregion Naher und Mitteler Osten* (Berlin: Verband für internationale Politik und Völkerrecht, 2005), 8; Hafez, "Von der nationalen Frage zur Systempolitik"; Lamm and Kupper, *DDR und der Dritte Welt.*

28. Martin Robbe, "Die DDR in Nah- und Mittelost: Eine Begegnung und ihre Spuren. Ein Rundtischgespräch mit Diplomaten," *Asien, Afrika und Lateinamerika* 21 (1994): 564.

29. Storkmann, *Geheime Solidarität*, 183, 389.

30. Lutz Maeke, *DDR und PLO: Die Palästinapolitik des SED-Staates* (Berlin: De Gruyter Oldenbourg, 2017). For a harsh critique of the GDR stance toward Israel, see Jeffrey Herf, *Undeclared Wars with Israel: East Germany and the West German Far Left, 1967–1989* (Cambridge: Cambridge University Press, 2016). A major argument for the FRG and Israel to close ranks was the so-called "Berlin-Jerusalem Komplex," namely the political analogy between the two cities "under siege" by authoritarian and socialist-leaning regimes, see Daniel Gerlach, *Die doppelte Front: Die Bundesrepublik Deutschland und der Nahostkonflikt, 1967–1973* (Berlin: Lit Verlag, 2006).

31. R. Hirschfeld, *Die Beziehungen der DDR zu Algerien, Syrien und der VAR zwischen 1953–1970: Theorie und Praxis der DDR-Außenpolitik in der 3. Welt*. Diss. Bonn, 1978; Massimiliano Trentin, *La Guerra fredda tedesca in Siria, diplomazia, economia e politica* (Padua: Cleup, 2015), ch. 2.

32. Wolfgang Schwanitz, "SED-Nahostpolitk als Chefsache: Die ZK-Abteilung Internationale Verbindungen 1946–1970 sowie die Nachlässe von Otto Grotewohl und Walter Ulbricht," *Asien, Afrika und Lateinamerika* 21, no. 1 (1993).

33. Trentin, *La Guerra fredda tedesca in Siria*, ch. 5. See the collection of diplomatic documents "Akten zur Auswärtigen Politik der Bundesrepublik Deutschland" (1965), "Institut für Zeitgeschichte, Munich-Berlin: Oldenbourg Wissenschaftverlag," 1996, hereafter AAPD.

34. Wippel, *Die Außenwirtschaftsbeziehungen der DDR zum Nahen Osten*, 21, 22.

35. Sapmo-BArchiv, DY30 IVA2/20, 874, *Vermerk über ein Gespräch am 19.10.1967 beim Genossen Hermann Axen über die weiteren Beziehungen der DDR mit der SAR*, ZK der SED, Abt. Int. Verb. October 20, 1967, translated by the author.

36. AAPD, 1969, ZB6-1-12408, VS-vertraulich, Legationsrat I. Mirow, z.Z Bagdad, an das Auswärtiges Amt, April 28, 1969; ZB6-1-12787, VS-vertraulich, Botschafter Lilienfeld, Teheran, an das Auswärtiges Amt, Betr.: Anerkennung der Zone durch Irak, May 20, 1969.

37. William G. Gray, *Germany's Cold War: The Global Campaign to Isolate East Germany, 1949–1969* (Chapel Hill: University of North Carolina Press, 2003), 196, 212.

38. Sapmo-BArchiv, DY30 A2/20 871, 3. AEA, *Konzeption für Verhandlungen für die diplomatische Anerkennung in arabischen Ländern*, Berlin, August 13, 1969; Wippel, *Die Außenwirtschaftsbeziehungen der DDR zum Nahen Osten*, 24.

39. Amélie Régnauld, "La SED et les gauches égyptiennes, 1969–1989: entre idéologie et pragmatism," in *Les Pays d'Europe orientale et la Méditerranée. Relations et regards croisés, 1967–1989*, eds. Nicolas Badalassi and Houda Ben Hamouda (Les Cahiers Irice, 2013) no. 10, 53.

40. Wippel, *Die Außenwirtschaftsbeziehungen der DDR zum Nahen Osten*, 29–31, 35.

41. Storkmann, *Geheime Solidarität*, 89; Archives of the Ministerium für Staatssicherheit in Berlin (hereafter BStU), HA I 18216, *Zahlenmäßige Übersicht über die in der DDR studierenden ausländischen Militärkader*, 63–64, November 28, 1984; HA I 18216, *Ausbildung ausländischer Militarkäder in der NVA*, 54–57, October 26, 1987; HA I 18216, *Kurzeinschätzung der erreichten Ergebnisse der Ausbildung syrischer Militärkader*, 11–41, November 13, 1987.

42. Winter, *Konfliktregion Naher und Mittlerer Osten*, 20–21.

43. Ibid., 14–15; Storkmann, *Geheime Solidarität*, 433, 490.

44. See also Lothar Rathmann, ed., *Geschichte der Araber: Von den Anfängen bis zur Gegenwart, Teil 3, Band 6* (Berlin: Akademie-Verlag, 1974), 541. For the PLO, see Maeke, *DDR und PLO*, 449; for Iraq, see Johan Franzen, *Red Star over Iraq: Iraqi Communism before Saddam* (New York: Columbia University Press, 2011), 233–243; as for the People's Republic of Yemen (also known as South Yemen), see Müller, *A Spectre Is Haunting Arabia*, 329.

45. Massimiliano Trentin, "Between Solidarity and Convenience: Socialist East Germany and Postcolonial Syria," in *Syria during the Cold War: The East European Connection*, eds. P. Gasztold-Sen, M. Trentin, and J. Adamec, St. Andrews Papers on Contemporary Syria (Boulder, CO: Lynne Rienner, 2014), 41–66.

46. Jan Adamec, "Czechoslovak-Syrian Relations during the Cold War" in Gasztold-Sen, Trentin, Adamec eds. *Syria during the Cold War*, 82, 84.

47. Pedro Ramet, *The Soviet-Syrian Relationship since 1955: A Troubled Alliance* (Boulder, CO: Westview Press, 1990), 106–110, 145.

48. Sapmo-BArchiv, DO1 11665, SAR–Information 4/80, 321–322; DO1 11665, *Bericht über den Einsatz in der SAR*, 420–429, June 30, 1980.

49. Sapmo-BArchiv, DL2 VA 1846, Konzeption, *Langfristige Sicherung des Bezuges von Erdöl durch die Aufnahme erdölgeologischer Arbeiten in der Republik Irak*, March 18, 1969, Kattner; DC20 16888, Botschaft DDR Bagdad, Jahresanalyse 1974, Schurath.

50. Sapmo-BArchiv, DC20 16888, Ministerrat DDR, Aufzeichnung, *Die Beziehungen mit Irak*, May 21, 1975; A. G. Samarbakhsh, *Socialisme en Irak et en Syrie* (Paris: Editions Anthropos, 1978), 195–197; Franzen, *Red Star over Iraq*, 206–215.

51. Saddam Hussein, *On Social and Foreign Affairs in Iraq* (London: Croom Helm, 1979), 19, 33. For detailed insights into Iraq, see Joseph Sassoon, *Saddam Hussein's Ba'th Party: Inside an Authoritarian Regime* (Cambridge: Cambridge University Press, 2012).

52. Artemy M. Kalinovsky, "The Soviet Union and the Iran-Iraq War," in *The Iran-Iraq War: New International Perspectives*, eds. Nigel Ashton and Bryan Gibson (London: Routledge, 2013), 230–240; Murray Williamson and Kevin M. Woods, *The Iran-Iraq War: A Military and Strategic History* (Cambridge: Cambridge University Press, 2014), 171, 205.

53. Joseph Sassoon, "The East German Ministry of State Security and Iraq, 1969–1989," *Journal of Cold War History* 16, no. 1 (2014): 17–23.

54. Massimiliano Trentin, "Tough Negotiations: The Two Germanys in Syria and Iraq from 1963 to 1974," *Cold War* History 8, no. 3 (Summer 2008): 353–380; Samarbakhsh, *Socialisme en Irak et en Syrie*, 146, 174.

55. Trentin, *La Guerra fredda tedesca in Siria*, 256. The same applied to Czechoslovakia, Adamec, 81, as well as between the GDR and Iraq, Joseph Sassoon, "The East German Ministry," 9; Storkmann, *Geheime Solidarität*, 433, 456.

56. Interviews conducted by the author with Syrian state officials trained in the GDR, Damascus, and Aleppo, 2005–2006. Tina Zintl, "Modernisierungspolitik durch Kompetenztransfer? Syrische Remigranten mit deutschem Hochschulabschluss als Katalysatoren von Brain Gain in Syrien unter Bashar al-Assad," in *Volkswirtschaftliche Diskussionspapiere* no. 104, eds. Dieter Weiss and Steffen Wippel (Berlin: Klaus Schwarz Verlag, 2009).

57. Roger Owen and Sevket Pamuk, *History of Middle East Economies in the XXth Century* (London: I. B. Tauris, 1998), 95–97.

58. See Sara Lorenzini, *Global Development. A Cold War History* (Princeton NJ: Princeton University Press, 2019).

MASSIMILIANO TRENTIN is Associate Professor of Modern History and International Relations of Western Asia at the Department of Political and Social Sciences, University of Bologna, Italy. He is author of *Engineers of Modern Development: East German Experts in Ba'thist Syria, 1965–1972* and *La Guerra fredda tedesca in Siria: diplomazia, economia e politica, 1963–1970*.

6 Entangling Agrarian Modernities: The "Agrarian Question" through the Eyes of Soviet Africanists

Steffi Marung

Introduction

Overcoming backwardness and the obstacles to the transfer of historically specific experiences between different world regions loomed large in the discussions of Soviet Africanists. These issues were from the start intricately intertwined in their research on rural development. While the other chapters in this section address entangled industrial and urban modernities, the focus here is on the transformations of agriculture. It is argued that the so-called agrarian question—that is the question of the development of capitalism in agriculture and thus also of the preconditions for a socialist transformation of it as part of a larger socialist revolution[1]—is a useful lens through which to apprehend an entangled history between East and South.

"Solving" the agrarian question was crucial to paving the way to socialist modernity in the Soviet Union. Yet it was not only important at home: after decolonization such transformations were also crucial to the promoting of the USSR as a powerful player in a new global order.[2] However, this posed a paradox from the outset: the Soviet ambition to be in the vanguard when addressing the agrarian question was intertwined with a perception of itself as a backward society, all traces of which had still not been completely eradicated. This tension also explains the interest in African agricultural developments, which seemed to mirror the modernization of the Soviet periphery, most notably Central Asia.

The African continent was not the only world region through which the Soviets reconsidered their developmental models. Soviet interest in the "foreign East"—under which Asia *and* Africa were usually subsumed—had first emerged with regard to India and China. As David Engerman has demonstrated, the Indian experience had been crucial for the formation of Soviet development aid and aid policy, including the rethinking of Stalinist "stageist" models of development.[3] At the same time, as Jerry Hough noted more than three decades ago, the "difficulties [of applying these orthodox models] were particularly great for Africanists."[4] And while "nearly all the hints of theoretical modification of the five-stage pattern[5] came from scholars who worked on Asia, [. . .] in many respects the fastest evolution of views was occurring among the Africanists."[6] Yet while Asia was studied intensively from the late 1940s, a decade passed before the same became true for Africa. This was partly the result of a mounting frustration at the failure of Soviet overtures to India and China. In the wake of such disappointments, African countries started to attract the interest of Soviet advisors, whose "missions of modernity" were from the 1960s onward increasingly shifted to the Middle East, northern Africa, and to countries such as Mozambique or Somalia.[7] In this context Africa thus became the first overseas context in which a rethinking of the relationship between agrarian and industrial modernization in the development processes in the Global South took place—a process that would boomerang back into discussions of development at home. This would further accelerate in the 1970s, driven forward by specialists on India (such as Viktor G. Tastiannikov), Egypt (such as Anatolii Ia. Elianov), and Ethiopia (such as Ruben N. Andreasyan).[8] But Africanists had seen the problem coming a decade earlier.

It may also have been the case that the deep challenges of the Soviet-African encounter explain why such a fruitful relationship developed. In Africa, Soviet experts were thus able to experiment with ideas of socialist modernity as they responded to the difficulties of translating their orthodox positions on African soil. Indeed, postcolonial African societies were in many ways the least plausible candidates for a socialist transformation, lacking as they did a powerful proletariat that could initiate a revolution. Furthermore, the importance of the question of race in African transformations and its vexed reconciliation with Marxist categories of class, which had been hotly debated since the times of the Communist International (Comintern), did not sit easily with the Soviet experts of the 1950s, most of whom had not been used to considering race a central category of their expert practice.[9] Finally, a transnational African elite did not receive the socialist gospel from the Soviets alone but had prior experience with the varieties of socialist and communist thought in London or Paris, through which they were well-equipped to contest Soviet orthodoxies.[10]

This chapter will thus suggest that debates over agricultural modernization increasingly brought Soviet and African modernities together. More particularly, the histories of both the Soviet and the global peripheries became closely related in the Soviet Africanists' perspective. The chapter starts by explaining how these debates emerged from the late nineteenth century onward as a transnational discourse. It will proceed by demonstrating how they became a topic on Soviet Africanists' agendas. The last part of the chapter is devoted to the complexities of academic transfers of the Soviet model of agrarian development. The Soviets faced considerable obstacles in exporting their model, both because it had repeatedly been adapted to fit the concrete dynamics in the Global South and because their ambition to dominate international scientific discourses far exceeded their capacity to do so.

Painful Transformations: The Agrarian Question in the Soviet Union

The efforts to solve the agrarian question in the Soviet Union had a long and often painful history: Central Asia was no exception, where, particularly during the first decades of the Soviet Union, such attempts resulted in enormous death tolls due to famine and the disruption of rural communities.[11] At the same time, the discussion surrounding the backwardness of the countryside and of farmers, peasants, and villagers had a long tradition in Russian political and academic discourse dating back to the late Tsarist period.[12] The countryside had been seen as a space for an internal civilizing mission[13] since the mid-nineteenth century. Liberal agrarianism before the October Revolution envisioned a "rural modernity" as an alternative to industrialization and urbanization, offering a specific, Russian version of modernization.

In particular, agrarianism as an intellectual and political movement, which aimed at developing a critical perspective on industrial modernization and suggested an alternative path for integrating rural communities, had developed as a transnational formation in Western and East (Central) Europe since the mid-nineteenth century.[14] For scholars and reformers from Belgium, France, Germany, and the United States, the German historical school of economics and the Austrian school of marginalism provided important theoretical foundations. Leading representatives of the agrarian movement in Russia—both more mainstream scholars such as Alexander Chaianov[15] and those of a Marxist orientation such as Mikhail Tugan-Baranovsky—tried to identify a path of agrarian development in Russia by investigating foreign cases, which they found mostly in Western Europe.[16] They did not concern themselves, however, with what would later become known as the Global South, as their intellectual geography was firmly rooted in a Western and transatlantic network of scholars.

The Bolshevik reforms after 1917 and in particular the New Economic Policy (NEP) in the 1920s modified these earlier visions of a rural modernity. The countryside became a space for ambitious modernizing interventions—as well as for a more "cooperative" transformation of rural societies.[17] Under Joseph Stalin in the 1930s, this approach fell out of favor in the face of rapid industrialization, to which agriculture was subordinated and under which specific social groups of farmers were persecuted, most notoriously after Stalin's call for "liquidating the Kulaks."[18] Yet during this same period Soviet efforts at agrarian modernization were again integrated into transatlantic movements, which were shaped by new motives and geographies. While the Comintern had modified the geopolitical context of Soviet thinking in general,[19] it had also made the Soviet Union a part of wider solidarity networks, which integrated African American experts. The most prominent case in this regard concerned a group of technical and agricultural specialists who traveled widely during the 1920s and 1930s, among them Oliver Golden, Robert Robinson, and George Washington Carver. Many of these specialists were of a Marxist orientation and had been educated at the Tuskegee Institute, one of the most renowned black institutions for higher education in the United States. Golden had also been enrolled at the Communist University of the Toilers of the East, a Comintern institution of higher education.[20] On his return, he recruited his fellow experts to assist with agricultural modernization in Central Asia, convinced that "the Uzbeks, Turkmen, Chukchawho had been colonized and who in American terms were 'coloured'"[21] were in need of international support on their way out of backwardness and marginalization. The emergence of Russian and Soviet concepts of agricultural modernization had thus been shaped since tsarist times by the transnational circulation of ideas and activism, in which the colonial world overseas had been emphasized more for the importation of ideas than on their export. A meaningful orientation toward the South, and Africa in particular, took place only with the onset of twentieth-century decolonization and with the globalization of the socialist project under Nikita Khrushchev.

Thus, it was only after Stalin's death that the debate around the agrarian question and development continued with a truly global geography. With Khrushchev's global ambitions, the acceleration of decolonization, and the widening and professionalization of Soviet area studies, the conditions were ripe for a broader international discussion, shaped by transfers and circulations in many different directions and beyond the mere import or export of ideas.[22]

The Stalinist trauma—which did not only concern agricultural transformations—was addressed in international terms and reflected in the discussions about agriculture in the Global South. The critique of Stalinist agricultural policy was propagated in international arenas, such as the UN Educational, Scientific, and Cultural Organization (UNESCO), where Soviet historians who were involved in the writing of a *General History of Mankind* drew attention to Leninist theories of collectivization which emphasized its voluntary and democratic character. These intellectuals were tireless in their efforts to correct the—in their mind too positive—interpretations of Stalin's policies.[23] These UNESCO discussions demonstrate how Soviet scholars sought to influence interpretations of the agrarian question in international discussions. In a similar vein, conceptual frameworks such as the noncapitalist path to development and the analysis of *mnogoukladnost'* (multistructurality)[24] did much to connect Soviet paths of development and those in the Global South.[25] Reinterpreting the Soviet past in a critical way and connecting and comparing it to agrarian developments in the

Global South represented an attempt to gain credibility and convince partners in newly independent countries of the validity of the socialist path of agricultural transformation. This was also a reaction on the part of Soviet scholars to the limited success of transferring the Soviet model to Africa.

Such debates were particularly pertinent for agrarian modernization. Indeed, it was no easy matter to sell the Soviet model abroad, in the light of the many failures it had suffered at home. There had been a number of food crises or even famines over the decades, and critics could also point to the creation of a Soviet dust bowl in the wake of the Virgin Lands Campaign.[26] Against this background the role of agriculture in relation to industrialization for development in the Global South was increasingly reevaluated during the 1970s,[27] a debate that was also connected to the critical assessment of domestic trajectories. In the early 1980s economists specializing in the (mainly European) socialist world, such as Yuriy Novopashin and Anatoliy Butenko, argued that domestic failures undermined the Soviet Union's claims as an attractive model of development for the Global South.[28] Rejecting the excessive enthusiasms of the 1960s, Novopashin in particular called for a rethinking of Soviet development policy abroad, advocating among other things an increased emphasis on agricultural production and modernization rather than on industry.[29] This debate predated the rapid decline of interest in African dynamics under Mikhail Gorbachev. However, among scholars specializing in African affairs, doubts concerning a Soviet-style solution to the agrarian question had already emerged in those earlier, more optimistic decades.

Struggling with Complexities: The Agrarian Question for Soviet Africanists

The late 1950s and early 1960s witnessed the tremendous expansion of Soviet Africanist production in a number of newly founded research and teaching institutions in the context of what became famous as "the thaw."[30] The major economic and political transformations of African states created an enormous demand for area-related expertise, given the relative lack of knowledge about the African continent in the Soviet Union. Furthermore, decolonization in Africa produced a vast space in which to test Marxist theories and models that could serve to explain and predict the (correct) path to development. Yet it soon became clear to Soviet Africanists that Marxist models and specific socialist experiences in the Soviet Union were not directly applicable elsewhere. The friction between theory and the reality in African countries led to the search for alternative models that were modified versions of the central Marxist claims.[31]

The area studies boom of the 1960s also reshaped research about agriculture. Reflecting domestic Soviet dynamics, agricultural reform, and the fundamental rearrangement of social and economic relations in the countryside likewise became central to the development of the newly independent states in Africa. The simultaneity of Soviet domestic reforms and the potential opening of Africa to Soviet modernization projects created fertile ground for academic ventures—although the region was not overly familiar to the Soviet political elite of that time.[32] Historian Ivan I. Potekhin—the first director of the Institute for African Studies at the Soviet Academy of Sciences, founded in 1960—immediately recognized the importance of the topic and organized a collaborative research effort in which most of the institute's members were involved. One of the first fruits of this endeavor was a major collective monograph, representing one of the first original Soviet publications on the agrarian question in Africa, which was published in 1964.[33]

The study, prefaced by a historical analysis of late colonial dynamics and constellations, employed Marxist categories and a Marxist theorization of agricultural development with regard to land tenure, the contours and shifts in feudalistic relations, the social structure of the village community, the emergence of an agricultural proletariat, and the farmers' political movements. The focus was on tropical Africa—contrasted with northern and southern Africa—the differences being accounted for in terms of the strong traditions of communal land tenure and the absence of feudalistic relations. Tropical Africa therefore displayed peculiar relations of production with a low level of capitalist development, as there was de facto no proletariat. The region therefore offered the conditions for a direct transition toward socialism, without passing through the stage of capitalism.[34]

Although the peculiarities of the region were emphasized, the narrative Potekhin and his colleagues presented highlighted parallels between the Russian and Soviet development and that of tropical Africa. Economic backwardness, they argued, made industrialization paramount. Yet in order to guarantee the supply of food for the urban population, increasingly crucial due to a massive rural exodus, agricultural reform was inevitable. The solutions they suggested clearly echoed the formula applied by the Khrushchevian elite. At the same time, the Soviet analysis displayed the limits of and alternatives to a socialist model in an African context. The cooperative movement, for example, as the authors explained, rested in tropical Africa on a tradition of communal land tenure. The socialization of land in the village occurred under conditions that were unfamiliar to them: the cultivated land was owned by the community, a private property to be socialized did not exist, and therefore the reorganization of land tenure could only concern "virgin lands" and former colonial tenures. The absence of feudalistic contexts, combined with the presence of no more than a minimal proletariat, posed a further challenge to the "stageist" theory of the path to socialist development. It is here that the need for alternative models became clear to Soviet

Africanists. Their efforts proceeded in parallel with a rethinking of developments in Central Asia by scholars specializing in that region.[35]

Potekhin emphasized the role of small-scale farming organized in cooperatives and recommended its promotion as an integral part of the socialist reconstruction of agriculture.[36] This was not congruent with Khrushchevian political doctrine, which emphasized the superiority of large-scale agricultural production in state farms, promoting the creation of "super collectives."[37] At the same time, Potekhin left the reader with no doubts in his subsequent presentations about the centrality of state intervention and the ultimate need to create large-scale farming structures to advance on the path to socialist modernization.[38] In this respect, he and his colleagues were positioned within a particular Soviet discourse and were challenged by—or rather, struggled with—observations of and encounters in newly independent African states on the road to independence in the early 1960s.

The work on this collaborative research project extended over several years. Almost all the members of the institute, who were able to travel to Africa for fieldwork, were in some way involved—collecting data; making ethnological observations; conducting interviews with state officials and farmers; gathering copies of books, brochures, journals and newspapers; and identifying archives.[39] Their reports not only demonstrate the main areas of interest geographically (West Africa) and thematically (the cooperative movement and the village) but also suggest an active role of the Soviet Union in the modernization of agriculture in the region. The scholars proposed translating Soviet literature on the topic into French and English to make it more easily accessible to the new elite, and they also argued for significant increases in Soviet aid in terms of technical equipment and expertise. They further advocated an intensification of research and the training of Soviet experts to be sent to the region to compete with Western projects of agricultural reform. At the same time, they made extensive use of data deriving from French and African sources, as well as that published by international organizations.

To a greater degree than in the published version, these unpublished reports demonstrate just how close the social and political upheavals in Africa and the Russian and Soviet past and present were presumed to be.[40] The African situation was thought to parallel two Soviet constellations, namely, prerevolutionary Russia and the contemporary Central Asian parts of the Soviet Union. This latter region was often cited as a model for African modernization projects, and "comrades from Central Asia" were mobilized to make African students and political delegations in the Soviet Union aware of the merits of the socialist path of development.[41] Links were thus posited between civilizing missions in the interior and those directed at Africa: "Speaking of pre-revolutionary Russia, Lenin said that it was necessary to clear the whole land of all 'medieval lumber'. The governments of the African states have to solve this problem," Potekhin explained.[42] Throughout the volume, however, Central Asia remains more a metaphor and shorthand than a thoroughly investigated case, serving as it did to confirm arguments about African dynamics. Few scholars had specialist knowledge of both regions.[43]

The prominence of their work notwithstanding, there can be no doubt that Africanist research on the agrarian question was a field for a small group of specialists, albeit a booming one in the 1960s and 1970s. Only 7 percent of the dissertations in history, geography, and economics defended between 1935 and 1980 addressed agriculture.[44] The majority were submitted in the 1960s[45] and 1970s[46]: before this, only four dissertations had been written on the topic. This was a consequence both of the general trend of professionalization within the discipline[47] as well as the increasing interest in agriculture. Africa north of the Sahara, Egypt in particular, but also Syria, Tunisia, Algeria, Morocco, and Iraq, were regions of major interest, as was Sub-Saharan Africa, although it comprised many more countries. Here West and East Africa were more often addressed than southern and Central Africa. The same pattern is confirmed for all Soviet publications about Africa.[48]

The themes reflect a focus on the role and situation of peasants (including peasant movements, the sociology of rural communities, and village life) and cooperatives but included questions of production and technical modernization, colonial policy, the role of the state and planning, as well as specific commodities. A number of studies explicitly dealt with questions of comparative or entangled developments in the Soviet Union (the Soviet South specifically) and Africa: in 1966 G. A. Gadzhiev, for example, investigated the participation of Azerbaijan in Soviet cooperation with the national democracies of Asia and Africa; in 1964 N. S. Petrov aimed to illuminate the historical importance of the socialist struggle in Kazakhstan and Central Asia for the countries of Asia and Africa; while in 1980 A. R. Junusov addressed agricultural transformation in the noncapitalist path of development in Africa in relation to the experiences in the Soviet East.

Comparison and entanglement were aspects not only of the research agenda but also of academic practice. A number of the registered theses were authored by scholars from African countries, most of them in economics. In the majority of cases, they address questions of planning and methods of calculation in agriculture. The scholars in question had often studied their own countries or regions in Africa, investigating cooperatives and the role of the state and socioeconomic relations in agriculture. Soviet knowledge of Africa was thus coproduced by Africans in the Soviet Union, although these did not always easily align with Soviet doctrines and interpretations. One prominent case in point was Osendé Afana (1930–1966), a Cameroonian economist and political activist who was assassinated by colonial armed forces in 1966 and later celebrated as a national hero of the liberation movement in Cameroon. Educated in Yaoundé as well as in Toulouse, he became the first (black) economist of his country. He interrupted the work on his thesis in

Toulouse in 1958 to return to his political activities in Cameroon but completed his studies in 1962 in Paris.[49] He defended his dissertation, which deals with the production of cocoa in West Africa, in Moscow in 1961.[50] Afana was also involved in the planning for the First International Congress of Africanists in 1962 in Accra, serving in this context as a mediator between African and Soviet colleagues.[51] At the same time, being the head of the Union of the Peoples of Cameroon (UPC), the most radical liberation party of Cameroon, supported by China, among others, he can be characterized politically as staunchly Maoist and radical, thus not neatly fitting into the Soviet universe: a French-educated radical Maoist would probably have been reluctant to simply confirm Leninist theories on the agrarian question.

Kenyan geographer Peter Mahende Sinda was less prominent and fiery, but his career sheds further light on the entangled trajectories of Soviet and African expertise on developments in African agriculture. Born in 1948 he left Kenya before the independence of his country to study at Moscow State University from 1961 to 1971. Sinda continued his studies there, which he completed in 1975 with a dissertation on the natural environment in Kenya and its agricultural potential. While in Moscow he lectured on the physical geography of eastern Africa and participated in Soviet expeditions to the region. After having left Moscow he worked for a UNESCO program in Kenya, subsequently taking an academic post at Kenyatta University in Nairobi.[52] To a greater extent than Afana, Sinda had been integrated into the Soviet academic community, facilitating Soviet research trips to eastern Africa and contributing to Africanist expertise on Kenya—a country that had followed a capitalist path of development. Sinda's career—like Afana's—further demonstrates how transnationally active and highly mobile African scholars, as well as activists, navigated both national and international arenas, leaving their mark on Soviet projects as well as on those of international organizations such as UNESCO. Like other academic migrants, such as (Joshua) Tsiu Selatile, a South African Communist and, according to Bernard Leeman, the only African member of the Soviet Academy of Sciences,[53] the scholars in question combined academic and political activity—a combination that their Soviet colleagues did not always find easy to digest. Selatile completed his dissertation at the Soviet Academy of Sciences in 1970 on relations in agriculture on South African reservations and became the vice president representing Lesotho at the African Economic Association of the UN Economic Commission for Africa (UNECA).[54] Academic exchanges between African and Soviet scholars—particularly in such spheres as agriculture—were not only driven by the ambition to export the Soviet model but to learn about African developments, as Soviet scholars were desperately aware of how limited their knowledge was.[55] And these models circulated in more complex networks than bilateral connections, insofar as African experts were qualified in the Soviet Union to work in international organizations that have shaped development policy on the continent to a considerable degree.[56]

Between Tashkent and Dakar: The Troubles and Limitations of Transfers

The challenge for Soviet scholars was twofold: to advertise the Soviet Union as a model and to gather insights into African developments, which might be used to bolster the prevailing Soviet interpretation and to serve as "academic currency" in the competition not only with Western—but also African—counterparts. This bifurcated agenda was realized quite differently depending on the forum of encounter and transfer. The tension between the Soviet ambition to be a model and the limits of Soviet knowledge concerning Africa to apply the model materialized in different encounters.

International conferences were among the most important arenas, but those organized by Soviet scholars to facilitate the exchange with their colleagues from different systems in the Global South and those offering a forum for colleagues specifically from the socialist world must be differentiated. The 1972 conference in Tashkent was a telling example of the first variant. This meeting in early February was prominently promoted as one of the hundreds of academic events celebrating the fiftieth anniversary of the foundation of the Soviet Union and as such intended to be yet another showcase to demonstrate the seminal success of the Soviet model of modernization. The conference had been initiated by the Soviet Academy of Sciences and the Soviet Committee of Afro-Asian Solidarity in close cooperation with the Uzbek Academy of Sciences and the Uzbek Central Committee of the Communist Party.[57] The pattern was an established one, bringing together scholars and activists from the Soviet Union and the Global South to meet in Central Asia, pursue a comparative investigation of regional trajectories, advertise the undertaking internationally, and sell this as proof of the exemplary character of the USSR. However, as was often the case, the proceedings brought certain contradictions to light. Undoubtedly, most of the participants from the Global South underlined the vanguard position of the Soviet Union and voiced their gratitude for its support and guidance. The tensions, however, were also obvious. For example, the Indian participant V. B. Singh not only observed that "no impact [. . .] is a one-way traffic" but also emphasized that the Indian-Soviet relationship was driven by the expectation of mutual benefit. The Soviet Union appeared in his contribution less as a role model and teacher than as a partner in economic development, for example, helping with technical equipment such as tractors—driven by economic self-interest in the light of the important position of the Indian economy in the international economic order. Simultaneously, Singh argued, Soviet scholars had profited from developments in Indian agricultural science and applied their knowledge in Soviet agriculture.[58]

Other participants were even more outspoken about the distance between the Soviet Union and newly independent countries in the Global South. From the Tanzanian delegation F. Myahoza emphasized: "Because of the differences between our background and those of other Socialist-oriented states our socialist paths will no wonder be different from those followed by other comrades. But the ultimate goal [emphasis in original] of all of us who are so dedicated is to develop, build and maintain classless nations in which every soul enjoys respect and dignity at and to the same degree as any other fellow being."[59] And another Tanzanian participant conceded that Ujamaa villages, analogous to Soviet collective farms, are geared to effect an agrarian revolution and rural development: "At the same time [i]t shoulnt [sic!] however be mistaken that Ujamaa village formation is the result of the liquidation of Kulaks [sic!],—for there, Kulaks are absent; we have and had mere peasants. Moreover even if the kulaks and big landlords were abundant, to us Ujamaa is a faith, an attitude of mind, and philosophy of life something that one can be convinced into joining but not forced to embrace."[60] This was a thinly veiled allusion to Stalinist excesses perpetrated in the very part of the Soviet Union where the conference met.

Other congresses, which gathered scholars exclusively from the Soviet Union or the socialist camp, followed a different logic. The fervor with which Soviet participants propagated the USSR as a model for the modernization of the Global South was tempered quite considerably, but the theoretical discussions intensified. A recurrent and hotly debated question concerned how best to characterize the role of African peasants and farmers in economic and political transformations. At the second All-Union Conference of Africanists in September 1974, Leonard V. Goncharov, deputy director of the Africa Institute, argued that during the 1960s insufficient attention had been paid to questions of agriculture—due to the well-known obsession with industrialization. It was high time, he suggested, to pay heed to its vital role in the transformation of African countries and to develop strategies of agricultural modernization that would have the interests of farmers in mind.[61] He connected this plea with a much more cautious evaluation of the pace and potential of socialist transformation in poorly developed African countries. Goncharov was joined by his colleague Nikolai I. Gavrilov, an expert in the agricultural transformation in Africa, who had left the Institute for Oriental Studies in 1960 to work at the Africa Institute, from which he had also been sent to the UN African Institute for Economic Development and Planning (IDEP). He elaborated on the question of alternatives to and variants of the path to socialism. The role of peasants was deemed crucial, serving as they might as strong partners in an otherwise fragile situation. This interpretation differed markedly from the skeptical account given of peasants in intra-Soviet debates. The call for differentiation and thorough investigation was aimed at researchers specializing in Africa but also at those concerned with Soviet development, in Central Asia in particular. Gavrilov concluded that even if one could discern a number of differences between the Central Asian situation in the 1920s and 1930s and current transformations in Africa (such as the role of political power and ideology), the time had come for closer investigation of both cases taken together.[62] Gavrilov and his colleagues would certainly concentrate on Africa and then draw on knowledge about Central Asia based on exchanges with colleagues from these republics—rather than from their own research. Yet the exchanges with colleagues from the region—some who were experts on Central Asia, others on Africa—played a crucial role in the formation of ideas about the plurality of social and economic transformations in previously backward and colonized regions heading toward some kind of socialist modernity. At the abovementioned conference in Tashkent, for example, experts on Central Asian developments were part of the group, but their colleagues from the region were welcome at other conferences of Soviet Africanists.[63] Furthermore, in the leading scholarly journals of the discipline, research results from Central Asia were published and discussed alongside findings on the countries of the Global South.[64] Indeed, frustrations with agricultural development in both regions occurred at similar moments. The 1970s and 1980s saw a flourishing of research by Central Asian scholars, who increasingly demonstrated the gap between ambition and the realities of the Soviet modernization project in the region and started to engage in in-depth micro-level studies to highlight and explain the specificities of Central Asian trajectories.[65] The parallel turns in the debates among Soviet Africanists and Central Asian economists was the result of simultaneous—perhaps even entangled—frustrations. It is important to note that the limits and contradictions of the Soviet modernization project were debated in Central Asia[66] at almost the same moment at which the high hopes for modernization and a socialist breakthrough in Africa had cooled off considerably.[67]

While congresses provided a collective arena for transfers and their complications, field trips and other visits to Africa produced a number of challenges.[68] More generally, such travels abroad were limited in number. It is certainly true that the majority of the hundreds of Soviet Africanists had neither received the permission nor the funding for lengthy field research in their chosen region. However, these difficulties can be overemphasized.[69] First, during the early 1960s only a third of the Africa Institute's staff were able to travel to Africa. Nevertheless, their stays were often short, and they had to be creative, using opportunities provided by friendship societies, women's committees, trade unions, or Soviet companies to visit these countries.[70] Second, Soviet Africanists in many cases crossed professional lines in the course of their careers, spending time as diplomats, journalists, or representatives of Soviet organizations abroad, often in the countries of their specialization.[71] And finally, the presence and visits of African scholars and activists in the Soviet Union, most of whom passed through the Africa Institute at one time or another, provided a not yet fully understood form of creating expertise based on "local knowledge."[72] Those peculiar patterns of Soviet-African academic mobility need to be more systematically explored elsewhere, but against this background, one of the central opportunities Soviet scholars were eager to take were invitations to teach at African institutions of higher education or international organizations in Africa. These trips, however, were not only undertaken by the elite of the academy but also extended to and keenly sought by other scholars. Yet limited resources, partial knowledge about local conditions, and the gap between ambition and reality in host institutions often resulted in enormous challenges for visiting lecturers. The experience of the economist Eduard Nuchovich provides a vivid insight into the complexities of these situations.[73] In August 1966 he had been sent by the presidium of the Academy of Sciences to lecture at the IDEP in Dakar on the development of agriculture in African countries. Prior to this he had mainly published on the foreign policy of Afghanistan,[74] so his qualifications for commenting on African developments were likely limited.[75] The material for the later books he wrote on Africa and development were in part collected on this trip to Dakar. He not only met with the French Africanist Claude Meillassoux—a student of Georges Balandier, a lecturer at the IDEP and a rising star in French anthropology[76]—but also with the American political scientist and specialist on the Soviet Union Robert Legvold, who was at that time doing fieldwork for what became the seminal monograph on Soviet policy in West Africa.[77] Furthermore, he visited the Dakar branch of the Institute Fondamental d'Afrique Noire (IFAN)—which was for him and many of his Soviet colleagues the first address to contact for archives and data. In the case of Meillassoux in particular, he thought to have found an ally in his critical view on the activities of the IDEP. For Nuchovich, the IDEP represented an altogether peculiar universe in which the cleavages and dynamics of the Cold War overlapped with those of the postcolonial condition.

The institute had been created in 1962 as a pan-African organization by the United Nations under the aegis of the Economic Commission for Africa, aiming to create in newly independent countries local elites competent in economic planning and development.[78] It found itself in the midst of the tectonic rifts emerging from the overlap of Cold War competition, decolonization, and the Western European metropoles' efforts to reorganize their former colonial spaces.[79] The permanent and temporary teaching staff of the institute[80] consisted mainly of a group of African economists, many of whom had started their careers in colonial administrations, were trained in the former colonial metropoles, and quickly rose in the hierarchy of international organizations such as the International Monetary Fund (IMF), the World Bank, or the United Nations.[81] They were subsequently joined by Western European scholars.[82] This was the context in which Nuchovich found himself in 1966, a universe that Soviet scholars certainly found difficult to navigate. In addition, Dakar was at the center not of socialist development, but of the Négritude movement, and thus the locus of an intellectual African elite whose vision of a postcolonial future was deeply shaped by experiences of entanglement with French political and cultural developments, quite distinct from the Soviet project. But it was because Dakar was at the heart of African intellectual and cultural dynamics that it was so attractive for Soviet scholars who came here to learn. The situation at the IDEP was thus complicated by the encounter "in the field," by the presence of a knowledge-hungry future African elite whom Soviet scholars hoped to guide, and also by the competition with Western and African scholars. The first setback Nuchovich suffered on arrival was the cancellation of the course he had been sent to teach on the development of agriculture in African countries.[83] With the agreement of the vice-director, David Carney, he developed a new course, which addressed questions of economic development, in particular the cooperation of the Soviet Union with African countries, principles of economic planning in the Soviet Union, and the results of the new Five-Year Plan in the USSR. Nuchovich dismissed the overall activities of the institute as well as the content of the courses as unduly academic and irrelevant for practical application, focusing on bourgeois' theories such as that of Walt Whitman Rostow on modernization. He shared his criticisms with Meillassoux, whose manuscript lectures had been removed from the library and whose permission to continue his course had been revoked. Reporting back on his teaching experience to his colleagues at home, Nuchovich offered insights into the manner in which the Soviet Union was viewed by the rising African elite, impressions that must have alarmed his seniors in Moscow. Some students associated the economic success of the Soviet Union with the plight of the Soviet population or had never heard of economic and political cooperation between the Soviet Union and African countries. Others recounted stories about the notorious snowplows delivered to Africa.

Nevertheless—or precisely in response to these challenges—Nuchovich lavished praise on the IDEP and welcomed the participation of Soviet scholars in its activities. The director, Mamadou Touré, had given him the hope that the IDEP would invite further colleagues—alluding to a lack of financial resources, Touré suggested that the USSR might contribute funds—and proposed to visit Moscow himself.[84] At least one other Soviet scholar had been invited to the IDEP again: Nikolai I. Gavrilov spend an entire year from spring 1967 to spring 1968 teaching on problems of agricultural planning in Africa. His habilitation on the same topic had most probably benefited from what had been by Soviet standards an unusually long stay.[85]

These few encounters illustrate broader patterns of transfer, which were often characterized by frustration and mutual puzzlement. It was not only political relations that complicated the "diffusion" of the Soviet model.[86] The limited Soviet knowledge about African conditions and developments was problematic too. The early setback in West Africa after attempts to implement Soviet agricultural (and other) models of modernization[87] was deeply felt by the Soviet authorities and added to the list of complaints against Khrushchev in 1964.[88] The failure of these ambitious plans for a socialist modernization in Africa contributed not only to a general dissatisfaction with the Khrushchevian project, which led ultimately to his fall from power, but also to more pragmatic approaches in the region under Leonid Brezhnev.[89] Soviet Africanists were well aware of these limitations and tried to mobilize further domestic support for their scientific activities.[90] Furthermore, African interest in the Soviet model was often driven by concerns over concrete material and financial aid, as well as over technical assistance to deal with the challenges of the postcolonial condition. More wide-ranging theorizations on the agrarian question were either beyond the agenda of African scholars and activists or countered by their own self-confident interpretations regarding the African and Soviet divergence in the solving of the agrarian question. And finally, Soviet scholars had to defend their expertise and theorizations vis-à-vis their Western counterparts, who were often, by virtue of their links to the former colonial power, much better connected to the new African elites.

Conclusion: Entangled Modernities

The limited applicability and effectiveness of the Soviet model of agricultural modernization in Africa has been emphasized in the scholarship produced during and after the Cold War.[91] This chapter, however, suggests a reformulation of the question: not *whether* the Soviet model has been successfully "applied" in Africa, but *how* it has been shaped and reformulated in this encounter. How did actors try to adapt the model to "African realities," and how were these adaptations shaped by their encounter with the backwardness of the Soviet peripheries? East-South relations during the Cold War in this regard provide important insights into the coproduction of modernities that were a core part of the history of twentieth-century globalization. The coproduction unfolded partly in the guise of the participation of African scholars in the shaping of Soviet knowledge of Africa, as the dissertations have demonstrated. More often, however, it resulted from a reflection of Soviet scholars on their experiences at international conferences or during trips in which they were confronted with competing understandings and their own limitations in knowledge and theoretical persuasiveness. Digesting both these frustrations and their enthusiastic discoveries of "Africa" resulted in a rethinking of Soviet models for the solution of the agrarian question in Africa. This observation problematizes assumptions on center-periphery relations in the postcolonial world of the twentieth century in two ways: first, "Africa" was not simply on the receiving end of the diffusion of models for development: Soviet Africanists learned from their African colleagues and struggled to translate this knowledge into the Soviet context. Second, the Soviet Union was in this respect not the leading academic player in the Global South.

Central Asia served as a projection screen for Soviet Africanists' visions and as a symbolic argument in the discussion with African colleagues. But by rethinking African developments—driven by their encounters "with the field"—limitations in their understanding of Central Asian trajectories became more obvious. Soviet Africanists were not the ones to close these gaps, but to some extent this permitted the opening of the field for Central Asian scholars to articulate their criticism of Soviet models of development.[92]

The reorientation of agricultural policy under Brezhnev may not have been the immediate result of academic encounters of the complexity of agricultural reform after decolonization in Africa. Yet African dynamics in this era posed both a tremendous challenge to and an opportunity for Soviet scholars. With regard to the agrarian question, Africanist research seemed to confirm the doubts raised by previously marginalized agronomists such as Chaianov and his followers. With the linking of Central Asian and African trajectories, Soviet Africanists contributed to a master narrative about the civilization of the domestic periphery by presenting it as a blueprint for African developments. In this sense, the Third World was also located in the Soviet Union.

Notes

1. For the Soviet perspective, see *Bolshai͡a sovetskai͡a ent͡siklopedii͡a*, 3rd edition (Moskva: Sovetskai͡a ent͡siklopedii͡a, 1969–1978). See also Henry Bernstein, "Agrarian Questions Then and Now," *Journal of Peasant Studies* 24, nos. 1–2 (1996): 22–59.

2. On the role of Central Asian actors in promoting the Soviet model in the Global South, see Kalinovsky, "Writing the Soviet South into the History of the Cold War and Decolonization," in this volume and Artemy Kalinovsky, "Not Some British Colony in Africa: The Politics of Decolonization and Modernization in Soviet Central Asia, 1955–1964," *Ab Imperio* 2 (2013): 191–222; and Masha Kirasirova, "'Sons of Muslims' in Moscow: Soviet Central Asian Mediators to the Foreign East, 1955–1962," *Ab Imperio* 4 (2011): 106–132.

3. David C. Engerman, *The Price of Aid: The Economic Cold War in India* (Cambridge, MA: Harvard University Press, 2018); David Engerman "Learning from the East Soviet Experts and India in the Era of Competitive Coexistence," *Comparative Studies of South Asia, Africa and the Middle East* 33, no. 2 (2013): 227–238.

4. Jerry F. Hough, *The Struggle for the Third World: Soviet Debates and American Options* (Washington, DC: Brookings Institution, 1986), 43.

5. Hough refers to Marxist-Leninist historical development, namely: primitive-communal, slaveholding, feudal, capitalist, and finally communist. See Hough, *The Struggle for the Third World*, 39.

6. Hough, *The Struggle for the Third World*, 46.

7. Antonio Giustozzi and Artemy Kalinovsky, *Missionaries of Modernity* (London: Hurst Publishers, 2014), 32, 59–62, 65.

8. Elizabeth Kridl Valkenier, "New Trends in Soviet Economic Relations with the Third World," *World Politics* 22, no. 3 (1970): 415–432, here 429.

9. Hakim Adi, *Pan-Africanism and Communism: The Communist International, Africa and the Diaspora, 1919–1939* (Trenton, NJ: Africa World Press, 2013); Holger Weiss, *Framing*

a Radical African Atlantic: African American Agency, West African Intellectuals, and the International Trade Union Committee of Negro Workers (Leiden: Brill, 2014).

10. Michael Goebel, *Anti-Imperial Metropolis: Interwar Paris and the Seeds of Third World Nationalism* (Cambridge: Cambridge University Press, 2017); Hakim Adi, *West Africans in Britain, 1900–1960: Nationalism, Pan-Africanism and Communism* (London: Lawrence & Wishart, 1997).

11. Viktor Danilov, *Tragediia͡ sovetskoĭ derevni: kollektivizatsiia͡ i raskulachivanie. Dokumenty i materialy v 5 tomakh, 1927–1939* (Moscow: ROSSPĖN, 1999); R. W. Davies and S. G. Wheatcroft, *The Years of Hunger: Soviet Agriculture, 1931–1933* (New York: Palgrave Macmillan, 2009).

12. Katja Bruisch, *Als das Dorf noch Zukunft war: Agrarismus und Expertise zwischen Zarenreich und Sowjetunion* (Cologne: Böhlau, 2014).

13. Christian Teichmann, *Macht der Unordnung: Stalins Herrschaft in Zentralasien 1920–1950* (Hamburg: Hamburger Edition, 2016).

14. Helga Schultz and Angela Harre, *Bauerngesellschaften auf dem Weg in die Moderne: Agrarismus in Ostmitteleuropa 1880 bis 1960* (Wiesbaden: Harrassowitz, 2010).

15. Alexander Chaianov, *The Theory of Peasant Co-operatives* (London: I. B. Tauris, 1991).

16. On the circulation of Western European debates on agrarian reform in tsarist Russia, see also Viktor Danilov, "Introduction: Alexander Chayanov as a Theoretician of the Co-operative Movement" in Chaianov, *The Theory of Co-operatives*, xi–xxxv.

17. Viktor Danilov, "The Issue of Alternatives and History of the Collectivisation of Soviet Agriculture," *Journal of Historical Sociology* 2 (1989): 1–13.

18. Sheila Fitzpatrick, *Stalin's Peasants: Resistance and Survival in the Russian Village after Collectivization* (New York: Oxford University Press, 1996).

19. Adi, *Pan-Africanism and Communism*; Weiss, *Framing a Radical African Atlantic.*

20. Joy Gleason Carew, *Blacks, Reds, and Russians: Sojourners in Search of the Soviet Promise* (New Brunswick, NJ: Rutgers University Press, 2010); Svetlana Boltovskaja, *Bildungsmigranten aus dem Subsaharischen Afrika in Moskau und St. Petersburg* (Herbolzheim: Centaurus Verlag & Media, 2015).

21. Cited in Lily Golden, *My Long Journey Home* (Chicago: Third World Press, 2002), 7.

22. For Soviet agronomy in transatlantic networks in the 1950s and 1960s, see in particular Marc Elie, "Formulating the Global Environment: Soviet Soil Scientists and the International Desertification Discussion, 1968–91," *Slavonic and East European Review* 93, no. 1 (2015): 181–204, 211.

23. Notes by Mikhail Tikhomirov and further unnamed Soviet historians, protesting against the interpretation of Stalin's collectivization program in *The Twentieth Century*, eds. Caroline F. Ware, K. M. Panikkar, and Jan Romein (London: Published for the International Commission for a History of the Scientific and Cultural Development of Mankind by Allen & Unwin, 1966), part 3: "The Self-Image and Aspirations of the Peoples of the World," chap. 30, "Drives for Individual Freedom and Human Dignity."

24. This concept went back to Lenin's theorization of development in tsarist Russia, suggesting its being a mixed economy in which centers of industrialization with an emerging Russian proletariat provided the motor for a socialist revolution. In a narrower Marxist view, the prerequisite for a socialist revolution would have been the capitalist transformation of the whole economy, which in the Russian case had not been achieved.

25. Steffi Marung, "The Provocation of Empirical Evidence: Soviet African Studies between Enthusiasm and Discomfort," *African Identities* 16, no. 2 (2018): 176–190.

26. Robert Kindler, *Stalin's Nomads: Power and Famine in Kazakhstan* (Pittsburgh, PA: University of Pittsburgh Press, 2018); Marc Elie and Carole Ferret, *Verte, la Steppe? Agriculture et Environnement en Asie Centrale* (Paris: Éditions de l'École des hautes études en sciences sociales, 2017).

27. Tanya Korovkin, "Soviet Strategies of Economic Development for the Third World: A Review Essay," *Canadian Journal of Latin American and Caribbean Studies* 10, no. 19 (1985): 59–72.

28. Thomas J. Zamostny, "Moscow and the Third World: Recent Trends in Soviet Thinking," *Soviet Studies* 36, no. 2 (1984): 223–235.

29. I͡uriĭ Novopashin, "Vozdeĭstvie real'nogo sot͡sialisma na mirovoĭ revolyut͡sionnyĭ prot͡sess: metodologicheskie aspekty," *Voprosy filosofii* 36, no. 8 (1982): 3–16.

30. Denis Kozlov and Eleonory Gilburd, *The Thaw: Soviet Society and Culture during the 1950s and 1960s* (Toronto: University of Toronto Press, 2014).

31. Hough, *The Struggle for the Third World.*

32. Jeremy Friedman, "Soviet Policy in the Developing World and the Chinese Challenge in the 1960s," *Cold War History* 10, no. 2 (2010): 247–272.

33. Ivan I. Potekhin, *Agrarnyĭ vopros i krest'i͡anstvo v tropiccheskoĭ* (Moscow: Nauka, 1964).

34. Ibid., 4–7; see also Colin Darch and Gary Littlejohn, "Endre Sik and the Development of African Studies in the USSR: A Study Agenda from 1929," *History in Africa: A Journal of Method* 10 (1983): 79–108.

35. Artemy Kalinovsky, "Tractors, Power Lines, and the Welfare State: The Contradictions of Soviet Development in Post-World War II Tajikistan," *Asiatische Studien—Études Asiatiques* 69, no. 3 (2015): 563–592; Kalinovsky, "Central Planning, Local Knowledge? Labor, Population, and the 'Tajik School of Economics,'" *Kritika* 17, no. 3 (2016): 585–620.

36. Ivan I. Potekhin, "Advance and Reconstruction of Agriculture in Independent African Countries," in *African Problems: Analysis of Eminent Soviet Scientist* (Moscow: Nauka, 1968), 79.

37. Lazar Volin, "Soviet Agriculture under Khrushchev," *The American Economic Review*, 49, no. 2, (1959): 16.

38. As his further explications demonstrate. Potekhin, *Agrarnyĭ vopros*, 79–80.

39. Otchety o komandirovke sotrudnikov Instituta za granit͡su za 1961–1962 gody. Archive of Russian Academy of Sciences ARAN f. 2010 op.1. d. 20.

40. Ibid.

41. Stenogramma rasshirennogo zasedanii͡a presidiuma SKSSAA s predstaviteli͡ami obshchestvennosti, 21.11.1961 goda. State Archive of the Russian Federation (GARF). F.R-9540. Op1. Delo 82.

42. Potekhin, *Agrarnyj vopros*, 90.

43. One example is Rachik M. Avakov, an economist, who had specialized in northern Africa at the Institute of World Economy and International Relations (IMEMO) and who started to work for UNESCO in 1984 and in this respect investigated education in Azerbaijan. Sofia D. Miliband, *Vostokovedy Rossii: XX - nachalo XXI veka: biobibliograficheskiĭ slovar' v dvukh knigakh. Vol. 2* (Moscow: Vostochnai͡a literatura RAN, 2008).

44. Calculations based on *Ukazatel' doktorskich i kandidatskich dissertacii po problemam Afriki, zashchishchenych v SSSR 1935–1980*, Moscow 1983, edited by the Scientific Council for the Problems of Africa at the Soviet Academy of Sciences, under the aegis of the Africa Institute.

45. 30 theses.
46. 42 theses.
47. Steffi Marung, "'Peculiar Encounters with the Black Continent': Soviet Africanists in the Global 1960s and the Expansion of the Discipline," in *Self-Reflexive Area Studies*, ed. Matthias Middell (Leipzig: Leipziger Universitätsverlag, 2013), 103–134.
48. Out of more than 17,000 Russian publications about Africa, 202 are devoted to the "agrarian question," mainly in the field of economics. The lion's share—130 titles—appeared between 1960 and 1967 and were related either to "Africa" and the "Arab East," while the most prominent countries were Ghana, Mali, Kenya, and Ethiopia: *Bibliografii͡a stran Afriki i Arabskogo Vostoka. Ukazatel' literatury na russkom Iiazyke, opublikovannoĭ v SSSR v 1917–1967 gg* (Moscow: Nauka, 1979).
49. Osendé Afana, *L'économie de l'ouest-africain* (Paris: Maspero, 1966).
50. A note on his defense in ARAN f. 2010 op.1. d. 77.
51. Letter of Afana to Potekhin, ARAN f. 2010 op.1. d. 14.
52. For his biography, see http://www.ku.ac.ke/schools/humanities/images/stories/docs/Dr_peter_mahende_sinda_updated_cv_27_4_2015.pdf.
53. Bernard Leeman, *Lesotho and the Struggle for Azania: Africanist Political Movements in Lesotho and Azania: The Origins and History of the Basutoland Congress Party and the Pan Africanist Congress* (London: University of Azania, PAC Education Off, 1985), http://historicalpapers-atom.wits.ac.za/tsiu-selatile-letters-to-leeman.
54. African Economic Association, *Report of African Economic Association: Inaugural Conference and Scientific Colloquium* (Addis Ababa, 1990), http://repository.uneca.org/bitstream/handle/10855/14158/Bib-55631.pdf?sequence=1.
55. Otchet o rabote mezhdunarodnogo kongressa po isuchenii͡u istorii Afiki. Dar-es-Salam, Tanzanii͡a, 26/IX–2/X- 1965 g., ARAN f. 2010 op.1 d. 66.
56. How this has evolved in detail and from the actors' perspective is a question for further research, including interviews with African alumni of Soviet institutions of higher education.
57. Tezisy dokladov na mezhdunarodnoĭ konferent͡sii "Opyt sot͡sialisticheskikh preobrazovaniĭ v SSSR i ego mezhdunarodnoe znachenie" (October 16–19, 1972, Tashkent). ARAN f. 2010, op. 1, d. 291.
58. He was referring to the development of high-yielding varieties of wheat by Indian scholars, which would have a great impact on Soviet crop farming in winter. V. B. Singh, "Soviet Impact on Indian Economic Development." Tezisy dokladov. ARAN f. 2010 op. 1, d. 291.
59. F. Myahoza, "Ujamaa: The Venue to Socialism in Tanzania." Tezisy dokladov. ARAN f. 2010 op. 1, d. 291.
60. "The Economic Experience of Non-Capitalist Reconstruction in Tanzania." Tezisy dokladov. ARAN f. 2010 op. 1, d. 291.
61. Stenogramma 2-i Vsesoiuznoi konferentsii afrikanistov, ARAN f. 2010 op. 1, d. 383.
62. Ibid.
63. Stenogramma nauchnoĭ konferent͡sii "Sel'skokhozi͡aĭstvennye rabochie razvivai͡ushchikhsi͡a stran Azii i Afriki" (April 24, 1967, Moskva). ARAN f. 2010 op. 1, d. 98.
64. Such as in the journals *Narodi Azii i Afriki* or *Afrika i Azija Segodni͡a*.
65. For the Tajik case, see Artemy Kalinovsky, "Central Planning."
66. Kalinovsky, "Tractors."

67. Crawford Young, *Ideology and Development in Africa* (New Haven, CT: Yale University Press, 1983).

68. Marung, "Peculiar Encounters."

69. Irina Filatova, "Some Thoughts on Soviet South African Studies under 'Stagnation' and Perestroika," *International Journal of African Historical Studies* 25, no. 1 (1992): 15–23; Karen Brutents, *Tridtsat' let na Staroj ploshchadi* (Moscow: Mezhdunarodnye Otnosheniia, 1998).

70. Marung, "Peculiar Encounters."

71. Elsewhere I have demonstrated this pattern for Oriental studies more broadly, under which African scholars have been subsumed: Steffi Marung and Katja Naumann, "The Making of Oriental Studies: Its Transnational and Transatlantic Past," in *The Making of the Humanities*, eds. Rens Bod, Jaap Maat, and Thijs Weststeijn (Amsterdam: Amsterdam University Press, 2010), 415–429, here 416–18.

72. Marung, "The Provocation of Empirical Evidence."

73. Otchet o nauchnoj komandirovke v Respubliku Senegal Nuchovicha E.S. and Cours d'ete pour etudiants 1966—Plan des cours du Professeurs de l'Universite de Moscou Mr. Noukhovich, ARAN f. 2010 op. 1, d. 87.

74. Eduard S. Nuchovich, *Vneshniaia politika Afganistana* (Moscow: Izdat. Inst. Medunarodnykh Otnosheniĭ, 1962).

75. Nuchovich, *No to Neocolonialist Diktat: A Study of Soviet Economic Cooperation with Developing Nations and Foes of This Cooperation* (Moscow: Novosti, 1969); Nuchovich, *Mezhdunarodnye monopolii v strategii neo-kolonializma* (Moscow: Mezhdunarodnye Otnosheniia, 1982).

76. Among his most influential books, see Claude Meillassoux, *Anthropologie de l'esclavage: le ventre de fer et d'argent* (Paris: PUF, 1998); *Mythes et limites de l'anthropologie: le sang et les mots* (Lausanne: Éd. Page deux, 2001).

77. Robert Legvold, *Soviet Policy in West Africa* (Boston: Harvard University Press, 1970). Until the publication of Sergej Mazov's *A Distant Front in the Cold War: The USSR in West Africa and the Congo, 1956–1964* (Washington, DC: Woodrow Wilson Center Press, 2010), this book was the most respected and comprehensive study on this question.

78. Alongside American, French, and Polish experts, Soviet scholars were directly involved in the consultations surrounding the establishment of this institute in October 1963: Otchet ob uchastii v soveshchanii v Dakare po voprosu sozdaniia Afrikanskogo instituta ekonomicheskogo razvitiia i planiovaniia, ARAN f. 2010 op. 1, d. 66; see further, Mogens Boserup, "The African Institute for Economic Development and Planning, Dakar," *The Journal of Modern African Studies* 2, no. 4 (1964): 573–575.

79. Peo Hansen and Stefan Jonsson, *Eurafrica: The Untold History of European Integration and Colonialism* (London: Bloomsbury Academic, 2015).

80. Commission Economique pour l'Afrique, Huitième session, Lagos, 13–25 février 1967, *Rapport du Conseil d'Administration de l'Institut Africain de Developpement Economique et de Planification*, UNECA repository, E/CN.14/367, November 8, 1966.

81. This was true for the Ghanaian Robert K. A. Gardiner, the Senegalese Mamadou Touré, who acted as the institute's director from 1964 to 1967, and David Carney, who replaced Touré as director in 1967. His successor, the Egyptian Samir Amin, called himself an "independent Marxist" and had been trained at French institutions of higher education.

82. Such as the German Karlernst Ringer, the Dutch Herman van der Tak, and the French Meillassoux.

83. See here and in the following: *Otchet o nauchnoĭ komandirovke v Rezpubliku Senegal Nuchovicha E.S.* and *Cours d'ete pour etudiants 1966—Plan des cours du Professeurs de l'Universite de Moscou Mr. Noukhovich*, ARAN f. 2010 op. 1, d. 87.

84. So far I have not found evidence to suggest that Touré had actually undertaken this visit.

85. Nikolai I. Gavrilov, *Problemy planirovanii͡a i razvitii͡a sel'skogo chozi͡aistva v stranach Afriki* (Moskow: Nauka, 1973).

86. Ragna Boden, *Die Grenzen der Weltmacht: sowjetische Indonesienpolitik von Stalin bis Brežnev* (Stuttgart: Franz Steiner Verlag, 2006); Oscar Sanchez-Sibony, *Red Globalization* (Cambridge: Cambridge University Press, 2017).

87. Iandolo, "The Rise and Fall"; Mazov, *Distant Front*.

88. D. C. Engerman, "The Second World's Third World," *Kritika* 12, no. 1 (2011): 183–212, here, 208; Engerman, "Learning from the East."

89. S. Lorenzini, "Comecon and the South in the Years of Détente: A Study on East-South Economic Relations," *European Review of History* 21, no. 2 (2014): 183–199.

90. Marung, "Peculiar Encounters."

91. Ernst Hillebrand, *Sowjetische Theorie, afrikanische Praxis: Zu den sowjetischen Konzepten einer sozialistischen Agrarpolitik in Afrika* (Hamburg: Institut für Afrika-Kunde, 1990); Marina Ottaway and David Ottaway, *Afrocommunism* (New York: Africana, 1986); Alessandro Iandolo, "The Rise and Fall of the 'Soviet Model of Development' in West Africa, 1957–64," *Cold War History*, 12, no. 4 (2012): 683–704.

92. Kalinovsky, "Central Planning."

STEFFI MARUNG is Senior Researcher at the Centre for Area Studies at the University of Leipzig. She is author of *Die wandernde Grenze: Die EU, Polen und der Wandel politischer Räume, 1990–2010* and co-author of *Spatial Formats under the Global Condition* and *In Search of Other Worlds: Essays Towards a Global Historical Reading of Area Studies.*

7 Socialist Worldmaking: Architecture and Global Urbanization in the Cold War

Łukasz Stanek

THIS CHAPTER PRESENTS the interim results of a research project that explores architectural mobilities among socialist Eastern Europe, West Africa, and the Middle East during the Cold War.[1] Against the prevailing tendency to reduce the globalization of architecture to nothing more than Westernization, this research draws attention to the contributions of architects, planners, engineers, and construction companies mobilized in state-socialist networks to worldwide urbanization processes after the Second World War. In so doing, it studies state-socialist networks bifurcating within a multiplicity of competing projects of worldwide cooperation and solidarity from the 1950s to the 1980s. By focusing on this multiplicity, this research does not simply add Moscow, Warsaw, or Belgrade to the Western centers from which architectural expertise was diffused. Rather, it replaces such a diffusionist model with a study of transactions between actors circulating in competing networks at a variety of scales and argues that such a heuristic is better suited to understanding their agency on the ground.[2] Consequently, rather than focusing on bilateral narratives—as Ryszard Kapuściński once quipped, "How are the Russians doing in Tanzania, [. . .] how are the Americans doing in Liberia?"[3]—four case studies focus on intersections of state-socialist networks with others in specific locations and at specific periods: Ghana under Kwame Nkrumah (1957–66), Nigeria between the First and the Second Republic (1966–79), Iraq from the coup of Abd al-Karim Qasim to the First Gulf War (1958–90), and Kuwait and the United Arab Emirates (UAE) during the last decade of the Cold War.

These case studies, explored in detail in my forthcoming book *Architecture in Global Socialism,* show how transactions across competing global networks in Ghana, Nigeria, Iraq, and the Gulf resulted in the deployment of architectural resources from socialist Europe, including construction materials and technologies, technical details and functional typologies, principles of design, images, and discourses. They also included the one resource that was both mobilized in socialist networks and was mobilizing others namely, the labor of architects, engineers, planners, technicians, economists, administrators, educators, foremen, and workers. By following architectural labor in each of the studied locations, this research shows how differences between various networks offered opportunities and constraints to assemble, accelerate, augment, or block the deployment of architectural resources. The results of these engagements include buildings and infrastructures still in use; master plans, regulations, and norms still applied; and curricula still taught. By revisiting them, this research contributes to a more heterogeneous and antagonistic genealogy of the globalization of architecture and, more generally, of urbanization conditions around the world.

Socialist Worldmaking

The global mobility of architecture after the Second World War has been a preoccupation of architectural and planning historians over the last two decades. In particular, scholars have shown how this mobility was accelerated by colonial and postcolonial networks, those of the United States, Western Europe, and international organizations such as the United Nations, and by economic globalization since the 1970s.[4] However, the socialist countries have been absent from this discussion until recently. Apart from the sheer difficulty of gaining access to archival sources that have often been destroyed or dispersed, this omission has been grounded in a series of conceptual decisions. In particular, they included the reduction of the worldwide mobility of architecture to the dominant narratives of "Westernization" or "Americanization," in which the role reserved for Eastern Europe is that of a "new market" for Western firms "created" after the fall of the Berlin Wall.[5]

By uncovering the role of socialist states in global urbanization processes, this research stresses the multiplicity, rather than bipolarity, of these exchanges. The questioning of the Western genealogy of globalization does not mean a return to Cold War discourse about "the world [. . .] split into two camps: the camp of peace, democracy, and socialism, and the camp of imperialism," as a resolution of East Germany's Socialist Unity Party put it in 1952.[6] Rather, the focus on global trajectories of architecture reveals differences between the political and economic interests of particular socialist countries and highlights various facets of socialist internationalism. For instance, a vital vehicle for the mobility of Yugoslavia's architecture, planning, and construction industry were networks of the nonaligned movement (NAM, since 1961). In the 1980s it was NAM diplomacy that leveraged the Belgrade-based design and construction company Energoprojekt (EP) into a group of the world's twenty largest engineering companies.[7] Like the Yugoslav-Soviet split in 1948, so too the Sino-Soviet split in the 1960s further diversified the trajectories of architecture from socialist countries. The townscape of a postcolonial capital, such as Conakry in Guinea under Ahmed

Sékou Touré (1958–84), was a case in point: it reflected assistance programs from both the Soviet Union (Conakry's Polytechnic Institute, L. Afanas'ev for Giprovuz, 1964) and China (National Assembly Building, Chen Deng'ao and Wang Rongshou for the Beijing Design Institute, 1960s), while the master plan was delivered by Yugoslav (Croatian) planners.[8] Competition between external powers opened a space for maneuvers much larger than the Cold War discourse about Soviet "proxies" would suggest. This concerned members of NAM in particular, with Indonesia under Sukarno (until 1967) and Egypt under Gamal Abdel Nasser (until 1970) being the two biggest recipients of Soviet aid, much of which was used for construction projects, sometimes against Moscow's advice.[9]

In order to capture the multiplicity and the antagonisms between architectural networks after the Second World War, I prefer to speak about the worldmaking (*mondialisation*) of architecture rather than about its "globalization." For Henri Lefebvre, who coined this term in the course of the 1970s, the "worldwide" (*le mondial*) was not an accomplished historical process but rather an emerging dimension of practice. Lefebvre argued that the worldwide was rendered operative in the world market, in transportation and communication technologies, in ecological threats on a planetary scale, in "right to the city" movements around the globe, and in the tendency toward complete urbanization. These latter contribute to the "worldwide experience" by conveying antagonistic practices of worldmaking—that is to say alternative visions of the world as a whole, its plural imaginations, and a variety of ways of "practicing" the world as an abstraction that is becoming "true in practice."[10] Along these lines, writing by the end of the Cold War, Martinican writer, poet, and theorist Édouard Glissant defined the world not by the logics of expansion but by the multiplication of possibilities of connection.[11] Following both authors, I insist on the difference between worldmaking and "globalization": the US-backed, global spread of economic and political phenomena since the 1970s known to Anglophone readers as "globalization" is to be seen as just one among many possibilities of worldmaking.[12]

Socialism offered other such possibilities: while the global dimension of socialism was explicitly present in the movement since its beginnings in the nineteenth century, after the emergence of the Soviet state and in particular after the Second World War, socialism became a global phenomenon conveyed by the political culture of socialist states and their geopolitical strategies and myths.[13] Architectural networks from socialist countries need to be seen as part of this global dimension of socialism, and their bifurcations reflected the worldmaking dynamics in play.

In Lefebvre's writings, worldmaking is an inchoate concept and hence each usage must be tailored to suit the case study in question. The first case study of this research project addresses the Soviet claim to the global applicability of the socialist model of development by focusing on the work of Soviet architects and engineers in Kwame Nkrumah's Ghana. Yet the application of this model did not exhaust the foreign engagements of Eastern European architects, engineers, planners, and contractors. Rather than referring to a global vision of socialist development, Hungarian, Polish, and Yugoslav architects working in Nigeria (1966–79) proposed a different type of commonality. It was based on the "worlding" of Eastern Europe, or the sharing of the Eastern European historical experience of overcoming cultural dependence and economic exploitation with the whole (Third) world. In countries that embarked on a noncapitalist (but not necessarily socialist) path of development, architects from Eastern Europe worked within what Soviet economists called the "World Socialist System," or a framework of global trade that was formulated by socialist countries in response to the bifurcations of socialisms during the 1960s. In so doing, these actors took advantage of the differences between the political economy of foreign trade in state socialism and the emerging, Western-dominated international market of design and construction services as the case study of Iraq shows (1958–90). The focus on Kuwait and the UAE (1979–90) allows us to retrace the integration of some actors from socialist countries into this increasingly globalized market. This integration, which I call "socialist globalization," was based on the previous experience of two decades of collaboration with Arab clients within the networks of socialist internationalism.

The socialist model of development, the worlding of Eastern Europe, the world socialist system, and socialist globalization were four historically specific instances of socialist worldmaking that both informed and were informed by the mobilities of architecture from socialist Eastern Europe. Before summarizing the ways in which the dynamics of worldmaking were articulated in these four case studies, I will contextualize them by means of a broad overview of their political economies, the geographic distribution, and the protagonists who mobilized architecture from Eastern Europe.

Motivations and Geographies

Preceded by Soviet technical assistance to the People's Republic of China and elsewhere in Central and Southeast Asia, the presence of architects, planners, and contractors from socialist countries in West and North Africa and the Middle East followed decolonization and nationalist revolutions in these regions, as well as the Soviet opening to the Third World after the death of Stalin. This opening was welcomed by the first generation of leaders in independent African and Asian countries, who were wary of the United States, an ally of former colonial powers that had assigned the Global South an unfavorable position within the world market.[14] These leaders were often intrigued by Soviet modernization programs. In spite of the similarities with, reflections of, and mutual borrowings from Western modernization theories and practice, the Soviet model of development distinguished itself by its emphasis on state-centered industrialization and justice-oriented welfare distribution within the framework of a command economy.[15]

However, collaboration with the USSR and other socialist countries was also attractive to those African and Asian governments that did not follow the socialist model of development. Besides military and geopolitical concerns shared with the USSR, governments of many developing countries appreciated the favorable terms on which the socialist countries offered their technology, goods, and services. By the 1970s socialist countries increasingly abandoned trade policies based on anti-imperialist solidarity and saw the Global South as a reservoir of raw materials and mobile labor.[16] Yet governments of several Asian and African countries continued to welcome Eastern Europeans as a means to stimulate economic competition between foreign investors. Another incentive to work with Eastern Europe were the notorious shortages in the professional workforce in West Africa and the Middle East that the socialist countries offered to fill.

The incentives for West African and Middle Eastern actors to collaborate with socialist countries were matched by a set of ideological aims, geopolitical objectives, and economic and industrial policy interests of the USSR and its satellites.[17] The shifts in foreign and economic policies were largely reflected in the trajectories of architectural transfers and their volumes, from a few, highly visible buildings donated by the Soviets under Nikita Khrushchev to a much more numerous production bartered by Soviet satellites according to the principle of "mutual advantage" under Leonid Brezhnev, even if the latter perpetuated the ambiguous relationship between aid and trade that characterized Khrushchev's "buildings-gifts." Geopolitical objectives and economic pressures in particular countries often differentiated the periodization of their architectural engagements abroad. For instance, assistance granted during the 1960s to developing countries by East Germany (GDR) in an attempt at subverting West Germany's Hallstein Doctrine was followed by the GDR's more economically oriented export policies in the following decade, when this doctrine was gradually abandoned.

In particular, the oil embargo of 1973 was a game changer, as the profits of Arab governments deposited in Western financial institutions were lent to socialist countries intent on modernizing their economies and financing their models of consumer societies. Yet the industrial leap that would have allowed them to pay back their debt never materialized, and Hungary, Poland, Bulgaria, and other socialist countries responded by boosting their exports in other areas, including design and construction.[18] For architects, planners, and managers of construction companies from non-Soviet socialist countries, this "kiss of debt" meant greater pressure from state leaderships to secure convertible currency that made them highly accommodating to the demands of their Middle Eastern and North African clients and led to a surge of their engagements in these regions. By contrast, export of design services did not play a comparable role in the foreign trade of the Soviets, who were able from the 1960s onward to obtain convertible currency by exporting fossil fuels to Western Europe.[19] There is also archival evidence showing that at least some governments (such as Libya) were wary of Soviet influence and preferred to trade with other Eastern European countries (such as Romania).

With these shifts in geography and in the motivations underlying architectural mobilities, the relationships between the architectures produced and the socialist project likewise changed. For instance, Soviet designs of two housing neighborhoods in Ghana were intended to be instrumental for the socialist modernization of the country.[20] Within a general vision of egalitarian welfare distribution, these neighborhoods featured nurseries, kindergartens, and canteens preparing precooked food, with the explicit aim of releasing women from domestic work and allowing their entrance into wage labor. The construction of these (unrealized) neighborhoods would have required a fundamental change in the Ghanaian construction industry to bring it in line with the Soviet model. Architecture under Nkrumah was also promoted in the Ghanaian mass media as a signifier of what a socialist everyday life could mean, thus staking out a field of debate that was relevant and meaningful for actors on the ground. However, West African and Middle Eastern architects, state authorities, intellectuals, and journalists also proposed other meanings for this architecture, including national identity and cultural emancipation. By the final decades of the Cold War, such readings had been embraced by Eastern European actors in Nigeria, Iraq, and the Gulf, and they often omitted any reference to socialism.

In contrast to these changing readings of architecture coproduced by Eastern Europeans, West Africans, and Middle Easterners, this production was consistently conditioned by the political economy of state socialism. All four case studies show that this political economy—governed by such principles as state monopoly on foreign trade, barter transactions, and the inconvertibility of Eastern European currencies—offered opportunities for and imposed constraints on the employment of distinct design procedures, research approaches, construction technologies, and construction materials. For example, barter agreements resulted in the Romanian practice of redrawing plans provided by the commissioners in African and Asian oil-producing countries to maximize the use of construction materials, technologies, and labor, which Romania bartered for crude oil. Another example may be found in the minutes of the negotiations regarding the contract for Baghdad's master plans by Poland's Miastoprojekt (1967, 1973). These minutes show how Polish negotiators exploited the inconvertibility of the Polish currency to offer a larger and more comprehensive team than their Western competitors could match. This team, working closely with the municipality of Baghdad, produced a plan that was survey-based, interdisciplinary, and collaborative. While there was nothing intrinsically anticapitalist about these features, they contrasted with the work of other actors on the ground, including the previous, British-delivered master plan of Baghdad (1956).[21]

Vessels of Architectural Resources

Three principal types of actors were mobilized as vessels of architectural resources from socialist countries. Besides large, state design institutes, they included state contractors offering design-and-build services and individual professionals directly hired by institutions abroad. All three answered to and collaborated with a wide network of other institutions in Eastern Europe, including ministries in charge of foreign trade, foreign affairs, construction, and others; Communist parties and their dependent organizations; foreign trade organizations (FTOs); research, training, and scientific institutions; trade unions; youth, women, and other mass organizations; producers of construction materials, equipment, and machinery; and cultural and sport organizations.[22]

As a result of the state monopoly on foreign trade in socialism, the activities of individual and institutional actors were mediated by FTOs; by the end of the Cold War, as attempts at "market socialism" were made in Hungary, Yugoslavia, and elsewhere, several contractors had obtained prerogatives previously reserved for FTOs. They sometimes recruited experts from the industry and from scientific institutes, including newly emerging research centers specializing in "tropical architecture" and planning in developing countries, such as the International Postgraduate Course of Urban and Regional Planning for Developing Countries in Szczecin (Poland) and the Institute of Tropical Architecture in Gdańsk (Poland). Research in tropical construction was carried out also at the Architecture and Civil Engineering University in Weimar (GDR) and at the Patrice Lumumba Peoples' Friendship University in Moscow. The capacity to recruit scholars from institutions such as these and, occasionally, their African and Asian graduates who had studied on scholarships granted by Eastern European governments, was presented to developing countries as a major advantage of a socialist planned economy.[23]

State design institutes that were closely monitored by, and sometimes directly connected to, particular ministries played the central role in delivering planning documentation and architectural designs to foreign countries. Many of them were in charge of large-scale projects, and so the Soviet Union's Gorstroiproekt (Institute for Town Construction Projects) and its predecessors and cooperators were responsible for master plans of cities in Cuba (Havana, 1960s), Mongolia (Ulaanbaatar, 1954, 1963, 1971), Afghanistan (Kabul, 1964), and Iran (Fuladshahr, 1968), as well as city districts elsewhere.[24] Planning offices from other socialist countries delivered master plans for Conakry (Zagreb Urban Planning Institute, 1963), the Tripolitania region in Libya and its individual cities

(Wadeco from Poland, 1983), and Tunisia's tourist development (Czechoslovak Institute of Regional Planning, 1966), among many others.[25] The projects delivered abroad reflected the particular specializations of architectural institutions, with Soviet Giproniizdrav, Giprovuz, and Giprostroiindustriia responsible for hospitals, university buildings, and prefabricated housing respectively. Yet from the 1970s, design institutes would often extend their areas of responsibility when working abroad; for example, the commissions of Hungary's Design Institute for Public Buildings (Közti) in Arab countries included not only medical, educational, and sports facilities but also housing neighborhoods.[26]

Most architectural exports from socialist countries were conveyed by two other types of actors. First, they included contractors who offered both design and construction services combined in one package. These companies had often been established during the postwar reconstruction period and put in charge of large-scale industrial works and civil engineering infrastructure; such tasks also dominated their export activities. This genealogy was sometimes reflected in their names. Consider, for example, Energoprojekt (EP) of Yugoslavia (Serbia), created in 1951 to provide design and consultancy services within hydro- and thermal power generation and water management. Other companies included Yugoslavia's Ivan Milutinović (PIM) and RAD from Serbia as well as Ingra from Croatia and Beton from Macedonia; Bulgaria's Technoexportstroy (TES); and Arcom and Romproiect from Romania. The design-and-build procedure that they offered had been often favored by West and North African and Middle Eastern governments, and it resulted in such highly visible projects as the National Arts Theatre (Stefan Kolchev for TES, 1977) and the International Trade Fair (Zoran Bojović for EP, 1977) both in Lagos, Nigeria; as well as the Sudanese parliament building in Khartoum (Cezar Lăzărescu and for the Design Institute Carpaţi, 1972–78).[27] Sometimes, commissions abroad for these actors were restricted to design tasks (Administration Center Hamma designed in Algiers by TES's Dimitar Bogdanov, 1987) or to construction (Ministries Complex built in Kuwait City by EP, 1981). In design-and-build commissions, EP, TES, and Romproiect lowered their costs by employing workers from their home countries and by producing building materials and components in factories set up near construction sites or in regional bases in North and West Africa and the Middle East.

The second type of actor common in many non-Soviet countries were individual professionals, directly employed by planning institutions, universities, authorities, and sometimes private offices in developing countries. For example, in the 1970s Polish planners and sociologists were hired by Comedor (Comité permanent d'études, de développement, d'organisation et d'aménagement de l'agglomération d'Alger), the body responsible for the master planning of Algiers.[28] Around the same time, a group of Romanian architects employed in Algeria as designers and educators at the University of Constantine shaped its architectural program according to the curriculum of the Ion Mincu University of Architecture in Bucharest. Such contracts with individual architects typically involved four signatories: the professionals in question, their home employer, their prospective employer abroad, and an FTO from the professionals' home country specialized in the export of labor (for instance, Limex in GDR, Polservice in Poland, Romconsult in Romania, or Polytechna in Czechoslovakia).

The motivations of Eastern Europeans for securing a contract abroad included professional ambition and the opportunity to practice architecture unhampered by the constraints imposed by party bureaucrats and state construction companies. The chance to travel, rare in most socialist countries, and to earn more than at home, were important incentives too. Professionals circulating in state-socialist networks sometimes branched out to other ones, including those of the United Nations, another mobilizer of architectural expertise from Eastern Europe.[29] For example, Croatian planner Vladimir Antolić was responsible for urban plans in Burma, Indonesia, and Malaysia as a UN expert (1953–63);[30] and among the collaborators of UN-Habitat was Soviet planner Anatolii Nikolaevich Rimsha, the codesigner of the Kabul master plan and professor at Patrice Lumumba University.[31]

Eastern European architects and planners working abroad for public institutions would have only a handful of colleagues from the West. Even when Western professionals sought opportunities in oil-producing countries in North Africa and the Middle East (which boomed after the 1973 embargo in difference to the economic crisis in Western Europe and the United States), they were typically operating from their headquarters, with brief local visits. By contrast, the lower fees requested by Eastern European FTOs allowed high-profile architects and planners from socialist countries longer periods of deployment, either in a branch office or in local institutions.[32] Whatever dissatisfaction this practice may have created among these professionals, it also facilitated design methodologies that engaged closely with the conditions on the ground, as in the case of extensive land-use surveys prepared for the master plans of Baghdad by Miastoprojekt or lightweight prefabricated systems fine-tuned by Miastoprojekt for the Iraqi construction industry.[33]

The focus on these actors shows the many forms assumed by architectural labor abroad. It was a fungible resource, whose export from Eastern Europe was defined by political-economic concerns; a technological expertise whose transfers were informed by concerns about stabilization and the reproduction of the expected performance; and a cultural competence translated into new contexts.[34] Each of these modalities of export, transfer, and translation applied to many, but not necessarily all, instances of architectural labor, and what could not be exported might well be translated. But this labor was also a lived, everyday experience from within which new collective subjectivities emerged and global visions of solidarity were tested, and, on occasion, challenged.

By studying the many forms assumed by architectural labor, this research takes its cue from architectural and planning history, global history, comparative urban studies, and science and technology studies. At the same time, the account of the various modalities of this labor (design, administration, supervision, research, and education) leads to a broader understanding of architecture beyond its manifestation in individual buildings. It brings to the fore actors that have largely been ignored by architectural historians, such as municipal planning institutions in Africa and Asia and foreign trade organizations from Eastern Europe. Such a reading of Eastern European architecture does not privilege "Central Europe" (Germany and the post-Habsburg space), which has been the focus of most architectural histories of the region. Rather, it pays attention to countries less discussed and yet deeply involved in urbanization processes in North Africa and the Middle East, such as Bulgaria and Romania.

Specialization, Cooperation, and Competition

During their work in West and North Africa and the Middle East, actors from socialist countries contributed to programs of industrialization and welfare distribution pursued by postindependence governments, with typical tasks including industrial plants, housing, and medical, educational, sports, and cultural facilities. These programs were sometimes explained by government officials in terms of socialist modernization (more often than not qualified as "African" or "Arab" socialism), and actors from Eastern Europe in charge of these projects drew on their experience of postwar, state-led reconstruction and development. At the same time, they were eager to argue the specificity of their national experience and competence, with Bulgarians promoting their tourist architecture at the Black Sea, Poles showcasing the reconstruction of Warsaw, and East Germans drawing attention to the merits of the "complex" (i.e., comprehensive) system of industrialized construction in the GDR.

These aspirations did not always coincide with attempts at specialization promoted by the Council of Mutual Economic Assistance (Comecon), which aimed at a "socialist international division of labor" as the basis of intersocialist economic integration.[35] Remits from Comecon agreements were sometimes extended to export activities, with Polish sugar plants built not only in member states but also around the Mediterranean and elsewhere; and Comecon's Permanent Commission for Construction coordinated technical assistance in architecture and construction to Comecon's least developed members, such as Mongolia.[36] However, there is little evidence of coordination among Comecon countries in commercial commissions in the Middle East and North Africa. Rather, by the 1970s many non-Soviet design institutes and state contractors found themselves competing against each other in open tenders organized by local governments, often setting aside their original institutional remits.

This does not mean that specific experiences of Eastern European architecture, planning, and construction were irrelevant to engagements abroad. Yet, rather than ready-made and available for export, these experiences need to be seen as actualized and reshaped when mobilized abroad. For instance, so-called type designs—designs constructed in various locations with small, if any, modifications—were privileged in export from socialist countries, above all from Romania. This was the case not only because these designs had dominated the country's architectural practice since the Second World War, but also because they proved to be a useful tool to coordinate the production of Romanian construction materials applied in buildings bartered for crude oil. The actors from the South were often decisive in shaping patterns of division of labor among Eastern European countries, for example, by soliciting engagement in a specific industry or by requesting that the scholarships offered to their students by a particular socialist country were assigned to a specific discipline.

Socialist Networks and Global Urbanization

The embedded character of the labor of architects from socialist countries means that their work needs to be understood from within their competition and collaboration with various local partners and with actors circulating in other networks. They included regional networks (for instance of Egyptian and Palestinian professionals in Cold War Middle East); those of other socialist countries; western European and North American; and emerging new actors (for instance, South and Southeast Asian contractors in the 1970s and 1980s Gulf). The need to account for these interactions in the framework of this research project resulted in a wide-ranging investigation conducted in public and private archives in West Africa, the Middle East, and Eastern Europe, as well as in the United Kingdom and the United States. The variety of engagements of architects from socialist countries abroad meant an extension of the investigation beyond architectural archives and toward, for instance, systematic enquiries into full runs of local newspapers, while the lived character of architectural labor came to the fore in semistructured interviews with actors in Eastern Europe and elsewhere. The four case studies summarized in what follows are based on this wide range of sources. They not only present a comparative perspective on the work of actors from various socialist countries but also offer glimpses into urbanization processes in Accra, Lagos, Baghdad, Abu Dhabi, and Kuwait, thus contributing to their respective urban histories.

The first case study, focused on Ghana under Kwame Nkrumah, argues that the claim to global applicability of the socialist model of development was

Fig. 7.1. Flagstaff House housing project, Accra, 1964. (GNCC, Vic Adegbite [chief architect], Charles Polónyi [project architect]. Photo by Łukasz Stanek, 2012.)

predicated on its adaptation to conditions outside the USSR, and that architecture, planning, and construction technology played a key role in this adaptation.[37] The reading of two Soviet large-scale housing designs in the cities of Accra and Tema shows how Soviet housing typologies, urban layouts, and prefabrication technologies were adapted to the climatic, social, and economic conditions of West Africa within the overarching attempt to industrialize Ghanaian construction. These projects, though never built, became a precedent for the mobility of Soviet architecture, planning, and construction to tropical regions around the world.

However, the Soviet Union did not dominate architectural production in Nkrumah's Ghana. Rather, the organization in charge of much of this production was the Ghana National Construction Corporation (GNCC), a state agency that was responsible for building and infrastructural programs. Besides being the local partner for the Soviet organizations, the majority of GNCC architects came from non-Soviet socialist countries, including Bulgaria, Hungary, Poland, and Yugoslavia. In this sense, while the work of the Soviets in Ghana was an instance of socialist multilateralism, in which nation-state organizations were the primary entity in architectural engagements, the GNCC may be viewed as an instance of socialist cosmopolitanism, an experience of an entangled transnational collaboration of Ghanaian actors with architects from various socialist countries.[38]

The argument that the transfer of the socialist model of development did not exhaust the international engagements of architects, planners, and contractors from socialist countries is reinforced in the second case study. It focuses on Nigeria, a country whose anglophile elite did not follow the path of socialist modernization. The presence of Eastern Europeans in Nigeria during the 1960s and 1970s arose out of an attempt by the federal government to diversify the set of foreign actors working in the country. Socialist states accepted the invitation, since they were eager to benefit from Nigeria's oil boom.[39]

Accordingly, rather than referring to a socialist model of development, Eastern European architects and planners who found themselves in Nigerian cities such as Lagos, Calabar, Zaria, and Jos, sought out ways of making sense of the tasks at hand. In particular, these architects pointed to analogies between the historical experiences of Eastern Europe and West Africa during the "long" nineteenth century. The argument that in both regions foreign domination by external empires resulted in economic backwardness and cultural dependency was part of state-socialist domestic propaganda and foreign diplomacy. But the protagonists of this case study referred to longer traditions of Eastern European architectural culture as useful precedents for confronting the tasks of economic modernization and cultural emancipation in Nigeria. Inspired by recent studies of the ways in which Africans deploy the city as a resource for operating at the level of the world, and how Asian cities reinvent urban norms that can count as "global," I call this practice the "worlding" of Eastern Europe.[40]

Such worlding informed the Nigerian work of a number of architects and planners from socialist countries. For example, study of the master plan of the city of Calabar (1969), delivered by a Hungarian team led by architect Charles Polónyi, shows how the latter drew on his earlier experience of architecture and regional planning in rural areas of postwar Hungary, which he saw as "not very far from what we later called a Developing Country."[41] Rural territories were also a preoccupation of Polish architect and scholar Zbigniew Dmochowski who studied vernacular building cultures in Nigeria by implementing drawing and survey techniques from prewar Poland to pave the way toward a "modern school of Nigerian architecture."[42] Finally, the Yugoslav designers and builders of the International Trade Fair in Lagos by Energoprojekt (1977) embraced the peripheral position shared by Eastern Europe and West Africa as an opportunity to work across multiple worlds and to mobilize resources from various centers. While showing how the protagonists of this case study employed historical analogies between Eastern Europe and West Africa, their work also reveals the limits to these analogies, not least Eastern Europeans' own colonial fantasies and practices of "internal colonization."

The openings and blockages inherent in socialist foreign trade are the focus of the third case study. It addresses the urbanization of Baghdad within the world

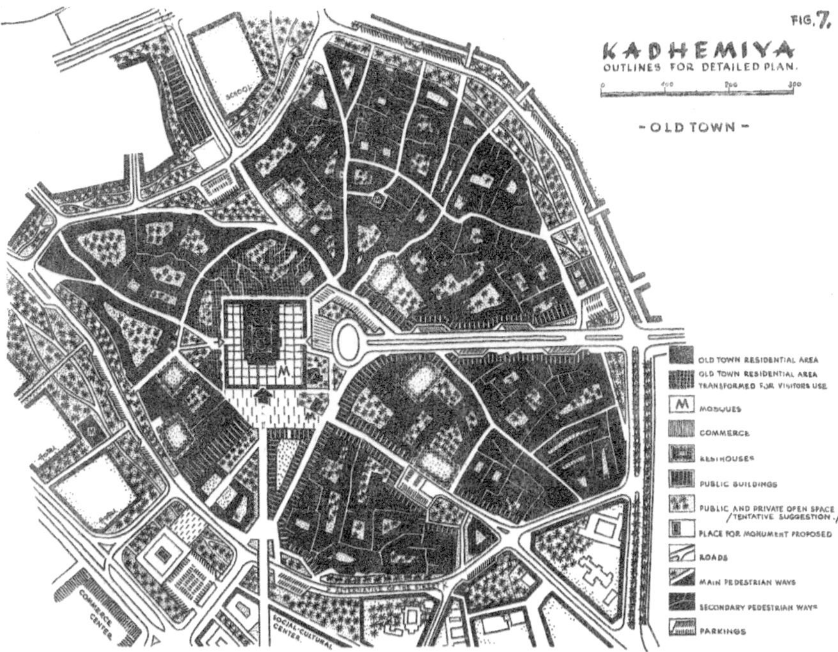

Fig. 7.2. "Kadhemiyah Old Town," 1967. (Miastoprojekt-Kraków, "Kadhemiyah Central District. Outlines for Detailed Plan. Short Report," 1967. Private archive of Kazimierz Bajer, Kraków, Poland.)

socialist system. The core of the system was the Comecon, but the system also included affiliated countries, among them Iraq (since 1975). This case study shows how architects, planners, and contractors from Comecon countries advanced their work in Baghdad by instrumentalizing the differences between the emerging global market of design and construction services and the political economy of state socialism.

This political economy defined the conditions of labor for actors from socialist countries on the ground, and, in turn, it facilitated the technopolitics of their work in Iraq.[43] These dynamics can be seen as the master plans of Baghdad delivered by Miastoprojekt and its General Housing Programme for Iraq (1976–80); housing neighborhoods by Romania's Arcom and Romproiect; infrastructure in Iraqi cities by Bulgarian, East German, and Soviet design institutes; public buildings by Yugoslav firms; and teaching curricula at the Department of Architecture in Baghdad to which architects from Czechoslovakia contributed.[44] The focus on collaboration and competition between actors from socialist countries in Iraq shows that their specific profiles resulted from path dependencies forged by economic instruments and political bargaining with their Iraqi counterparts.

Fig. 7.3. Main bus terminal, Abu Dhabi, 1980–91. (Bulgarproject, Kuno Dundakov, Stanka Dundakova [project architects]. Photo by Łukasz Stanek, 2015.)

The final case study starts with one of the most prominent buildings in Abu Dhabi (UAE): the Municipality and Town Planning Department. Designed by Bulgaria's TES, it was constructed in 1985 by an Abu Dhabi–based contractor and a number of subcontractors from the region and elsewhere. This building, as well as others delivered by Eastern Europeans in the UAE and Kuwait during the last decade of the Cold War, differs from those discussed above. It did not result from intergovernmental agreements but from increasingly adamant attempts by state-socialist companies to enter foreign markets. In so doing, their managers left aside references to socialist internationalism and introduced themselves to prospective clients as carriers of technological expertise on a par with their Western competitors. Furthermore, the Abu Dhabi building broke with the tradition of modern architecture that characterized the foreign work of architects from socialist countries in the previous decades. Instead, it reflected the requirement of "Arab-Islamic culture," formalized in the UAE and Kuwait by the late 1970s in response to the disenchantment with post-oil urbanization in the Gulf.

Such a combination of technological and cultural expertise was the precondition of the integration of Eastern European architects and contractors into the Western-dominated and increasingly globalized market of design and construction services in the Gulf.[45] This double expertise had been acquired by Eastern Europeans during their engagements in North Africa and the Middle East since

Fig. 7.4. Site C, Sabah Al-Salem, Kuwait, 1982. (Shiber Consult and INCO, Andrzej Bohdanowicz, Wojciech Jarząbek, Krzysztof Wiśniowski [project architects]. Photo by Łukasz Stanek, 2014.)

the 1960s. In the course of their work abroad, they had learned to comply with Western building norms, specification standards, financial regimes, technological systems, and construction management procedures; but they also became acquainted with the aesthetic and cultural proclivities of governmental clients in Arab countries. In so doing, they became agents of "socialist globalization," understood not as an autarkic system but as an integration into the Western-dominated global economic order.[46] With the Gulf becoming one of the paradigmatic places of architecture's globalization since the end of the twentieth century, this case study rewrites the genealogy of these processes by situating them within a longer history of socialist projects of worldwide solidarity.[47]

Globalization by Weak Actors

The focus on Accra, Lagos, Baghdad, Abu Dhabi, and Kuwait City shows how architects, planners, and contractors from Eastern Europe, West Africa, and the

Middle East practiced worldmaking. While studies of architectural transfers during the Cold War have typically been informed by the metaphor of a curtain, either iron or nylon, the conceptual framework of worldmaking offers a different image.[48] In this study, the Cold War appears as a clockwork mechanism in which the cogs of the antagonistic visions of global cooperation sometimes crash and grind and sometimes complement each other to a mutually productive effect.[49]

What was produced was urbanization, and the results of these engagements continue to condition urbanization processes around the world. In West and North Africa and the Middle East, they include buildings and infrastructures, some of which have become a symbolically charged heritage of the decolonization processes. But they also include urban planning documents, building legislation, and teaching curricula still used by administrators, designers, contractors, and educators. Architectural mobilities affected urbanization in postsocialist Europe too. In particular, by the end of the Cold War, working abroad was a genuine learning experience for architects from stagnating Eastern European countries. The knowledge of modern building materials, technologies, functional programs, and construction management provided individual and institutional actors returning to Eastern Europe after 1989 with a competitive advantage, and so too did their familiarity with the architectural idiom of postmodernism, embraced by clients and the public after socialism.[50]

This persisting entanglement of urbanization processes in West and North Africa, the Middle East, and Eastern Europe concerns also the persisting entanglement of their actors. When entering postsocialist countries, Western contractors sometimes reactivated their links with Eastern European architects and enterprises with whom they had worked in the Middle East and North Africa, while Middle Eastern developers invest in Eastern Europe, and Eastern European firms continue to operate in Middle Eastern and North African countries. These firms, now privatized, include EP, Wadeco, and TES; the latter typically works on middle-size contracts, while smaller contracts are operated by local firms, and larger ones are granted to Western companies. Eastern European architects who stayed in the Gulf after 1989 often occupy a similar middle ground on the labor market, expressed in the range of their salaries which are typically related to the passport of the employee.

The agency of these actors has been covered neither by architectural studies of star architects and "global" offices, nor by ethnographies of migrant workers and "inhabitants"—just as professionals and firms from North Africa, the Middle East, and South Asia have been largely invisible to the scholarship on architectural globalization in spite of the key roles they have played in the urbanization of the Gulf and elsewhere. In the case of Eastern Europeans, their specific place in these processes has been path-dependent on their original placements by means of state-socialist networks during the Cold War. This placement concerned both institutional entrance points, in public or private offices, but also the "weak" bargaining position of non-Soviet actors. As this research shows, such a weak position was typically shared by a state-socialist company under pressure to fulfill the compulsory "convertible currency plan" and by individual architects employed by a local planning agency for whom a dismissal would inhibit career prospects and deprive them of the opportunities that went with contracts abroad.[51] This "weakness" was structural and hence independent of the personalities and abilities of the individuals involved, including such exceptionally skilled designers as Dimitar Bogdanov of TES or Zoran Bojović of EP. Yet it was precisely this "weakness" and its corollaries, such as flexibility and adaptability, that made these actors highly instrumental, and sometimes indispensable, within development road maps of local administrators, planners, and decision makers. This instrumentality resulted in an impact on urbanization processes around the world often far greater than that of powerful centers of the Cold War, thus constituting one of the most relevant legacies of twentieth-century socialism's global visions.

Notes

1. This project was launched in 2009 at the Institute of History and Theory of Architecture (GTA), Swiss Federal Institute of Technology in Zurich (ETH), and since then developed with the support of the Museum of Modern Art in Warsaw, the Center for Advanced Study in the Visual Arts (CASVA), National Gallery of Art in Washington, DC, and the Manchester Architecture Research Centre (MARC), University of Manchester. The results of this research will be presented in Łukasz Stanek, *Architecture in Global Socialism: Eastern Europe, West Africa, and the Middle East in the Cold War* (Princeton, NJ: Princeton University Press, forthcoming in 2020). For collected volumes on this theme, see Łukasz Stanek and Tom Avermaete, eds., "Cold War Transfer: Architecture and Planning from Socialist Countries in the 'Third World,'" *The Journal of Architecture* (London) 17, no. 3 (2012); Łukasz Stanek, ed., "Socialist Networks and the Internationalization of Building Culture after 1945," *ABE Journal* 6 (2014), published online on January 30, 2015, https://journals.openedition.org/abe/1266.

2. For a critique of the diffusionist model, see Jane M. Jacobs, "A Geography of Big Things," *Cultural Geographies* 13, no. 1 (2006): 1–27.

3. Ryszard Kapuściński, *Heban* (Warsaw: Czytelnik, 1998), 138.

4. See, for instance, Patsy Healey and Robert Upton, eds., *Crossing Borders: International Exchange and Planning Practices* (London: Routledge, 2010); Jeffrey W. Cody, *Exporting American Architecture, 1870–2000* (New York: Routledge, 2003); Donald McNeill, *The Global Architect: Firms, Fame and Urban Form* (New York: Routledge, 2009); for overview, see Stanek, "Socialist Networks."

5. McNeill, *Global Architect*, 1.

6. Harald Möller, *DDR und Dritte Welt: Die Beziehungen der DDR mit Entwicklungsländern, ein neues theoretisches Konzept, dargestellt anhand der Beispiele China und Äthiopien sowie Irak/ Iran* (Berlin: Köster, 2004), 4.

7. According to the US-based Engineering News Report (ENR), see "Energoprojekt, 60 Years of Success," (Belgrade: Energoprojekt, 2011), 32, 38.

8. "Sovetskaia arkhitektura za rubezhom," *Arkhitektura SSSR* 6 (1984): 109; Cole Roskam, "Non-Aligned Architecture: China's Designs on and in Ghana and Guinea, 1955–92," *Architectural History* 58 (2015): 261–291; Guanghui Ding and Charlie Q. L. Xue, "China's Architectural Aid: Exporting a Transformational Modernism," *Habitat International* 47 (2015): 136–147; Urbanistički institut, "Conakry: Plan directeur d'urbanisme" (Zagreb, 1963).

9. Ragna Boden, "Cold War Economics: Soviet Aid to Indonesia," *Journal of Cold War Studies* 10, no. 3 (2008): 110–128.

10. Henri Lefebvre, "The Worldwide Experience" (1978), in *State, Space, World: Selected Essays*, eds. Neil Brenner and Stuart Elden (Minneapolis: University of Minnesota Press, 2009), 274–289. Łukasz Stanek, *Henri Lefebvre on Space: Architecture, Urban Research, and the Production of Theory* (Minneapolis: University of Minnesota Press, 2011).

11. Édouard Glissant, *Poetics of Relation* (Ann Arbor MI: University of Michigan Press, 1997).

12. Stuart Elden, "*Mondialisation* before Globalisation: Lefebvre and Axelos," in *Space, Difference, Everyday Life: Reading Henri Lefebvre*, eds. Kanishka Goonewardena, Stefan Kipfer, Richard Milgrom, and Christian Schmid (New York: Routledge, 2008), 80–93.

13. Silvio Pons, *The Global Revolution: A History of International Communism 1917–1991* (Oxford: Oxford University Press, 2014).

14. Odd Arne Westad, *The Global Cold War: Third World Interventions and the Making of Our Times* (Cambridge: Cambridge University Press, 2005).

15. David Engerman, "The Second World's Third World," *Kritika: Explorations in Russian and Eurasian History* 12, no. 1 (2011): 183–212.

16. James Mark and Quinn Slobodian, "Eastern Europe," in *The Oxford Handbook of the Ends of Empire*, eds. Martin Thomas and Andrew Thompson (2017), https://doi.org/10.1093/oxfordhb/9780198713197.013.20.

17. Martin Rudner, "East European Aid to Asian Developing Countries: The Legacy of the Communist Era," *Modern Asian Studies* 30, no. 1 (1996): 1–28.

18. Stephen Kotkin, "The Kiss of Debt: The East Bloc Goes Borrowing," in *The Shock of the Global: The 1970s in Perspective*, eds. Niall Ferguson, Charles S. Maier, Erez Manela, and Daniel S. Sargent (Cambridge, MA: Belknap Press of Harvard University Press, 2011), 80–93.

19. Andrey Kaftanov, "From International Architecture to Architectural Internationalism," *Project Russia* 16 (2000): 19–24; Oscar Sanchez-Sibony, *Red Globalization: The Political Economy of the Soviet Cold War from Stalin to Khrushchev* (Cambridge: Cambridge University Press, 2014).

20. Sergey Mazov, *A Distant Front in the Cold War: The USSR in West Africa and the Congo, 1956–1964* (Washington, DC: Woodrow Wilson Center Press, 2010).

21. Łukasz Stanek, "Miastoprojekt Goes Abroad: Transfer of Architectural Labor from Socialist Poland to Iraq (1958–1989)," *Journal of Architecture* 17, no. 3 (2012): 361–386.

22. Andreas Butter, "Showcase and Window to the World: East German Architecture Abroad 1949–1990," *Planning Perspectives* 33, no. 2 (2018): 249–269, https://www.tandfonline.com/doi/full/10.1080/02665433.2017.1348969.

23. L. Z. Zevin, *Economic Cooperation of Socialist and Developing Countries: New Trends* (Moscow: Nauka, 1976), 59.

24. Kaftanov, "From International Architecture."

25. Warsaw Development Consortium (Wadeco), no date, W. Piziorski Archive, Warsaw; Zagreb (Croatia), Urbanistički institut, "Conakry"; Oldřich Kolář and František Přikryl, "Rozvoj cestovního ruchu v Tunisku," *Architektura ČSSR* 5 (1967): 282–289.

26. András Ferkai, ed., *KÖZTI 66. Egy tervezőiroda története (1949–1991)* (Budapest: Vince Kiadó, 2015), 2 vols.

27. "35 godina arhitekture Energoprojekta," Energoprojekt Archive, Belgrade (Serbia); "Technoexportstroy," catalog, no date (1980s), Technoexportstroy Archive, Sofia (Bulgaria); "S.C. Romproiect S.A.," catalogue, no date (2000s), Romproiect Archive, Bucharest (Romania).

28. Jean-Jacques Deluz, *L'Urbanisme et l'architecture d'Alger* (Liège: P. Mardaga, Algiers: Office des publications universitaires, 1988); Bohdan Jałowiecki, *Procesy rozwoju społecznego współczesnej Algerii* (Warsaw: Państwowe Wydawictwo Naukowe, 1978).

29. Bogdan Wyporek, *Daleko od Warszawy: architekta zapiski z trzech kontynentów* (Warsaw: Akapit, 2009); Ulrich van der Heyden, Ilona Schleicher, and Hans-Georg Schleicher, eds., *Die DDR und Afrika. Zwischen Klassenkampf und neuem Denken* (Münster: Lit, 1993).

30. Mojca Smode Cvitanović and Marina Smokvina, "Hrvatski arhitekti i urbanisti u zemljama Trećega svijeta/ Croatian architects and urban planners in Third World countries," *Razvojna suradnja kroz nasljeđe Pokreta Nesvrstanih/ Development cooperation through the legacy of the nonaligned movement* (Zagreb: Croatian Platform for International Citizen Solidarity, 2015), 83–96.

31. Anatolii Nikolaevich Rimsha, *Gorod i zharkij klimat* (Moscow: Stroiizdat, 1975).

32. By contrast, industrial facilities from socialist countries were sometimes chosen by local authorities in spite of the fact that they were not the cheapest ones on offer. They were favored because Eastern European companies offered to train local staff and to use local resources. Technological compatibilities and path dependencies were another reason to choose Eastern European deliveries, which were often part of larger barter agreements.

33. Stanek, "Miastoprojekt."

34. On technology transfer in science and technology studies, see Andrew Barry, "Technological Zones," *European Journal of Social Theory* 9, no. 2 (2006): 239–253; for a bibliographical overview on cultural transfer, see Manuela Rossini and Michael Toggweiler, "Cultural Transfer: An Introduction," *Word and Text: A Journal of Literary Studies and Linguistics* 4, no. 2 (December 2014): 5–9.

35. Sara Lorenzini, "Comecon and the South in the Years of Détente: A Study on East–South Economic Relations," *European Review of History* 21, no. 2 (2014): 183–199.

36. Gerhard Kraft, *Die Zusammenarbeit der Mitgliedsländer des RWG auf dem Gebiet der Investitionen* (Berlin: Akademie-Verlag, 1977); "Einheitliche technische Bedingungen für die Projektierung von Betrieben und anderen Objekten, die in der Mongolischen Volksrepublik mit technischer Hilfe der Mitgliedsländer des RGW errichtet werden" (Berlin: Bauakademie der DDR, 1976).

37. Łukasz Stanek, "Architects from Socialist Countries in Ghana (1957–1967): Modern Architecture and Mondialisation," *Journal of the Society of Architectural Historians* 74, no. 4 (December 2015): 416–442.

38. For the distinction between socialist multilateralism and socialist cosmopolitanism, see Quinn Slobodian, "The Uses of Disorientation: Socialist Cosmopolitanism in an Unfinished DEFA-China Documentary," in *Comrades of Color: East Germany in the Cold War World*, ed. Quinn Slobodian (New York, Oxford: Berghahn Books, 2017), 222.

39. The military support obtained by the federal government from the Soviet Union and some of its satellites during the civil war (1967–70) was an important gate opener to Nigeria for several state-socialist contractors.

40. AbdouMaliq Simone, "On the Worlding of African Cities," *African Studies Review* 44, no. 2 (2001): 15–41; Aihwa Ong, "Worlding Cities, or the Art of Being Global," in *Worlding Cities: Asian Experiments and the Art of Being Global*, eds. Ananya Roy and Aihwa Ong (Chichester: Wiley-Blackwell, 2012), 1–26.

41. Charles Polónyi, *An Architect-Planner on the Peripheries: The Retrospective Diary of Charles K. Polónyi* (Budapest: Műszaki Könyvkiadó, 2000), 12.

42. Zbigniew Dmochowski, *An Introduction to Nigerian Traditional Architecture* (London: Ethnographica; Lagos: National Commission for Museums and Monuments, 1990), vol. 1, ix.

43. For the concept of technopolitics, see Gabrielle Hecht, ed., *Entangled Geographies: Empire and Technopolitics in the Global Cold War* (Cambridge, MA: MIT Press, 2011).

44. Stanek, "Miastoprojekt"; "Technoexportstroy," catalogue (n.d.), TES Archive, Sofia (Bulgaria); "S.C. Romproiect S.A.," catalogue (n.d.), Romproiect Archive, Bucharest (Romania); Života Perišić et al., *Građevinarstvo Srbije* (Belgrade: Ministarstvo građevina Srbije, 1997).

45. See also Stephen J. Collier and Aihwa Ong, "Global Assemblages, Anthropological Problems," in *Global Assemblages: Technology, Politics, and Ethics as Anthropological Problems*, eds. Ong and Collier (Malden, MA: Blackwell, 2005), 3–21; Barry, "Technological Zones."

46. Łukasz Stanek, *Postmodernism Is Almost All Right: Polish Architecture after Socialist Globalisation* (Warsaw: Fundacja Bęc-Zmiana, 2012).

47. Łukasz Stanek, "Mobilities of Architecture in the Global Cold War: From Socialist Poland to Kuwait and Back," *International Journal of Islamic Architecture* 4, no. 2 (2015): 365–398; Stanek, *Postmodernism*.

48. Ákos Moravánszky et al., eds., *East West Central: Re-building Europe 1950–1990* (Basel: Birkhäuser, 2017), 3 vols.

49. I owe this comment to a conversation with Quinn Slobodian, Hong Kong, March 2017.

50. Stanek, *Postmodernism*.

51. See also Dana Vais, "Exporting Hard Modernity: Construction Projects from Ceaușescu's Romania in the 'Third World,'" *Journal of Architecture* 17, no. 3 (2012): 438.

ŁUKASZ STANEK is Senior Lecturer at the Manchester School of Architecture, The University of Manchester, UK. He is author of *Henri Lefebvre on Space: Architecture, Urban Research, and the Production of Theory*

Part III

Cultural Encounters: Discovering Similarities, Defining Difference, Creating Identities

8 Writing the Soviet South into the History of the Cold War and Decolonization

Artemy M. Kalinovsky

In 1932 the African American poet Langston Hughes traveled through Soviet Central Asia. He had been in Moscow to work on a film project about the plight of black workers in the United States, but when that collapsed he decided, as he put it, to take a journey into the "Soviet South." Among the results of that trip was a pamphlet called "A Negro Looks at Soviet Central Asia," which positively assessed Soviet achievements in economic development and racial equality.[1] Hughes returned to the trip in his 1956 memoir, *I Wonder as I Wander.* By the mid-1950s, many communist fellow travelers had abandoned their earlier convictions, dismayed by the crimes of Stalinism. Hughes, however, used his memoir to expand on the reasons he had found what was happening in Central Asia attractive in the first place. At one point, Hughes, a deeply empathetic writer, reflects on his mixed emotions regarding a former Russian aristocrat assigned to help him after a bout of illness:

> Something hard and young in me could not help thinking, now had come the hour of those from the desert, who once had to work seven years for the beys in order to afford a wrinkled worn-out old wife that some richer man had first enjoyed, in the days when women were bought and sold like cattle. Today women are free, and men, too, for now has come the time of those who formerly had to till the overlord's vast acres in return for the use of just a little water to irrigate a single barren acre of their own. The overlords have fled, along with the Emirs, the Khans and the Tzarist officers. Now it is the turn of those who in former days had to beg of the Cossacks, "Please, master! No more lashes, please! White master, no more! Please!"[2]

Hughes's memoir appeared just as Joseph Stalin's crimes were becoming public knowledge, and the Soviet Union was once again engaging with the Third World. And while he shows awareness of Soviet repressions as well as some of the economic shortcomings of socialist development throughout, he insists on a more apologetic reading of the Soviet experiment in Central Asia. For Hughes,

Central Asia was a land that had been oppressed by its own rulers and then conquered by a European empire, but was now beginning to see radical progress, something that still seemed a long way off in his own South.

It was this kind of favorable reading that Soviet leaders counted on when they revived the idea of using Central Asia in the Global Cold War. From the early days of the Soviet state, it was understood that these republics would have an important role to play in the broader world revolution that would sweep through European empires. The Soviet reengagement with the Third World in the 1950s once again thrust these republics onto the front lines of Soviet foreign policy, with important consequences also for their domestic politics. The republics were meant to serve as showcases of Moscow's commitment to anticolonialism, demonstrating that the Soviet model had found a way to preserve "national" culture while bringing societies into technological modernity. In other words, Moscow's bid for leadership of the postcolonial world was premised on the notion that it could make people in these countries see the Soviet South as Hughes saw it in 1932.

Some fifteen years ago historian Mathew Connelly urged his colleagues to "take off the Cold War lens" when approaching the study of decolonization and the international history of US relations with the so-called Third World.[3] Connelly's point was that neither postcolonial elites nor US policy makers thought in explicitly Cold War terms when they engaged each other and that forcing their actions into Cold War frameworks would blind researchers to other dynamics at play. As we will see, however, the framework of Cold War competition was very much on the mind of Soviet policy makers when they began to engage the postcolonial world; moreover, it had an impact on how they related to their own periphery.[4] To neglect the nexus of the Cold War and decolonization in the history of Central Asia, then, would be to miss a central and transformative feature of the region's history; to ignore the region in the history of the Cold War would be to neglect a key aspect of Soviet engagement with the world in the latter half of the twentieth century.

This chapter will explore some of the ways we can write the history of the Soviet South, that is, the republics of Central Asia and the Caucasus, into the international history of the Cold War and decolonization. The leaders and intellectuals in these southern republics were in many ways similar to other (post) colonial elites—they thought of themselves as leaders in defining national culture and the putative transformation of their own societies, were integrated into professional and intellectual networks of the larger Soviet Union, and in most cases owed their professional status to a system that assigned them a peripheral status. There are thus a number of opportunities for comparison. However, because of the centrality of these republics (and their representatives) to Moscow's Third World policy, there is also an opportunity to consider how they affected each other. Presenting the history of the Soviet South in this way is not simply a question of shedding new light on a neglected area of study. Rather, it allows us to consider the histories of the Soviet Union, postcolonialism, and the Cold War in a new way. Looking outward from the Soviet periphery, we begin to appreciate how Soviet globalization ran not only through Moscow but also through Tashkent, Dushanbe, and Alma-ata (Almaty), and how the Soviet claim to lead the struggle against colonialism shaped politics in the region.[5] At the same time, the comparisons drawn by Central Asians and others from the Soviet "South" or "East" (the terms could be interchangeable, as we shall see), between their own lands and those of the so-called Third World were not always favorable—which in turn played an important role in political mobilization in the late Soviet era. Indeed, the Soviet strategy of instrumentalizing Central Asia for outreach to the postcolonial world ended up demonstrating the shortcomings of Soviet development projects in Central Asia and contributing to domestic resistance against the regime. It is therefore an apt example of how "dangerous" transnational and global projects can become for empires and hegemonic states as well as how profound an effect these projects can have for changing hegemonic regimes.

Central or Isolated?

As the Central Asia region was (re)incorporated into the Soviet Union through an often brutal civil war, two contradictory impulses seemed to guide Bolshevik policy. On the one hand, the idea that the colonies of the former Russian Empire could be used as a showcase to prove that the Soviet Union offered a radically new solution to the problem of imperialism and economic backwardness was frequently celebrated in propaganda. On the other hand, fears about local discontent and the ways this region might be used by British, German, or other potential Soviet enemies prompted Soviet officials to place the area "under lock and key," as one historian described the situation of the 1930s.[6] One could travel to Moscow or other Soviet centers, but (legal) travel beyond the USSR's borders became nearly impossible after the 1920s. Indeed, the Great Terror brought together Europeans and Central Asians in an unprecedented way. Thousands of forced laborers were brought in from across the USSR to take part in construction projects, and thousands of Central Asian victims of the Great Terror wasted in labor camps in Siberia.[7]

The 1930s were arguably the decade in which the anticolonial promise of the USSR hit its nadir. In a sense, forced collectivization and the forced mobilization of people for dangerous and often unfruitful projects of that decade only made the region more like the rest of the Soviet Union. Both Kazakhstan and Ukraine endured a famine; both the Vakhsh Valley and the Volga were sites of forced labor and personal tragedy as well as environmental destruction. If the 1920s had seen some genuinely anticolonial policies (such as the promotion of local cadres and the shifting of land from European settlers to locals), then the 1930s saw the elevation of Russian culture above other national cultures, European cadres replacing those swept up in different phases of the Great Terror, and the Russian language obtaining a primacy in administration and education it would not lose until the end of the Soviet period. The 1930s also set an economic pattern that remained at the heart of controversies concerning Central Asia's coloniality right up until the Soviet collapse, namely, the cotton complex. From the first Five-Year Plan onward, Uzbekistan, Tajikistan, and Turkmenistan, and to a lesser extent Kyrgyzstan and southern Kazakhstan, were assigned cotton production as their primary task, so that Soviet textile industries (located in European parts of the USSR) would not have to rely on exports. The cotton complex had many terrible side effects, from pollution caused by the excessive reliance on fertilizers to the widespread use of child labor, but it also made the region a commodity producer for the more developed parts of the union.

Yet even in the 1930s—the decade during which more open Soviet internationalism gave way to isolation and stricter cultural control—the region was still celebrated as a focal point in the broader connections between the Soviet Union and the wider proletarian world. Although the 1920s are seen as a decade of freedom and experimentation in the arts and the 1930s that of Stalinist bureaucracy bringing the arts under strict control, Katherine Clark reminds us that the latter decade, despite a creeping xenophobia and isolationism, witnessed the biggest push not only to engage with "universal" culture in literature, architecture, and other arts; but also to make Moscow (and by extension the Soviet Union) that culture's center. This bid for cultural leadership took place in the context of continued insecurity over Russia's culture advancement relative to that of Europe.[8] In the 1930s the Soviet Union invested heavily in developing local culture in the national republics, including those in Central Asia and the Caucasus, while simultaneously highlighting the global connections of these cultures. Moscow invested resources in regional opera, theater, ballet, and the novel, all of which were intended to fuse national forms and traditions with European (or universal) ones. These new "cultural achievements" were showcased in Moscow in ten-day festivals aimed at both domestic and foreign audiences. And while there was more than a hint of imperialism in attempts to bring in European forms such as opera (and in celebrating them as the pinnacle of cultural achievement), Moscow's investment in these cultural institutions and the vagueness of the new cultural concepts gave local musicians, composers, and writers an opportunity to pursue their own ambitions for cultural experimentation and renewal within the new Soviet context.[9]

Globalization and the Khrushchev Years

During the Cold War, Central Asia and the Caucasus held particular interest for certain Western scholars who saw in the region a potential for a resistance to Soviet communism that seemed to have been extinguished elsewhere in the USSR. Skeptical that the USSR could actually convince its people that it had found a way to shake off the colonial legacy of the Russian Empire, they thought that the peoples of the region would draw inspiration from the anticolonial struggle in places such as Algeria and eventually rise up against Moscow. Without much access to the region, such Western scholars obtained information from émigrés and from the Soviet press and on this basis created a kind of imaginary South. The most prominent representative of this school, Alexandre Bennigsen, was particularly drawn to the idea of a nationalism fused with religious feeling that could never accept Soviet communism for long.[10]

Where Western scholars saw a threat for Moscow, however, Soviet leaders saw an opportunity. Stalin had largely ignored the Third World, with the exception of an ill-fated attempt to separate off Iranian Azerbaijan after the Second World War (a venture spearheaded, incidentally, by party leaders in the Soviet Republic of Azerbaijan).[11] But Nikita Khrushchev, who had consolidated his power in the years after Stalin's death in 1953, was much more enthusiastic about the possibilities of Soviet engagement with countries in Asia, Africa, the Middle East, and even Latin America. Khrushchev and Nikolai Bulganin made their trip to India, Burma, and Afghanistan in 1955 and were inspired enough to commit the USSR to millions in economic aid. Yet the Bandung Conference earlier that same year had demonstrated that many of the postcolonial states were suspicious of the USSR's anti-imperialist credentials.[12]

In the years that followed Khrushchev's first trips, local politicians as well as Soviet specialists on international relations urged him to make use of the Central Asian example in reaching out to the Third World. Politicians who also had experience in journalism and scholarship, such as the Uzbek Sharof Rashidov and the Tajik Bobojon Gafurov, were particularly active in this regard. They argued that many Third World countries had extensive cultural links with the Central Asian republics, which could be exploited to strengthen connections with decolonizing states. In addition, the republics' material progress and the prominence of its intellectuals and party leaders could serve as proof that they represented a desirable vision for other postcolonial states and that the USSR would be their most reliable and trusted friend. Foreign policy professionals in Moscow echoed this view. In a lengthy memo circulated to Central Committee members, the prominent journalist and head of the State Committee on Cultural Ties with Foreign Countries Georgii Zhukov urged Soviet leaders to make better use of Central Asia and the Caucasus for propaganda purposes. Rather than allowing the imperialists to call themselves the "free world" in opposition to the USSR, the Soviet Union needed to demonstrate its own democracy at work, first in Central Asia and the Caucasus.[13] The people to carry out this propaganda work, Zhukov argued, were "wonderful [Central Asian and Caucasian] writers, economists, historians, philosophers, people who know Asia and Africa, speak and write in the languages of these countries."[14]

Soviet officials spoke about using their own "East" to reach out to the "foreign East" in discussing cultural diplomacy, but what did this mean in practice? The domestic East almost always meant Central Asia and the Caucasus,[15] and demographers and geographers often referred to the same region as the "South" to distinguish it from the western (European) USSR and the Siberian "east." The most obvious connections were between Uzbekistan and Tajikistan and South Asia—a shared Persianate literary culture, centuries of trade, circulating religious leaders, and the legacy of the Mughal Empire, which traced its origins to the region. All served to underline the links between these two republics and the modern states of Afghanistan, Pakistan, and India. In practice, politicians and cultural figures from the region were sent to many Muslim majority countries and beyond. The most important connection was the one noted by Langston Hughes—Central Asians had once been colonized but were now "free," and thus they could be held up as models for all of the oppressed peoples of the world.

Khrushchev quickly saw the importance of using the Russian Empire's former colonies in this struggle.[16] The only problem was that the promise of equality and development did not (yet) match the reality. As of 1955, when Khrushchev made his first whirlwind tour of India, Burma, and Afghanistan (which shared a border with three of the Central Asian republics), there were no Central Asians in the Presidium (as the Politburo, the highest decision-making body in the Communist Party) was known at the time) or even in the Central Committee, nor were there any in highly visible roles in international affairs. Economically, the region looked much more like a producer of primary commodities than a developed and equal economic partner in the union. Khrushchev's outreach to the postcolonial world would have important consequences for both situations. Khrushchev began to promote the "Sons of Muslims" (as he called them) to positions in the Presidium, the Central Committee, and other highly visible positions in the world of scholarship and foreign policy.[17] Some became diplomats, serving in countries such as Syria, Togo, South Yemen, and Mauritania. Others, like the Tajik poet Mirzo Tursunzade, played leading roles in, for example, the Committee for Solidarity with Countries of Asia and Africa, set up outside the formal foreign policy apparatus to strengthen ties with the postcolonial world and mobilize domestic support. Many more were expected to play host to foreign delegations that passed through Central Asia, which came to be a crucial part of the itinerary for visiting dignitaries from the Third World and for newly appointed ambassadors. Central Asians themselves became regular members of high-level delegations to Asia, Africa, and the Middle East.

Another way to strengthen those links was to develop scholarship on Central Asia, thereby accomplishing three distinct goals: to provide knowledge for policy makers to guide them in interstate relations, propaganda, and economic policy; to prove Soviet commitment to honoring and preserving the inheritance of the past in former colonial areas; and to highlight the long-term cultural connections between the Soviet South and the broader "East." Sharof Rashidov, an Uzbek writer and politician who accompanied Khrushchev on his first eastern trip, urged the Soviet leader to invest in the preservation of ancient mosques and madrassas in the region to prove to the world that the USSR respected and preserved its ancient heritage. Khrushchev appreciated and accepted the advice, later helping Rashidov become first secretary of the Communist Party of Uzbekistan. The Tajik politician and historian Bobojon Ghafurov took over the Institute of Oriental Studies in Moscow in 1956, transforming it in the following decades into a dynamic institution engaged with scholars all over the world. Institutes based in the republics were also expanded and given resources to contribute to this work. Study of the domestic and foreign Orient, with its attendant possibilities for travel and exchange and the publication of research in various languages, was considered one of the most successful examples of Soviet public diplomacy. As the Afghanistan specialist Iurii Gankovskii noted with satisfaction in 1972, "One could cite many examples that prove that the flowering of Oriental science (vostokovednaia nauka) in Tajikistan is attracting the sympathy of the foreign progressive intelligentsia in Iran, in Afghanistan, in India, in Pakistan, as well as in Arab countries, in Bangladesh, [arousing sympathy] towards those social, cultural, economic and political conditions that make such research possible [in the Soviet republics of Central Asia]."[18]

Scholarly exchanges were not limited to the field of Oriental studies, however. Economists, engineers, and public health specialists hosted their counterparts from around the world and went to conferences and lectures abroad, where they spoke of Soviet achievements from their position as specialists in a given area. Such exchanges were not just propaganda junkets, however. Whether they traveled to Eastern Europe, the capitalist world, or postcolonial states, Soviet specialists were expected to take note of practices in their field and offer suggestions for implementing these practices at home.

Mobilization for Soviet engagement with the foreign East *through* Central Asia was not limited to politicians and famous intellectuals. In the 1950s and 1960s, access to higher education expanded throughout the Soviet Union, but particularly in Central Asia. In Tajikistan, the first university was founded in 1948. A technical college was founded in 1956. In the context of the political and cultural thaw of the late 1950s and 1960s, both institutions hosted literary evenings and debates. Visiting politicians, writers, and scholars from India, Pakistan, and even farther came to address the student bodies.[19] Some students, especially those active in the Communist Youth Movement (Komsomol) were drawn in as translators or guides. Years later they remembered the exciting atmosphere of the meetings and the pride they felt in knowing that, as Soviet citizens, they were in the vanguard of the fight against anticolonialism.[20]

In the years that followed, as these students became specialists and went to work in various government organizations, they were often called on to lend their expertise abroad. As the Soviet Union expanded its aid and cooperation programs with postcolonial states such as Afghanistan and India, it tried to make use of agencies and specialists based in the Soviet South, for practical and propaganda reasons. Some of these specialists were sent as part of bilateral arrangements with Central Asian organizations or agencies, while others worked through the State Committee for Foreign Economic Relations (Gosudarstvennyi komitet po vneshnim ekonomicheskim sviaziam, GKĖS).[21] As Steffi Marung argues in this volume, it was thought that Central Asian agencies were particularly well placed to assist in fields such as irrigation or crop management, since they shared similar climatic conditions with the countries in which they went to work.

Even more important for Soviet public diplomacy was the fact that Central Asian specialists were living proof of Soviet achievements in development and were in a prime position to demonstrate the Soviet commitment to anticolonialism in economic, social, and cultural terms. A Tajik professor of education at a Soviet fair on education in Kabul was thus able to debate with visitors who doubted whether the USSR allowed for study in languages other than Russian, pointing to the number of Tajik language primary and secondary schools in his republic and the possibility of completing university study in one's native language.[22] An Uzbek irrigation engineer working in Afghanistan, meanwhile, was able to answer questions from members of the royal family about the preservation of historic monuments in Samarkand and Bukhara.[23] Successful cultural figures used their performances to underline the shared heritage of Soviet Central Asian culture and that of their host country, while at the same time showcasing achievements made under Soviet rule. Thus the actor Mahmud Vahidov, part of a delegation sent to Afghanistan in 1966, recited classic Persian poetry by Rudaki, Hofiz, and Jomi, along with contemporary Tajik poets such as Mirzo Tursunzoda and Loiq Sherali.[24]

Another way to bring the Soviet South into contact with the broader Third World was to organize literary and film festivals that positioned the USSR as the chief patron of non-Western art. Organizers of literary festivals could build on an obvious shared heritage. Cinema, too, provided opportunities, as each republic had its own film studios and somewhat distinct cinematic traditions. Whereas Soviet-Russian cinema was associated with established European and American conventions, cinema from Tajikistan, Uzbekistan, or Georgia could more easily be linked with established and emerging film cultures of Asia and Africa. As Rossen Djagalov and Masha Salazkina write in their study of the Tashkent Film Festival, first organized in 1968, "The agenda that united most participants,

Soviet cultural bureaucracies and Afro-Asian filmmakers alike, was the common sentiment that these cinemas suffered unfairly from their peripheral status vis-à-vis Western (Hollywood, but also west European) cinematic hegemony."[25] Such occasions also provided many opportunities for Soviets and visitors to meet informally, discuss and debate art, and form lasting connections.

Construction sites could also become sites of exchange, especially since, unlike scholarly meetings or cultural excursions, they presented an opportunity to develop and demonstrate solidarity among working people of different cultures. The Nurek Dam became one such site. In the 1950s, Tajik officials had cleverly used the Soviet opening to the Third World to argue for the building of a large dam on the Vakhsh River that would jump-start the republic's industrialization and expand its agricultural base. Tajik politicians pointed out to skeptical officials in Moscow that such a dam would demonstrate to other Eastern countries (and especially Afghanistan) that the Soviet Union was serious about overcoming backwardness in its own periphery. In the years that followed, construction proceeded in fits and starts, but by the late 1960s it was well under way, and a city to house the workers was taking shape as well. Nurek became a destination for tourists, delegations from Eastern countries, and even engineering students from Asia, Africa, and Latin America who came to Nurek to do their practical work. The site's growing importance for demonstrating domestic and foreign internationalism in turn spurred officials to invest more in the city and the surrounding villages. Even if Soviet internationalism was performative, a kind of pageant reenacted repeatedly for domestic and foreign audiences, it had real effects on people's lives.

Not all republics were equal in the Soviet South–Global South exchange. Uzbekistan, the most developed economically and with the most visible number of cultural artifacts (Timurid architecture in Samarkand and Shahrisabz, famed madrassas and forts in Bukhara and Khiva) played the greatest role. Tashkent's airport received international flights. Sharof Rashidov, the first secretary of the republic's Communist Party from 1959, was also a candidate member of the Politburo, making him one of the most influential Central Asian politicians. The city of Tashkent was considered a crown jewel for foreign visitors, because it combined ancient sites, an old city composed of traditional neighborhoods (*mahallas*), and plenty of modern buildings and infrastructure.[26] Tashkent even hosted the peace negotiations that ended the 1965 war between India and Pakistan. All of the republics were involved in one way or another, though. Delegations from Muslim countries in Africa were brought to Azerbaijan and the Central Asian republics to show what their future might look like if they chose to adopt Moscow's advice and patronage.[27] Tajikistan, as the only republic in which the official language was a variant of Persian (rather than a Turkic language), was particularly important

Fig. 8.1. Fidel Castro visiting the Hungry Steppe in Uzbekistan in 1963, with Uzbek first secretary Sharof Rashidov, who frequently represented the USSR in Third World fora, to his right. (Sputnik Photo Archive, Moscow, Photo 2652936.)

for relations with Afghanistan and India.[28] Both Kyrgyzstan and Kazakhstan hosted international conferences and fora on issues such as agriculture and public health.

The mobilization of Central Asians for the anti-imperialist struggle also offered an opportunity to complete the region's integration into the USSR. When they went abroad as experts and advisers, young Central Asian intellectuals were no longer the "younger brothers" of Russians; they were being encouraged to think of themselves as playing a leading role in a global struggle for justice and equality. Writers, artists, and party members all took part in extensive tours and returned home to write about their experiences in newspaper articles, brochures, and books.[29] Abdullahad Kakhorov, who spent many years working in planning and served as chairman of the Council of Ministers between 1964 and 1974, coauthored a book, published in Tajik in 1959, called *Economic and Technical Cooperation of the USSR with the Poorly Developed Countries of the East*, which included a chapter highlighting how Tajikistan and the other Central Asian republics compared favorably to the countries of South and Southeast Asia, and "set an example for the weakly developed countries . . . the Republics of the Soviet east will be torches lighting the way to progress and civilization for less developed countries."[30] Kakhorov later traveled to South and Southeast Asia and parts of

Africa and wrote about his experiences in a series of pamphlets published in Dushanbe, all of them in Tajik.[31] Such publications differed in details but followed similar arcs: the writer described the suffering of these countries under colonialism and their struggle for freedom, supplementing facts gleaned primarily from Soviet publications with some eyewitness accounts. Inevitably, the writer also pointed to the yearning he or she found for friendship with the Soviet Union, and Moscow's willingness to extend a helping hand. Sometimes, in more private settings, the accounts of Central Asian travelers took on a more overtly paternalistic and Orientalist tone. Thus the Tajik poet Mirzo Tursunzoda, the chairman of the Soviet Afro-Asian Solidarity Committee, told his colleague that Guinea was "full of natural gifts, pineapples, bananas, coconuts, but with illiterate people [who were] simply big kids." Now that they were free from colonialism, they were "out in the streets, singing and dancing." It was up to the Soviet Union, nevertheless, to "give them correct education and enlightenment, so that their country takes the right path."[32]

To summarize, by the mid 1960s, the Central Asian republics were firmly on the front line of the Soviet struggle for influence in the Third World. Their history as former colonies of the Russian Empire made them a potential liability in the USSR's attempts to establish friendly relations with newly decolonizing states, but it also presented an opportunity. By running its relations with the postcolonial world through Tashkent, Dushanbe, and other Central Asian sites, Moscow created many opportunities for interaction and comparison.

Comparisons

How did the Soviet South compare to the countries Moscow hoped to lead? The Soviet Union, naturally, claimed that Central Asia offered a positive model both in terms of its own achievements and in the relationship between the old imperial center and the periphery. Indeed, aid plans put together by GKĖS starting in the late 1950s explicitly included references to learning from the Central Asian experience in the mechanization of agriculture and industrialization.[33] For a period in the 1960s, economists in Moscow and in the Central Asian capitals even produced articles, dissertations, and monographs on the applicability of a Central Asian model of development to countries of the Third World, although this stream of scholarship petered out by the early 1970s.[34] Among Western scholars, there were those who saw the Soviet South as just another colonial region that would eventually rise up, but also those who thought the Soviet Union provided a worthy example to underdeveloped countries, particularly in its achievements in areas such as public health and education.[35]

The reality is that, while the Soviet Union did invest heavily in the region after Stalin's death, in part with a view to overcoming earlier inequalities, the relationship between Central Asia and the European Soviet Union retained many features of a colonial relationship, while developmental efforts led to many of the same problems and contradictions faced by postcolonial states. First, the cotton complex remained firmly in place, and even expanded. The attempts under Khrushchev and later Leonid Brezhnev to expand the availability of consumer products, including clothing, only added to the demand for cotton. Because the Central Asians grew cotton but then shipped most of it to secondary producers, they collected no turnover tax on the crop. Meanwhile, its production led to the wasting of water and the degradation and pollution of soil. Moreover, despite numerous initiatives, cotton remained reliant on manual labor, which often meant pulling in children to work during peak harvest periods.[36] In this sense, the Central Asian republics remained trapped in the same patterns former colonies struggled to escape in the 1960s and 1970s.[37]

Central Asian politicians and those of postcolonial states had similar visions and reasons for pursuing investments in industry and infrastructure. Industrialization was supposed to help overcome neocolonial social and economic conditions by drawing the population into the labor force, diversifying the economy, raising standards of living, and thus decreasing dependence on wealthier foreign powers. Central Asian politicians did not speak of ending dependence on Moscow, of course, but they did talk about making their republics more self-sufficient and believed firmly that industrialization and diversification were a prerequisite for raising living standards. Supporters of industrialization often had in mind a social goal as well: by bringing peasants into the industrial workforce, they could shape them into modern citizens who would form the backbone of the new nation-state. Working in industry would expose yesterday's peasants to technology, education, modern conveniences, and everything else that modernity had to offer.

Few postcolonial countries successfully pulled off this feat, however. Indeed, by the 1970s many postcolonial countries that had pursued a policy of rapid industrialization found themselves in economic trouble. Although the reasons varied, it is important to remember how often the promise of industrialization fell short in the postindependence decades. Zambia's mining industry allowed that country to achieve standards of living approaching those of poorer European countries by the 1970s. Yet Zambia never developed an urban industrial economy and suffered when commodity prices crashed.[38] Ghana, which had hoped to use its cocoa export to fund a broader industrialization, similarly suffered when the price for its main cash crop collapsed. The Central Asian republics never faced such drastic crises, cushioned as they were by budget transfers and price guarantees from the federal center. Yet here too industrialization did little to raise the standard of living for the local population.

Rather than fulfilling the promise of decolonization, as Central Asian politicians had hoped to do in the postwar years, industrialization produced what we might term a "colonial pattern," while also creating problems seen in many postcolonial states. To get factories up and running quickly, managers preferred to avoid drawing on the Central Asian workforce, relying instead on imported labor, especially for jobs requiring skills and experience. As housing in the Soviet Union was usually tied to employment, the newcomers were assigned scarce housing in cities. The cities thus became primarily Russian-speaking and were often alienating to the local population, which found some success at the top of the hierarchy (as party leaders, academics, and so on) but mostly occupied the bottom (unskilled labor, often commuting from nearby villages).[39] Just as the cotton complex turned the republics into commodity producers, industrialization, which was supposed to help overcome that economic condition, instead created a situation in which a settler, European elite dominated the industrial sector as well as the cities, while the local population was largely employed for manual labor in the countryside.

Even education, an area Soviets were particularly proud of and foreigners often admired, created highly problematic imbalances. Postsecondary institutions struggled to recruit Central Asians for technical studies. Language was a major part of the problem, as was the divide between schools that taught primarily in Russian and those offering instruction in indigenous languages. The latter—which were sometimes the only option outside of major cities and towns—often lacked good textbooks and teachers, especially in math and science subjects. As a result, students were not well prepared to pursue these subjects in higher education. Preparatory courses helped some students, but not many. The result was that the industrial managerial class remained European. For this reason, planners urged expanding Russian language instruction and phasing out or reducing education in the indigenous languages, but that was logistically difficult and threatened to exacerbate another colonial pattern in the countryside, something local intellectuals would not accept. Meanwhile, the universities were producing more specialists in the humanities and the social sciences, who often sought work in the bureaucracy. Here, the pattern conformed to that in other postcolonial and developmental states, where investment in education intended for economic development instead produced a growing number of underemployed and overeducated young men and women, who often grew frustrated with a system that could not provide scope for everyone's ambition. The similarity between the problems of the developing world and that of Central Asia was something to which Moscow-based and Central Asian observers began to draw attention from the late 1970s, and particularly forcefully during perestroika.[40]

By the late 1970s the consensus on development that had originally led scholars and officials to think of the Soviet South as a model for the Third World was coming apart. Soviet politicians had found that development aid often meant throwing good money after bad and not only led to poor economic results but also failed to buy political loyalty.[41] Religion turned out to be a much greater mobilizing force than Soviet specialists had anticipated two decades earlier, especially in the Middle East. At the same time, disappointment over results in Central Asia, while rarely voiced publicly, made officials reluctant to use the region as a basis for a model of development. Indeed, in the perestroika era, some scholars began turning to their knowledge of the Third World to explain the economic problems of Central Asia and to predict the political problems that might arise as a result. For example, they began to wonder whether urbanization, which had been touted as evidence of progress, might actually lead to inequality and urban unrest, as had been the case in Iran and a number of other countries since the 1970s.[42]

Learning from the East?

Not surprisingly, from the 1970s onward many Central Asian intellectuals began to notice that the comparison between their republics and the postcolonial world was often not in their favor. Those people who were most involved in international contacts were often the first to note that, while they had in common with the postcolonial world a shared road to progress (on which the Central Asians were supposedly a few steps ahead), development had not fulfilled its promise and had simultaneously brought with it enormous social and environmental costs.

Already in the 1960s, however, the kind of interactions encouraged by Soviet Cold War policies began to bring unexpected consequences. For the students of a more literary bent at Tajikistan's universities and colleges, for example, the cultural thaw and engagement with the East meant access, on the one hand, to previously unavailable works by Russian poets such as Sergei Yesenin, Marina Tsvetaeva, and Anna Akhmatova, and to the ancient and contemporary literature of the Persian-speaking world on the other. (As part of Soviet engagement with the East, Tajik publishers began producing Persian-language works in the Tajik script, a modified form of Cyrillic, making them available to a growing reading public that could not read Arabic-Persian script).[43] While not making dissidents out of communist youth, this literature inevitably broadened the scope for many who came in contact with it. For at least one Komsomol activist, working as a translator with an Indian delegation and traveling to India led her to lose interest in practical work for the youth movement and politics and to devote herself instead to scholarship on cultural ties between Europe and the Persianate world.[44] Other young intellectuals began to question whether the version of national culture presented by official Soviet cultural authorities represented the most genuine version of their cultural tradition. In particular, they resented what they saw as the elevation of Russian literature and language in the USSR as a whole.[45]

Some scholars and specialists sent abroad to give technical advice found that their own way of doing things was inferior to practices in the places they had gone to assist. An engineer from Nurek who went to work in Libya found that Soviet technology was outdated compared to the Western technology he and his colleagues found there.[46] Such experiences were not limited to those from the Soviet South, however—sometimes Russian engineers also found that methods of water management in Egypt and Syria, for example, had much to teach the Soviet Union about how it handled its own increasingly polluted water supply.[47] Russian and Central Asian social scientists, meanwhile, found they had much to learn from their Indian colleagues. Hojamamat Umarov, a Tajik economist who engaged with Indian colleagues in Tashkent in the late 1970s and later lectured in India, credited Indian economists with introducing him to the idea of studying poverty as an indicator within Central Asia (something Soviet social scientists had never done, at least not explicitly) and to the idea of family planning as a way to raise standards of living in the region.[48]

Moreover, some of these intellectuals noted that their ability to define and articulate their own culture was actually inferior to that of their counterparts in postcolonial states, and more reminiscent of truly colonial relationships, marked by more overt domination. Central Asians working in the Middle East and other majority-Muslim countries were often asked whether one could truly be a practicing Muslim back home. They had stock answers ready, and when they reported to Moscow, they naturally portrayed themselves as winning over their interlocutors. The diplomat Mirzo Rahmatov recalled that as ambassador to Yemen he was asked whether one could live "as Allah willed" in the Soviet Union. Rahmatov explained, "If they wanted, [Muslims in the USSR] could live according to the sharia," but added that progress achieved in the USSR was breaking down the "insularity" of religious communities.[49] Later memoirs and oral histories suggest that things were not that simple. Tajiks working in Afghanistan, in particular, were challenged about whether what they reported about life back home represented reality. Prior to the Soviet invasion in 1979, contacts between the Central Asian interpreters and specialists who worked in the country and various locals were open, allowing for plenty of unscripted encounters and even genuine friendships to form. The literary historian Hudoynazar Asozoda, for example, recalled that some Afghans insisted that groups like the Tajiks had little real autonomy in the Soviet Union. Asozoda knew that both Soviet and Afghan secret services were probably keeping an eye on him, so he could not really engage in such discussions. Still, he noted "the views [of his interlocutors] were not without effect on my world view."[50]

The Soviet intervention in Afghanistan (1979–89) would draw on Central Asians in an unprecedented way. Thousands went to the country as interpreters, officers, ordinary soldiers, party advisers, and technical specialists. In recent years, several oral history projects and a trickle of memoirs have greatly expanded our understanding of the range of experiences and contacts engendered by the war experience.[51] In the United States, opponents of détente and those who thought that Central Asia and the Caucasus formed the "soft underbelly" of the Soviet Union believed that their hour had come, and that the war would inevitably lead to growing resistance against Moscow, and even pushed the Carter and Reagan administrations to fund programs designed to accelerate the process.[52] No such resistance materialized on any real scale, and many returned as loyal Soviet citizens who were proud of their war service. For some Central Asians, the cruelty of the war, the corruption they witnessed among Soviet officials, or the racist attitudes of Russian officers forced them to reevaluate their place in the Soviet Union and question its policies and its claims about anticolonialism and equality.

During perestroika, many of these individuals became increasingly vocal in their critiques of the Soviet Union, and some went on to become involved in activist groups that pushed for fundamental changes in the relationship between the periphery and the center. They employed explicitly anticolonial rhetoric as well as comparisons between their own republics and the postcolonial world that were actually to the advantage of the latter. While this rhetoric may have been used selectively to get Moscow to fulfil certain promises in earlier periods, it was now being used to question the fundamental ordering of economic and ethnic relations in the Soviet Union. In Tajikistan, one economist who had engaged frequently with Indian colleagues complained that decades of Soviet development had actually created patterns akin to those in Third World countries.[53] Another, who had worked in Afghanistan during the war, argued that Moscow had only developed the region for its own benefit and generally behaved in a classic colonial manner with regard to its Muslim periphery. He would go on to lead Tajikistan's first real opposition group, Rastokhez.[54] Like analogous groups in other republics, Rastokhez combined a critique of Soviet economic management and political control with environmentalism and calls for laws that would support cultural authenticity.[55]

These individuals were not just reacting to their experiences abroad, however. Nor should we assume that mobilization around this anticolonial rhetoric was a mass phenomenon, or that it necessarily translated into calls for full independence. Indeed, referenda carried out in 1991 showed widespread support for keeping a reformed USSR together throughout the Soviet republics.[56] Still, it is clear that part of the intellectual elite, who had been socialized to lead their own societies toward a socialist future and to encourage other postcolonial societies to follow Moscow's lead, drew on their experiences as they articulated a new critique of the Soviet system. Through their contacts in intra-Soviet intellectual networks, they also engaged with various discussions about language, sovereignty, and culture that were taking place across the USSR, including in Russia itself. The Kyrgyz novelist Chingiz Aytmatov, a veteran of Soviet engagement with the postcolonial world, became one of the most articulate spokespeople for the revival of national culture and language and served as a model to others throughout the

USSR. The anticolonial rhetoric of the late Soviet era thus had diverse sources. Nevertheless, the anticolonial critiques that emerged in the late Soviet era and were directed *at* Moscow were shaped in part by the interactions and comparisons promoted by the USSR from the 1950s in its bid to prove that it offered a model of development, welfare, and justice for the postcolonial world.

Conclusion

From the 1950s onward, the Soviet Union presented its republics in Central Asia and the Caucasus as a model for postcolonial states. Soviet leaders seemed genuinely to believe that their cultural policies, economic achievements, and models of limited sovereignty for the national republics would prove to postcolonial regimes that the Soviet Union was not an empire but an anti-imperialist power. At the same time, Soviet leaders recognized that the region had a long way to go before these claims were truly credible, a realization that had important consequences for politics, culture, and economic development in the region.

The problem was that Moscow was vulnerable on all aspects of this contest. Its models of limited sovereignty held little attraction for postcolonial elites. The possibilities for national cultural development were impressive up to a point, but at the same time were seen as far too limited by some intellectuals, as Asozoda found in his travels. Economically, too, the Soviet South increasingly seemed like a model of the problems of development in the Third World rather than something to emulate. It is not surprising, therefore, that some of the people who had gone abroad to tout Soviet achievements were among the most vocal critics of the Soviet regime in the late 1980s.

Notes

1. Langston Hughes, *A Negro Looks at Soviet Central Asia* (Moscow: Cooperative Publishing Society of Foreign Workers in the USSR, 1934).

2. Langston Hughes, *I Wonder as I Wander* (New York: Hill and Wang, 1993), 147; David Chioni-Moore, "Local Color, Global 'Color': Langston Hughes, the Black Atlantic, and Soviet Central Asia, 1932," *Research in African Literatures* 27, no. 4 (Winter 1996): 49–70.

3. Mathew Connelly, "Taking Off the Cold War Lens: Visions of North-South Conflict during the Algerian War for Independence," *American Historical Review* 105, no. 3 (June 2000): 739–769.

4. See, for example, Odd Arne Westad, *Global Cold War: Third World Interventions and the Making of Our Times* (Cambridge: Cambridge University Press, 2005).

5. The South Caucasus, especially Azerbaijan, must ultimately form a part of this story as well. However, since there is little secondary literature on that region's engagement with the postcolonial world and my own work has focused on Central Asia, this chapter will focus only on the latter. Much of the material in this chapter was collected in the process of

writing Artemy M. Kalinovsky, *Laboratory of Socialist Development: Cold War Politics and Decolonization in Soviet Tajikistan* (Ithaca, NY: Cornell University Press, 2018).

6. Charles Shaw, "Friendship under Lock and Key: The Soviet Central Asian Border, 1918–34," *Central Asian Survey* 30, no. 3–4 (2011): 331–348.

7. Christian Teichmann, "Canals, Cotton, and the Limits of De-colonization in Soviet Uzbekistan, 1924–1941," *Central Asian Survey* 26, no. 4 (December 2007): 499–519. Benjamin Loring, "Building Socialism in Kyrgyzstan: Nation-Making, Rural Development, and Social Change, 1921–1932" (PhD diss., University of Chicago, 2008). Botakoz Kassymbekova, "Humans as Territory: Forced Resettlement and the Making of Soviet Tajikistan, 1920–38," *Central Asian Survey* 30, no. 3–4 (2011): 349–370.

8. Katerina Clark, *Moscow—The Fourth Rome: Stalinism, Cosmopolitanism, and the Evolution of Soviet Culture, 1931–1941* (Cambridge, MA: Harvard University Press, 2011), 26–27.

9. Artemy M. Kalinovsky, "Opera as the Highest Stage of Socialism: Soviet Cultural Modernization in Tajikistan," *International Institute for Asian Studies Newsletter* 74 (Summer 2016). See also Michel Rouland, "Music and the Making of the Kazak Nation, 1920–1936" (PhD diss., Georgetown University, 2005); Theodore Levin, *The Hundred Thousand Fools of God: Musical Travels in Central Asia (and Queens, New York)* (Bloomington: Indiana University Press, 1999); Marina Frolova-Walker, "'National in Form, Socialist in Content': Musical Nation-Building in the Soviet Republics," *Journal of the American Musicological Society* 51, no. 2 (Summer 1998).

10. Will Myers, *Islam and Colonialism: Western Perspectives on Soviet Asia* (London: RoutledgeCurzon, 2002).

11. Natalia Yegorova, "The 'Iran Crisis' of 1945–46: A View from the Russian Archives," Cold War International History Project Working Paper 15 (Washington, DC, 1996); Jamil Hasanli, *Iran at the Dawn of the Cold War: The Soviet–American Crisis over Iranian Azerbaijan, 1941–1946* (Lanham, MD: Rowman & Littlefield Publishers, 2006).

12. On the tension between Moscow's commitment to the European proletariat and its anti-imperial policies, see Jeremy Friedman, *Shadow Cold War: The Sino-Soviet Competition for the Third World* (Chapel Hill: University of North Carolina Press, 2015).

13. RGANI, f. 5, op. 30, d. 273, 43.

14. RGANI, f. 5, op. 30, d. 273, 41.

15. See Masha Kirasirova, "'Sons of Muslims' in Moscow: Soviet Central Asian Mediators to the Foreign East, 1955–1962," *Ab Imperio* 4 (2011): 106–132.

16. This and the following paragraph are based on Artemy M. Kalinovsky, "'Not Some British Colony in Africa': The Politics of Decolonization and Modernization in Soviet Central Asia, 1955–1964," *Ab Imperio* 2 (2013): 191–222.

17. See also Kirasirova, "'Sons of Muslims' in Moscow," 114–115.

18. "Regarding the Activity of the Institute of Oriental Studies of the Tajik SSR," discussion in the Sector of Social Sciences of the Academy of Sciences of the USSR, April 29, 1972. Archive of the Russian Academy of Sciences, fond 1731, opis' 1, delo 157, 74.

19. Hudojnazar Asozoda, *Ta'rihi Adabieti Tojik* (Dushanbe: Maorif va Farhang, 2014), 462–463.

20. Author's interviews.

21. From the beginning of the USSR's decades-long aid relationship with Afghanistan, for example, specialists, institutes, and agencies from the Central Asian and Caucasian republics were called on to take a leading role in projects. RGANI, f. 5, op. 30, d. 272, 132–133.

22. RGANI, f. 5, op. 35, d. 225, 7.

23. RGAE, f. 365, op. 9, d. 185.

24. Holmorod Sharifov, *Tolei baland* (Dushanbe: 2010), 32–34.

25. Rossen Djagalov and Masha Salazkina, "Tashkent '68: A Cinematic Contact Zone," *Slavic Review* 75, no. 2 (2016): 294.

26. On Tashkent, see Paul Stronski, *Tashkent: Forging a Soviet City, 1930–1966* (Pittsburgh, PA: University of Pittsburgh Press, 2010). As frontline republics, Uzbekistan and Tajikistan also sent more tourists of the titular nationality abroad, particularly from the 1970s.

27. Alessandro Iandolo, "The Rise and Fall of the 'Soviet Model of Development' in West Africa, 1957–64," *Cold War History* 12, no. 4 (2012): 693, 695.

28. Bukhara and Samarkand, located in Uzbekistan, were also part of this broader Persianate culture.

29. Mirzo Rakhmatov, *Afrika idet k svobode* (Moscow: 1961).

30. A. Kakhorov and G. Prohorov, *Xamkorii iqtisodi va texnikii SSSR bo mamlakatxoi susttaraqqiardai sharq* (Stalinobod: Nashriete davlatii Tojikiston, 1959), 44.

31. A. Kakhorov, *Dar avstralia va Ceylon (qaydhoi safar)* (Dushanbe: Nashrieti davlatii Tojikiston, 1962).

32. Quoted in Constantin Katsakioris, "The Soviet-South Encounter: Tensions in the Friendship with Afro-Asian Partners, 1945–1965," in *Cold War Crossings: International Travel and Exchange across the Soviet Bloc, 1940s-1960s*, eds. Patryk Babiracki and Kenyon Zimmer, (College Station: Texas A&M University Press, 2014), 148.

33. RGANI, f. 5, op. 30, d. 305, 116–288. Cited in Iandolo, "The Rise and Fall of the 'Soviet Model of Development,'" 692.

34. See, for example, G. Ia. Kurzer. "K voprosu ob ispol'zovanii razvivaiushimisia stranami opyta sotsialisticheskoi industrializatsii respublik srednii azii," *Izvestiia Akademii Nauk Tadzhikskoi SSR*, no. 2 (1965): 45–59.

35. See, for example, Alec Nove and J. A. Newith, *The Soviet Middle East: A Communist Model for Development* (New York: Frederick A. Praeger, 1966).

36. See Artemy M. Kalinovsky, "Tractors, Powerlines, and the Welfare State: The Contradictions of Soviet Development in Post–World War II Tajikistan," *Asian Survey* 69, no. 3 (2015): 563–592.

37. Iandolo, "The Rise and Fall of the 'Soviet Model of Development.'"

38. James Ferguson, *Expectations of Modernity: Myths and Meanings of Urban Life on the Zambian Copper Belt* (Berkley: University of California Press, 1999), 4–10.

39. The classic work remains Nancy Lubin, *Labour and Nationality in Central Asia* (London: Macmillan, 1984).

40. See also Artemy M. Kalinovsky, "Central Planning, Local Knowledge? Labor, Population, and the Tajik School of Economics," *Kritika: Explorations in Russian and Eurasian History* 17, no. 3 (2016): 585–620.

41. Elizabeth Kridl Valkenier, *The Soviet Union and the Third World: An Economic Bind* (New York: Praeger, 1983).

42. See the roundtable in the authoritative party journal *Kommunist* in May 1989, and especially Georgy Mirsky's comments on pages 40–41.

43. Hoduynazar Asozoda, *Ta'rihi Adabieti Tojik* (Dushanbe: Maorif va Farhang, 2014), 462–463.

44. Munira Shakhidi interviews, Dushanbe, 2013.

45. See Diana T. Kudaibergenova, *Rewriting the Nation in Modern Kazakh Literature: Elites and Narratives* (London: Lexington Books, 2017), 123–148.

46. Amirkul Erov interview.

47. RGANI f. 5, op. 34, d. 403, 50–62.

48. Author's interviews with H. Umarov, 2013, 2015.

49. Mirzo Rakhmatov, *Na diplomaticheskoi sluzhbe* (Dushanbe: Irfon, 1991), 18–19.

50. Ibid., 291.

51. Markus Gorranson, *At the Service of the State: Soviet-Afghan War Veterans in Tajikistan, 1979–1992* (PhD Thesis: Aberystwyth University, 2016).

52. Artemy M. Kalinovsky, "Encouraging Resistance: Paul Henze, the Bennigsen School, and the Crisis of Détente," in *Reassessing Orientalism: Interlocking Orientologies in the Cold War Era*, eds. Michael Kemper and Artemy M. Kalinovsky (London: Routledge, 2015).

53. Kalinovsky, "Central Planning, Local Knowledge?"

54. Abdujabbor's speeches and various documents regarding Rastokhez are collected in Ahmadshohi Kamilzoda, ed., *Me'mori istikloli Tojikiston* (Dushanbe: 2010).

55. For more on nationalist mobilization, see Mark Beissinger, *Nationalist Mobilization and the Collapse of the Soviet State* (Cambridge, Cambridge University Press, 2002); Geoffrey Wheeler, *Nationalism in Uzbekistan: A Soviet Republic's Road to Sovereignty* (Westview Press, 1991); Kirill Nourzhanov and Christian Bleuer, *Tajikistan: A Political and Social History* (Canberra: Australian National University Press, 2013).

56. Beissinger, *Nationalist Mobilization*, 420–421. Although it should be noted that referenda later that fall, after the August 1991 coup attempt, showed overwhelming support for independence in some of these same republics.

ARTEMY M. KALINOVSKY is Senior Lecturer in East European Studies at the University of Amsterdam. He is author of *Laboratory of Socialist Development: Cold War Politics and Decolonization in Soviet Tajikistan* and *A Long Goodbye: The Soviet Withdrawal from Afghanistan.*

9 Internationalizing the Thaw: Soviet Orientalists and the Contested Politics of Spiritual Solidarity in Asia 1954–1959*

Hanna Jansen

On December 30, 1956, Soviet foreign minister Viacheslav Molotov sent a letter to Luther Evans, director-general of the United Nations Educational, Scientific and Cultural Organization (UNESCO), to confirm his support for the UNESCO Major Project for the "Mutual Appreciation of Eastern and Western Cultural Values." Molotov stressed that in the past year the Soviet Union had hosted "many hundreds of foreign delegations and thousands of tourists" and that "a great number of Soviet delegations that included Soviet scholars, engineers, agronomists, creators of culture and art" had traveled abroad to participate in international meetings and conferences. While Molotov was "disappointed" that the organization did not represent "such a great country" as the Chinese People's Republic (PRC), he nevertheless "fully agreed" with the project's aims to advance world "international relations with an enlightening, scientific and cultural character."[1]

Molotov's declaration of support for a UNESCO project that aimed to advance global cultural awareness and improve cultural exchange between East and West illustrates the fundamental changes Joseph Stalin's death had brought to Soviet intellectual and cultural life. In the post-Stalinist thaw, Soviet intellectuals and artists began to present art, creativity, and imagination as central aspects of human development, embracing culture as a source of socialist progress and international solidarity. This approach to culture was at least partly rooted in the radical internationalisms that had inspired various reform and revolutionary circles in Asia and Russia in the interwar period. Soviet activities in the Asia-initiated UNESCO East-West Project show that, throughout the Cold War, international organizations such as UNESCO allowed Soviet intellectuals to actively align themselves with scholars and representatives from decolonizing countries, negotiating an anti-Stalinist and anti-imperial vision of socialist development and modernity. This chapter demonstrates how in the years of the thaw, Soviet scholars and writers brought their perspectives to the international stage, thereby contributing to a global critique of imperialism and Eurocentrism.

In their international efforts, Soviet academics were supported by the aim of the new Communist Party leader Nikita Khrushchev to establish friendly relations with the countries of Asia, Africa, and the Middle East. Breaking with Stalin's isolationism, Khrushchev embarked on a diplomatic mission to spread socialism in the decolonizing world. As he mobilized Soviet scholarship for the "Break to the East," Khrushchev's diplomacy in Asia was much influenced by the thaw's embrace of culture as a source of progress by Soviet scholars working in the humanities. In the mid-1950s Khrushchev phrased the socialist international mission in the East in language that acknowledged the continued relevance of cultural and spiritual traditions for modern international solidarity and that also emphasized orthodox revolutionary themes of decolonization, development, and class struggle.

By focusing on the response of the communist leadership of the Chinese People's Republic (PRC), this article highlights the fact that Khrushchev's new language of spiritual solidarity was contested within the socialist camp. In his famous speech at the November 1957 meeting for Communist parties in Moscow, Chairman Mao rejected "metaphysical" approaches to international solidarity. Historians have traditionally analyzed Mao's famous speech on this occasion within a political context of ideological revisionism and Cold War dynamics: as a key moment heralding the return of a confrontational two-camp approach in world politics. This chapter situates Mao's defense of historical materialism in a context of the cultural and intellectual thaw. An analysis of Soviet Orientalist discourses illustrates that, responding to Mao's critiques, the rehabilitation of spiritual and cultural solidarities as a progressive force in world historical development was partially reversed in the USSR. Consequently, in the work of Soviet academic Orientalists, two different narratives of Asian history emerged: the one presenting the countries of Asia and the world as culturally and spiritually entangled; the other presenting the history of Asian countries as separated by clear historical and political boundaries.

As this chapter concludes, Mao's critiques had a profound influence on Soviet international conduct. At the level of state diplomacy, by the early 1960s the theme of spiritual unity and solidarity had disappeared from Soviet discourse. At the substate level of cultural and intellectual networks, however, Soviet scholars continued to emphasize the theme of spiritual or cultural solidarity with the East as a key aspect of socialist progress. For these figures, the institutional infrastructure of UNESCO provided a crucial international arena: allowing Soviet cultural experts and diplomats to continue and advance a critical, anti-Eurocentric spiritual internationalism on a global scale.

Internationalizing the Cultural and Intellectual Thaw

At the first Afro-Asian Congress organized in Indonesian Bandung in April 1955, the world witnessed the great appeal that ideals of African-Asian solidarity and nonalignment had among political representatives in the decolonizing world. While the Soviet Union, being viewed as a Western country, was not invited to the Congress, in these same years the new party leader Nikita Khrushchev positioned himself as a strong supporter of Afro-Asian solidarity and decolonization. After Stalin's death in 1953, the earlier confrontational two-camp politics gave way to a politics of peaceful coexistence with both nonaligned and capitalist countries.

Peaceful coexistence ushered in a new era of international cultural and scientific engagement. In 1954 the Soviet Union became a member of UNESCO. Programs of cultural and educational exchange were set up between the Soviet Union and the countries of Asia, Africa, and the Middle East. As the Soviet Union obtained membership in international organizations, Soviet delegates defended the goal of decolonization within international organizations that had traditionally been oriented toward the West.[2] Soviet participation in international organizations was strongly connected with Khrushchev's "Break to the East." In his letter of December 1955 to the UNESCO director-general, Molotov called for a reorientation toward non-Western countries and peoples in particular: ". . . alongside the study of languages such as Russian, English, French and German, more attention should be given to the study of languages of other peoples and, in particular of the great peoples of Asia and Africa such as the Chinese, Indian and Arabic peoples."[3] Molotov framed the proposed reorganization in terms of anticolonial struggle and national liberation: it "would deepen the mutual understanding between East and West, and meet the legitimate efforts of the peoples of the countries of Asia and Africa who aim to safeguard their national independence in line with the principles of the equality of peoples and nations."[4] As such, Soviet UNESCO membership held the promise of strengthening the position of non-Western countries within the organization.

One of the first Soviet delegates to UNESCO was Alexander Guber, an academically trained Orientalist and head of the "eastern section" of the All-Union Society for Cultural Relations with Foreign Countries (known as VOKS, Vsesoiuznoe obshchestvo kul'turnoi sviazi s zagranitsei). In 1954 Guber became a member of the Soviet research committee for the multivolume "History of Mankind" project that Julian Huxley, formerly the director general of UNESCO, had launched.[5] The Presidium of the Communist Party of the Soviet Union (CPSU) had ordered Soviet participation in this international research project to ensure that "the history of the peoples of the USSR and the development of their economy and culture were correctly described."[6] Around this time Guber was also installed as director of the Institute for Oriental Studies (IVAN, Institut

Vostokovedenie Akademii Nauk) in Moscow.[7] Guber's dual leadership role as a VOKS official and director of a prestigious academic research institute for the history and culture of the "East" illustrated the growing priority accorded to the non-Western world in Soviet cultural relations in the aftermath of Bandung.

Guber was quick to realize the potential of the UNESCO infrastructure for socialist agitation in the East. At the inaugural convention of the Soviet Committee for Solidarity with the Countries of Asia (SKSSA, Sovetskii komitet solidarnosti stran Azii) in November 1956, he pleaded for an explicitly anti-Eurocentric cultural policy in Asia. Echoing the mood at the UNESCO Asian Regional Conference that had been held that same spring in Tokyo, he claimed that projects of cultural "enlightenment" or education were burning issues for Asian member states. He warned of the dissatisfaction among Asian leaders with the Europe-centered orientation of UNESCO, calling to mind the fact that, at the UNESCO Regional Conference in Tokyo, Asian representatives had been greatly outnumbered by their European colleagues.[8]

At its ninth session in December 1956, the UNESCO General Conference approved the plan for the Major Project for "Mutual Appreciation of Eastern and Western Values," which had resulted from a proposal of the Indian delegation at the Asian Relations Conference in Tokyo. An implicit aim of the program was to correct the Eurocentric bias in various UNESCO projects by spreading awareness of the cultures of the East in the West.[9] With the adoption of the East-West Project, UNESCO's cultural and educational exchange program took a Eurocritical turn. In the USSR, the Institute for Oriental Studies was granted a special role in the program. When the UNESCO executive board approved the draft of the East-West Project in July 1956, Guber was replaced as director of the IVAN by a representative of the Soviet "East": the former first secretary of the Tajik Soviet Socialist Republic (SSR), Bobojon Ghafurovich Ghafurov.[10] Under Ghafurov's leadership the cultural research profile of the IVAN was further refined. Most importantly, under his directorship, the humanistic study of Eastern cultural history and philology was rehabilitated as a priority research field at the IVAN.[11] The thaw's embrace of culture as a source of progress was reflected in Orientalist discourses that granted historical religions and literatures a progressive role in world history.

In the Soviet Orientalist tradition, the study of historical literatures was controversial. Scholarship in the Soviet Union was meant to support the socialist mission.[12] In the first decades of Soviet state building, a strict historical materialism had thus dominated the Soviet sciences, and as a consequence the philological study of historical texts and literatures had been marginalized. In 1934 Stalin had canonized the *piatichlenka*, which taught that human history passed through five universal stages of material (rather than spiritual) development.[13] In this train of thought, all modern cultural and spiritual solidarities were to pass through a process of national becoming.[14] If received cultural traditions were appreciated as being in any sense progressive, it was only insofar as they carried popular, motivational themes, celebrating romantic heroism, military vigor, and local folklore.[15]

Stalin's suspicion of historical literary and spiritual traditions was due in part to their association with bourgeois elite cultural models and to his conviction that they would inevitably weaken the revolutionary struggle. Indeed, in the prerevolutionary past, studies of local religious and cultural traditions had been used in the service of empire: emphasizing the "special connection" between Russia and Asia in support of territorial annexation or for privileging specific local communities in order to divide and rule.[16] Furthermore, in colonial Asia local groups and ruling elites had mobilized cultural and spiritual sentiments in support of their nationalist or regionalist agendas.[17]

Not all communist revolutionaries in Stalin's time had, however, believed that prerevolutionary cultural solidarities and traditions would undermine the socialist project. In the early postrevolutionary period, various reform-oriented and revolutionary individuals and groups backed the Bolshevik struggle in the Russian Empire while also maintaining that cultural and religious traditions had progressive revolutionary value, regarding them as a potential source of international recognition and solidarity.[18] In Soviet Central Asia and the Transcaucasus, revolutionaries used cultural arguments to criticize Western worldviews and to emphasize the unity of colonized countries against imperial rule. Their efforts were supported by the studies of Russian Orientalists who argued that world history had a complex, inclusive character and accused Western models of suffering from a Eurocentric, discriminatory bias.[19] These Eurocritical scholars rejected the stereotypical division between the modern, secular West and the traditional, spiritual East, arguing that religious traditions constituted an important source of historical change of equal historical value to the secular intellectual traditions of ancient Greece and Renaissance Europe.[20] This critical position encouraged them to adopt a complex interdisciplinary research method, which would be taken up and further refined by Soviet Orientalists in the aftermath of the October Revolution. The complex method was intended to allow Russian and Soviet Orientalists to analyze world history as an integrated process in which different cultural and material traditions interacted, overlapped, and cross-fertilized.[21] In this approach, cultural and religious traditions were often grouped together under the label "spiritual" and presented as a potential source of international solidarity and unity.

After Stalin's death, various intellectuals in the USSR rehabilitated the idea that historical international solidarities could be of relevance to international revolutionary development. One of these was Ghafurov, the new director of the Institute for Oriental Studies. At the Twentieth Congress of the Soviet Communist Party in February 1956, Ghafurov had defended a vision of modernization that centered not only on historical-material development and technological achievements but also on cultural and spiritual enrichment. He argued for the need to improve Tajik cultural education, primarily in the field of literature. In his opinion, the development of literature had fallen behind that of the economy in the Tajik Republic, and this had "increased" the "spiritual demand" among the Tajik population. To resolve this, Ghafurov proposed, cultural education in Tajikistan should involve the study of classical Islamic literature.[22] At the first All-Union Congress for Orientalists in June 1957, Ghafurov explicitly traced the Soviet tradition of Oriental studies to the school of prerevolutionary Orientalists who had argued for the value of Eastern traditions for world civilization.[23]

Cold War Encounters

In this period of post-Stalinist thaw, Soviet diplomacy at the interstate level likewise deployed a language that stressed spiritual and cultural solidarities. In November 1955 Khrushchev led a Soviet delegation on a diplomatic tour through India, Burma, and Afghanistan. At several public appearances he emphasized a "spiritual" connection between peoples. Indeed, at a banquet at Indian prime minister Jawaharlal Nehru's house on November 20, he presented Soviet commitments to peaceful coexistence in near-religious terms: "The word 'peace' is just as sacred for the people of India as it is for the people of the Soviet Union."[24] One day later he told the Indian Parliament: "Our peoples are brothers in spirit and in all their aspirations."[25] And at a meeting in Calcutta, he claimed that the new Soviet-Indian friendship would have both material and spiritual value: "Our friendship enriches the peoples of India and the Soviet Union materially and spiritually."[26]

In Khrushchev's approach, spiritual unity was strongly entangled with the understanding that, at the common level of everyday life, there was something uniting all of humankind, powerful enough to transcend religious and ethnic boundaries. In Kashmir Khrushchev stated that he had encountered "Hindus, Moslems and Sikhs" as well as people from "Kashmiri, Dogra and Ladkhi nationalities." Despite these differences, the Soviet leader claimed, on the "streets of Srinagar," he had been "greeted equally by men and women of all creeds and nationalities."[27] Emphasizing this common unity, Khrushchev observed that religious and cultural diversity could readily be reconciled with socialism: "In what way do Muslems [*sic*] differ from the other creeds? In our country we have no such differences, because all peoples of our country are worthy members of the great Soviet Union and make a united family of the peoples."[28]

Of course, Khrushchev had a variety of political reasons to stress popular solidarities transcending religious and ethnic divisions. In Asia he used the language of spiritual and cultural solidarity to fend off claims to religious and national exclusivism. Blaming the partition of British India on a political situation in which "passions were fanned around the differences in the religions of the peoples of India," he accused "official representatives" in Asian politics of trying to "sow discord between the peoples of India, fomenting national enmity or dividing the peoples according to the principle of religious denomination." As Khrushchev reminded his audience, modern state borders did not need to run parallel to religious lines: "problems of religion have never been the cardinal questions in creating a state."[29]

Soviet officials actively tried to persuade other communist states to endorse the new diplomacy of cultural or spiritual solidarities. In April 1954 the Soviet Union urged the PRC to step up its cultural diplomacy (to "expand the influence of New China").[30] Initially the PRC welcomed Soviet and Indian political and cultural representatives' attempts to take part in the new international cultural trend that emphasized cultural exchange and cooperation.[31] Soviet writers were published regularly in Chinese literary journals and were in correspondence with Chinese intellectuals.[32] Peaceful coexistence and the growing appeal of the movement for Afro-Asian solidarity and nonalignment provided Mao with new opportunities to present the PRC as an important player on the stage of global politics. At the April 1955 Afro-Asian Congress in Bandung, Indonesia, the PRC was invited while the USSR was not, and from the mid-1950s onward, Chinese visibility in international relations grew steadily.[33]

Also within UNESCO, Soviet representatives aimed to improve the position of their communist ally in Asia. In his letter to Luther Evans, Molotov had argued that the influence of the PRC "in the development of world general-humanistic culture" was hugely significant, and that therefore the importance of PRC participation in UNESCO "needs no further specific explanation."[34] India, for its part, seeing in the PRC an important partner in the politics of Eurocritical Afro-Asian solidarity, supported Chinese membership in UNESCO. In his address to the Second Conference of the Indian National Committee for UNESCO, held in February 1956 in New Delhi, Indian minister of education Maulana Azad expressed disappointment with that organization's "failure to accord recognition to the true representatives of the Chinese people."[35] In May 1957 acting director of the UNESCO Department for Cultural Activities Prem Kirpal argued in a report to the director general that it "is natural and desirable" that "artists and scholars from the mainland of China will be invited to participate in activities organized within the scope of the major project by all countries of Eastern Europe and many countries of Asia," adding that "without due stress on Chinese civilization and culture the Project will remain somewhat farcical."[36]

PRC self-presentation on the international political stage suggests that the communist Chinese leadership accepted the thaw's cultural narrative that emphasized "spiritual" solidarities between people, embracing it as a tool of anti-imperial struggle. At the Bandung Congress, the PRC foreign minister

Zhou Enlai presented China as a multicultural and multifaith country: "China is a country where there is freedom of religious belief. There are, in China, not only seven million Communists, but also tens of millions of Moslems and Buddhists and millions of Protestants and Catholics. Here in the Chinese Delegation, there is a pious Imam of the Islamic faith."[37] The PRC would seem here to be supporting the view that cultural (or religious) traditions were still relevant to modern life. At the same time, in Zhou Enlai's speech, the secular (atheist) nation-state was placed at the root of modern spiritual and cultural freedoms. Zhou Enlai emphasized that the attainment of modern nationhood allowed popular cultural and religious solidarities to flourish, not the other way around: "Freedom of religious belief is a principle recognized by all modern nations."[38] PRC officials may thus be said to have only met the scholarly narrative of anti-Eurocentric "spiritual" solidarity halfway. Indeed, in his speech Zhou Enlai reaffirmed the atheist character of modern communist society: "We Communists are atheists, but we respect all those who have religious belief. We hope that those with religious belief will also respect those without."[39] While acknowledging the world's cultural and religious diversity, the PRC leadership continued to uphold the materialist narrative of historical development that the complex tradition of thaw Oriental studies in the USSR had aimed to correct.

In the course of the next few years, the differences between Soviet orientalist and Chinese political approaches to the language of spiritual solidarities became more marked. A key moment was the international meeting between Communist parties of November 1957. In his speech, Mao questioned the spiritual approach to international solidarity, calling instead for the rehabilitation of a strict materialist understanding of popular unity. First, Mao reaffirmed a two-camp approach by distinguishing between socialist unity and unity "of another type."[40] Second, he claimed that diversity could only be approached from within a framework of dialectic materialism: "diversity" should be acquired by adopting a "dialectical, not a metaphysical, approach." He did acknowledge the need for a humane approach to diversity, but to his mind this had little to do with appreciating spiritual diversity or accepting culture as a source of popular unity across ethnic or political boundaries. Rather it came down to "acknowledging that human beings all make mistakes and not negating a person completely just because he has made mistakes."[41] To Mao, cultural and spiritual diversity was a temporary societal phenomenon to be overcome in the forward march of historical progress. Cultural and intellectual emancipation had to follow the trajectory of dialectical materialism: in the sphere of "ideology," he claimed, "idealism will be replaced by materialism and theism by atheism."[42] This was far from the UNESCO East-West principle that aimed to critically expand the Western vision of modernity and to include non-Western cultural and spiritual traditions. Finally, Mao attacked the role of cultural and intellectual elites in advancing a new world order: "I say dialectics should be moved from the small circle of philosophers to the broad masses of the people."[43]

Historians have traditionally understood Mao's attempts to rehabilitate a two-camp approach at the November 1957 meeting of Communist parties as a response to the chairman's growing sense of a security threat, both at home and abroad.[44] Focusing in particular on the political and ideological implications, such accounts have presented Mao's speech as a political turning point, reversing elements of socialist ideological revisionism and the politics of peaceful coexistence.[45] However, Mao's speech also had an intellectual dimension that challenged the new course in Soviet Oriental studies that had been made possible by Stalin's death.

Mao's critiques affected the new structure, organization, and research agenda of Soviet academic Oriental studies that had been adopted as part of the Soviet thaw. In February 1958 Ghafurov submitted a modified research plan for the IVAN to the Central Committee of the CPSU, citing the November 1957 meeting as his inspiration.[46] In the new plan, elements of Stalin's confrontational two-camp politics reappeared, with the plans emphasizing the need to "unmask the colonial politics of imperialism" (that of the United States in particular) and to highlight the "international relations between the countries of Asia and Africa and the struggle of these countries with the imperial blocs."[47] In the revised IVAN research agenda, a renewed emphasis on orthodox themes of socioeconomic history and the history of the "communist and workers' movement" in the East went hand in hand with the marginalization of classical philological studies at the institute.[48]

Mao seems to have interpreted the scholars' revisionist reading of history as a particular challenge. The thaw's embrace of cultural traditions affected the way Chinese history was written by Soviet Orientalists. This can be illustrated with the research proposal to rewrite the "History of Asia," which had been submitted to the East-West secretariat in Paris in November 1957. A coworker at the Soviet Institute for Oriental Studies had acted as a member of the advisory committee.[49] The aim of the project, as drafters of the proposal had put it, was to write an "integrated" and "comprehensive" history of Asia that focused on the dynamic processes unifying Asian "civilizations and cultures." The cultural focus was meant to provide a new, international reading of Asia's past. As far as the drafters were concerned, humanistic education in Asia had been tainted by an imperial, Eurocentric reading of Asia's history. They claimed this had led to a "lack of appreciation among Asian peoples themselves of the inter-linking of their several national histories and developments with each other."[50]

At the 1957 meeting for Communist parties, Mao pleaded for the rehabilitation of historical materialism. This was intended to reverse the approach of history that presented Asia's peoples and cultures as culturally or spiritually united. A materialist approach to the past emphasized the distinct cultural identity of the

PRC, separating the state from the cultural and spiritual traditions of neighboring countries, and most importantly, perhaps, of the Republic of China across the Taiwan Strait.[51] The PRC claim to distinction had an interesting parallel in the Soviet academic institutional landscape—as the IVAN's research agenda moved further toward the study of religious traditions and heritages in Asia, a separate Institute for China Studies (IKAN, Institut Kitaevedeniia Akademii Nauk) was set up. Such an institutional arrangement officially distanced modern Chinese studies from the integrated approaches of humanistic, classical Oriental studies.[52]

Implicitly, in his speech, Mao reminded his audience that historical materialism provided a strong legitimizing narrative for centralized statehood and the Communist Party leadership's claims that the rise of communist states was an objective outcome of historical development. In the years of Soviet construction, Stalin had rejected the view that international cultural and spiritual solidarities could serve as a stable foundation for popular socialist unity and progress. Instead he had maintained a strongly territorialized approach to the popular links that served as a stable foundation for socialist statehood: identifying these as the ties of mutual dependency that existed between strong regional state centers and their tributary peripheries.[53] At the international meeting for Communist parties Mao similarly seemed to suggest that successful centralized leadership rested on the support of tributary states and nations: "Another Chinese proverb says: with all its beauty the lotus needs the green of its leaves to set it off." In so doing, he explicitly compared the situation of the PRC with that of the USSR in the Soviet Bloc: "You, comrade Khrushchev, even though you are a beautiful lotus, you too need the leaves to set you off. I, Mao Zedong, while not a beautiful lotus, also need leaves to set me off."[54]

The timing of Mao's critiques suggests that they were a response to events unfolding in the Chinese borderlands and stemmed from the desire to reestablish the state as the sole historical force that united the various Chinese peoples. Throughout 1957 Tibetan uprisings had spilled over into PRC territory, and Mao was greatly worried by signs of CIA involvement in the rebellions. Within the PRC the mood against minority emancipation movements was growing, and as Iurii Andropov, head of the KGB, also noted, Mao viewed the situation in the PRC borderlands as comparable to that of the USSR in Eastern Europe and regarded Tibet as an "Asian Hungary."[55] PRC officials consistently stressed the historical character of current state relations. In 1959 Chinese foreign minister Zhang Hanfu denied the relevance of spiritual and humanist readings of human relations, presenting history as the main legitimating narrative for the current map of China. "The residents are all Chinese as these areas have been a part of China historically. Most of them are Tibetans. This is the situation on China's border with India."[56] Approached through the prism of historiography, Mao's efforts to rehabilitate Stalinist historical materialism can be understood as an attempt to rehabilitate an approach to the past that emphasized the primacy of strong states as centers of territorialized processes of development and regional stability. For the PRC a cultural or spiritual approach to popular solidarity undermined the legitimizing narrative of PRC statehood that was rooted in historical materialism.

Spiritual Solidarity Contested

In the words of Vladislav Zubok, the thaw had unleashed a "cult of humanism" in the Soviet Union, with writers emphasizing the progressive role of cultural and intellectual activity and claiming that "great ideas" could "transform the world."[57] Participation in international organizations such as UNESCO allowed Soviet representatives to recreate this cultural and intellectual thaw on an international scale. Projects sponsored by UNESCO offered new opportunities for cultural reformers and revolutionaries from across the world to meet and engage and to renegotiate prewar visions of modernity. A prime example of this was Julian Huxley's "History of Mankind" project, which had been intended to inspire a new, Eurocritical humanism and was rooted in the intellectual legacy of radical internationalist intellectuals and artists of the interwar period.[58] At Moscow State University, students of Africa and Asia were introduced to the work of radical cultural reformers such as the Orientalist and painter Nikolai Roerich and the famous writer Leo Tolstoy (originally trained as an Orientalist), who had embraced spiritual traditions as a source of cultural renewal.[59] In 1957, after years of emigration, Iurii Roerich, the son of the painter, was invited back to the IVAN as head of the new section of Ancient Cultural and Spiritual Traditions that was set up in the Indology department. The Roerich family had been friends with the Bengali writer and Nobel Prize winner Rabindranath Tagore, who shared with them a commitment to a spiritual progressive universalism.[60] In 1957 Tagore's collected works were published in the USSR for the first time, and in 1961 celebrations were organized all over the Soviet Union to honor Tagore's one hundredth birthday.[61]

Soviet Orientalists celebrated Tagore but without implying that they also embraced the "reified versions of national civilizations" that Prasenjit Duara attributes to such Asianist thinkers as Tagore and his generation.[62] Soviet writers espoused culture (or "spiritualism") as a source of progress and change, granting it the ability to unite people across cultural, religious, and geographic borders. Exemplary in this regard was the work of Il'ia Erenburg, one of the most prominent writers of the thaw generation, who presented human creativity as a source of transcendence, having the capacity to elevate people above their material circumstances.[63] In his travelogue *Indian Impressions*, the writer presented his readership with two contrasting images of India: one based on material characteristics, the other on immaterial ones. In the first case India was depicted as remote and exotic: "Any book devoted to India will tell you that this country, fenced off from others by the Himalayas and the ocean, is a special world."[64] In the other case, cultural recognition and inspiration served to make the country appear close and familiar: "In the songs [a Russian traveler] would hear melodic similarities, he would recognize many of the customs as familiar to him, and he would look at the minaret of Qutub Minar with eyes that had also seen the Gur-Emir and Shah-i Sindh."[65]

Erenburg's essay highlighted the shortcomings of a materialist worldview for achieving a sense of international understanding. In his opinion, popular unity was based on more than strong, unifying state structures, military conquests, or trade relations. People also needed a shared sense of culture: "It is not only in the campaigns of Alexander the Great or the lively relations between India and Hellas at the time of Asoka and later, but it is the fact that Greece, like India—is one of the sources of our civilization, and that an introduction to the inhabitants of Olympus teaches us to understand the harmony of ancient Indian art."[66] In Erenburg's *Indian Impressions* we see how the thaw's embrace of culture as a basis for international solidarity served to undermine narratives of distinct statehood. Moreover, the essay criticized the Western materialist worldview. Describing a scene in which a bewildered European traveler visits India for the first time, Erenburg remarked: "Perhaps, if he had seen the Arab immersed in thought and listening to the sound of running water, the traveler would have been better prepared for his first interview with a resident of Madras, who assured the French merchant that there is more of value in this world than the stock market."[67] While the essay conjures up a stereotypical image of the East as inherently spiritual or ethical, this nevertheless served as a critical reminder that culture or spirituality provided an important potential source of popular understanding and recognition across borders.

Similar critiques of Western worldviews were voiced by African and Asian writers at the Asian-African Writers Conference held in Tashkent in October 1958.[68] At the conference, Soviet representatives tried to facilitate both the two-camp approach and the spiritual, thaw-inspired response to international Afro-Asian solidarity. In his plenary speech, Nuriddin Mukhitdinov, former first secretary of the Uzbek SSR and the first Soviet "Asian" to have been granted a seat at the Presidium of the Central Committee of the Party in the USSR, addressed the African and Asian writers as the "sons and daughters of the Eastern people" who had "for ages been creating invaluable material and spiritual wealth."[69] He had emphasized the centrality of anti-imperial struggle, presenting cultural solidarity as supporting this higher cause: "Progressive literature has always been in the forefront of the struggle for peace and progress. So may more and more writers join the ranks of the mighty movement for peace. May the voice of the writer-fighter, the writer-citizen resound ever louder. May they, through the great force of their pens, fight ever more actively for the triumph of the bright ideals of friendship and peace, freedom and progress."[70] At the same time, however, Mukhitdinov had emphasized the importance of spiritual culture, or humanism, in the pursuit of peace and Afro-Asian solidarity: "It is essential that the unity of the peoples in the struggle for peace, for the freedom and happiness of the whole of mankind, should grow stronger and become tempered day by day. And in this great cause, you, who have chosen to devote your lives to serve the lofty ideas of humanism, are called upon to play a tremendous role."[71] As such, he had presented the event as a celebration of cultural and spiritual solidarities in the current age.

Erenburg's work and that of other Soviet writers was popular among intellectuals and artists in the PRC. In December 1957 his Chinese translator wrote him a letter of appreciation, emphasizing the international meaning and appeal of his work: "For many years I have been impressed by your talent, and I have been reading your work in Chinese and English translation. When I lived across the border, I met with many people who agreed with me, that you are the greatest author of our times."[72] Even so, by late 1957 a trend was well under way in Chinese literature that rejected the language of Afro-Asian spiritual connections and cultural unity. A few weeks after the second Asian-African Writers Conference, a Chinese periodical published a scathing review of the event, arguing that at the conference, "bourgeois" writers had aimed to make the "oppressed peoples decadent."[73] Taking issue with assertions of the continued relevance of shared Asian cultural or spiritual traditions, the author of the article argued: "The backward, passive, so-called 'spiritual civilization' of the East is one of the cankers they have been pushing hard in order to paralyze the fighting spirit of the Eastern peoples and leave them intoxicated by this empty, passive 'spiritual civilization', contented with the world as it is, with no desire to advance, no determination to resist oppression, like sheep to be slaughtered."[74] To the communist leader it appeared as if the spiritual trend in Soviet cultural diplomacy in the East had rekindled nineteenth-century imperial imaginings of Asia as passive and docile, unfit for national independence and self-determination.

In this review the thaw language of cultural or spiritual unity between the peoples of Asia was presented as a perpetuation of Western practices of cultural imperialism. As Sino-Soviet relations continued to deteriorate, Soviet political figures gradually abandoned this language. On the substate level of Soviet intellectual and cultural life, however, Soviet scholars, writers, and artists still espoused the complex approach to world historical development and embraced cultural and spiritual solidarities as a potential source of internationalism. In late 1959 Ghafurov published his own review of the Conference for Asian and African Writers in a Soviet literary journal. In the article he stressed the value of "immaterial" solidarities between peoples, claiming that the ties uniting the African and Asian writers transcended material and political divisions and were "deeper than the ocean, higher than mountain peaks, costlier than gold, firmer than iron and stronger than the wind." As he concluded: "The spirit of Tashkent will prevail!"[75]

The Afro-Asian Writers Conference had been partly sponsored by UNESCO; this was not the last time this organ's infrastructure enabled Soviet Orientalists to negotiate a cultural approach to Asian history and development at a global level. In the next few years, Soviet researchers launched various projects that continued to emphasize international, culturally integrated perspectives on history. At the final meeting of the UNESCO East-West Project, Ghafurov proposed a new research project designed to analyze the cultural history of the broader Central Asian region, preliminarily entitled the "Contribution of Central Asian Peoples to World Civilization."[76] Ghafurov defended the project as contributing to international understanding and solidarity and argued that the project assumed "an especially urgent character" in this current period in which "problems of [the] cultural intercourse of peoples are burning issues of the day."[77] In 1962 a special research group was established at the Central Asian State University in Uzbekistan, bringing together members from the different Soviet Central Asian Republics for the purpose of research into the literary and cultural ties of Central Asia to surrounding countries.[78] The Soviet archaeologist Galena A. Pugachenkova conducted research into the ancient shrine of Khoja Abu Nasr Parsa in the ruined city of Balkh in Afghanistan. While a flirtation with fascism in the mid-1930s had led the Afghan authorities to attempt a rebuilding of the shrine as a glorious center of a new Pashto "Aryan" nation-state (Balkh supposedly having been a historical center of Aryan culture), Pugachenkova's work displaced this nationalist, state-centered cultural narrative by restoring the Islamic, Sufi identity of the shrine.[79] In her research Pugachenkova supported an internationalism based on spiritual solidarities. By subsequently disseminating her findings in UNESCO publications, she, and Soviet scholars like her, persisted in the attempt to convince a global audience of an internationalism that acknowledged transformative cultural and spiritual solidarities.[80]

Conclusion

This chapter has presented the rehabilitation of spiritual approaches to historical development as a central part of the post-Stalinist thaw in Soviet intellectual and cultural life. In this period Soviet historians and Orientalists argued that spiritual and cultural traditions might serve as a foundation for solidarity and unity between peoples. This approach had strong roots in the anti-Eurocentric visions of progress and modernity sustained by critical Russian academics and radical anticolonial circles in the interwar period. After Stalin's death the

Institute for Oriental Studies was mobilized in support of Khrushchev's "break to the East," and Soviet Orientalists came to rehabilitate elements of such radical anti-Eurocentric thinking in their work. At a political level Soviet diplomatic conduct in countries such as India, Afghanistan, and the PRC was also strongly affected by the spiritual trend in Soviet Oriental studies. Soviet participation in international organizations such as UNESCO allowed Soviet Orientalists to convey certain aspects of the values of the "thaw" concerning history and international solidarity to a global audience.

What this chapter has further demonstrated is how Soviet Eurocritical cultural diplomacy was contested at the level of state politics. Analyzing the critiques of Soviet revisionism advanced by Chairman Mao of the Chinese People's Republic, this chapter has shown that the cultural history of Asia was a politically sensitive issue and played a role in the political conflicts between the Soviet Union and the PRC in the late 1950s. Historians have interpreted Mao's critiques of Soviet cultural diplomacy in terms of his resistance to what they tend to regard as a chauvinistic attitude on the part of the Soviets toward their Asian ally. This chapter has added another perspective, in that it suggests that Mao perceived the language of cultural and spiritual internationalism as undermining PRC claims to historical legitimacy. Tibetan rebellions in the region further heightened Mao's fears that the narratives of spiritual solidarity threatened the stability and security of the Chinese People's Republic and would play into the hands of the forces of imperialism in the region.

Finally, this chapter has illustrated that Khrushchev's abandonment of the diplomacy of spiritual solidarity in Asia did not end Soviet support for "thaw approaches" to historical development and modernity. On the substate level of cultural and scholarly networks, Soviet intellectuals and artists were still prepared to advance and negotiate an internationalism that was critical of Eurocentrism. In their everyday professional lives, Soviet Orientalists continued to research internationally shared cultural and religious traditions. International institutions such as UNESCO enabled them to disseminate their findings on a global level and thereby to contribute to an international debate regarding an understanding of world history and modernity that acknowledged the agency of (formerly) colonized and marginalized groups.

Notes

* Research for this chapter has been conducted as part of the joint project "The Legacy of Soviet Oriental Studies: Networks, Institutions, Discourses," directed by Michael Kemper (UvA, Amsterdam) and Stéphane A. Dudoignon (EHESS, Paris) and funded by the NWO (The Netherlands Organization for Scientific Research). Following the example of M. Kemper and S. A. Dudoignon, this article distinguishes the term *Oriental studies* as describing a

specific academic discipline, from Edward Said's use of the term *Orientalism* (Said, 1978) as indicating processes of subjectivization and essentialization in scholarly representations of the Orient. Again after Kemper and Dudoignon (Kemper & Dudoignon, 2009), the term *Oriental studies* will be used for the Soviet period, and the term *Orientology* for the Russian and European Imperial period.

1. Letter from Viacheslav Molotov to Luther Evans, December 30, 1955, 008 (470) MP 03, East-West Major Project, Participation USSR part 1, Archives of the United Nations Educational Scientific and Cultural Organization (UNESCO), Paris, France.

2. On UN organizations specifically, see Akira Iriye, *Global Community. The Role of International Organizations in the Making of the Contemporary World* (Berkeley, Los Angeles, London: University of California Press, 2002).

3. Letter from Viacheslav Molotov, December 30, 1955, 008 (470) MP 03, East-West Major Project, Participation USSR part 1, UNESCO Archives, Paris, France.

4. Ibid.

5. Guber's candidature was approved by Suslov. See V. Iu. Arfiani and V. D. Esakov, eds., *Akademiia Nauk v Resheniiakh TsK KPSS* (Moscow: ROSSPEN, 2010), 312.

6. Arfiani and Esakov, *Akademiia Nauk*, 314; Zapiskaby, P. N. Pospelova, K. V. Ostrovitianova, A. M. Pankratovoi, and A. M. Rumiantseva, dated no later than July 20, 1955, fond 3, opis 8, delo 279, RGANI, Moscow, Russia.

7. Guber was selected for the position of director in 1954, but he was only installed in August 1955; see Oded Eran, *Mezhdunarodniki: An Assessment of Professional Expertise in the Making of Soviet Foreign Policy* (Ramat: Turtledove Publishing, 1979). There is a rich Russian-language literature surveying the evolution of academic Orientology during the Soviet period. Key recent English-language publications that address the history of Oriental studies in the Soviet Union are Michael Kemper and Artemy M. Kalinovsky, eds., *Reassessing Orientalism: Interlocking Orientologies during the Cold War* (London: Routledge, 2015); Michael Kemper and Stephan Conermann, eds., *The Heritage of Soviet Oriental Studies* (London: Routledge, 2011); Vera Tolz, *Russia's Own Orient: The Politics of Identity and Oriental Studies in the Late Imperial and Early Soviet Periods* (Oxford: Oxford University Press, 2011). For a recent work exploring the international context of the Soviet discipline, see S. Marung and K. Naumann, "The Making of Oriental Studies: Its Transnational and Transatlantic Past," in *The Making of the Humanities. Volume III: The Modern Humanities*, eds. R. Bod, J. Maat, and T. Weststeijn (Amsterdam University Press, 2014), 415–429.

8. Stenogramma Zasedaniia Sovetskogo Komiteta Solidarnosti Stran' Azii, November 1, 1956, fond 9540, opis 1, delo 2, Gosudarstvennyi Arkhiv Rossiiskoi Federatsii (GARF), Moscow, Russia.

9. Laura Wong, "Cultural Agency: UNESCO's Major Project on the Mutual Appreciation of Eastern and Western Values, 1957–1966," (PhD diss., Harvard University, 2006), 63.

10. For how Central Asians played crucial roles as mediators in Soviet foreign relations, see Masha Kirasirova, "The Eastern International: The 'Domestic East' and the 'Foreign East' in Soviet-Arab Relations, 1917–68," (PhD diss., New York University, 2014); Artemy Kalinovsky, "Not Some British Colony in Africa: The Politics of Decolonization and Modernization in Soviet Central Asia, 1955–1964," *Ab Imperio* 2 (2013): 191–222; Masha Kirasirova, "'Sons of Muslims' in Moscow: Soviet Central Asian Mediators to the Foreign East, 1955–1962," *Ab Imperio* 4 (2011): 106–132. Also see my "Negotiating Russian Imperial Aryanism? Soviet Oriental

Studies in the Cold War," in *Decolonization and the Cold War: Negotiating Independence*, eds. Leslie James and Elisabeth Leake (London: Bloomsbury Academic, 2015), 145–166.

11. For the rehabilitation of classical philology in Soviet Oriental studies, see Michael Kemper, "Propaganda for the East, Scholarship for the West: Soviet Strategies at the 1960 International Congress of Orientalists in Moscow," in *Reassessing Orientalism*, eds. Kemper and Kalinovsky. For Soviet Orientalists presenting the new philological turn as a central aspect of de-Stalinization, see N. A. Kuznetsova and L. M. Kulagina, eds., *Iz istorii sovetskogo vostokovedeniia 1917–1967* (Moscow: Nauka, 1970), 156. For Ghafurov's speech, see B. G. Gafurov, *Sostoianie i zadachi sovetskogo vostokovedeniia v svete reshenii XX S'ezda KPSS: Doklad na vsesoiuznoi konferentsii vostokovedov* (Tashkent, 1957).

12. For a thorough analysis of how the writings of Soviet academically trained Orientalists and foreign policy experts were influenced by and entangled with Soviet foreign relations in the world, and decolonizing countries in particular, see Eran, *Mezhdunarodniki*.

13. Francine Hirsch, *Empire of Nations: Ethnographic Knowledge and the Making of the Soviet Union* (Ithaca, London: Cornell University Press, 2005).

14. Nation formation was understood as an unavoidable by-product of the modern, capitalist stage of development. See Terry Martin, "Modernization or Neo-Traditionalism? Ascribed Nationality and Soviet Primordialism," in *Russian Modernity: Politics, Knowledge, Practices*, eds. David L. Hoffmann and Yanni Kotsonis (New York: St. Martin's Press, 2000).

15. For a recent article addressing the links between Stalinist historiography and Soviet national policy, see David Brandenberger and Mikhail V. Zelenov, "Stalin's Answer to the National Question: A Case Study on the Editing of the 1938 Short Course," *Slavic Review* 73, no. 4 (Winter 2014): 859–880.

16. For the way culture and scholarship on the East supported Russian imperial rule, see David Schimmelpennick van der Oye, *Russian Orientalism: Asia in the Russian Mind from Catherine the Great to the Emigration* (New Haven, CT: Yale University Press, 2010).

17. For an overview of different ideologies of Asian unity and distinction, see Carolien Stolte and Harald Fischer Tiné, "Imagining Asia in India: Nationalism and Internationalism (ca. 1905–1940)," *Comparative Studies in Society and History* 54, no. 1 (2012): 403–423.

18. For a discussion of the various and variegated ideologies of internationalism that inspired anticolonial radicals and revolutionaries in the interwar period, see Ali Raza, Franziska Roy, and Benjamin Zachariah, eds., *The Internationalist Moment: South Asia, Worlds, and World Views, 1917–1939* (New Delhi: Sage Publications, 2014).

19. For the anti-Eurocentric commitments of prerevolutionary Orientalists, see Vera Tolz, "European, National, and (Anti-)Imperial: The Formation of Academic Oriental Studies in Late Tsarist and Early Soviet Russia," *Kritika: Explorations in Russian and Eurasian History* 9, no. 1 (Winter 2008): 53–81. Also see Tolz, *Russia's Own Orient*.

20. See Tolz, *Russia's Own Orient*.

21. Yuri Bregel, "Barthold and Modern Oriental Studies," *International Journal of Middle Eastern Studies* 12, no. 3 (November 1980): 385–403.

22. V. Gurevich, ed., *XX s'ezd Kommunisticheskoi Partii Sovetskogo Soiuza: Stenograficheskii otchet Tom I* (Moscow: Gosudarstvennoe izdatel'stva politicheskoi literatury, 1956), 333.

23. Gafurov, *Sostoianie i zadachi*.

24. *N. A. Bulganin and N. S. Khruhschev: Full Texts of Speeches and Statements in India, Burma and Afghanistan* (Soviet News: London, 1955), 4.

25. Ibid., 11.
26. Ibid., 21.
27. Ibid., 23.
28. Ibid., 23.
29. Ibid., 24.
30. Telegram, Zhang Wentian to PRC vice foreign minister Li Kenong, April 6, 1954, Wilson Center Digital Archive, www.digitalarchive.center.org (last accessed January 14, 2014).
31. For recent works highlighting the cooperative character of early post-Stalinist PRC-USSR relations, see Austin Jersild, *The Sino-Soviet Alliance: An International History* (Chapel Hill: University of North Carolina Press, 2014); Odd Arne Westad, *Restless Empire: China and the World since 1750* (London: Bodley Head, 2012). For India-PRC relations in this period, see for instance Benjamin Zachariah, *Nehru* (London: Routledge, 2004).
32. See D. W. Fokkema, *Literary Doctrine in China and Soviet Influence 1956–1960* (The Hague: Mouton & Co., 1965).
33. Westad, *Restless Empire*.
34. Letter from Viacheslav Molotov, December 30, 1955, 008 (470) MP 03, East-West Major Project, Participation USSR part 1, UNESCO Archives, Paris, France.
35. Report on the Second Conference of the Indian National Commission for Cooperation with UNESCO, March 13, 1956, 008 (540) MP 03, East-West Major Project, Participation India part 1, UNESCO Archives, Paris, France.
36. Ibid.
37. Supplementary speech of premier Zhou Enlai at the Plenary Session of the Asian-African Conference, April 19, 1955, Wilson Center Digital Archive, https://digitalarchive.wilsoncenter.org, (last accessed February 7, 2015).
38. Ibid.
39. Ibid.
40. Mao Zedong speech at a meeting of the representatives of sixty-four Communist and Workers' Parties, November 18, 1957, Wilson Center Digital Archive, https://digitalarchive.wilsoncenter.org, (last accessed January 14, 2015).
41. Ibid.
42. Ibid.
43. Ibid. Mao had fought against a metaphysical approach to international relations before. As Austin Jersild pointed out, in 1938 Mao had already argued against a metaphysical approach to socialist unity, claiming that the socialist approach to the historical path of development should be sensitive to "concrete" circumstance; see Jersild, *The Sino-Soviet Alliance*, 116.
44. For the view that Mao's orthodox turn was primarily a response to domestic pressures, see Westad, *Restless Empire*.
45. For the claim that the meeting was a pivotal moment in intercommunist relations, since here Soviet Bloc leadership was reaffirmed, see Jersild, *The Sino-Soviet Alliance*. For the notion that the meeting was a turning point in international relations with peaceful coexistence partially replaced by the orthodox two-camp approach, see Westad, *Restless Empire*.
46. Postanovlenie o dal'neishem razvitii sovetskogo vostokovedeniia, February 21, 1958, fond 5, opis 35, delo 78, Russian State Archive of Contemporary History (RGANI), Moscow, Russia.

47. Ibid.
48. Ibid.
49. Memorandum of the "History of Asia" Project, November 18, 1957, 008 (470) MP 03 East-West Major Project, Participation USSR part 1, UNESCO Archives, Paris, France.
50. Ibid.
51. For cultural and spatial politics in 20th-century Asia see Paul H. Kratoska, Remco Raben, and Henk Schulte Nordholt, eds. *Locating Southeast Asia: Geographies of Knowledge and Politics of Space* (Singapore: Singapore University Press, 2005).
52. See N. A. Kuznetsova and L. M. Kulagina, eds., *Iz istorii sovetskogo vostokovedeniia* 1917–1967 (Moscow: Nauka, 1970).
53. For this argument, see Alfred Rieber, *Stalin and the Struggle for Supremacy in Eurasia* (Cambridge: Cambridge University Press, 2015).
54. Mao Zedong speech, November 18, 1957, Wilson Center Digital Archive.
55. For Andropov's note, see the report by Yuri Andropov "On the Situation in Tibet," March 31, 1959, Wilson Center Digital Archive, https://digitalarchive.wilsoncenter.org (last accessed October 15, 2014).
56. "Meeting Minutes between Chinese Vice Foreign Minister Zhang Hanfu and Ambassadors from Fraternal Countries on the Tibet Issue," September 9, 1959, Wilson Center Digital Archive, https://digitalarchive.wilsoncenter.org (last accessed May 6, 2016).
57. As quoted in Vladislav Zubok, *Zhivago's Children: The Last Russian Intelligentsia* (Cambridge, MA: Harvard University Press, 2009), 71.
58. For Huxley's humanist plans for UNESCO, see Laura Wong, "Cultural Agency." For more on Huxley's universalist worldview, see Glenda Sluga, "UNESCO and the (One) World of Julian Huxley," *Journal of World History* 21, no. 3 (September 2010): 392–418. For a discussion of Julian Huxley's History of Mankind Project in particular, see Poul Duedahl, "UNESCO and the Invention of Global History, 1945-1976," *Journal of World History* 22, no. 1 (March 2011): 101–133. For ideas of internationalism popular in the interwar years, see Raza, Roy, Zachariah, eds., *The Internationalist Moment.*
59. As Irina Smilianskaia, a later prominent Arabist at the IVAN remembered, one of the most popular writers studied by students at the Moscow State University was Leo Tolstoy; interview by the author with Irina Smilianskaia (May 15, 2010). For more on the Roerichs, see Anita Stasulane, *Theosophy and Culture: Nicholas Roerich* (Rome: Pontificia Universita Gregoriana, 2005); John McCannon, "In Search of Primeval Russia: Stylistic Evolution in the Landscapes of Nicholas Roerich 1897–1914," *Cultural Geographies* 7, no. 271 (2000): 271–297.
60. For Roerich's friendship with Rabindranath Tagore, see Stasulane, *Theosophy and Culture.* For more on Tagore's popularity in Central Europe in the interwar period, see Ana Jelnikar, "Srecko Kosovel and Rabindranath Tagore: Universalist Hopes from the Margins of Europe," in *The Internationalist Moment*, eds. Raza, Roy, Zachariah, 188–228.
61. RGANI fond 5, opis 35, delo 78, RGANI, Moscow, Russia; Tagore honored in the Soviet Union (undated), 008 (470) MP 03, East-West Major Project, Participation USSR part 1, UNESCO Archives, Paris, France. For an assessment of Tagore as a universalist, whose ideas of Asian unity revolved around a "creative ideal of universality rather than the readily available nationalisms that were the easier choices at the time," see Raza, Roy, Zachariah, eds., *The Internationalist Moment*, xi.
62. For this interpretation of the visions of Asia held by prominent Asianist intellectuals such as Rabindranath Tagore (India), Okakura Tenshin (Japan), and Zhang Taiyan (China),

see Prasenjit Duara, "Asia Redux: Conceptualizing a Region for Our Times," *Journal of Asian Studies* 69, no. 4 (November 2010): 963–983.

63. The Soviet writer and poet Il'ia Erenburg was at the forefront of the post-Stalin intellectual revisionist movement. In 1960 the essay cited in this article appeared as "Indian Impressions," ("Indiiskie vpechatleniia") in a volume together with two other essays, one on the writer's travels to Japan ("Japonskie zametki") and one on his travels to Greece (entitled "Razmyshlenniia v Gretsii"), see Il'ia Erenburg, *Putevye zapisi: Iaponiia, Gretsiia, Indiia* (1960), http://nippon-history.ru/books/item/foo/soo/zoooo016/st003.shtml (accessed on June 3, 2016).

64. Ibid.

65. Ibid.

66. Ibid.

67. Ibid.

68. For more on the Afro-Asian Writers Conference, see Rossen Djagalov, "The People's Republic of Letters: Towards a Media History of Twentieth-Century Socialist Internationalism" (PhD diss., Yale University, 2011).

69. 008 (470) MP 03, East-West Major Project, Participation USSR part 1, UNESCO Archives, Paris, France.

70. Ibid.

71. Ibid.

72. V. S. Miasnikov, ed., *Drug i soiuznik novogo Kitaia: Kitaiskiaia Narodnaia Respublika v 1950-e gody, sbornik dokumentov v dvukh tomakh, tom 2* (Moscow: Pami͡atniki istoricheskoĭ mysli, 2009), 417–418.

73. As quoted in Fokkema, *Literary Doctrine in China*, 195.

74. Ibid.

75. B. G. Gafurov, "Dukh Tashkenta," in *Inostrannaia Literatura* 11 (November 1959), 211.

76. Contribution of Central Asian peoples to world civilization: Organization of study (undated), 008 (470) MP 03, East-West Major Project, Participation USSR part 1, UNESCO Archives, Paris, France.

77. Ibid.

78. N. G. Kalinin, ed., *Spetsialnyĭ Biulleten' No. 6* (Moscow: Nauka, 1991), 21.

79. R. D. McChesney, "Architecture and Narrative: The Khwaja Abu Nasr Parsa Shrine. Part 2: Representing the Complex in Word and Image, 1696–1998," *Muqarnas* 19 (2002): 85–87.

80. Ibid., 90.

HANNA JANSEN is PhD Candidate in Eastern European and Russian History at the Amsterdam School for Regional, Transnational, and European Studies.

10 Soviet Antiracism and Its Discontents: The Cold War Years

Maxim Matusevich

Of all the ideological battles waged during the Cold War, none should have been easier for the Soviet Union to win than the struggle for the "soul of the Third World." When it came to upholding the principles of antiracism and anticolonialism, the Soviets were on solid ground, as an adherence to these values constituted one of the fundamentals of Marxism-Leninism. Marxists eschewed racism as a matter of course and, on the very eve of the great October Revolution, V. I. Lenin famously proclaimed imperialism to be the "highest stage" of the "parasitic" and "decaying" capitalism.[1] From its early days, the new socialist state engaged in massive propaganda campaigns decrying the evils of Western racism and colonial oppression. The Communist International (Comintern), formed in 1919—just as the first Red Scare and its accompanying wave of antiblack violence hit the United States—sought to spread the gospel of colorblind internationalism and proletarian solidarity; it also set out to formulate a global strategy for black liberation and forced the leadership of various Communist parties, including the American one, to address the "Negro Question."[2] Soviet antiracism campaigns would continue more or less unabated until the arrival of perestroika in the late 1980s; in fact, they would serve as an essential element of the Soviet Union's anti-American critique. To be fair, the United States and its European colonial allies provided an almost endless supply of incriminating evidence (Jim Crow segregation, colonial violence, public and covert persecution of black radicals, etc.) ready-made for Soviet use against them. As the historian Meredith Roman recently observed, putting American racism on trial helped the Soviets to build a more convincing case for the moral superiority of their own model of modernity.[3]

Yet the Soviet Union's engagement with race was hardly unproblematic. A number of scholars have noted the tension between the aspirations of Soviet antiracism and the complexity of new postcolonial identities.[4] Africa's nationalist elites readily denounced racism and colonialism, but they also recognized the opportunities offered to independent Africa by the Cold War and the rivalry between its main antagonists. Western racism was just as likely (or even more likely) to inspire demands for reform as calls for revolution. In the United States, for example, the most recognizable face of the black struggle for equality was that of a Baptist minister Martin Luther King Jr., who preached nonviolence and integration and whose influence and political clout far surpassed the appeal of such radicals as the card-carrying Communists Harry Haywood, Angela Davis, or the Soviet Union's devoted friend Paul Robeson. In other words, rejection and critique of racism and colonialism by black Americans and the new elite class of African nationalists did not automatically entail their uncritical acceptance of Soviet "socialist development" or an immediate adoption of the Soviet Union as a natural ally.

As their Cold War involvement in the developing world deepened, the Soviets had to tread carefully to avoid any unflattering comparisons with their ideological opponents in the West while emphasizing the Soviet Union's exceptional status as the only industrialized nation free of the historical taint of racism. More often than not, these arguments were cast in explicitly ideological terms, yet as a number of scholars observed, a cultural case could be made for the Soviet Union tapping into an antiracist (and thus anti-Western) tradition articulated by segments of Russian and Russian-speaking educated elites since before the revolution.[5] The Soviets routinely pitched the socialist model of development to the nonwhite world by highlighting their nation's commitments to antiracism and its history of ethnic and racial diversity and coexistence. Independent Africa appreciated the sentiment, but when it came to choosing (or not choosing) sides in the Cold War, African elites often preferred pragmatism to ideology or idealism.[6]

Curiously, the vociferousness of Soviet antiracist campaigns sometimes rendered the USSR vulnerable to the criticism of failing to live up to its own professed ideals. Martin Luther King Jr., for example, famously castigated Moscow for its treatment of Soviet Jews.[7] And there were other unanticipated challenges. African and other Third World students in the Soviet Union would eventually number many thousands, and their presence in the midst of a highly insular society would become a source of great anxiety. After all, the Soviet authorities were steeped in dogma and hampered by parochialism. In the aftermath of Soviet collapse, Russian and Ukrainian archives have yielded a wealth of materials that reveal the degree to which these postcolonial actors subverted the Soviet status quo and even emerged as conduits for dissent and a variety of liberation discourses that called into question the rigidity of Marxism-Leninism.[8]

Scholars have noted the significance of the often strained interactions between the Soviet authorities, habitually crusading against Western racism, and the postcolonial subjects of their ideological concern. Incidentally, sociologist Nikolay Zakharov has found at least some of the sources of the virulent racist backlash that would sweep across post-Soviet spaces after the Cold War in this tension.[9] By recognizing the complexity and limitations of Soviet engagement with race during the crucial phase of decolonization, with all the attendant hopefulness, ideological experimentation, naiveté, and inevitable frustrations, we gain an insight into an important and insufficiently understood aspect of the global Cold War.

Not surprisingly, among those who responded most enthusiastically to Soviet antiracist propaganda were the citizens of the West whose lives were defined and sometimes dominated by racial oppression. In the 1920s and 1930s, the Soviet Union became a popular destination for African American, Afro-Caribbean, and African radicals and intellectuals anxious to experience its alleged racial utopia. Starting with poet Claude McKay's widely publicized 1922 journey to the Fourth Comintern Congress in Moscow, black activists, public intellectuals, professionals, students, and adventurers trekked to Soviet Russia. There were those who, like the communists Lovett Fort-Whiteman, George Padmore, Otto Hall, his brother Harry Haywood, or the lawyer William L. Patterson, arrived to receive ideological training and work on the "Negro Question" at the Comintern.

But there were others whose motivations to embark on a Soviet sojourn had little to do with Soviet ideology and a lot to do with the reality of North American racism. The budding journalist Homer Smith (pen name Chatwood Hall), or the young Detroit toolmaker Robert Robinson, or some of the members of the cast of the projected (and eventually unrealized) antiracist propaganda film *Black and White* came to the Soviet Union in the early 1930s to have an adventure in a land free of racism and also to escape the Depression-era unemployment back home.[10] According to most existing accounts, these sojourners often found what they had sought—a new country undergoing an unprecedented social experiment of multiethnic coexistence that afforded them dizzying opportunities for economic and personal advancement. The sense of exuberance at the discovery of this El Dorado of racial equality is palpable in the accounts by black travelers in the Soviet Union. Claude McKay returned from his triumphant visit overwhelmed by the experience of being accepted—both as a person and as a representative of his race: "Never in my life did I feel prouder of being an African, and black . . . I was like a black icon in the flesh. . . . Yes, that was exactly what it was. I was like a black icon."[11] The great Pan-Africanist W. E. B. Du Bois was similarly impressed following his 1926 trip to the socialist mecca. "I stand in astonishment and wonder," he editorialized in the NAACP publication the *Crisis*, "at the revelation of Russia that has come to me. I may be partially deceived and half-informed. But if what I have seen with my eyes and heard with my ears in Russia is Bolshevism, I am a Bolshevik."[12]

Poet Langston Hughes and actor and singer Paul Robeson visited the country during the prewar decade and remained sentimentally attached to Russia and its people for the rest of their lives. Robeson's Soviet commitments ran particularly deep, reflecting his conviction that black liberation causes had no better friend than the Soviet Union. Even when confronted with the well-documented horrors of Stalin's purges (which incidentally claimed the lives of some of his close Jewish-Russian friends), he refused to reconsider or even modify his stance; the Soviet Union's very existence, he insisted as late as 1950, "has given us Negroes the chance of achieving our complete liberation within our own time, within this generation."[13]

The Second World War ushered in a novel geopolitical reality dominated by two new superpowers. The war period deepened the conservative, nationalist tendencies first revealed during the prewar decade. The dreams of an internationalist, colorblind utopia had given way to a hard-nosed nationalism. Having rallied the people around the Russian center and the memories of imperial military glories (a new Soviet anthem supplanted the "International" in 1944 and proclaimed "Great Russia" to be the guarantor of the socialist union), Stalin also embarked on a series of campaigns of ethnic cleansing, which resulted in the expulsion of hundreds of thousands of ethnic Chechens, Crimean Tatars, Volga Germans, and others from their traditional homelands. The extent to which the regime had abandoned its early internationalist principles was further exposed in the course of a vicious anti-Semitic drive that claimed the lives and liberty of some the country's most prominent Jewish figures (including such friends of Paul Robeson's as theater director Solomon Mikhoels and poet Itzik Feffer).[14] From the "affirmative action empire" of its prewar years, the Soviet Union had evolved into a more Russian-centric nation-state in which national particularisms and local nationalist aspirations were treated with an ever-increasing suspicion.[15]

Just as the Soviet Union was growing more isolationist during the late Stalinist period, two major geopolitical developments put to the test its ideological commitment to decolonization. First, the Cold War between the Soviets and their American rivals had come to replace the European-centered international order. And second, while the Cold War was heating up, the European colonial empires began to unravel in real time—the very process of decolonization the Soviets had anticipated and championed so incessantly through their massive anticolonial propaganda campaigns. However, when faced with the rise of nationalist movements in the colonies, particularly in Africa, Soviet ideologues could not quite decide whether they were dealing with friends or foes and viewed with apprehension the rise of some of the new African nationalist leaders. If Jomo Kenyatta had long since compromised himself in the eyes of the Kremlin by abandoning his early infatuation with Marxism (he briefly studied in Moscow in 1932) for other, more nationalistic pursuits, Kwame Nkrumah of the Gold Coast became the target of intemperate official criticism. Writing in 1953, just four years prior to Ghana's independence, the leading light of Soviet African studies Ivan Potekhin denounced Nkrumah as a British "puppet" prone to dubious double-dealing with his "colonial masters": "The government of the People's Party is basically a screen concealing the actual role of English imperialism. . . . The People's Party, representing the interests of the big national bourgeoisie of the Gold Coast, deceived the confidence of the people, and the leaders of the party made a sharp turn to the right, to the side of collaboration with English imperialism."[16] Similarly, the Soviets took a generally dim view of the early nationalist leaders in British Nigeria, with Nnamdi Azikiwe, for example, castigated as a compliant stooge of British imperialism. In a paper presented at the Soviet Institute of Ethnography on Stalin's seventieth birthday (1949), Ivan Potekhin spoke plainly: the views of Nigerian nationalists, in his opinion, were nothing more than a "colonial edition of the reactionary American philosophy of pragmatism," and as such they failed to reflect the interests of the toiling masses. Apparently the very fact that new African elites were negotiating the terms of transition to independence and constitutional reforms with European colonial powers condemned them in the eyes of the stern Kremlin ideologues, committed as they were to a class-based interpretation of decolonization. From their point of view, a search for compromise and adherence to nonviolence (Gandhi had few sympathizers in Moscow at the time) marked African nationalists as bourgeois sellouts, "feudal marionette princes," and "reactionaries."[17]

Such interpretive rigidity stemmed from an inflexible view of world affairs divided into two antagonistic camps with little leeway for compromise. Genuine decolonization could be achieved only through a direct confrontation with imperialists, and only a broad coalition of patriotic workers, preferably led by a Communist party, could secure true independence. The Stalinist theory of colonial revolutions allowed no place for moderate nationalists, insisting that "the solution of colonial slavery is impossible without a proletarian revolution and the overthrow of imperialism." Any attempts to chart an independent course and avoid the ideological contest between the superpowers and any claims to neutrality were met with dismissive or openly hostile rejoinders.[18] At the time, the incongruity between the Soviet Union's antiracist rhetoric and the excoriation of African and black "bourgeois" nationalism by its propaganda outlets put off such former allies and fellow travelers as the abovementioned George Padmore or the famed black American novelist Richard Wright. Clearly, the idea of African and black emancipation proceeding in accordance with the theory of proletarian revolution and under the aegis of Moscow satisfied neither the nationalists like Nkrumah, who demanded "self-rule now," nor the Pan-Africanists like Padmore.[19] Soviet analysis of the African colonial condition and the state of race relations in the colonies and in the United States additionally suffered from the dearth of serious scholarship on these subjects. Among the lesser known casualties of Stalin's purges was the burgeoning discipline of African studies. Most of the early Soviet experts on Africa, some of them previously associated with the Comintern, fell victim to Stalin's growing xenophobia and wariness of area studies research: some were executed and others jailed or forced to seek less hazardous occupations, with survivors often looking for refuge in the innocuous field of African linguistics.[20]

On the very eve of African independence, the Soviet Union could justifiably congratulate itself on its ideological commitment to antiracism and anticolonialism, and it could cite its well-documented and even better publicized antiracist campaigns and point to the vociferous (and often highly effective) propaganda crusades of previous decades as proof of this enduring commitment. The Soviet critique of Western racism was central to Moscow's efforts to occupy the moral high ground in the ongoing Cold War context. As Meredith Roman recently argued, Soviet antiracist propaganda served as a marketing tool to promote the "new Soviet man," a figure free of the blemishes of capitalism, of which racism was but the most visible. The first generation of Soviet writers, especially those who had visited the United States, decried racial inequities in the West. Such prominent cultural figures as poet Vladimir Mayakovsky, writers Ilya Il'f and Yevgenii Petrov, and journalist Ilya Ehrenburg left accounts of their American sojourns that not only emphasized the prevalence of American racism but also argued for the moral superiority and progressive nature of Soviet modernity.[21] In their popular travelogue *Single-Storied America*, Il'f and Petrov, for example, recount a conversation they held with a white Southern hitchhiker, whom they (to no apparent avail) instruct in the basics of white privilege and Jim Crow injustices.[22]

But while Soviet writers and propagandists sought to expose the depravity of race relations in the West, Soviet scholarship on Africa remained parochial and burdened by ideological interpretive models (e.g., Stalin's insistence on the necessity of proletarian revolutions in the colonies) that mirrored the prevailing party line in Moscow but in no way reflected local African conditions. Importantly, Soviet Africanists seldom set foot in Africa and tended to lump together all race-related issues, including those pertaining to North America, under the generic rubrics of Negro, Asian, and even Eastern "questions." Ivan Potekhin, the doyen of Soviet African studies, did not visit the continent to which he had devoted his professional and scholarly life until 1957, when he was already in his mid-fifties.[23]

Stalin's demise and the subsequent rise of Nikita Khrushchev marked a transition from Stalinist dogmatic rigidity to a period of relative relaxation, commonly known as the "Khrushchevian thaw." To be sure, the Cold War rivalry between the superpowers continued largely unabated, but the Kremlin's approach to foreign affairs, which increasingly included dealing with the emerging Third World, underwent a major overhaul. To his credit, Khrushchev recognized the necessity to reconsider the previously inflexible approach toward African (and Third World) nationalism. Whereas Stalin had treated Third World nationalists with profound distrust and even animosity, the new leader leaned toward optimism. A wake-up call came at the 1955 Bandung Conference of the leaders of nonaligned African and Asian countries, where at least some delegates, while condemning Western colonialism, were also quite candid in expressing their suspicion of Soviet motives: the Soviet Union's efforts to obtain representation for its Central Asian and Caucasian republics were stymied by the champions of "positive neutralism."[24] Undoubtedly, faced with a similar challenge, Stalin would have branded the offenders as fascists and Western lackeys, but now Khrushchev demonstrated a far greater sensibility and willingness to accept the indisputable fact that many, if not most, Third World leaders were not all that interested in Soviet ideology. If Moscow desired to remain on cordial terms with the emerging Third World, it had to soften its ideology.

The change of heart arrived in the immediate aftermath of the Bandung Conference and is easily detectable in a call for a more nuanced study of Africa appearing in a May 1955 editorial in *Kommunist*, the party's primary theoretical journal: "It should be noted that the study of African countries on the whole has been so far inadequately organized . . . the study of history, economics and culture of the African peoples, their national liberation struggle, and the exposure of the colonial policies of the imperialists in Africa is one of the important tasks of Soviet Oriental studies."[25] No other event better captured this new spirit of openness than the International Youth Festival that took Moscow by storm in late summer 1957. For the first time in decades, the Muscovites were treated to a parade of colorful foreigners filling the streets, squares, and parks of their city. The festival's contemporaries would later compare the cultural import of the event to the 1945 V-Day parade and the 1980 Moscow Olympics. Apollon Davidson, one of the founding fathers of Soviet African studies, recalled in his memoir the sense of euphoria that accompanied the arrival of foreign guests in Moscow: "This was a turning point. . . . After the decades of Stalinist isolationism we saw the festival as something unusual, extraordinary, fantastic. It is hard to imagine now but at the time the majority of the Muscovites had never met a foreigner. Especially someone from Africa!"[26]

The impact of the festival proved to be long-lasting. If the Kremlin had planned the festival to showcase its internationalist credentials and refurbish its international image, particularly in the decolonizing world, the festival's most enduring influence was probably domestic. In August 1957 Soviet citizens received their first exposure to the lifestyles, mannerisms, aesthetics, cultural expressions, and political debates that contrasted most sharply with the Soviet norm. Just seeing foreign fashions on display and observing the public displays of affection by the uninhibited festival guests made for an unforgettable and strangely liberating experience—the first ripples of the sexual revolution, including some of the initial forays into the realm of interracial love, had finally reached the puritanical Soviet shores.[27]

On a more practical level, the festival rejuvenated the study of Africa and restarted the long-dormant substantive conversation about race at the highest levels of Soviet power. Besides the generally relaxed atmosphere during the "thaw," much credit belonged to the Soviet Union's prominent African American friends in the United States, particularly Paul Robeson and W. E. B. Du Bois. Barred from foreign travel during the McCarthy years, Robeson had his US passport reinstated by the State Department in 1958 and almost immediately left for the Soviet Union, where he addressed the country's growing TV audience as part of a predictably tendentious film project on race relations in the United States.[28] That same year, the elderly Du Bois visited Nikita Khrushchev in the Kremlin, and the two apparently discussed at length the prospects for the creation of a new research center dedicated to the study of Africa under the auspices of the Soviet Academy of Sciences. Du Bois later claimed credit for the founding of the Africa Institute in Moscow under the directorship of the indefatigable Ivan Potekhin.[29] The institute was a legacy of the thaw and would play an important role in formulating new theoretical frameworks to reorient Soviet foreign policy toward a more direct engagement with postcolonial Africa.

This engagement became based on a more optimistic assessment of the national liberation movements and an expectation that they could yet mature as part of the "world revolutionary process" and thus evolve into the Soviet Union's natural allies. As Sergey Mazov has recently shown, the reorientation from castigating the national bourgeoisie in the colonies to embracing previously dismissed political forces, such as the Convention People's Party in the Gold Coast, had been completed by the time of Ghanaian independence in 1957.[30] Ivan Potekhin, who had not so long ago been dismissive of the "colonizers' minions" in the Gold Coast, was now prepared to view Nkrumah as progressive and anti-imperialist.[31] A Soviet correspondent, reporting from the first Conference of Independent States of Africa (April 1958), asserted most enthusiastically that "Africa has spoken for the first time in its history," while Potekhin, having attended the 1958 All-African People's Conference in Accra, had few doubts regarding the impending collapse of the "colonial system in Africa."[32]

Under such changed circumstances, the idea of nonalignment now found more understanding and even acceptance among Soviet policy makers. The non aligned nations were far from irredeemable in terms of their ideological potential: in fact, the new model envisioned a Third World "state of national democracy" that, despite the prominence of the national bourgeoisie, still held a promise of developing in accordance with the logic of Marxist-Leninist theory, even though for the time being there was no need to press the issue.[33] The Soviet Union had thus adopted the degree of doctrinal flexibility needed to navigate the delicate postcolonial milieus. The Soviets still spoke of the inevitability of socialism in the Third World but conceded the leadership role of the national bourgeoisie.

Instead of imagining a wave of "proletarian revolutions" sweeping across Africa, the Kremlin was now prepared to settle for a more moderate approach, which recognized alternative paths toward socialism. The new theory allowed Moscow to seek contacts even with those regimes that held little immediate promise of transition to socialism; the stark Stalinist terminology had been discarded and supplanted by vague euphemisms that described such nations as pursuing a "non-capitalist road of development" or, later, as having adopted a "socialist orientation."[34]

Probably no other Soviet institution at the time better captured the high hopes of the Soviet Union forging a lasting "natural" alliance with independent Africa than the newly created Peoples' Friendship University, named after the martyred Congolese prime minister Patrice Lumumba. A February 1960 Communist Party of the Soviet Union (CPSU) resolution stipulated the founding of a new university to cater to the needs of Third World students, particularly those from Africa, Asia, and Latin America.[35] The Lumumba University became one of the most visible symbols and expressions of the Soviet charm offensive in the developing world. By signing off on the creation of an educational institution oriented toward foreign youth, Khrushchev tapped into the prewar Comintern tradition of providing training to friendly foreigners. But while the Comintern schools in Moscow had overwhelmingly privileged ideological education, the new cohort of students arrived primarily for professional training. In this case, pragmatism clearly trumped ideology.

The first African students made their appearance in Moscow in the immediate aftermath of the youth festival. But as late as January 1, 1959, there were only seven African students officially enrolled at Soviet institutions of higher learning. By the end of that year, 114 young Africans were studying in the Soviet Union. Just a year later, in 1961, Soviet officials put the number of African students in the country at well over 500.[36] According to the figures presented in a recently published piece of research by Constantin Katsakioris, by 1965 the number of Africans enrolled in Soviet universities and institutes approached 3,000, and a decade later close to 18,000 Africans were studying in the Soviet Union (as compared with 20,000 Arab, 17,000 Latin American, and 27,000 Asian students).[37]

The accelerating battle for the hearts and minds of the Third World proceeded against the background of ever-expanding propaganda campaigns. There was nothing particularly new in Soviet efforts to portray the state as the protectors of the oppressed. Meredith Roman, among other scholars recently engaged with the subject, has produced a comprehensive study of Soviet antiracist propaganda drives, particularly as they took shape prior to the Second World War.[38] However, a deepening Cold War and the arrival of new technologies at the time of global decolonization added a special urgency and vigor to such campaigns. Numerous Soviet propaganda materials published and disseminated at the time presented the Soviet Union not just as the "Red Mecca" of the prewar years but rather as a new beacon of modernity, whose technological achievement went hand in hand with its egalitarian principles and was not tainted by a history of capitalist and imperialist exploitation. In effect, Soviet antiracist propaganda persistently linked the Soviet Union's alleged scientific preeminence with its progressive politics, a claim rendered more credible following the successful 1957 launch of the first satellite, *Sputnik*. A typical cartoon of the era from the popular humor magazine *Krokodil* depicted a pair of oppressed Third-Worlders toiling under the lash of a dastardly imperialist. Suddenly a Soviet spaceship crosses the sky high above palm trees. The next frame shows these dark-skinned toilers of the East reasserting themselves and casting off the imperialist yoke. The message could not be any clearer: the salvation of the oppressed Third World masses will issue from an alliance with a technologically advanced and politically enlightened Soviet Union.[39]

There was no more straightforward and seemingly effective way to raise the Soviet Union's visibility and improve its fortunes in the developing world than by opening the doors of Soviet educational institutions to the very people at whom Soviet antiracist and anticolonial agitation was directed. The generous educational scholarships extended by the Soviet government to the citizens of newly independent nations were driving home the same point repeatedly articulated in the official propaganda output: the Soviet Union had more to offer than simply a lofty ideology of liberation; it could also provide technical and professional training, scientific expertise, and access to new technologies. And Moscow could justifiably refer to its own experience of rapid prewar industrialization and postwar reconstruction, making the Soviet Union's example relevant to the development concerns of the new nations and their educated elites. Even though contemporary Western observers never failed to focus on the ideological content of Soviet curricula and often alleged attempts at wholesale indoctrination of the incoming foreign students, the real story appears to have been less straightforward.[40] There is little evidence that the majority of Third World students arriving in the Soviet Union readily embraced or ended up being indoctrinated into Marxism-Leninism. The propaganda value of providing free education to thousands of former colonial subjects and "people of color" in general and manufacturing new "friends of the Soviet Union" in the process probably far outweighed any temptation to convert the arrivals to the cause.[41]

But there existed another problem. As a number of contemporary observers and several recent researchers have pointed out, the decimation of African studies during the purges and the lack of a systematic nonideological study of race and racial relations in the colonies and in the West in general (something that had infuriated such early Soviet backers as George Padmore and Jomo Kenyatta) had left the Soviet authorities woefully ill prepared to deal with the influx of Third World foreigners arriving in the country on educational scholarships or to attend conferences organized by Soviet ideological or cultural outfits.[42] In their dealings with the postcolonial world, the Soviets had to tread carefully to avoid falling into a trap of Orientalist paternalism and thus compromising their standing with the developing nations. Yet they repeatedly fell into this very trap. Using the 1958 Afro-Asian Writers' Conference in Tashkent as a case study, Constantin Katsakioris has found examples of Soviet authorities' multiple failures to address the unique racial and cultural sensibilities and concerns of at least some of the attendees. Conceived as a grand assembly of Soviet and Afro-Asian intellectuals to form an anti-imperialist alliance, in some ways the conference became a "crash landing for Soviet cultural policy."[43] The Soviets, for example, showed scant understanding of or appreciation for black cultural nationalism, describing at one point Alioune Diop, the secretary-general of the Société Africaine de Culture (SAC), as a "bourgeois nationalist Negro" keen on "undermining" the conference. Commenting on the incident, Ivan Potekhin was dismissive of black culture and poetics, particularly of the notions of "négritude" first formulated by prominent SAC members Aimé Césaire and Léopold Sédar Senghor. "The heads of African intellectuals," he warned, "are filled with an immense quantity of prejudice."[44] Senghor, in his capacity as Senegal's first president, never visited the Soviet Union and apparently bore a grudge on account of Potekhin's criticisms. While welcoming a delegation of Soviet writers in Dakar in 1961, he used the occasion to lecture them on the future of socialism, arguing that the brand he represented (African socialism) would ultimately prevail over the Marxist-Leninist one advocated by Potekhin. A man of letters, Senghor clearly preferred the company of Soviet writers and poets to that of Soviet ideologues. The bard of the Khrushchevian thaw, poet Yevgenii Yevtushenko, visited Senegal twice during the 1960s and conversed at length with his fellow poet—who also happened to be the country's president. In the course of these conversations, Senghor played down the utility of Soviet modernity for African nations. He insisted that the Soviet Union's most important and positive contribution to African culture stemmed not so much from its ideology as from the riches of "Russian literature" and "the most sparkling sources of Slavdom."[45]

Even the Soviet Union's bona fide friends in Africa had to be approached with a degree of caution; their loyalty could not be taken for granted, and the depth of their ideological commitments remained questionable at best. Independent Guinea under Sékou Touré became a major recipient of Soviet development largesse, hailed by Khrushchev as "a sort of window to the new life in Africa" and assumed by the West to have become a Soviet satellite.[46] As late as November 1961, no other independent African leader inspired in the Soviets more hope and confidence than Touré, and yet that December he expelled the Soviet ambassador and accused Moscow of meddling in Guinea's internal affairs and promoting Marxism-Leninism, especially among the "anti-national elements."[47] Following the debacle in Guinea, the Soviets assiduously cultivated three other "promising" leftist African leaders—Ahmed Ben Bella of Algeria, Kwame Nkrumah of Ghana, and Modibo Keita of Mali. All three became recipients of the highest honor the Soviet Union bestowed on foreign dignitaries and prominent cultural personalities, namely, the Lenin Peace Prize. The citation for the prize eulogized Ben Bella as an "ardent champion of peaceful coexistence" and the genuine "voice of Africa."[48] But the commendation hardly turned Ben Bella into Moscow's flunky. Even though he once famously proclaimed that "if the Soviet Union did not exist, we would have to invent one," Ben Bella was not about to embrace his Soviet friends uncritically. The Algerian ruling elites may have rejected Western colonial domination, but they remained apprehensive of Soviet political and cultural hegemony. During a 1965 visit of Soviet writers to Algeria, the hosts expressed incredulity at some of the Soviets' cultural practices, insisting that their own country adopted a much broader vision of national culture, inclusive of a variety of artistic forms of expression, including abstract art, a tendency much derided in the Soviet Union. They specifically referred to the sad case of the disgraced Soviet poet and celebrated author of the novel *Doctor Zhivago*, Boris Pasternak. Awarded the Nobel Prize in literature in 1958, Pasternak was immediately subjected to a vicious campaign of slander by Soviet authorities and fellow writers; his novel, published in the West without the Kremlin's permission, did not altogether fit the straightjacket of socialist realism—the one artistic form stamped for approval by Soviet officialdom. Apparently "no such conflicts like the 'Pasternak case'" could have happened in Algeria—at least that was the view of the delegation's Algerian hosts.[49] The limits of Moscow's influence and its ability to expertly negotiate and interpret postcolonial political and cultural discourses were even more demonstrably put on display when the three Lenin Prize recipients in Algeria, Ghana, and Mali were forcibly removed from power by their far less Soviet-friendly opponents within a short three-year period (1965–68).[50]

One gains a more nuanced understanding of the nature of the difficulties experienced by Soviet foreign policy in many parts of the Third World (particularly in Africa) as well as the limitations of Soviet appeal within the civil rights and black nationalist movements in the West by examining the place of former colonial and postcolonial actors within Soviet society. As mentioned earlier, the creation of the People's Friendship (Lumumba) University in Moscow inaugurated an era of increased contacts between Soviet bureaucracies and citizenry and the subjects of their internationalist concern. The thousands of Third World students who enrolled in the Soviet Union's institutions of higher learning constituted a distinct subgroup within a country still largely isolated from the wider world. Soviet newspapers and information bulletins emphasized the appeal of Soviet education for the underprivileged *deti trudyashchikhsia* (workers' children). However, limited access to secondary education and low literacy rates throughout former European colonies ensured that the arriving students hailed from a wide variety of social backgrounds. A 1964 *Izvestia* article, for example, described the Third World students at Moscow State University as "children of poor peasants, prosperous people, the bourgeoisie, landowners, and the intelligentsia."[51] While Lumumba University exercised some control over the selection process of freshman students from the Third World and at least tried to give preference to those deemed more disadvantaged, other Soviet universities and institutes often knew or understood precious little about the social backgrounds of their incoming foreign students. These students' political sensibilities and privileged status within colonial and postcolonial power hierarchies back home sometimes made them dubious candidates for their imputed role as a "metaphorical proletariat," representing their nations' strivings toward modernity through Soviet education.[52]

By refashioning their country from the Red Mecca of the two prewar decades into an educational destination, Soviet authorities opened themselves up to a new kind of competition with Western nations—they needed to demonstrate more than just the moral superiority of their system but also the attractiveness of Soviet society. Black travelers in Stalin's Soviet Union had enjoyed the status of highly valued guests, with all the attendant perks and even material comforts. Those African American and African intellectuals who visited the USSR during its prewar decades often benefited from the Soviets' eagerness to highlight their antiracism by providing the visitors with access to unprecedented social and professional opportunities. In the mid-1930s Soviet propagandists could credibly claim that in comparison to Jim Crow America or the European colonies, people of color fared better under the Soviet system, which accorded them respect, opportunities for advancement, and both formal and informal protection against racism.[53] But the situation proved to be decidedly different with the new arrivals. Admittedly, few of the scholarship recipients were fleeing racism and persecution. On the contrary, many of them were arriving from postcolonial locations steeped in political activism and animated by the liberation ethos and nationalism. For Moscow to earn their loyalty and appreciation, it was not sufficient to simply engage in public denunciations of racism. The Cold War competition with the West made it imperative for the Soviets to make a convincing case for the superiority of their own educational project and its utility for the professional goals and nation-building aspirations of Third World youth. And here, as the Soviets were quick to discover, they had to deal with some tough customers.

A journey from a Third World location to one of the major cities in the USSR was full of symbolism—these young people were heading to a nation that presented itself as a moral and economic alternative to their former colonial masters. That was undoubtedly the vision embraced by Khrushchev and, possibly with less enthusiasm, by his successors. But spending a few years in the Soviet

Union also meant an extensive and often intimate encounter with the new society, and such encounters often veered far from the official scripts contained in Soviet propaganda materials. One of the more noticeable differences between Soviet and Third World students was the latter's lack of inhibition in expressing their displeasure with authorities and the rules imposed on them by university administrators. African students in the Soviet Union complained openly about drab lifestyles, everyday regimentation, substandard dorm accommodations, and even alleged spying by Soviet roommates.[54] On his arrival in Moscow in 1959, an East African student named Everest Mulekezi had to share his fourteen-by-sixteen-foot dorm room with three other students, two of whom were Russians handpicked by Soviet university authorities. His hopes for a hot bath after a long and arduous journey were quickly dashed—hot water was only available once a week on Wednesdays from five to eleven o'clock in the evening.[55] Fifty-five air force cadets from Guinea enjoyed even fewer creature comforts at a training base in Soviet Kirghizia. Their complaints triggered an inspection by the CPSU Central Committee, whose conclusions confirmed the wretched living conditions in the barracks: "The cadets are housed 6–7 persons per room, living quarters are poorly furnished with little to no furniture. Most buildings lack plumbing and heating." According to the report, the cadets grumbled about the empty shelves at the local grocery and stationery store: "This is the country of sputniks but look at this poverty." Alarmed, the party inspector warned that the low living standards at the installation could potentially tarnish the image of the country abroad and supply its foes with an effective "propaganda weapon against us, against the socialist community."[56]

In stark contrast with the prevailing climate of complacency and the relative timidity of their Soviet peers, Africans protested vociferously against poor living conditions, racist incidents, and restrictions on travel within the USSR, dating Russian girls, and forming national and ethnic student associations. As early as March 1960, African students in Moscow petitioned the Soviet government to curb Soviet citizens' expressions of crude racism.[57] On another occasion, two African students refused to be part of a long-established Soviet practice—an annual dispatch of thousands of Soviet students to work in the countryside during the harvest. The objectors from Chad and Morocco appealed to the Soviet authorities' cultural sensitivity and argued (in all likelihood facetiously) that their respective traditions compelled them "to engage in leisure activities."[58] At about the same time, in September 1960, four African students (Theophilus Okonkwo of Nigeria, Andrew Richard Amar and Stanley Omar Okullo of Uganda, and Michel Ayieh of Togo) were expelled from Moscow State University. The four defied an administrative ban on unauthorized student organizations by forming the Black African Student Union. Their expulsion and subsequent departure from the country received wide coverage in the Western press. The students publicly accused university officials of suppressing the union and of imposing severe restrictions on the circulation of "books and jazz records." Okonkwo, Amar, and Ayieh challenged the Soviet authorities in a scathing open letter: "For the Soviet leaders to pose before the world as champions of oppressed Africa while they oppress millions in their own country and their satellites is hypocrisy at its worst." The expelled students left the Soviet Union under a cloud of scandal but, once safely outside the country, sought to capitalize on their notoriety. Amar quickly penned a book while Okonkwo gained minor celebrity by publicizing his Soviet travails in a series of interviews and lengthy newspaper articles.[59]

As Rossen Djagalov and Christine Evans noted, Third World students at Lumumba University, where the concentration of foreign students was the highest of anywhere in the USSR, articulated a variety of political opinions not observed on other Soviet campuses.[60] The freedom with which at least some of these students expressed their dissent must have astonished the Soviet authorities (and their Soviet fellow students). The death of a Ghanaian student in Moscow in December 1963, which his friends suspected to have been a homicide, occasioned an exceptionally angry reaction among African students in the USSR.[61] They staged a protest march on the Kremlin demanding a "bill of rights" for African students in the country (the first unauthorized demonstration in the Soviet Union since the expulsion of Leon Trotsky in 1927). The press was also up in arms at home: "Why did our students . . . protest in Moscow recently?" asked a particularly incensed African observer. "Was it not because . . . our boys had been insulted and attacked on trams, on the streets, in restaurants, in most public places? Could it be that our students have grown tired of the hypocrisy of Communism and the Soviet system?"[62] In 1965 in an episode that was particularly embarrassing for the Soviet authorities, several dozen African students organized an eight-day sit-down strike at the railway station in Baku; they protested the death of a fellow student from Ghana who had apparently fallen victim to an intense rivalry over a girl. The strike in Baku reverberated throughout the community of African students across the length and breadth of the Soviet Union, with solidarity protests reported in Moscow, Leningrad, and Minsk. Eventually twenty-nine students insisted on being repatriated and on their return to Nairobi painted a highly unflattering picture of their Soviet sojourn. They accused their Soviet hosts of suffering from the same Western affliction they had so publicly set out to vanquish—institutional and everyday racism.[63]

One is tempted to view these sporadic confrontations between Africans and other postcolonials and the Soviet authorities as an unintended subversion of the original intent to modernize the Third World based on the Soviet model. A number of recent studies have addressed this issue by focusing on the tension between the theory and practice of Soviet antiracism. Soviet antiracist rhetoric and support for a variety of "liberation causes" (particularly in southern Africa) did not necessarily guarantee the Soviet Union's acceptance by postcolonial subjects and their governments.[64] African students in the Soviet Union became emblematic of Soviet antiracist discontents. The "friendship of the peoples" symbolism of their presence in the Soviet Union at the time of decolonization and liberation struggles was intended for a variety of audiences—both domestic and international, with the Soviets playing the part of socialist modernizers, teachers, and emancipators. But the reality of these encounters often defied the neat logic of ideological pronouncements. Undoubtedly African students were eager to learn, but many of them emerged as de facto educators of their hosts. Their politics, in many cases, tended toward the syncretic and the unorthodox. At least some of them had the kind of cosmopolitan backgrounds that few of their Soviet peers could claim. In a country largely walled off from the outside world, these Third Worlders became the veritable links to alien (and therefore alluring) forms of artistic, cultural, and political expression. It is also important to note that a good number of the Third World students enjoyed an economic and social status that by Soviet standards could be considered privileged. When compared to their Soviet peers, they had far greater freedom to enjoy domestic (often sponsored by Soviet authorities) and foreign travel; they could pick up summer jobs in the West and thus gain legal access to hard currency and bring back Western-made material goods, which could be resold at significant profit or used/worn as a status symbol; most of them spoke at least one European language. Third World undergraduates received generous state stipends—90 rubles per month as compared to 30–35 rubles paid to Soviet students. And in the course of their studies, foreign students had far less exposure to ideological subjects and curricula.[65] All of the above problematized the task of "modernizing" subjects who in some significant respects looked and acted in a more modern fashion than their hosts did. This generated tensions, but also a fair amount of fascination. Marriages between Third World students and Soviet women were becoming more common—much to the consternation of their own families and of the Soviet authorities.[66] In class, African students were sometimes more eager than their Soviet peers to challenge their professors: they asked "uncomfortable questions," not to subvert the educational process but rather out of a simple wish to "know the answers." Fascinated by such displays of uninhibited conduct, some Russian students reportedly attempted to emulate them.[67] Everest Mulekezi remembered intense political discussions he used to hold in his dorm room with some of his Russian friends, who were bewildered by the openness and nonchalance with which he and his fellow Africans discussed politically sensitive matters. From the Soviet perspective, Mulekezi, by encouraging his Russian friends to question authority and read the Western press, clearly acted as an agent of political subversion. By introducing them to jazz, he effectively sabotaged Soviet cultural values. It was in the course of one such "sedition session" that a Russian friend of Mulekezi's "buried his face in his hands" and conceded the truth of the African's argument: "It is true we're not free . . . I am not free to read what Westerners read. I am not free to visit the West or even travel in my own country without a permit."[68] African students in Moscow articulated ideas manifestly at odds with Soviet sensibilities, as may be seen in the pages of *Russian Journal*, Andrea Lee's perceptive memoir of her time in Russia. Lee records, for example, a memorable conversation she had in a smoke-filled Moscow kitchen with a stern-looking Eritrean student: "In my five years in Russia, I've come to hate everything about the Soviet system. Life here is a misery of repression—you yourselves know it. . . . The Soviet Union has educated me, though not in a way it intended."[69]

Conclusion

We should be careful not to succumb to the tendency, commonly displayed by the Western media and political analysts during the Cold War, to dismiss all Soviet claims of antiracism as propaganda or to cast Soviet society as fundamentally racist, the regime's internationalist rhetoric and the pronouncements regarding the "friendship of the peoples" notwithstanding. It would appear to be more appropriate to view the discontents of Soviet antiracism as indicative of the sheer complexity of Soviet engagements with the Third World during the Cold War. As the ambivalence and occasional hostility with which Soviet commentators responded to such iconic civil rights figures as Malcolm X and Martin Luther King Jr. would seem to suggest, the Soviets often found themselves ideologically constrained when dealing with non-Marxist movements for racial emancipation in the West.[70] They struggled to reconcile Marxist-Leninist internationalism with the necessity of dealing with black radicalism. During the Cold War years, an American black radical who also happened to be a Marxist-Leninist (someone like Angela Davis) was a relative rarity. As the Soviet Union learned, simplistic Marxist-Leninist prescriptions rarely worked when addressing the question of race in the United States and across the Third World. The Soviets, it seems, had some difficulty "connecting" to the postcolonial sensibilities of their Third World friends and intended beneficiaries, routinely underestimating and underappreciating the centrality of race in postcolonial discourses, including the liberation discourse that they claimed to articulate and champion. The presence of Third Worlders, especially Africans, in the midst of Soviet society and the idiosyncratic and often unpredictable foreign policy initiatives of Moscow's supposed allies and sympathizers in the Third World (not to mention their opponents) defied the Soviet Union's expectations of forging a "natural" internationalist alliance with nonwhite populations oppressed by Moscow's Cold War Western rivals.

Notes

1. V. I. Lenin, "Imperialism, the Highest Stage of Capitalism (January–June 1916)," https://www.marxists.org/archive/lenin/works/1916/imp-hsc/ (accessed on October 3, 2018).

2. See Jacob Zumoff, *The Communist International and US Communism, 1919–1929* (Leiden: Brill, 2014).

3. See Meredith L. Roman, *Opposing Jim Crow: African Americans and the Soviet Indictment of U.S. Racism, 1928–1937* (Lincoln, NE: University of Nebraska Press, 2012).

4. Constantine Katsakioris, "Burden or Allies?: Third World Students and Internationalist Duty through Soviet Eyes," *Kritika* 18, no. 3 (Summer 2017): 539–567; Maxim Matusevich, "Expanding the Boundaries of the Black Atlantic: African Students as Soviet Moderns," *Ab Imperio*, no. 2 (2012): 325–350.

5. See Dale Peterson, *Up from Bondage: The Literatures of Russian and African American Soul* (Durham, NC: Duke University Press, 2000); John MacKay, *True Songs of Freedom: Uncle Tom's Cabin in Russian Culture and Society* (Madison, WI: University of Wisconsin Press, 2013); Nathaniel Knight, "Geography, Race and the Malleability of Man: Karl von Baer and the Problem of Academic Particularism in the Russian Human Sciences," *Centaurus: An International Journal of the History of Science and Its Cultural Aspects* 59, no. 1/2 (May 2017): 97–121.

6. See S. V. Mazov, *A Distant Front in the Cold War: The USSR in West Africa and the Congo, 1956–1964* (Washington, DC; Stanford, CA: Woodrow Wilson Center Press; Stanford University Press, 2010); Maxim Matusevich, *No Easy Row for a Russian Hoe: Ideology and Pragmatism in Nigerian-Soviet Relations, 1960–1991* (Trenton, NJ: Africa World Press, 2003).

7. Martin Luther King Jr., "Speech from MLK about Jews Living in the Soviet Union," (December 1966), quoted in Albert Chernin, "Focus on Issues: Martin Luther King and Soviet Jews," *JTA Daily News Bulletin* (January 8, 1986), 4; also, see King's original notes at the King Center Archive: https://thekingcenter.org/archive/document/speech-mlk-about-jews-living-soviet-union# (accessed on October 6, 2018).

8. See Ewa Dabrowska and Margaret Litvin, "Soviet Dormitories as a Prism for Interpreting Cultural Ties between the Soviet Union and the World," Blog for Transregional Research (Forum Transregionale Studien, February 21, 2018), https://trafo.hypotheses.org/9093 (accessed on February 21, 2018); Katsakioris, "Burden or Allies?"; Svetlana Boltovskaja, *Bildungsmigranten aus dem subsaharischen Afrika in Moskau und St. Petersburg: Selbst- und Fremdbilder* (Herbolzheim: Centaurus, 2014).

9. See Nikolay Zakharov and Ian Law, *Post-Soviet Racisms (Mapping Global Racisms)* (New York: Palgrave Macmillan, 2017); Nikolay Zakharov, *Attaining Whiteness: A Sociological Study of Race and Racialization in Russia* (Uppsala: Uppsala University, 2013).

10. See Roman, *Opposing Jim Crow*; Maxim Matusevich, "Harlem Globe-Trotters: Black Sojourners in Stalin's Soviet Union," in *Harlem Renaissance Revisited: Politics, Arts, and Letters*, ed. Jeffrey Ogbar (Baltimore, MD: Johns Hopkins University Press, 2010), 211–244.

11. See Claude McKay, *A Long Way from Home* (New York: L. Furman, 1937).

12. W. E. B. Du Bois, "Editorial," *The Crisis*, no. 8 (1926).

13. Paul Robeson, *The Negro People and the Soviet Union* (New York: New Century Publishers, 1950).

14. Paul Robeson Jr., "How My Father Last Met Itzik Feffer," *Jewish Currents* (November 1981): 4–8.

15. Terry Martin, *The Affirmative Action Empire: Nations and Nationalism in the Soviet Union, 1923–1939* (Ithaca, NY: Cornell University Press, 2001).

16. Woodford McClellan, "Africans and Black Americans in the Comintern Schools, 1925–1934," *The International Journal of African Historical Studies* 26, no. 2 (1993): 371–390; Ivan Potekhin, "Etnicheskij i Klassovyj Sostav Naseleniya Zolotogo Berega," *Sovetskaya Etnografiya*, no. 3 (1953): 113.

17. I. I. Potekhin, "Manevry Angliiskogo Imperializma v Zapadnoi Afrike," in *imperialisticheskaia Bor'ba za Afriku i Osvoboditel'noye Dvizhenie Narodov*, eds. V. Ya. Vasilieva, I. M. Lemin, and V. A. Maslenniko (Moscow: Gospolitizdat, 1953): 229–230.

18. I. I. Potekhin, "Stalinskaia Teoriia Colonial'noi Revolyutsii i Natsional'no-osvoboditel'noe Dvizhenie v Tropicheskoi i Yuzhnoi Afrike," *Sovetskaya Etnografiya*, no. 1 (1950): 24–50; Ye. M. Zhukov, "Voprosy Natsional'no-osvoboditel'noi Bor'by posle Vtoroi Mirovoi Voiny," *Voprosy Ekonomiki*, no. 9 (1949): 57–58.

19. See Padmore, *Pan-Africanism or Communism?*; R. H. S. Crossman and André Gide, *The God That Failed* (New York: Bantam Books, 1965).

20. For a history of Soviet African studies, see Apollon Davidson and Irina Filatova, "African History: A View from behind the Kremlin Wall," in Maxim Matusevich, ed., *Africa in Russia, Russia in Africa: Three Centuries of Encounters* (Trenton, NJ: Africa World Press, 2006), 111–131; also Lily Golden, *My Long Journey Home* (Chicago, IL: Third World Press, 2002).

21. Meredith L. Roman, "Forging Soviet Racial Enlightenment: Soviet Writers Condemn American Racial Mores, 1926, 1936, 1946," *Historian* 74, no. 3 (2012): 528–550; Meredith L. Roman, "Race, Politics and US Students in 1930s Soviet Russia," *Race & Class* 53, no. 2 (2011): 58–76.

22. Ilya Il'f and Yevgenii Petrov, "Negry,"*Ogonyok*, no. 22 (August 10, 1936): 14–17; Il'f and Petrov, *Odnoetazhnaya Amerika: Pis'ma iz Ameriki* (Moscow: Tekst, 2003).

23. See R. R. Viatkina, A. B. Davidson, and G. V. Tsypkin, eds., *Rossiya i Afrika: Dokumenty i Materialy, XVIII v. – 1960 g.* (Moscow: Institute of Global History RAN, 1999); Apollon Davidson, Sergey Mazov, and Georgii Tsypkin, eds., *SSSR i Afrika: Dokumentirovannaya Istoriia Vzaimootnoshenii, 1918–1960* (Moscow: Institute of Global History RAN, 2002); A. B. Davidson, ed., *The Formative Years of African Studies in Russia* (Moscow: RAN, 2003).

24. Robert Strausz-Hupé and Harry W. Hazard, *The Idea of Colonialism* (New York: Praeger Publishers, 1958).

25. Editorial, "Za Dal'neishii Pod'em Sovetskogo Vostokovedeniia," *Kommunist*, no. 8 (May 1955): 77.

26. A. B. Davidson and L. V. Ivanova, *Moskovskaia Afrika* (Moscow: Teatral'nyi Institut, 2003).

27. Melanie Ilič, Susan Emily Reid, and Lynne Attwood, eds., *Women in the Khrushchev Era* (New York: Palgrave Macmillan, 2004, 2013); Melanie Ilič and Jeremy Smith, eds., *Soviet State and Society under Nikita Khrushchev* (New York: Routledge, 2009); Davidson and Ivanova, *Moskovskaia Afrika*.

28. "Robeson on Moscow TV," *New York Times* (August 17, 1958).

29. See W. E. B. Du Bois, *The Autobiography of W. E. B. Du Bois: A Soliloquy on Viewing My Life from the Last Decade of Its First Century* (New York: International Publishers, 1968);

David L. Lewis, *W. E. B. Du Bois: The Fight for Equality and the American Century, 1919–1963* (New York: Henry Holt and Company, 2000); Yu. M. Ilyin, *Institut Afriki, 1960–2004* (Moscow: Africa Institute RAN, 2005); S. V. Mazov, "Sozdanie Instituta Afriki," *Vostok*, no. 1 (1998): 80–88.

30. Mazov, *A Distant Front.*

31. Ivan Potekhin, "Politicheskoye Polozheniie v Stranah Afriki," *Sovetskoe Vostokovedenie*, no. 1 (1956): 25.

32. See *International Affairs*, Moscow, no. 2 (February 1958): 57 and *International Affairs* Moscow, no. 2 (February 1959): 90.

33. K. Brutens, "The October Revolution in Africa," *New Times* (Moscow), no. 45 (November 7, 1962): 10; see also Dan C. Heldman, *The USSR and Africa: Foreign Policy under Khrushchev* (New York: Praeger Publishers, 1981).

34. Davidson and Filatova, "African History," 111–131.

35. Mazov, "Sozdanie Instituta Afriki"; S. V. Mazov, "Afrikanskie Studenty v Moskve v God Afriki," *Vostok*, no. 3 (May–June 1999): 91–93.

36. Cited in Maxim Matusevich, "Expanding the Boundaries of the Black Atlantic: African Students as Soviet Moderns," *Ab Imperio*, no. 2 (2012): 325–350.

37. Constantin Katsakioris, "The Soviet-South Encounter: Tensions in the Friendship with Afro-Asian Partners, 1945–1965," in *Cold War Crossings: International Travel and Exchange across the Soviet Block*, eds. Patryk Babiracki and Kenyon Zimmer (Arlington, TX: University of Texas, 2014); for earlier Soviet statistics, see O. M. Gorbatov and L. Ya. Cherkasskii, *Sotrudnichestvo SSSR so Stranami Arabskogo Vostoka i Afriki* (Moscow: Nauka, 1973).

38. See Roman, *Opposing Jim Crow.*

39. Milan Korzhava, "Bez Slov o Sputnike," *Krokodil*, no. 2 (January 20, 1958): 8.

40. Roger E. Kanet, "African Youth: The Target of Soviet African Policy," *Russian Review* 27, no. 2 (1968): 161–175.

41. Mazov, *Afrikanskie Studenty*, 91–93.

42. Davidson and Ivanova, *Moskovskaia Afrika*; Maxim Matusevich, "Black in the USSR," *Transition*, no. 100 (2008): 56–75; Maxim Matusevich, "An Exotic Subversive: Africa, Africans, and the Soviet Everyday," *Race & Class* 49, no. 4 (2008): 57–81.

43. Katsakioris, "The Soviet-South Encounter"; for more on Tashkent as the site of Soviet-South cultural contacts during the Cold War, see Rossen Djagalov and Masha Salazkina, "Tashkent'68: A Cinematic Contact Zone," *Slavic Review* 75, no. 2 (Summer 2016): 279–298.

44. *African Commission of the Soviet Afro-Asian Solidarity Committee (SKSSAA)* (January 15, 1959), 12–13.

45. Leopold Senghor, "Russian-Language Copies of Letters to Yevgenii Yevtushenko and Andriel Voznesensky" (January 7, 1966), 103.

46. V. A. Brykin, ed., *SSSR i Strany Afriki, 1946–1962: Dokumenty i Materialy* 1–2 (Moscow: Gosudarstvennoe izdatel'stvo politicheskoi literatury, 1963).

47. See Brykin, *SSSR i Strany Afriki*; Mazov, *A Distant Front.*

48. Henry Tanner, "Lenin Peace Prize Given to Ben Bella," *New York Times* (May 1, 1964).

49. For more on the controversy, see Katsakioris, "The Soviet-South Encounter."

50. See S. V. Mazov, *Politika SSSR v Zapadnoi Afrike: Neizvestnye Stranitsy Istorii Kholodnoi* Voiny (Moscow: Nauka, 2008); Mazov, *A Distant Front.*

51. "Spasibo za Znania," *Izvestia* (January 29, 1964).

52. Rossen Djagalov and Christine Evans, "Moskau, 1960: Wie man sich eine sowjetische Freundschaft mit der Dritten Welt vorstellte," in Andreas Hilger, ed. *Die Sowietunion und die Dritte Welt: UdSSR, Staatssozialismus und Antikolonialismus im Kalten Krieg, 1945–1991* (München: R. Oldenbourg Verlag, 2009), 83–106.

53. See Glenda Gilmore, *Defying Dixie: The Radical Roots of Civil Rights, 1919–1950* (New York: W.W. Norton, 2008); Joy Gleason Carew, *Blacks, Reds, and Russians: Sojourners in Search of the Soviet Promise* (New Brunswick, NJ: Rutgers University Press, 2008); Matusevich, "Harlem Globe-Trotters"; Roman, "Race, Politics and US Students"; for firsthand autobiographical accounts, see Homer Smith, *Black Man in Red Russia: A Memoir* (Chicago: Johnson, 1964); and Robert Robinson and Jonathan Slevin, *Black on Red: A Black American's 44 Years inside the Soviet Union* (Washington, DC: Acropolis Books, 1988).

54. Richard Andrew Amar, *A Student in Moscow* (London: Ampersand, 1961); Olabisi Ajala, *An African Abroad* (London: Jarrolds, 1963); Jan Carew, *Moscow Is Not My Mecca* (London: Seckler and Warburg, 1964); Nicholas Nyangira, "Africans Don't Go to Russia to Be Brainwashed," *New York Times* (May 16, 1965); William Anti-Taylor, *Moscow Diary* (London: Robert Hale, 1967).

55. Everest Mulekezi, "I Was a Student at Moscow State," *Reader's Digest* 79, no. 471 (1961): 99–104.

56. In Mazov, *Politika SSSR v Zapadnoi Afrike.*

57. See Mazov, "Afrikanskie Studenty v Moskve."

58. RGASPI, f. 1M, op. 46, d. 295 (1961).

59. Chukwuemeka Okonkwo, "Behind the Iron Curtain," *Sunday Times*, Lagos (October 23, 1960); Okonkwo, "Life in Moscow University," *Sunday Times*, Lagos (November 6, 1960); Okonkwo, "I Meet Imoudu in Moscow," *Sunday Times*, Lagos (November 13, 1960); Okonkwo, "The Russians Try to Hold Me Back," *Sunday Times*, Lagos (November 20, 1960).

60. Djagolov and Evans, "*Moskau* 1960," 83–106.

61. Julie Hessler, "Death of an African Student in Moscow: Race, Politics, and the Cold War," *Cahiers Du Monde Russe* 47, no. 1 (2006): 33–63.

62. "Students Demand Bill of Rights," *West African Pilot*, Nigeria (December 30, 1963); Sunny Odulana, "Our Students in Moscow," *West African Pilot*, Nigeria (January 2, 1964).

63. "Kenya Students Go Home after Mysterious Death of Youth from Ghana," *Pittsburgh Courier* (April 17, 1965); Lawrence Fellows, "Kenyans Charge Brutality," *New York Times* (April 7, 1965).

64. Matusevich, *Africa in Russia*; Katsakioris, "The Soviet-South Encounter"; Davidson and Ivanova, *Moskoskaya Afrika*; Mazov, "Afrikanskie Studenty"; Mazov, *A Distant Front*; Djagolov and Evans, "Moscau, 1960"; V. G. Shubin, *ANC: A View from Moscow*, Mayibuye History and Literature Series 88 (Bellville, South Africa, 1999); V. G. Shubin, *The "Hot" Cold War: The USSR in Southern Africa* (London: Pluto Press, 2008).

65. See Nyangira, "Africans Don't Go to Russia"; Katsakioris, "The Soviet-South Encounter"; Seymour Rosen, *The Development of People's Friendship University in Moscow* (Washington, DC: Institute of International Studies, 1973).

66. Ilič, Reid, and Attwood, *Women in the Khrushchev Era*; N. L. Krylova, *Russkie Zhenshshiny v Afrike: Problemy Adaptatsii* (Moscow: ROSSPEN, 1996).

67. See Okonkwo, "Behind the Iron Curtain."

68. See Mulekezi, "I Was a Student at Moscow State."

69. Andrea Lee, *Russian Journal* (New York: Random House, 1981).

70. See James Zeigler, *Red Scare Racism and Cold War Black Radicalism* (Jackson, MS: University Press of Mississippi, 2015).

MAXIM MATUSEVICH is Professor of History and Director of the Russian and East European Studies Program at Seton Hall University. He is author of *No Easy Row for a Russian Hoe: Ideology and Pragmatism in the Nigerian-Soviet Relations, 1960–1991* and editor of *Africa in Russia, Russia in Africa: Three Centuries of Encounters.*

11 Southeast by Global South: The Balkans, UNESCO, and the Cold War

Bogdan C. Iacob

In 1976 the director general of the United Nations Educational, Scientific and Cultural Organization (UNESCO), Amadou-Mahtar M'Bow, visited Sofia where he received the most flattering welcome possible. In the presence of Todor Zhivkov, general secretary of the Bulgarian Communist Party, M'Bow was awarded the distinction Stara Planina First Class.[1] As recognition of his role in the relationship between Bulgaria and UNESCO, M'Bow soon after received the title of doctor honoris causa of Sofia University. What stood out was the speech that M'Bow delivered on accepting the honor. Highlighting the persistence of underdevelopment across the globe, he declared that the situation was caused "by old political inequalities as well as by the persistence of serious economic disparities which are contrary to both the most basic notions of justice and the general interest of humanity with a view to its long perspectives for the future." He reminded his audience that, for these very reasons, in 1974 the General Assembly of the United Nations had passed a declaration on the establishment of a New International Economic Order (NIEO).[2]

But what does this have to do with the Balkans? Before the Second World War, Southeastern European expert exchange and interaction hardly went beyond the limits of this geographical region.[3] By the 1960s, however, Balkan scholars were increasingly playing roles in international organizations that enabled regular exposure to the intellectual currents of a rapidly decolonizing world. The same period saw the rise of cooperation among countries in Southeast Europe (Albania, Bulgaria, Greece, Romania, Turkey, and Yugoslavia) that sought to find a space in the global order that allowed them to bypass the East-West divide. Yet few have noted that this phenomenon—the so-called Balkan détente—also consisted of significant interaction between Southeast Europe and the Global South. Addressing this relationship between "peripheries" sheds fresh light on the new regional configurations—and interregional relationships—that emerged to challenge marginalization and/or dependency in the postwar order.

These initiatives found a global stage at UNESCO, which became *the* bridge between Southeastern Europeans and decolonized peoples. Balkan countries joined UNESCO around the same time as the wave of decolonization that fundamentally altered the United Nations and its specialized institutions. Even though Turkey (1946), Greece (1948), and Yugoslavia (1951) had a head start in comparison with Albania, Bulgaria, or Romania, by 1958 all of them were full members of UNESCO. After 1960 the Global South became a force to be reckoned with inside the organization. During the next decade, with the nomination of M'Bow as director general and his enthusiastic embrace of the NIEO, the Third World had a significant impact on UNESCO. This development led to acrimonious exchanges with some Western countries. In the mid-1980s, the United States and United Kingdom withdrew from UNESCO, accusing it of anti-Westernism and mismanagement.

Yet for Southeastern European states, it remained important: their cultural cooperation within UNESCO, as a hub of knowledge production, offered them the possibility to rethink Balkan identity in the light of new ways of conceptualizing regional identity that were emerging in the Global South. Here Balkan intellectuals advocated alternative visions of Europe distinct from those anchored in the continent's northwest. In these imaginaries, the Balkans were no longer on Europe's civilizational fringe. The Southeast was seen as a channel for communication between Mediterranean territories and northern areas of the continent, an account that became essential to regional narratives of Europeanness that challenged the dominance of Western visions. Yet by 1989 such reactions to globalization—deperipheralizing as they did former fringes of Europe—lost out to European integration. The European Union, for its part, remarginalized the Balkans as an outlier of liberal modernity.

The Southeast Rises with the South

From the late 1950s regional and international organizations offered new possibilities for collaboration in the Balkans. Such cooperation was institutionalized with varying degrees of success. The most prominent of these developments was the International Association for Southeast European Studies (AIESEE). It was a supragovernmental scholarly body created in 1963 by academics from the Balkans (Albania, Bulgaria, Greece, Romania, Turkey, and Yugoslavia) under the aegis of UNESCO and affiliated with the International Council for Philosophy and Humanities (CIPSH). In its heyday, during the mid- to late 1970s, it brought together twenty-four national committees of Southeast European or Balkan studies from Europe, North America, and the Middle East. This association was the result of local scholars taking advantage of early détente to internationalize regional knowledge production and cultural diplomacy. From the 1960s other forms of cooperation flourished as exchanges across the Balkans significantly expanded. They comprised the humanities, medicine, engineering, seismology, education, trade, film, folklore, book exchanges, sports and exhibitions, and midlevel state experts' meetings.

Nevertheless, the Balkans were riven with political division. Some bilateral relationships functioned better than others, such as the Yugoslav-Greek connection, Turkish-Bulgarian bilateralism (until the late 1970s), or Yugoslav-Romanian ties. Yet Albania remained reluctant to engage with multilateralism and rejected nonalignment. Though Bulgaria was perceived (justifiably) as a proxy for Soviet interests, Yugoslavia was one of the initiators of the nonaligned movement (NAM—its first conference in Belgrade in 1961). Romania and Albania embarked on individualized paths to building socialism in one country, while the latter was China's protégé from 1960 until the mid-1970s. Greece struggled with the legacy of the Civil War (1946–49) and with building sustainable pluralism. Between 1967 and 1974 it was ruled by a military junta. After the military coup d'état in 1960, Turkey made some progress toward democratic pluralism. It suffered setbacks, however, because of two subsequent coups; in 1971 and in 1980.

At the same time, all Balkan states courted the Third World. In the nonaligned movement, Josip Broz Tito found "the 'constituency' he lacked in Europe" as Yugoslavia embraced its role of intermediary between North and South.[4] In 1964 Romania considered joining the Group of 77 at the first UNCTAD conference and flirted with the status of "developing country" until officially defining itself as one in the early seventies.[5] Bulgaria intensified its military and economic aid programs, mainly in decolonized countries on the path to their own socialist revolution, while nonetheless remaining closer to the Soviet Bloc.[6] After the US involvement in the Cyprus crisis of 1964, Greece[7] and Turkey[8] experienced waves of anti-Americanism and looked to forge new relationships with Arab countries.[9]

The initial expressions of intra-Balkan cooperation opened up new channels of exchange with their counterparts in the Third World. Despite earlier pronouncements, the first global display of this potential collaboration was at the Fifteenth Session of the UN General Assembly in September 1960. The Romanian Communist leader Gheorghe Gheorghiu-Dej, seconded by the Bulgarian leader Zhivkov, put forward a draft resolution entitled "Regional Actions concerning the Advancement of Good Neighborly Relations among European States Belonging to Different Socio-Political Systems." It would be approved by the General Assembly in 1965. Central to this proposal was the idea of "a Balkan entente" that could go beyond the Socialist Bloc but "did not presuppose giving up on [military] alliances to which the states involved belong." Multilateral relations among Balkan countries would not exclude bilateral ones.[10] Nevertheless, lingering geopolitical and ideological suspicions often made the development of a regional entente difficult. Domestic political turmoil fueled Turkey's and Greece's reservations toward the initiative.[11] Tito was a keen supporter of the project, particularly as his attempted rapprochement with the Soviet Union was not going well; nevertheless, Yugoslavia's relationship with Bulgaria and Albania was difficult, to say the least.[12]

The 1960 resolution concerning good neighborly relations coincided with the joint appeal of Tito, Jawaharlal Nehru, Gamal Abdel Nasser, Sukarno, and Kwame Nkrumah to the United Nations that the United States and USSR end the Cold War. Gheorghiu-Dej remarked in an interview for the *Daily Mirror* that "one cannot simply be a bystander in our contemporary, complicated world. Look at the neutral countries, they have such an important part to play within the UN and this is so because they are vitally interested in peace."[13] In 1960 and 1965, this Dej-Zhivkov Balkan initiative elicited positive reactions from UN representatives of Ethiopia, Iraq, Syria, Pakistan, Lebanon, and Afghanistan. A member of the Ghanaian delegation declared that "the Africans are inspired by the ideas of the resolution at a time when they strive for stronger unity on their continent."[14] The Greek journalist Christos Nikolopoulos thought that Balkan leaders could learn from Africa too: if it was difficult to solve several international problems simultaneously, perhaps various regions ought to take on the task of resolving their own issues. The next step was obvious: "The Balkans had better adopt Nkrumah's slogan 'Africa for the Africans' and declare 'the Balkans for the Balkan peoples with no foreign bases or diktats.'"[15]

At the United Nations from around 1960, one can discern a mutual recognition on the part of both southeastern Europeans and the representatives of newly decolonized peoples. A Romanian official from the local League for Friendship with the African and Asian Peoples reported that he had had the opportunity "to meet people, to infer more straightforwardly what they thought, to better figure out what could be done in the future." The potential solidarity based on the shared consciousness of being peripheral was apparent during his discussion with Mali's representative, Demba Diallo. Commenting on the protests against Gheorghiu-Dej's presence in New York, Diallo told his colleague that "it seems that Americans see you 'as black' as well. Only that, obviously, we like the color black."[16] At a meeting with Dej in 1963, Tito insisted that their countries' collaboration with African countries had to take into account the latter's "sensibility . . . their experience vis-à-vis the whites, thus avoiding anything that would make them feel underappreciated."[17]

Southeast European countries and newly decolonized ones shared a common experience of being on the periphery of postwar political, economic, and cultural hierarchies. Unsurprisingly, the Bandung Era—generally considered to have lasted from 1955 until 1975—overlapped with the heyday of Balkan cooperation.[18] Right from the start, the participant countries at the Bandung Conference were explicitly compared with the Balkans. British expert in international affairs Martin

Wight argued that the new wave of states "may be the dream-transformation of the historical experience called Balkanisation, which means a *Kleinstaaterei* of weak States, fiercely divided among themselves by nationalistic feuds, governed by unstable popular autocracies, as unaccustomed to international law and diplomatic practice as they are to parliamentary government and a battle-ground for the surrounding Great Powers."[19] If one considers the domestic tribulations of democracy in Greece and Turkey along with the post-Stalinist national paths to state socialism in Albania, Bulgaria, Romania, and Yugoslavia, one can discern similarities to the evolution of parts of the "developing world" in this same era. According to historian Prasenjit Duara, decolonization in the context of the Cold War generated "an undemocratic, authoritarian, if not military, ruling structure committed in varying degrees to building a developmental nation-state."[20] Similarly, we need also to look at the Cold War Balkans in terms of the construction and nationalization of their nation-states in this period. Yet NAM and Balkan countries responded to such characterizations by emphasizing that international cooperation could be founded on a shared sense of national identity, socioeconomic developmentalism, and cultural emancipation. Initiatives within the UN institutional system offered a window of opportunity for the periphery—in a South-Southeast alliance—to reorganize the world, putting the hegemonic powers in the West and East under pressure.

Furthermore, the attraction within the Balkans to the developing world was a result of the region's sense of its own inbetweenness in an otherwise bipolar world. With the exception of Bulgaria, other Southeast European states' membership in ideological and military blocs had proved tumultuous. Romania boasted an ambivalent track record in participation within the Warsaw Pact and opposed supragovernmental socialist integration.[21] The European Economic Community suspended its association agreement with Greece in 1967 because of the Colonels' dictatorship. Accusing NATO of inaction over the landing of Turkish troops in the Cyprus crisis of 1974, Greece withdrew from the organization's command structures (and remained outside of them until 1980). Turkey had a tenuous relationship with NATO and the United States where the Eastern Mediterranean and the Middle East were concerned.

In September 1960, just after the military coup, Selim Sarper, the Turkish foreign minister and former UN representative, declared that his country belonged "to the Asia-Africa bloc and always supports the cause of these nations within its commitments."[22] Not all Turkish politicians were as enthusiastic about such a nonaligned position. Nevertheless, the idea of regional cooperation with Balkan and Arab countries as a counterbalance to the vagaries of the relationship with the United States can be seen across the ideological spectrum in Turkey. In Greece, after rapprochement with Yugoslavia, Bulgaria, and Romania, politicians attempted to obtain Third World support during successive Cyprus crises (as did

Turkey). In 1976, during Greece's accession negotiations with the European Community, a historian remarked in the review of the local institute of Balkan studies that the common market was not the only option for the country. There were plenty of "developing countries that find themselves at clearly inferior levels to our own, and this accelerates the pace of their imports."[23] A year later, Andreas Papandreou, who in 1981 would become prime minister, called for a liberated and socialist Mediterranean while lambasting the country's dependence on the United States. Within the Turkish State Planning Organization (SPO), an institution created to manage the local version of a five-year plan (1963), there was intense criticism of the Association Agreement with the European Community, to the effect that it was in fact a source of underdevelopment.

In 1966 the *New York Times* remarked among Southeast European diplomatic circles "a spirit of optimism unequaled since the war about the opportunities for establishing closer cooperation across geographical and ideological borders." Collaboration was an alternative to what Nicolae Ceaușescu considered these countries' statuses as "pawns in [the Great Powers'] policy of domination and seizure."[24] Eight years later, the Greek prime minister, Konstantinos Karamanlis, during a trip to Sofia, invoked the same principle: "The fact that we know we can have such close cooperation even with rival systems lessens our need to depend on others."[25] There was considerable identification with what Tito and Ceaușescu considered a typical phenomenon of the times: "In general all these small and middle-sized countries are fed up, if I may put it like this, with politics imposing upon them certain orientations."[26] The United States and the USSR did not look kindly on such claims to regional autonomy. Yet Balkan countries saw their spirit of cooperation as comparable to that articulated by the nonaligned movement or the Group of 77. Southeastern Europe shared with many newly decolonized societies the drive to overcome their own histories of imperial subjection and contemporary experiences of subordination inherent in Great Power politics during the Cold War.

UNESCO: A Bridge between Two Regions

Cooperation between Southeast European states with different social and political systems was possible under the aegis of UNESCO. The organization was a global arena, offering Balkan representatives opportunities to find common ground with the newly decolonized countries. In the Third World and in the Southeast, UNESCO was a crucial partner and stage for the internationalization of local agendas.

During his trip to Sofia in 1958, Malcolm S. Adiseshiah, UNESCO's assistant director general, remarked that the Bulgarian national commission's program of activities "is very comprehensive and it mobilized the enthusiasm and support of intellectuals, institutions and public leaders. This kind of cultural cooperation . . . is given full rein and unlimited resources." Adiseshiah concluded that if similar enthusiasm spread across the region, "We may have a situation where their participation might rapidly outstrip those of Asia and other parts of Europe."[27] Mircea Malița, former Romanian deputy foreign minister, underlined in his memoirs the same enthusiasm for UNESCO among local intellectuals: the institution enabled an exit from pre-1955 isolation; it defied the frontiers of bipolarism; and, according to Malița, "what could be more promising than participating at gatherings and establishing contacts within an organization which functioned on the principle of equality?"[28]

Similar attitudes can be discerned in Greece and Turkey. In 1964 a position paper on the activities of the Greek UNESCO National Commission drew attention to its members' attempts to expand contacts and collaboration with various countries such as Romania or Turkey, as well as France and India.[29] In 1955 Turkey requested to be moved from the Middle East into the European region. Because of widening activities within UNESCO and the evolution of the country's relations with Muslim countries, in 1982 Turkey also asked to participate in the meetings and projects organized within the scope of activities relating to Asia and the Pacific.[30]

In 1963 the Balkan countries' National UNESCO Commissions met for the first time in Bucharest. They would gather every two years from 1965 onward to discuss regional projects and prepare larger intergovernmental conferences. The six states in Southeast Europe embraced UNESCO with a view to fostering closer relations with each other and with the decolonizing world. To paraphrase one Yugoslav scholar's optimistic remark at AIESEE's founding colloquium in Sinaia (July 1962), "The old discordant harmony" in the region seemed to be turning, under the inspiration of UNESCO, into a "more serene harmony."[31]

Emancipation was the defining aspect of AIESEE's various activities. During its inaugural session, the association's general secretary, Romanian archaeologist Emil Condurachi, stressed the obscurity forced on the Balkans as a consequence of their peripheral status: "This contribution [of Southeast Europeans to universal culture], so rich and diverse, has unfortunately been not only less known, but from certain points of view, entirely ignored and, is, by implication, contested."[32] In 1966, at the first Congress of Southeast European Studies (in Sofia, opened by UNESCO's director general, René Maheu), Greek legal scholar Dimitrios Evrigenis stressed that such interactions "could finally reverse the meaning of what we call, with a heavy dose of contempt, Balkanisation and recast this term as a slogan of unity and cooperation."[33]

What brought together the Southeast and the Global South intellectually was the perception of "a homogeneous condition of dependency."[34] Third World politicians and intellectuals saw themselves as victims rather than agents of history. In the Balkans, history was thought to hold the key to *décalage*, that is, the social, economic, cultural, and political discrepancies that sustained underdevelopment.

Condurachi remarked in Istanbul, on the association's tenth anniversary, that Southeast Europeans could not be blamed for what, at the beginning of the twentieth century appeared to be, "with little justification in reality, massive instability as they seemed gripped by incessant territorial, political, and linguistic quarrels." He considered it equally "unjust and illogical to condemn" these peoples for aspiring to the same "ideal of political liberty and national sovereignty as their fellow peoples on the old continent."[35] Condurachi and his Southeastern European colleagues within AIESEE criticized the fact that other Europeans or North Americans narrated Balkan peoples' self-determination predominantly as conflict, thus implicitly questioning the region's right to emancipation. To make matters worse, once independent, Southeast Europeans had become victims of struggles between the Great Powers.

Third World solidarity evolved from the image of a "tiers état . . . a third pole of influence ('third force') in the contemporary international order"[36] to "a de-Europeanized concept, a nodal point for political identities inside, but most of all *outside* the West." Societies in the Global South were able "to speak *for* themselves in a terminology that initially had been created to talk *about* them" [original emphasis].[37] Similarly, the emancipation from the shadow of empires in Southeast Europe was the foundation on which transnational solidarity was built within AIESEE. In 1974 social scientist George Constantacopoulos argued that various forms of regional integration functioned as "effective weapons against colonial subordination and underdevelopment." He defined *Balkanization* as the product of "historical circumstances . . . particularly intervention from the side of empire builders or the so-called Great Powers," which resulted "in some kind of colonialism or semi-colonialism."[38]

Misrepresentations of the Balkans were rooted in a historical fallacy, it was argued. The director of the Romanian Institute of Southeast European Studies and chair of AIESEE's Commission for the History of Ideas, Mihai Berza, stated that "these [forms of cooperation] have been more numerous than those of strife. Generally speaking, the image that we have on the matter is false because our attention is captivated to a large extent by state-to-state relations and it pays little heed to those between peoples."[39] At the third Congress of Southeast European Studies (Bucharest, 1974), Berza proclaimed the triumph of multilateralism in the field of the humanities. He declared that "we have made immense progress toward the enlargement of our cultural horizon, in our understanding of the past, which, following older attempts to escape former Eurocentrism, translated into a fortuitous 'dearistocratization' of history."[40] Echoing the criticism leveled by developing countries at Western-centric universalism and historiography, Balkan scholars affirmed within AIESEE their cultures and societies' significance, originality, and right to visibility on the world and European stage. In this way, they were attempting to break the perceived hegemony of former imperial cultures, whether located in the East or the West.

Southeast European and Third World intellectuals were brought together by the recasting of the mission of international institutions functioning under UNESCO's umbrella. CIPSH, a nongovernmental organization (NGO) associated with UNESCO that dealt with global humanities and to which AIESEE was affiliated, reassessed its tasks in the context of decolonization. In 1965, during the meeting of CIPSH's General Assembly in Copenhagen, Cambridge professor S. C. Aston called for the enlargement of contemporary conceptions of humanism to encompass China, India, and Islam. The new humanism had to comprise "the totality of its [the world's] cultures and societies."[41] In 1967 the gathering of the same body took place in Bucharest, and it included AIESEE's colloquium "Tradition and Innovation in the Culture of Southeast European Countries." Endorsing the call made two years earlier for an extended notion of humanism, secretary-general Ronald Syme stressed that one of CIPSH's main tasks was "to encourage a spirit of collaboration . . . among the various cultures in different spiritual regions, among the various perspectives of a divided spirit whose unity it is urgent to recover."[42] His stance was endorsed by vice president C. C. Berg (University of Leiden), who argued that, in the context of decolonization, humanity was "more and more aware of its responsibilities towards the underdeveloped communities."[43]

A new idea shaped CIPSH's activities and the agendas of its affiliate bodies, namely, "humanism of development." This concept was introduced in 1961 by René Maheu, UNESCO's director general until 1974. He argued that development should not be interpreted solely in economic terms but also in social and cultural terms.[44] In 1972, on the heels of the first Intergovernmental Conference on Institutional, Administrative, and Financial Aspects of Cultural Policies (Venice, 1970), the conclusions of UNESCO's General Conference proclaimed: "Development is endogenous or it does not exist. [. . .] Each nation, small or big, has something to give and to receive."[45] Cultural development in UNESCO's vision had to bring together national traditions and progress into a common heritage of humankind.

UNESCO and CIPSH were milieus through which Southeastern Europe and the Global South could "rebuild their histories from within," to paraphrase C. C. Berg.[46] They were stages for local scholars to internationalize national and regional narratives. Contemporaries dwelled on the similarities between past and present stances of the Third World and the Balkans. After listening to the proceedings of AIESEE's colloquium in 1967, Alassane N'Daw (Senegal), secretary-general of the International Congress of Africanists, remarked: "We, who presently experience, perhaps with greater intensity than others, the problems raised by the double necessity of maintaining our cultural heritage and of making our people join the general movement of history, we have been shocked by the analogies, similarities, even the identity of the situations described here. By this I mean that we have the strong feeling that we have received precious lessons concerning our own undertakings." African historians could emulate AIESEE's focus on history of ideas, the evolution of literary languages, the permanence of traditional culture and its role in education, or linguistic unity as the basis for political unity.[47]

N'Daw's intervention was seconded by statements made at the same event by N. Bammate, UNESCO's liaison with the cultural commission of the Arab League and the World Muslim Congress. One could, he declared, draw a parallel between the nineteenth-century Balkans and present-day developing countries.[48] The Balkans could be emulated in both epistemic practice and historical *exemplum*. Two years after its creation, at the CIPSH Copenhagen meeting, Japanese scholar T. Yamamoto considered AIESEE a fortunate but rare instance of the successful affiliation of non-Western institutions to international specialized bodies. He reminded his colleagues that there were numerous academic gatherings in the Far East. In contrast to AIESEE, despite their scientific worth, they had not been affiliated to international organizations.[49]

There were instances in this period of the narrating of Southeastern European national struggles within an anticolonial framework. Indeed, there was a convergence during the 1960s between the determination of the decolonized to obtain cultural and historiographical recognition at a global level and the Balkan peoples' concern to do the same. For example, in 1965 Yugoslav historian Dimitrije Djordjević published a book on national revolutions among Balkan peoples during the nineteenth and early twentieth centuries. It was a volume prepared for the International Congress of Historical Sciences in Vienna. Djordjević presented the region's emancipation under the heading of "the Balkans belonging to the Balkan peoples." Revolutions in Southeast Europe represented unique movements that had a "liberating and anti-colonial" character rooted in "national self-determination." The involvement of Balkan peoples in the First World War might readily be compared with the enrollment of African and Asian ones. They were drawn into "a four-year slaughter" that had been motivated not simply by "the death of an Austrian archduke, but by colonial interests." Djordjević's volume basically stated that the nation-states of Southeast Europe had undergone their own decolonization.[50] Until 1970 Djordjević was the president of the Yugoslav Committee for Southeast European Studies. Afterward, he immigrated to the United States, obtained a professorship at the University of California, Santa Barbara, and continued to serve as a point of contact between scholars based in the Balkans and American area studies. His book coincided with an extensive report prepared by the International Committee for Historical Sciences on the state of the sources available to assist in writing histories of Africa. Influenced by developing countries' narratives of decolonization at UNESCO and its associated NGOs, Balkan historians rethought their anti-imperial pasts in an anticolonial context.

AIESEE and the Third World—Together but Apart

The common ground and synchronization between cultural discourses from Southeast Europe and newly independent countries had institutional foundations. In 1957 UNESCO launched the Major Project on the Mutual Appreciation of Eastern and Western Cultural Values (Major Project).[51] It was the original milieu within which the AIESEE came into being. One of the initiators of the Major Project was Japan. Accordingly, the "East" or the "Orient" initially meant Asia. As decolonization gathered steam, socialist countries became more involved with UNESCO. As the geocultural balance within the organization tilted in favor of the Global South, the East/Orient turned into a catchall conceptualization of alterity, of non-Western-ness.

To give an example regarding the possibilities of such an ambiguous geography, in 1959 a UNESCO official's report of his mission to Albania described the rationale used by local representatives to justify the country's worthiness as a partner. They underlined that Albania was ideally positioned to participate in the "Major Project": "its history . . . , its language, the original basis of which combined contributions from the Orient and the Occident, its geographical position, as well as its political [circumstances], all this will play a role in the implementation of the project."[52] Such a trope of hybridity, the centrality of inbetweenness, would be the key mechanism for scholars and officials from the region in appending the Southeast to the Major Project.

The UNESCO project aimed to reformulate concepts that it considered essential for constructing a new foundation for interaction between cultures/civilizations. These were "nationalism, imperialism or colonialism; borrowings and influences; domination and isolation."[53] It was implemented through a network of "associated institutions" that had "to respond to: (a) the need for more comparative studies of cultures; (b) the need for an interdisciplinary approach in the study and presentation of cultures."[54] As its associate institution, AIESEE adopted within the Major Project global themes that reinforced pre-1945 regionalist scholarly discourses. First, it placed value on the individuality and originality of national cultures; second, the critique of Western-centrism; third, deperipheralization by emancipation from imperial/colonial legacies; and finally, the importance, if not centrality, of each national/regional civilization in the "unity in diversity" of the concert of world civilizations.

Southeastern European scholars refuted a "Western Europeanism" perceived to have suffocated the cultures of the Southeast of the continent, for "it continued to treat them as poor relatives that, of course, do not know how to be emancipated."[55] A commission dealing with the history of ideas was founded in late 1965 within AIESEE. Its members argued that, in the multiplicity of Balkan syntheses, individual cultures produced their own historical cultures that could not be judged on a spectrum of advanced to backward. It rejected the concept of "delays" (*retards*) of a region or society, considering them "mechanical" interpretations of the diffusion of ideas across time and space. Such interpretations hid the belief that "the accomplishments of the 'delayed' ('*attardés*') only confirm the things already known through the accomplishments obtained by the 'advanced.'"[56]

Starting with the budgetary year 1971–72, AIESEE advocated studying the Balkans through the notion of hybridity, as a "pathway of cultural communication between the Mediterranean Europe, the Slavic world, and Asia Minor." Its programs turned attention to more contemporary topics and problems.[57] UNESCO attempted to transform the Balkans into "a model Europe" that embodied cultural détente and solidarity together with the Third World's drive to overcome neocolonialism and underdevelopment. This reading was evident in the closing remarks of N. Bammate, the chief of the Coordinating Unit for the East-West-MP, at AIESEE's 1968 conference "The Archeological Sources of European Civilization": "Because of Balkan studies all the countries of the world (Asia, Africa, and the Americas included) are presently curious about Europe."[58]

The hybridity of Southeastern Europe was embedded in the new ways that Balkan intellectuals chose to conceptualize the very notion of Europe, not as a distinct bordered region with a core in its northwest, but rather as a looser geographical space with porous borders. Its so-called peripheries became civilizational conduits between the rest of the continent, Asia, and North Africa. The internationalization of Balkan scholarly cooperation within UNESCO did not articulate a new universalism but rather a new form of European identity founded on the Southeast's connections to the world through the Mediterranean, Adriatic, and Black seas. The importance of the Mediterranean space and the Ottoman Empire to Balkan symbolic geographies, which seemingly broke down the East-West divisions between Europe and non-Europe, was used to reinforce national and regional claims of their own centrality in Europe. The Mediterranean was primarily tied to the grand theme of Byzantium as "second Europe."[59] The Ottoman Empire was approached either as a counterbalance to European supremacy, especially by Turkish scholars, or from a Balkan-centric viewpoint rooted in national experiences of imperial rule.[60]

Working within such a framework, AIESEE began to support cultural projects that articulated this vision of a more open Europe with a liminal Balkans at its center, for example, specialization courses for young archaeologists from Algeria, Morocco, and Tunisia. The program was an outgrowth of UNESCO's "Save Carthage Project." Condurachi and Yugoslav archaeologist Miliutin Garašanin represented the association in this CIPSH project. They collaborated with the École Française de Rome, where, during the late 1970s and mid-1980s, young North Africans undertook residences while visiting digs in the Balkans.

The initial enthusiasm concerning the program generated proposals for similar initiatives within CIPSH for Southeast Asia and Sub-Saharan Africa. They did not materialize, however, because the council had obtained UNESCO funding for North Africa only as part of the organization's focus on Carthage.[61]

Perhaps the most significant attempt to translate the debates about an open-bordered vision of Europe, one not centered on the West, into AIESEE's programs was the colloquium "Istanbul at the Intersection of Balkan, Mediterranean, Slavic, and Oriental Cultures" (October 1973). According to N. Bammate, the event was greatly appreciated by the cultural sector of the Arab League. It brought together four epistemic groups: AIESEE; specialists in Slavic and Central Asian studies; the International Commission of Maritime History (represented by French and Italian historians); and Arab scholars. It was an opportunity to affirm the historical connections of European lands with the Middle East and North Africa via the *pars Orientis* (eastern half) of the former Roman Empire, which had survived through the latter's Byzantine and Ottoman incarnations. The event in Istanbul witnessed the articulation of a debate regarding the Europeanization of the Ottoman Empire, defined in terms of its integration into world capitalism. According to Balkan scholars, this process precipitated the modernization of Southeastern Europe and its turn toward the West, which meant both progress and exploitation.[62] American-Turkish historian Kemal Karpat best exemplified this idea by describing Istanbul in the nineteenth century as "not very different from that of many other larger cities in Asia, Africa, and South America . . . a semi-colonial post of exchange of goods."[63]

While Balkan scholars used decolonizing narratives to throw off victim status, they nevertheless did this primarily to assert their region's centrality to European history and to showcase stories of national greatness. Their interest in connecting Southeastern representations and histories to extra-European territories (e.g., North Africa or western Asia) was secondary. This may account for the fact that the attendance of extra-European scholars (North Americans not included) at AIESEE's events steadily declined. The first Congress of Southeast European Studies, in Sofia, gathered participants from Japan (3), Lebanon (3), and Israel (2). The second, in Athens, brought attendance from Egypt (1), Ghana (2), Israel (3), and Lebanon (4). The third, in Bucharest in 1974 included approximately 1,300 researchers from thirty-two countries. Its global flavor was enhanced by participants from Algeria (1), Israel (7), India (1), Japan (1), Lebanon (5), Mexico (1), and New Zealand (2). It seemed that this congress reflected an upward turn. However, by 1979, at the fourth congress in Ankara, only one researcher from Israel and two from Lebanon took part.

The problems in co-opting non-Western scholars reflected AIESEE's difficulties, since its inception, in creating consistent transregional cooperation. In 1962 at the Sinaia colloquium, the Romanian organizers and UNESCO invited countries viewed as having historical ties to Turkey or the Balkans. Lebanon and Iran sent representatives; the United Arab Republic and Iraq did not. A fundamental paradox characterized AIESEE's activities. Despite the fact that it "went beyond the usual regional classifications" by situating the Balkans in relation with the Middle East, Central Europe, and the Mediterranean,[64] it failed to increase thematic or institutional connections beyond its Eurocentric embeddedness and national particularisms. The main reason was the persistent geocultural bias among regional scholars. As an institution, AIESEE was envisaged to aid a cultural return to Europe. Its general secretary described it as "our [scholars from the region] common effort to reintegrate this part of our continent into the great European family."[65]

While AIESEE embraced UNESCO's nonterritorial and ambiguous vision of Orient and Occident, scholars associated with it rewrote their region's history within a specific Eurocentric worldview set against the long shadow of Great Power dominance. Their geographical purview remained embedded in the East-West axis, while embracing the emancipatory ethos of the North-South dialogue. In 1976 Nikolai Todorov (director of the Bulgarian Institute of Balkan Studies and AIESEE president 1974–79) postulated that European capitalism reduced "to the status of colonies or semi-colonies not only the countries detached [from empires], but entire continents."[66] The Balkans and the Third World suffered, in a diachronic perspective, from the same historical affliction: as imperial peripheries, their autonomous development had been stunted, which resulted in dependency and alienation.[67]

By the end of the Cold War, AIESEE's regionalist narratives based on challenging hegemonic representations of Europe from either West or East lost their visibility and influence. The fate of the association remained tied to that of UNESCO. When the latter experienced a systemic crisis in the mid-1980s, AIESEE was unable to obtain enough international and domestic support to preserve its relevance without the international organization's tutelage. UNESCO cut the association's budget to USD 10,000 for the 1982–83 biennium (five times less than its funding in the early 1970s) with further reductions until 1989. In 1990 and 1991 the association did not receive any support at all. The limited response to UNESCO's transregional objectives made it a casualty of the organization's prioritizing funding for extra-European regions. The dwindling international prestige of AIESEE brought about the disengagement of local actors. For instance, the Romanian government cut the endowment for the association's secretariat, which was in Bucharest.

In this context, Southeastern European scholars gradually lost the initiative in the production of regional representations to their Western peers. In 1982 at a conference of experts in Balkan studies held in Belgrade, American historians lamented what they considered the disconnectedness of Southeastern

European from Central European and Russian/Soviet studies. They proposed a division of labor within common editorial enterprises: locals would deal with national case studies, while foreign academics would take on the task of generalists—translators of regional specificity in broader European and world contexts.[68] The event reflected Yugoslav scholars' interest in North American connections at the expense of regional Balkan or Mediterranean collaborations. By the late 1980s AIESEE had lost its capacity to aggregate and represent regional and international expertise. The economic downturn in socialist states combined with the worsening of minority conflicts among the region's countries accelerated the demise of the association's counterhegemonic regionalism. Since its creation, the association's activity had been premised on the capacity of its members to accept the coexistence among various historiographies in the region. By the last decade of the Cold War, such fragile equilibrium was increasingly unsustainable.

The hardening Western turn of AIESEE at the expense of transregional themes was noticeable at international congresses of Southeast European studies from the mid-1980s onward. In Belgrade (1984) the thematic focus was the link between the Balkans and Central Europe. In Sofia (September 1989) the assembly dealt with European progressive traditions and was connected with the bicentenary of the French Revolution. The association's vision of the Southeast as the core of Europe due to its Mediterranean heritage was marginalized as two new conceptualizations of regional grouping came to the fore—Southern and Central Europe. Inherent in both these terms was the idea of a peripheral region converging toward the West. The Balkans' self-assigned liminality between the Orient and Occident—once, in the age of high decolonization, deemed a strength and a position from which to become global—now turned into a liability as Balkan intellectual elites sought to align themselves with a new regional vision of Europe grounded on the European Community/European Union.[69] Ironically, in the early 1970s, AIESEE had been the model for several attempts to create a similar association for Central European studies. Condurachi criticized one of these projects, proposed by Austrian, Czechoslovak, and Hungarian scholars, for its excessive focus on historical studies and the Habsburg Empire. In his view it ignored UNESCO's emphasis on interdisciplinarity, and it sought to build an exclusionary parochial regionalism.[70] In the late 1980s and early 1990s, Central Europe became a concept that refuted the idea that the countries of this area were in any way associated with the Orient or non-European territories. It was defined by its proximity and similarity with the West rather than, as in the case of the Balkans, by differences based on original, local syntheses of transregional influences.[71] In 1994 AIESEE organized its first post–Cold War congress in Thessaloniki (with three hundred attendees) after UNESCO had resumed its funding, but it was woefully insufficient. The association's future initiatives now depended on Western and North American support and, as some suggested in Thessaloniki, on the European Union.[72]

Conclusion

Balkan and Third World ideas of emancipation often appeared as mirror images one of the other. The vision from UNESCO of unity in diversity and its embrace of the cause of formerly peripheral peoples resonated among both constituencies. Their reenfranchisement via UNESCO presupposed the economic, political, and cultural democratization of international relations. Southeastern Europe and the Global South found themselves on the same side as they strove for "increased, real access to the natural condition of active, sovereign, and independent subjects, rejecting the limited, local, regionally peripheral role that, historically, they were often condemned to play."[73]

AIESEE was an important example of how an emancipatory discourse and practice from the Global South was transferred to a periphery of Europe. Through UNESCO, Balkan scholars were able to appropriate transregional initiatives to assert the worth of their own region in the face of its cultural peripheralization by the West. Balkan academics developed an institutional springboard that allowed them to take advantage of the openings in the global politics of culture engendered by decolonization and to contest forms of European identity that had left them on the cultural fringes. Nevertheless, these remained essentially Eurocentric discourses, important for claiming a role for the Balkans in a broader European civilization. However, by the late 1980s, all this had changed: as the Global South's challenge to the postwar hierarchies dissipated, AIESEE's calls for a self-assertive Balkan regional identity were eclipsed by competing national self-representations and the idea of a postsocialist "return to Europe," based on the values of its northwestern core. As the Cold War ended, the Balkans were once again at the margins.

Notes

1. This work was supported by a grant of the Romanian National Authority for Scientific Research and Innovation, CNCS—UEFISCDI, project number PN-II-RU-TE-2014-4-0335.

2. "Le Directeur général de l'UNESCO, A-M. M'Bow—docteur honoris causa de l'Université de Sofia," *Etudes balkaniques*, no. 4 (1976): 7–8.

3. Diana Mishkova, "The Politics of Regionalist Science: The Balkans as a Supranational Space in Late Nineteenth to Mid-Twentieth Century Academic Projects," *East Central Europe* 39, nos. 1–2 (2012): 266–303.

4. Alvin Rubinstein, *Yugoslavia and the Nonaligned World* (Princeton, NJ: Princeton University Press 1970), 61.

5. Mircea Maliţa, *Secolul meu scurt* (Bucureşti: RAO Class, 2015), 348–350; and Colin W. Lawson, "National Independence and Reciprocal Advantages: The Political Economy of Romanian-South Relations," *Soviet Studies* 35, no. 3 (July 1983): 363.

6. Jordan Baev, "Bulgarian Arms Delivery to Third World Countries, 1950–1989," April 30, 2007, http://www.ocnus.net/artman/publish/article_28787.shtml (last accessed January 17, 2015).

7. Evanthis Hatzivassiliou, *Greece and the Cold War Frontline State, 1952–1967* (London: Routledge, 2006).

8. Feroz Ahmad, *Turkey: The Quest for Identity* (Oxford: One World Publications, 2003).

9. Eyüp Ersoy, "Turkish Foreign Policy toward the Algerian War of Independence (1954–62)," *Turkish Studies* 13, no. 4 (2012): 683–695; John Sakkas, "The Greek Dictatorship, the USA and the Arabs, 1967–1974," *Journal of Southern Europe and the Balkans* 6, no. 3 (December 2004): 245–257.

10. ANIC, C.C. al P.C.R., Relaţii Externe, 46/1960, vol. 1, 137.

11. ANIC, C.C. al P.C.R., Relaţii Externe, 39/1965, vol. 2, 172.

12. Spyridon Sfetas, "The Bulgarian-Yugoslav Dispute over the Macedonian Question as a Reflection of the Soviet-Yugoslav Controversy (1968–1980)," *Balcanica* 43 (Belgrade: Institute des études balkaniques 2012), 241–271; and Tchavdar Marinov, "In Defense of the Native Tongue: The Standardization of the Macedonian Language and the Bulgarian-Macedonian Linguistic Controversies," in *Entangled Histories of the Balkans: National Ideologies and Language Policies*, eds. Roumen Daskalov and Tchavdar Marinov, vol. 1 (Leiden: Brill, 2013), 419–487.

13. ANIC, C.C. al P.C.R., Relaţii Externe, 50/1960, 179.

14. Maliţa, *Secolul*, 363–364.

15. ANIC, C.C. al P.C.R., Relaţii Externe, 50/1960, 99.

16. ANIC, C.C. al P.C.R., Relaţii Externe, 53/1960, 2 and 5.

17. ANIC, CC al P.C.R., Relaţii Externe, 7I, 159.

18. Samir Amin, *Eurocentrism* (London: Zed Press, 1989), 143. Eirini Karamouzi, "Managing the 'Helsinki Spirit' in the Balkans: The Greek Initiative for Balkan Co-operation, 1975–1976," *Diplomacy & Statecraft* 24, no. 4 (2013): 597–618.

19. Quoted in Mark Mazower, *Governing the World. The History of an Idea* (London/New York: Allen Lane, 2012), 269.

20. Prasenjit Duara, "The Cold War as a Historical Period: An Interpretive Essay," *Journal of Global History* 6, no. 3 (November 2011): 469.

21. Bogdan C. Iacob, "Is It Transnational? A New Perspective in the Study of Communism," *East Central Europe* 40, no. 1 (2013): 114–139.

22. Ersoy, "Turkish Foreign Policy," 689.

23. Maria Negreponti Delivanis, "Structures du développement économique de la Grèce," *Balkan Studies* 17, no. 1 (1976): 291.

24. David Binder, "Balkan Nations Spur Contacts within the Region," *New York Times*, August 21, 1966, 15.

25. Steven V. Roberts, "Détente Even in the Fractious Balkans," *New York Times* (October 26, 1975), 206.

26. ANIC, C.C. al P.C.R., Relaţii Externe, 153/1966, 24.

27. UNESCO/Box X07.21 (497.2), 4.

28. Maliţa, *Secolul*, 504.

29. UNESCO/Box X07.21 (495) NC Relations with Greece—National Commission, part 2 from 1/I/1964, 2.

30. UNESCO/Box X07.21 (560), Relations with Turkey—Official, part 3—from 01/I/1982.

31. Historian Svetozar Radojčič in Commission Nationale Roumaine Pour L'UNESCO, *Actes du Colloque International de Civilisations Balkanique* (Bucharest, 1962), 198.

32. Emil Condurachi, "Un programme de connaissance et compréhension mutuelles par la coopération scientifique," *Bulletin AIESEE*, nos. 1–2 (1963): 8.

33. Dimitros J. Evrigenis, "Réflexions sur une coopération des pays balkaniques dans le domaine du droit," *Balkan Studies* 7, no. 2 (1966): 362.

34. B. R. Tomlinson, "What Was the Third World?" *Journal of Contemporary History* 38, no. 2 (April 2003): 307–321.

35. Emil Condurachi, "L'AIESEE à son Xe anniversaire—esquisse d'un bilan du passée et de ses perspectives d'avenir," *Bulletin AIESEE*, nos. 1–2 (1973): 39.

36. Marcin Solarz, "'Third World': The 60th Anniversary of a Concept that Changed History," *Third World Quarterly* 33, no. 9 (2012): 1562.

37. Christoph Kalter, "A Shared Space of Imagination, Communication, and Action: Perspectives on the History of the 'Third World,'" in *The Third World in the Global 1960s (Protest, Culture and Society)*, eds. Samantha Christiansen and Zachary Scarlett (London: Berghahn Books, 2013), 27–29.

38. George Constantacopoulos, "Cultural and Economic Bases of Balkan Cooperation in Connection with Prewar Movements," *Bulletin AIESEE*, nos. 13–14 (1975–1976): 32 and 27.

39. Ion Sion, "Interviu cu prof. Mihai Berza: Pe marginea unui mesaj adresat congresului," *Buletinul Comisiei Naţionale a R.S.R. pentru UNESCO*, an. 16, nr. 3–4 (1974): 50.

40. Mihai Berza, "Les études du Sud-Est européen, leur rôle et leur place dans l'esemble des sciences humaines," *Revue des Études Sud-Est Européennes* 13, no. 1 (1975): 14.

41. "8e Assemblée générale, 15–18 septembre 1965, Copenhague," UNESCO/Box CIPSH 8, 20–21.

42. "Report of the Secretary General on the Activities of CIPSH at the 9th General Assembly, 9–13 September 1967, Bucharest," UNESCO/Box CIPSH 9, 4.

43. C. C. Berg, "Relations avec l'Unesco et suggestions concernant le programme de l'Unesco pour 1969–1970, 9th General Assembly, 9–13 September 1967, Bucharest," UNESCO/Box CIPSH 9, 28.

44. Vincenzo Pavone, *From the Labyrinth of the World to the Paradise of the Heart: Science and Humanism in UNESCO's Approach to Globalization* (Lanham, MD: Lexington Books, 2008), 97–124.

45. "Conclusions du débat de politique générale à la XVIIe session de la Conférence Générale," *Buletinul Comisiei Naţionale a R.S.R. pentru UNESCO*, an 15, nr. 1 (1973): 18.

46. "10th General Assembly of the CPISH (Palermo, 8–11 September 1969)," UNESCO/Box CIPSH 10, 31.

47. *Tradition et innovation dans la culture des pays du sud-est européen* (Bucharest: AIESEE, 1969), 138–139.

48. "9th General Assembly, 9–13 September 1967, Bucharest," UNESCO/Box CIPSH 9, 47.

49. "8th General Assembly, 15–18 September 1965, Copenhagen," UNESCO/Box CIPSH 8, 21.

50. Dimitrije Djordjević, *Révolutions nationales des peuples balkaniques 1804–1914* (Belgrade: Institute d'Histoire, 1965), 226 and 239–240.

51. Laura Wong, "Relocating East and West: UNESCO's Major Project on the Mutual Appreciation of Eastern and Western Cultural Values," *Journal of World History* 19, no. 3 (September 2008): 349–374.

52. Jean Chevallier (BMS) à Directeur General, 'Mission en Albanie (25–28 avril 1959),' Box X07.21 (496.5) Relations with Albania-official, 4.

53. UNESCO, NGO/Conf. 6 (June 17–20, 1958), 4–5.

54. UNESCO/CUA/96 (June 17, 1959), 4.

55. Emil Georgiev, "Le développement des études balkaniques en Bulgarie," *Actes du IIe Congrès International des Etudes du Sud-est Européen, Tome I, Chronique du Congrès, Rapports* (Athens: AIESEE, 1972), 200.

56. Alexandru Duţu, "L'étude comparée des cultures europeennes et la recherche interdisciplinaire," *Revue des Études Sud-Est Européennes* 12, no. 2 (1974): 195, 203, 200.

57. Moënis Taha-Hussein, "L'UNESCO et l'étude des cultures du sud-est européen," *Bulletin AIESEE* 1 (1972): 41, 45.

58. *Sources archéologiques de la civilisation européenne* (AIESEE: Bucharest, 1970), 300.

59. Denis A. Zakythinos, "La synthèse Byzantine dans l'antithèse Orient-Occident," in *Actes du Colloque International de Civilisations Balkanique (Sinaia, 8-14 juillet 1962)* (Bucarest: Commission Nationale Roumaine pour l'Unesco, 1962), 107–115; and Berza, "Les études du Sud-Est européen," 13.

60. Association Internationale des Etudes Balkaniques et Sud-Est Européennes, *Actes du Premier Congrès International des Etudes Balkaniques et Sud-Est Européennes, vol. I, Manifestations officielles* (Sofia : BANU, 1967), 617.

61. "CIPSH Assemblée générale, Dubrovnik, 23–25 septembre 1975," box UNESCO/CIPSH 11, 20; and "Procès-verbal Provisoire, XXXIVe Réunion du Bureau, Paris, 13–14 décembre 1976," UNESCO/CIPSH 30, 14.

62. The proceedings of the event in Istanbul were published in issues 1 and 2 of the *Bulletin AIESEE* in 1974.

63. Kemal H. Karpat, "The Social and Economic Transformation of Istanbul in the Nineteenth Century," *Bulletin AIESEE*, no. 2 (1974): 297.

64. I am paraphrasing N. Bammate's characterization of the colloquium in Sinaia. PHS/Memo/62.170, UNESCO/Box 21(498) AMS, Romania-Participation Program, part 1 up to 31/XII/74.

65. "Information sur les decision prises par le Comité International de l'AIESEE," *Actes du Premier Congrès International des Etudes Balkaniques et Sud-Est Européennes, vol. I, Manifestations officielles* (Sofia, 1967), 47.

66. Nikolai Todorov, "La révolution industrielle en Europe Occidentale et les provinces balkaniques de l'Empire Ottoman. Le cas bulgare," in *La révolution industrielle dans le Sud-est européen—XIX s* (AIESEE: Sofia, 1976), 114.

67. Similar interpretations by Valentin Georgescu (Romania), Nikola Vuco (Yugoslavia), or Vassilis Panayotopoulos (Greece) in *La révolution industrielle.*

68. *Conférence Internationale des Balkanologues*, Belgrade, 7–8 septembre 1982 (Belgrade: Académie Serbe des Sciences et des Arts, Institut des Etudes Balkaniques, 1984).

69. The accession of southern Europe (Greece, Spain, and Portugal) to the European Community (EC) generated criteria that would later be applied to former socialist states. This triggered the elimination of any representational inbetweenness from the territories at the margins of the EC. Kim Christiaens, James Mark, and José Faraldo, "Entangled Transitions: Eastern and Southern European Convergence or Alternative Europes? 1960s–2000s," *Contemporary European History* 26, no. 4 (2017): 577–599.

70. ANIC, CC al P.C.R., Secţia Agitaţie şi Propagandă, May 1970, 137–138.

71. Diana Mishkova, Bo Stråth, and Balázs Trencsényi, "Regional History as a 'Challenge' to National Frameworks of Historiography: The Case of Central, Southeast, and Northern Europe," in *Transnational Challenges to National History Writing*, eds. Matthias Middell and Luís Roura (New York: Palgrave MacMillan, 2013), 257–314.

72. "Rapport Sexennal AIESEE 1988–1994," UNESCO/File 288, BBC/CISH AIESEE 1994–1995, 3.

73. Radu Pascal, "O idee-forţă a lumii noastre. Democratizarea relaţiilor internaţionale," *Lumea*, no. 12 (1974): 15.

BOGDAN C. IACOB is Researcher at the Institute of History, Romanian Academy of Sciences and fellow at the Aarhus Institute of Advanced Studies.

Part IV

Global Encounter and Challenges to State Socialism

12 A Prehistory of Postcolonialism in Socialist Poland*

Adam F. Kola

Introduction

In the immediate wake of the fall of state socialism in 1989, postcolonialism had few takers in Poland. It would only arrive as a powerful intellectual project with political resonance in the 2000s: not as an import from the Third World, but rather from Western humanities and social sciences—and used by the anticommunist right as much as by the left to make sense of Poland's present as a condition shaped by the experience of "Soviet colonization." Despite its increasing usage in contemporary Poland, there has been little investigation into its origins; this chapter will present an archeology of knowledge, a prehistory of postcolonial studies and literatures in a postsocialist society.

Postcolonialism in fact took many different forms in late socialist Poland, although these were political and cultural manifestations marked by tensions and ambivalences. The communist state had promoted a sympathy with anticolonial movements since its inception. The term *postcolonial* was in fact used in academic texts and encyclopedias, usually to denote neocolonial practices in former colonies or the allure of an Eastern European style of socialism to those who were throwing off the chains of empire.[1] Despite this, official figures expressed little interest in promoting a "postcolonial studies" of the sort that had emerged in the Global South and West. Nevertheless, over two hundred works of postcolonial literature were published during the communist era.[2] In the 1950s and 1960s, there were already Polish translations of books by Aimé Césaire, Mahatma Gandhi, Frantz Fanon, Chinua Achebe, and Kavalam Madhava Panikkar.[3] The Polish edition of Edward W. Said's *Orientalism* was prepared before 1989, although it did not appear until 1991—after the collapse of communism but long before the later interest in postcolonial theory in Poland.[4]

Moreover, tropes that we might today recognize as postcolonial—the idea of enslaved nations or groups, for instance—had widespread resonance in late communist Poland: Alex Haley's book *Roots*, published in Polish in 1976, and the TV series that followed were immensely popular, partly because its account of resistance to slavery quickly became understood as analogous to the country's own contemporary struggle against "Soviet colonization." Yet these works did not provide an intellectual language of resistance to communism that placed the national experience in the context of broader struggles against authoritarian and imperial power. Neither the Polish humanities (especially those that may have been termed "underground") nor the politically engaged democratic, anticommunist opposition made such connections. This was not only the result of the Communist state's appropriation of anticolonialism in the cause of bolstering its own legitimacy but also the absence of a theoretical framework of postcolonial studies—which at that time was largely unknown in Poland.[5] Why, given the relative popularity of "postcolonial literature" in late socialist-era Polish popular culture, did it have little resonance among the dissenting intelligentsia? It is a story that deserves thorough study. The gap becomes even more puzzling when we consider that other theories (postmodernism in particular) that had been foreign to the East European communist "traditions" of the time had already started to resonate in academic milieus. In fact, one can speak of an unwillingness or even refusal during this period to employ a postcolonial approach to the Polish experiences of empire, whether historically or under contemporary conditions of Soviet influence. This late communist-era rejection still has ramifications today.

The Postwar Growth of a Common Anticolonialism

Global anticolonial movements in the postwar period had only a limited resonance in Poland in the immediate aftermath of the Second World War. Despite the country's own history of partition, colonization and Nazi recolonization, the lack of extra-European colonies in Poland, and its postwar monoethnic society, rendered the implications of the struggle against European empires a distant—if not irrelevant—development. Nevertheless, by the end of the 1940s, this situation had begun to change. From the first years of Communist rule, the intimations of a "durable friendship" between the Eastern Bloc and the so-called Third World brought these issues into Polish public debate. The idea of a communist struggle against Western imperialism expanded to make sense of the anticolonial resistance and decolonization on a global scale, in a framework that presented Eastern Europe's own past struggles as a forerunner of what was now occurring globally.[6] One of the first manifestations of this tendency could be observed at the World Congress of Intellectuals in Defense of Peace and in the Recovered Territories Exhibition held in Wrocław in 1948.[7] The congress itself was a major Soviet-inspired propaganda event, organized in the so-called just recovered Wrocław (formerly German Breslau) by Communist writer and activist Jerzy Borejsza (1905–1952). Among notable left-wing intellectuals who attended were Pablo Picasso, Irène Joliot-Curie, Bertold Brecht, György Lukács, as well as Polish delegates such as Jarosław Iwaszkiewicz, Maria Dąbrowska, Zofia Nałkowska, and Tadeusz Kotarbiński. The stated purpose of this congress was to discuss possible solutions to the nuclear arms race, and thereby to slow an increasingly evident Cold War division of the world. In this it failed: due to Soviet attempts to manipulate the proceedings, some of the Western intellectuals in attendance decided to leave early.[8] What occurred instead was the mapping out of a new political agenda linking the Eastern Bloc to a decolonizing world. This same agenda gave rise to many of the frameworks that would be developed by leftist Polish intellectuals over the following decade. It was at the congress—in the documents prepared beforehand by communist intellectuals, both the reports and party bulletins—that the anti-imperialist idea of relations between socialist and postcolonial nations was formulated and widely publicized.[9] Both Soviet and Polish socialist propaganda began to articulate the idea that socialist solidarity should extend beyond Europe—in global alliances capable of mounting a challenge to the capitalist Western colonial system.[10]

The Korean War was likewise a crucial moment for the political consolidation of the idea of a broader anticolonial struggle within Polish society. Mass anti-imperialist, anti-American solidarity movements were organized for the first time.[11] Poles were thus encouraged to believe that the struggle of North Korean soldiers echoed their own fight against Nazi occupation. Lucjan Pracki's (1923–2016) book *Korespondent wojenny z Korei donosi* (War correspondent from Korea reports) was typical in this regard: American troops were, he implied, the new Nazis.[12] A struggle that had been won on Eastern European soil now needed to be supported in other areas of the world. Such a link also had domestic motivations: in the postwar years the Recovered Territories in western Poland had large German minorities—who were soon expelled. Anti-imperialist propaganda was often used to demonstrate that German Nazism was still alive, albeit displaced: such links could be used to reinforce the ideological necessity of the de-Germanization of "eternal" Polish Recovered Territories.[13] In this sense, the first postwar Polish interest in non-European territories and the process of decolonization was partly motivated by a domestic project of ethnic homogenization.

It is important to note here that Poles, when attempting to clarify their anti-imperialism, looked not eastward but westward, invoking their historical experience of resisting German expansionism. The Polish western Recovered Territories were thus a crucial space by virtue of which such linkages could be articulated. By contrast, there is little evidence to suggest that communists in Poland used earlier traditions of Polish "'Eastness" to fashion propaganda images of Polish relations with non-European territories. They were not inclined to invoke an anti-imperialist Orient. This latter could not be deployed imaginatively to forge relationships with non-European territories and to build alliances between the Second and the Third Worlds, because the Eastern Borderlands (the so-called Kresy) had been subsumed within the Soviet Union.[14]

Vietnam would subsequently play a crucial role in deepening the connection between Poland and a postcolonial world. The stories of struggle against imperial Japan, of postwar French recolonization, of the Vietnamese victory over the European forces in the 1950s, and of the struggle of the North, supported by the Eastern Bloc and China, against the South were widely publicized and had an impact that went beyond a socialist elite—particularly among a younger generation.[15] Travel writing played a particularly important role. In the case of Asia, Wojciech Żukrowski (1916–2000), who traveled extensively in China, India (where he worked at the Polish embassy), and Southeast Asia, was a key figure. The result of his 1954 trip to Vietnam was the book *Dom bez ścian* (House without walls), which included high-quality illustrations by the outstanding Polish socialist realist painter Aleksander Kobzdej (1920–1972). This was a closely monitored anti-imperialism: *House without Walls* was published by the Ministry of National Defense. Nearly all anticolonial writing was the product of official publishing houses, owned and run by the state, and the text as a whole had to be vetted by censors. The book is full of exemplary moral tales, confirming the official friendship between the Polish and Vietnamese nations and communist support for the latter's resistance in the anticolonialist and anti-imperialist war against the French. Strikingly, it sought—as many contemporary texts did—to intimate close parallels between the experiences of Poles and those of the Vietnamese. The Vietnamese struggle against the colonial oppression of the Japanese and the French was rendered comprehensible to Polish readers using stories and imagery that called to mind both the manner in which the reestablishment of a sovereign Polish state in 1918 had come to be narrated in independent Poland and the still-raw memories of the Nazi occupation of Poland during the Second World War. At the beginning of the book, a Vietnamese student, Ha Quej, recounts a short history of his own country during the previous decades. "In August 1945 we declared our country's independence. The French lacked even the [minimal] notion of right that is dictated by power and violence. . . . They gave away our country to the Japanese."[16] And he continues: "In 1949 the colonists started their invasion of our fertile plains. [. . .] They shot our men, raped our girls, confiscated our rice and, while withdrawing, stopped by the partisans, they set peasant huts on fire" (pp. 9–10). The history of violence, known all too well in anticolonial literature, returns in this Polish book from the first half of the 1950s. "The French fort threatened the area. People were forced to provide necessities: workers, cattle, bamboo . . . They hunted for the girls by themselves" (p. 10). Workers, cattle, and bamboo placed in this sequence clearly reflect, in a descending scale, the assumed hierarchy of values. Human beings, animals, and plant life are in another sense rendered equal, in that to the colonists they are seen as equivalent, subservient, and destined to be acquired by white people. In addition, there are constant intimations of sexual violence, with women being hunted like wild animals or caught like fish.

The book drew frequent parallels between the experiences of occupied nations fighting for independence. Poland and Vietnam, the reader might infer, would be bound together as two countries in which Communist parties would realize a humanitarian future of liberty, independence, self-determination, and human rights. The last sentence of the main part of the book is of crucial significance in this regard: "And then I understood—the People's China is for those people [the Vietnamese], for the whole of Asia, for the PEACE [that the whole world desires]" (p. 398, capitals in the original). The shared experience of resistance was often essential to establishing such parallels. In the photographic album *Niepokonani* (The invincible), published in 1971, an introduction by Ryszard Frelek (1929–2007; writer, professor, diplomat, and member of Parliament before 1989) noted: "First [resistance in Vietnam], in the years of World War II, was directed at the Japanese invaders. [The Vietnamese] liberated their country by themselves and, what is more, it was their struggle that made it possible to set free the French prisoners of war from the camps established by the Japanese. Then, there was another stage of resistance—against French colonialism."[17] The album shows the war as seen by the enslaved, oppressed subalterns and gives voice to the marginalized. The semiperipheral position of Poland gave the Poles a privileged insight into the peripheral situation of Vietnam during these wars. The historical experience of partitions and occupation strengthened and honed Poles' instinctive sympathies, while the friendship of the authors with Vietnamese people justified their claims to speak in their name. When Jean-Paul Sartre was writing his afterword to Frantz Fanon's *Les damnés de la terre*, he looked through the eyes of an Algerian revolutionary by choice and an Afro-French intellectual from Martinique by birth, but he did so as a reflexive intellectual and from the vantage point of a colonial metropolis—Paris. The Poles, with their traumatic experience of repeated partition, were only too well-placed, or so Frelek imagined, to truly comprehend colonialism. Zbigniew Staszyszyn's photographs presented the grassroots perspective, the everyday life of ordinary people during the war. *Invincible* presents a photographic history of the third Vietnamese resistance movement, this time against the Americans. In this war—as Frelek, who had traveled around Vietnam previously, recounted—the Vietnamese did not feel abandoned. Bolstered by the support of socialist countries, the Soviet Union in particular, and by expressions of "solidarity on the part of socialist countries," they were convinced that "in the case of the Vietnam war, there is a front encompassing the entire world" (p. 8). In this album from the 1970s, with its fine black-and-white images, as in the book from the 1950s, we can discern a feature characteristic of the socialism of this period, namely, a mixture of propagandist jargon with a humanist and pacifist message. Frelek seems to have been aware of this when mentioning other anticolonial wars, for example, in Africa, where the invading soldiers of colonizer armies had transformed ordinary people into murderers. This phenomenon was described by Hannah Arendt in her famous but controversial study of 1963, *Eichmann in Jerusalem: A Report on the Banality of Evil*, but also at an earlier date, it may be argued, in Poland. Leon Kruczkowski, in his play *Niemcy* (The Germans), first performed in 1949, had likewise raised the problem of the banality of evil. This literary and cultural background provided Frelek with the means to pose similar questions concerning the colonization process and struggles for independence. He began with the example of American soldiers in Vietnam, extending the list and adding that "they became [murderers]—French soldiers in Vietnam and Algeria, British soldiers in Malaya, Dutch soldiers in Indonesia, the Belgians in the Congo, as did the Portuguese in Angola and Israeli soldiers in the occupied Arab territories" (p. 7). He concluded: "Such is the logic of all these wars, named long ago as 'dirty wars'" (p. 7). The Polish picture of Vietnam's anticolonial and anti-imperialist struggle after the Second World War was heavily infused with the rhetoric of the socialist state, which rendered it difficult for the democratic opposition later to identify with this kind of struggle—or to recognize its revolutionary potential.

Anticolonialism and Anticommunism: A Rendezvous Manqué?

Yet elements of anticolonial and postcolonial thinking were not absent from a leftist culture that extended well beyond the controlling grasp of the state. Indeed, in the 1960s, some radicals of the younger generation, such as Jacek Kuroń and Karol Modzelewski, did invoke the struggle against colonial oppression as they sought to reform bureaucratic socialism at home.[18] The historian Marian Małowist (1909–1988) was a key figure too[19]—said by Immanuel Wallerstein to be the main inspiration and founding father (along with Fernand Braudel) of so-called world-systems theory.[20] Małowist suggested a reverse order of knowledge in historiography through a questioning of those historical models that had made Western Europe the normative model from which other regions had deviated. This still preeminent Eurocentric approach was for him a consequence of European claims to world domination and was based on feelings of moral superiority over non-Europeans.[21] In the 1960s Małowist formulated the idea of core/center-(semi)peripheries and called the hegemony of the West a form of continuing colonial domination over colonized peoples. His books were concerned with European-African relations in the early era of colonization, the Portuguese conquistadors, Tamerlane (Timur), the East-West division of Europe, and the problem of slavery.[22] For Małowist this domination was not only restricted to the political and economic spheres but also influenced the field of culture—much as Edward W. Said would argue a decade later in *Orientalism*. And finally, Małowist argued that Eastern Europe was also a part of this global system of dependence as a territory dependent on the West.

Similar parallels were also drawn in popular culture. Alex Haley's *Roots: The Saga of an American Family*,[23] originally published in 1976, and the television miniseries *Roots* (1977), based on this novel, were popular in 1980s Poland. Both Polish-language editions of the book, published in 1982 and 1988 respectively, had a print run of over a hundred thousand copies, and the main character of the novel, Kunta Kinte, played an important part in the social imaginary. One contemporary popular verse had it that: "Polak nosi nos na kwintę, bo chce żyć jak Kunta Kinte, / ale Gierek wszystko robi, żeby Polak żył jak Tobi" (A Pole mopes about, wishing to live like Kunta Kinte, / but Gierek and his mates prepare for him Toby's fate). This couplet, in one version or another, is still widely known in Poland and recalls a memorable scene in the TV version. Kunta Kinte is caught in an attempt to escape from the plantation. He receives a flogging, and his overseer repeatedly insists: "Your name is Toby." When asked what his name is, he answers: "Kunta. Kunta Kinte." After another blow, the overseer asks him again and adds: "When the master gives you something—you take it. They gave you a name. It's a nice name. It's Toby. And it's going to be yours till you die. And now you understand me? And I want to hear it." Kunta Kinte resists a series of blows until the whipping becomes unbearable, and eventually he says with resignation that his name is Toby. The overseer concludes: "That's a good nigger." In the parallel drawn by the couplet, Edward Gierek (1913–2001), the first secretary of the Polish United Workers' Party in the 1970s who fell from power in 1980 with the rise of Solidarity, became the slave owner. Kunta Kinte—the true name of the slave—is an epitome of individual freedom, enshrined in the depths of his heart and mind, in his sense of his identity, whereas Toby is a name for an object, the personal property of the owner of the plantation and of the overseer administering it on his behalf. Submission is enforced by violent power. The analogy to Poland under the Communist regime was clear. Poles were deprived of freedom and of their true Polish identity. This identity remained hidden, like the true name of Kunta Kinte. But the communist authorities—acting as the overseers on behalf of the Soviet rulers—were ready to use violence to transform Poles into a new socialist people, in a similar way to Kunta Kinte, who was forced to become Toby.

Polish submission to Soviet domination is summed up in another popular verse that referred to Kunta Kinte's daughter Kizzy, who was sexually abused by plantation owners: "Polak gwałcony jest jak Kizzy / i skubany jest jak kura / przez wschodniego pana Moora" (A Pole is raped like Kizzy / plucked like a chicken / to serve as a feast for Mr. Moore from the East). It is obvious who the real master in this system is—the Soviet Union, whereas Poles are slaves in the "communist plantation." This dependence is also built on sexual violence as a tool used by whites for asserting masculine power and domination over black women. Rape is an instrument of hegemony, metaphorically also of Soviet hegemony over the Polish nation.

Yet while such borrowings existed, they remained limited in their scope and impact. Anticolonialism in non-European countries and anticommunism in Europe might have developed in closer symbiosis: one can imagine how the democratic opposition in Poland could have appropriated postcolonial studies as a weapon in their own struggle. Nevertheless, with the emergence of a democratic opposition in the late 1970s, such a language disappeared—both anticolonialism and Western postcolonial critique were negatively associated with a type of Marxism that dissidents tended to disavow.[24] There is little evidence of the use of this analogy in samizdat, clandestinely circulated by the opposition in the 1980s. The antiregime opposition did not inaugurate a serious intellectual debate in Poland on anticolonial issues and postcolonial theory, even though they might well have judged their own experience as that of subalterns living under the Communist regime and yet supported by forces from outside the country.

Instead, when resistance to communism was interpreted in anticolonial terms, no attempt was made to link it to the struggles of the decolonization era outside Europe. Some of the Polish opposition of the 1980s admittedly understood their opposition as directed against an external colonial power—yet to make sense of it, they drew on a highly national memory of resisting quasicolonial rulers, as during the partition period, when Poland was divided between Russia, Prussia, and Austria, or later against the Nazi occupiers. The struggle against communism was perceived as part of a national (and supposedly unique) tradition, implying transgenerational continuity in the constant and unrelenting fight against invaders, waged in the name of the partitioned nation. From this perspective, the analogy to the process of decolonization was not needed. The specific Polish context might have helped Poles to understand the plight of those battling empires elsewhere: but by the 1980s the analogy was not felt to offer anything particularly illuminating to an oppositional intellectual culture.

Drawing such parallels was in some ways a perilous undertaking: the affiliation of Poland's anticommunist opposition with anticolonial movements was perceived as hazardous, since it risked being seen as being too close to the regime and the official discourse of power. As a consequence, postcolonial theory would not feature in Polish academic and political discourse until the end of the twentieth century. And when it finally did appear in Poland, it was stripped of its Marxist background and emerged as part of conservative discourse and right-wing politics.

This reluctance to engage with postcolonial theory also reflected a sense of the vast cultural chasm between the Polish opposition and struggles against racism, slavery, or colonialism outside Europe. Extra-European movements were often distanced from Polish realities by being exoticized. In this sense, the fascination with *Roots* was instructive: unlike contemporaneous anticolonial struggles, such as that of the South African opposition under apartheid, *Roots* was situated in the distant past—it allowed society to dream, but it did not demand a present political commitment that would be problematic ideologically, being insufficiently removed from the contemporary language of the regime.

Yet this exoticization had deeper roots that the politicization of anticolonialism by the communist state never really overcame—indeed, one can argue that in many ways such modes of viewing the extra-European world were reproduced in the communist era. The origins of this lay partly in Poland's lack of a colonial empire and the corresponding want of expertise. This is not to argue that there was no interest at all—there were Polish travelers who wrote about their experiences. One could mention the stories of the Jesuit Michał Boym and his mission to seventeenth-century China;[25] or the Polish (or in fact Polish-Slovak-Hungarian) "king" of Madagascar—the story is known from his own memoirs, which later became a motif used by the Polish Romantic poet Juliusz Słowacki in his epic poem *Beniowski*—that is, Count Maurice Benyovszky in the eighteenth century. One could also mention Wacław Sieroszewski, a Polish writer exiled to Siberia in the late nineteenth century and a traveler to the Far East, whose writings included a historical novel about the abovementioned figure, entitled *Beniowski*; or the reportage of Ryszard Kapuściński from the latter half of the twentieth century. Yet these glimpses were usually fleeting and not backed up by sustained and substantial intellectual traditions of engagement. Notwithstanding important figures such as Stanisław Schayer, the founding father of the Warsaw Indological school in the 1930s, there were few Polish experts in the field of non-European studies (not only in anthropology but also in other fields)—at least compared to countries in Western Europe. The handful of famous Polish contributors to the worldwide debate about empire—such as Joseph Conrad or Bronisław Malinowski—became important because of their global and international perspective yet had a limited impact on Polish attitudes "at home."

Even so, popular representations of the world of European empires from the mid-nineteenth century emphasized adventure as the key to understanding non-European countries and are replete with exoticization and Orientalization of otherness and difference. Such patterns were first created by the highly popular book series about Winnetou by the German writer Karl May from the second half of the nineteenth century and the German-Yugoslav movie series from the 1960s based on these books (a kind of spaghetti Western). Exoticizing representation of the extra-European Other continued to thrive in popular culture under communism—even as the regime was promoting a more political conception of the relationship with Africa and Asia. While the Western left was developing a new postcolonial lens through which to view the extra-European world, the communist state still promoted representations that continued to draw heavily on the exoticizing and politically distancing tropes of older European traditions. Alfred Szklarski's series of adventure books about Tomek Wilmowski and his expeditions in faraway lands—from Kenya and Uganda, through Mexico and Brazil, to India, Tibet, and Siberia—were published in the 1950s through the 1980s and were widely consumed. There were TV series and books by Tony Halik, a traveler and explorer from the postwar era; another TV show, *Klub sześciu kontynentów* (Six continents club), produced by Ryszard Badowski from the late 1960s till the end of the 1980s; or the series *Naokoło świata* (Around the world), which was very popular in socialist Poland, with about two hundred books published since 1956 and edited for decades by Krystyna Goldbergowa. Even in the more political works on Vietnam—which we encountered above—we find this same exoticization, particularly in the illustrations that draw on longer-term tropes of the exotic Other.[26] It was these stories that continued to shape the Polish imagination, as opposed to politically oriented anticolonial literature and postcolonial theory. Thus the political potential of *Roots* did not constitute, or only to a limited extent, an appropriate frame of reference for Polish readers and audiences, nor was there any contextual and cultural code for a political reading, interpretation, and use of this novel. The expectations of Poles during the communist era were vastly different from those of anticolonial activists and postcolonial critics.

Conclusion

These understandings of postcolonialism have survived in the ways in which Poles make sense of the journey out of communism. The comparison between the protagonist of *Roots*, Kunta Kinte, and Poland under the Communist regime is still highly resonant. In 2000, twenty years after the strike in the Gdańsk Shipyard and the ensuing agreement on August 31, 1980, which enabled the existence of the Solidarity Labor Union, a local newspaper, *Gazeta Ustrońska*, published an article about the anniversary celebrations. It featured a quote from a Solidarity activist and member of the Społem state cooperative, Henryk Kania: "Before 1980 we were all like Kunta-Kinte, slaves who could do nothing. (. . .) There is nothing to discuss now, we did regain our freedom in 1980."[27] In this interpretation, Solidarity's foundation in 1980 was the beginning of Polish freedom, even though Poles had to wait almost a decade for what they saw as independence. On December 13, 2008, the anniversary of martial law, Witold Kowalczyk recalled his memories of the days of 1981 and his own involvement in Solidarity as an employee of a manufacturing company, FMG Pioma. "On 12 December I was staying up late writing another letter to Lech Wałęsa and complaining that Solidarity was so indifferent to the special teams of the so-called 'Workers-peasant inspections' supervising our enterprises and factories, and I wrote that if we allowed them to do that, we would not be called Kunta Kinte, but Toby."[28] In this example the difference between Kunta Kinte and Toby is preserved, as well as the analogy between *Roots* and the Polish situation.

Postcolonialism has in the postcommunist era remained highly nationalist—its protagonists have been reluctant to connect the Polish experience to broader postcolonial struggles. This can be seen in the way in which the oeuvre of world historian Marian Małowist has been remade for a new Poland. His contention that Poland has long been marked by an economically peripheral position has again proved attractive for a nation attempting a reintegration into Europe.[29] Yet for the most part, Poles have ignored his plea to be global and to connect Poland to other peripheral experiences. Most of Małowist's recent followers have concentrated exclusively on Polish reality, past and present, and limited themselves to Polish problems using a postcolonial perspective developed elsewhere.[30] A truly global perspective is still rare in Polish national discourse: postcolonial history is simply a Polish history in which a succession of symbolic political events, such as the end of the Second World War or the collapse of the Soviet-supported Communist regime in 1989, are considered moments of liberation.

Nor have leftist Western postcolonial thinkers received much acclaim in late socialist or postsocialist Poland. As we have seen in this article, the subversive and revolutionary potential of anticolonial literature and postcolonialism was rarely used by the anticommunist prodemocratic movements in Poland, largely due to the fact that Communist power had appropriated what Westerners called decolonization within the language of its official propaganda. As a consequence, postcolonial theory appeared on the Polish intellectual scene as late as a decade after communism had collapsed, and its influence could hardly be compared to the success of other trends such as neopragmatism or feminism. When postcolonial theory made its first appearance in Poland, it tended to be in the guise of a right-wing and conservative discourse in politics, in academic texts, and in the media.[31]

This does not mean that there is no other postcolonial discourse in contemporary Poland. [32] However, postcolonial categories are still for the most part used in political discourse by right-wing parties, such as Prawo i Sprawiedliwość (PiS; Law and justice), for whom postcolonial concepts provide a coherent political language. Postcolonial discourse undergirds a politics of memory in which foreign empires, whether (Soviet) Russia or (Nazi) Germany, were trying to colonize Poland. What is more, postcolonial theory helps to explain mechanisms and processes of domination and hegemony and of defeat and loss. The role of traitors or—in postcolonial categories—of "comprador elites" is crucial in this process, as well as the global betrayal of Poland by other forces. Such a framework is also employed to make sense of contemporary politics: postsocialist political transformation and the economic transition become understood in a global context as a new colonialism, and so an earlier postcolonialism provides an accurate vocabulary to describe this new situation. From the right-wing perspective, European Union (EU) institutions are trying to colonize Poland and to exploit it for their own political and economic profits. Of course, the idea that the EU is nothing more than a façade for the interests of German business is not rare in this kind of narrative. I cannot hope to cover every aspect of this discourse here. I would merely note that such an anticommunist, conservative, and right-wing revival of this communist-era language of colonization means that there is simply no place for the left to invoke such postcolonial categories, to the extent that anyone who describes a leftist postcolonialism becomes demonized as an unreformed communist stooge.

Notes

*I am grateful to a number of people who have aided me during the last few years when this text arose, including Ebony Coletu in offering a source of inspiration to take Alex Haley's *Roots* into account; the translator of the book into Polish—Blanka Kuczborska; as well as Jan Zieliński and Krzysztof Brzechczyn. I also owe a special thanks to activists of the Solidarity movement for answering my questions related to these themes.

1. Compare with postcolonialism as neocolonialism, Zdzisław Szpakowski, "Biafra—kamyk czy lawina?" *Więź* 114, no. 10 (1967): 90–97; "Socjalizm," in *Wielka Encyklopedia Powszechna PWN* 10 (Warszawa: PWN, 1967), 630–637.

2. Dorota Goluch, "Postcolonial Literature in Polish Translation (1970–2010): Difference, Similarity and Solidarity" (PhD diss., UCL, 2015).

3. Aimé Césaire, *Rozprawa z kolonializmem*, trans. and foreword Zofia Jaremko-Żytyńska (Warszawa: Czytelnik, 1950 [1950]). This text was published in Polish just a few months after the French original. Mahatma Gandhi, *Autobiografia: dzieje moich poszukiwań prawdy*, foreword for Polish edition Jawaharlal Nehru, trans. from English Józef Brodzki (Warszawa: Książka i Wiedza, 1958, next editions 1969, 1973, 1974, 2013 [1925–1929]). Frantz Fanon, *Algieria zrzuca zasłonę*, trans. Zygmunt Szymański (Warszawa: Iskry, 1962 [1959]); Fanon, *Wyklęty lud ziemi*, trans. Hanna Tygielska, foreword Elżbieta Rekłajtis, afterword Jean-Paul Sartre (Warszawa: PIW, 1985). Chinua Achebe, *Boża strzała*, trans. Maria Skibniewska (Warszawa: PAX, 1967); Achebe, *Czcigodny kacyk Nanga*, trans. Zofia Kierszys (Warszawa: Książka i Wiedza, 1968); Achebe, *Świat się rozpada*, trans. Małgorzata Żbikowska (Warszawa: Iskry, 1989)]. His other books were translated after 1989. It is interesting and significant that *Things Fall Apart* and *Arrow of God* were published in 2009 and 2013 respectively in new translations by (respectively) Jolanta Kozak and Jerzy Łoziński. Kavalam Madhava Panikkar, *Azja a dominacja Zachodu: epoka Vasco da Gamy w dziejach Azji 1498–1945*, trans. Klemens Kęplicz, foreword Andrzej Bartnicki (Warszawa: PWN, 1972).

4. Edward W. Said, *Orientalizm*, trans. Witold Kalinowski, foreword Zdzisław Żygulski (Warszawa: PIW, 1991). In the Polish translation of Leela Gandhi's *Postcolonial Theory: A Critical Introduction* [1998], Ewa Domańska included a selected bibliography of postcolonial studies in Poland. Almost all texts were published after 2000, with a few exceptions from the 1990s and one book by Fanon from 1985; see Leela Gandhi, *Teoria postkolonialna: Wprowadzenie krytyczne*, trans. Jacek Serwański, afterword Ewa Domańska (Poznań: Wydawnictwo Poznańskie, 2008), 179–187. However, if we take into account a range of other

sources, it is clear that there were more postcolonial texts translated into Polish than initially meet the eye. In Domańska's bibliography only 1 percent of "postcolonial texts" in Poland were published before 1989. Other scholars have challenged this. Edyta Krajewska and Grzegorz Koneczniak assert that the correct figure is 27 percent (Edyta Krajewska and Grzegorz Koneczniak, "Bibliografie literatury dostępnej w przekładach," in *Studia postkolonialne w literaturoznawstwie i kulturoznawstwie anglojęzycznym*, ed. Mirosława Buchholtz (Toruń: Wydawnictwo Adam Marszałek, 2009), 312–401, whereas in Dorota Gołuch's list of postcolonial texts, 40 percent were published before the collapse of communism (Goluch, *Postcolonial Literature*). For further discussion, see Adam F. Kola, *Socjalistyczny postkolonializm: Rekonsolidacja pamięci* (Toruń: Nicolaus Copernicus University Press, 2018), 164–174.

5. I fully agree with those postcolonial authors who construe postcolonialism broadly in connection with decolonization and anticolonial movements, among them Ali Behdad, who mentions "Fanon, Césaire, Memmi, and other founders of postcolonial discursivity" [see Ali Behdad, "*Une Pratique Sauvage*: Postcolonial Belatedness and Cultural Politics," in *The Pre-Occupation of Postcolonial Studies*, eds. Fawzia Afzal-Khan and Kalpana Seshadri-Crooks (Durham/London: Duke University Press, 2000), 71]; and Leela Gandhi (1998), who cites Mahatma Gandhi and Fanon as crucial figures for postcolonialism. See also Robert J. C. Young, *Postcolonialism: An Historical Introduction* (Oxford/Malden: Wiley-Blackwell, 2001). If we take into consideration the fact that many of these authors were translated into Polish before 1989—Fanon, Césaire, and Mahatma Gandhi, for example—there is no simple explanation for this neglect of postcolonial studies as such.

6. For this point in relation to Hungary, see James Mark and Péter Apor, "Socialism Goes Global: Decolonization and the Making of a New Culture of Internationalism in Socialist Hungary 1956–1989," *Journal of Modern History* 87 (December 2015): 859–860.

7. The Recovered Territories (*Ziemie Odzyskane*) was the official name for the western part of postwar Poland, which had belonged before the war to Germany. It was an important focus for Polish socialist, anti-German, and anti-Western propaganda, linked as it was to the notion of an eternal Polish character, embodied in the concept of the Piasts, the first Polish ruling dynasty from the Medieval period in these western territories. Władysław Gomułka (1905–1982), subsequently the first secretary of the Communist Party and one of the leaders of the more nationalistic orientation in Communist Party, was a minister of Recovered Territories at that time.

8. Jacek Ślusarczyk, *Powstanie i działalność ruchu obrońców pokoju w latach 1948–1957* (Wrocław: Zakład Narodowy im. Ossolińskich, 1987); Zygmunt Woźniczak, "Wrocławski Kongres Intelektualistów w Obronie Pokoju," *Kwartalnik Historyczny* 2: 131–157.

9. See, e.g., Bolesław Bierut, "O upowszechnianiu kultury," "Biuletyn Prasowy" Światowego Kongresu Intelektualistów w Obronie Pokoju (25–28 sierpnia 1948 roku, Wrocław), vol. 2 (from August 13, 1948); Tadeusz Borowski, "Pisarz i pacyfizm," "Biuletyn Prasowy" Światowego Kongresu Intelektualistów w Obronie Pokoju (25–28 sierpnia 1948 roku, Wrocław), vol. 2 (from August 13, 1948).

10. Patryk Babiracki, *Soviet Soft Power in Poland: Culture and the Making of Stalin's New Empire, 1943–1957* (Chapel Hill: University of North Carolina Press, 2015). By way of example, see the Soviet propaganda pamphlets and books that were translated into Polish, e.g., Grigorij Akopian, *W. I. Lenin i J. W. Stalin o ruchu narodowo-wyzwoleńczym narodów kolonialnych i zależnych* (Warsaw: Książka i Wiedza, 1951).

11. *Imperializm amerykański wróg ludzkości i polski: Materiały dla prelegentów* (Warsaw: Wydział Propagandy KC PZPR, 1951).

12. Lucjan Pracki, *Korespondent wojenny z Korei donosi* (Warsaw: Wydawnictwo Ministerstwa Obrony Narodowej, 1953). The book was published by the Ministry of National Defense.

13. Władysław Gomułka, *O problemie niemieckim* (Warszawa: Książka i Wiedza, 1971).

14. For a more extended discussion regarding the "Eastness" of Poland, see Tomasz Zarycki, *Ideologies of Eastness in Central and Eastern Europe* (London/New York: Routledge, 2014). For further treatment of "Europe" in Poland (by which I mean not only Polish Occidentalism but also other notions of East and Central Europe, including the so-called *Kresy*), see Adam F. Kola, *Europa w dyskursie polskim, czeskim i chorwackim: Rekonfiguracje krytyczne* (Toruń: Nicolaus Copernicus University Press, 2011). And finally, on socialist Orientalism, see Agnieszka Sadecka, "A Socialist Orientalism? Polish Travel Writing on India in the 1960s," in *Postcolonial Europe? Essays on Post-Communist Literatures and Cultures*, eds. Dobrota Pucherová and Robert Gáfrik (Leiden/Boston: Brill, 2015), 315–333.

15. See James Mark, Péter Apor, Piotr Osęka, and Radina Vučetić, "'We Are with You, Vietnam': Transnational Solidarities in Socialist Hungary, Poland and Yugoslavia," *Journal of Contemporary History* 50, no. 3 (2015): 439–464.

16. Wojciech Żukrowski, *Dom bez ścian* (Warszawa: Wydawnictwo Ministerstwa Obrony Narodowej, 1954), 9.

17. Ryszard Frelek, foreword, in *Niepokonani . . . Wietnam Północny w fotografiach Zbigniewa Staszyszyna* (Warszawa: Wydawnictwo Artystyczno-Graficzne, 1971), 6. When North Vietnamese delegations visited Warsaw in the 1960s, solidarity rallies were often held at sites of the Warsaw Uprising to further cement the sense of parallel struggle. See Mark et al., "We Are with You," 446.

18. Mark et al., "We Are with You," 459. On an anticolonial socialism, see Marla Zubel, "Black Stars, Red Stars: Anti-Colonial Constellations in Ryszard Kapuściński's Cold War Reportage," *Postcolonial Studies* 19, no. 2 (2016): 131–149.

19. For a fuller account of Małowist, see Adam F. Kola, "Marian Małowist's World History and Its Application to World Literature," in *The Routledge Companion to World Literature and World History*, ed. May Hawas (London/New York: Routledge, 2018), 57–68.

20. Immanuel Wallerstein, *The Modern World-System I: Capitalist Agriculture and the Origins of the European World-Economy in the Sixteenth Century* (Berkeley/Los Angeles/London: University of California Press, 2011), xi.

21. The history of colonial conquest is the best example of such claims used as a political tool; see Iza Bieżuńska-Małowist and Marian Małowist, *Niewolnictwo* (Warszawa: Czytelnik, 1987); Marian Małowist, *Europa i jej ekspansja XIV–XVII w.*, foreword and edition by Antoni Mączak, ed. Hanna Zaremska (Warszawa: PWN, 1993). See also Sven Lindqvist, *"Exterminate All the Brutes": One Man's Odyssey into the Heart of Darkness and the Origins of European Genocide*, trans. Joan Tate (New York: New Press 1996).

22. See also, e.g., M. Małowist, *Tamerlan i jego czasy* (Warszawa: Państwowy Instytut Wydawniczy, 1985); M. Małowist, *Wschód a Zachód Europy w XIII–XVI wieku: konfrontacja struktur społeczno-gospodarczych* (Warszawa: PWN, 1973).

23. Alex Haley (1921–1992), American writer, author of the bestseller *The Autobiography of Malcolm X* (1965) and his best known work *Roots: The Saga of an American Family* published in 1976 (Pulitzer Prize in 1977). The story starts in eighteenth-century Gambia with a detailed description of the life of African tribes. The main character, Kunta Kinte, is kidnapped and transported as a slave to the United States; the second part of the book presents the story of

his adult life on a plantation. Haley presented this story as the genealogy of his own family of African American citizens.

24. See Dipesh Chakrabarty, *Provincializing Europe: Postcolonial Thought and Historical Difference*, with a new preface by the author (Princeton/Oxford: Princeton University Press, 2008); Kevin B. Anderson, *Marx at the Margins: On Nationalism, Ethnicity, and Non-Western Societies* (Chicago/London: University of Chicago Press, 2010); Aijaz Ahmad, *In Theory: Classes, Nations, Literatures* (London/New York: Verso, 2008).

25. Edward Kajdański, *Michał Boym: Ambasador Państwa Środka* (Warszawa: Książka i Wiedza, 1999); Kajdański, *Perłowy Trójkąt* (Warszawa: Książka i Wiedza, 1987), 63–87.

26. In the categories introduced by David Spurr, we can talk about aestheticization; see David Spurr, *The Rhetoric of Empire: Colonial Discourse in Journalism, Travel Writing, and Imperial Administration* (Durham/London: Duke University Press, 1993), 43–60.

27. Henryk Kania, "Solidarność sprzed dwudziestu lat," *Gazeta Ustrońska* 39 (476) (September 28, 2000): 2, accessed July 31, 2014, https://www.yumpu.com/pl/document/view/16968002/gazeta-ustronska-nr-39-00.

28. Witold Kowalczyk, "Do późnych godzin 12 grudnia," http://www.trybunalscy.pl/node/701#comment-562, accessed July 31, 2014.

29. For a recent example of this approach in Poland, see Adam Leszczyński, *Skok w nowoczesność: Polityka wzrostu w krajach peryferyjnych, 1943–1980* (Warsaw: Instytut Studiów Politycznych PAN, Wydawnictwo Krytyki Politycznej, 2013).

30. Jan Sowa, *Fantomowe ciało króla: peryferyjne zmagania z nowoczesną formą* (Kraków: Universitas, 2011). It is significant that in his earlier book, written from a truly global perspective about Japan, India, Turkey, Congo, and Poland, he did not quote Małowist but postcolonial criticism and world-systems theory, see Sowa, *Ciesz się, późny wnuku! Kolonializm, globalizacja i demokracja radykalna* (Kraków: Korporacja Ha!art, 2008).

31. E.g., Ewa M. Thompson, "Sarmatyzm i postkolonializm: O naturze polskich resentymentów," *Europa: Tygodnik Idei*, 46, November 18, 2006; Thompson "Said a sprawa polska," *Europa: Tygodnik Idei*, 26, June 29, 2005.

32. An excellent exception is the collection of essays edited by Max Cegielski titled *Polska i Azja. Od Rzeczpospolitej Szlacheckiej do Nangar Khel: Przewodnik interdyscyplinarny* (Poznań: Fundacja Malta, 2013).

ADAM F. KOLA is Assistant Professor at Nicolaus Copernicus University, President of the Polish Comparative Literature Association, and Visiting Scholar at the University of Chicago. He is author of *Socialist Postcolonialism: The Reconsolidation of Memory, Europe in Polish, Czech, and Croatian Discourse: A Critical Reconfiguration*, and *Comparing Czech and Russian Slavophilism*, both in Polish.

13 Competing Solidarities? Solidarność and the Global South during the 1980s

Kim Christiaens and Idesbald Goddeeris

Reviewing his struggle against state socialism in his memoirs, the prominent Polish dissident Adam Michnik equated the oppressive rule of General Wojciech Jaruzelski during the 1980s with two other international pariahs of the era, namely the South African apartheid regime and the dictatorship of Augusto Pinochet in Chile.[1] Presenting the socialist system in his country as another apartheid and comparing the communist General Jaruzelski to his Chilean counterpart, Michnik conjured up a vision that had been widely drawn on in public and academic analyses since the Polish crisis erupted in the 1980s. After the declaration of martial law and the outlawing of the Polish trade union Solidarność (Solidarity), it was a topos among many observers to speak about a "Pinochetization" of Poland.[2] Others discerned in the Polish events another Central America, threatened by superpower involvement and state terror, as demonstrated by the comparisons that contemporaries drew between the murder of Polish priest Jerzy Popiełuszko and the fate of Archbishop Óscar Romero in El Salvador.[3]

Polish historians and opinion makers now cherish these global dimensions of Solidarność, alongside its contribution to European freedom.[4] Among foreign scholars, however, a debate has developed concerning whether the transnational linkages posited between Eastern European dissent and other global causes were more than a matter of mere rhetoric or later invention. Padraic Kenney portrayed the trade union as a nationally embedded and rather introverted movement, which "never staged such a public campaign in defense of a foreign movement. Solidarity was in general slow to react to external events."[5] The American academic-cum-activist Noam Chomsky asserted that Eastern European dissent was above all self-absorbed, cherished its privileged access to Western support, and lacked any real feeling for, or connection with, the struggles of the Global South.[6] In such accounts, the "two utopias" that emerged from the "1968 moment"—Marxist revolution and liberal democracy—were seen to mark a dividing line between the struggles of the Third World and East European dissent.[7]

Accounts that focus on the development of a so-called global civil society frame movements such as Solidarność differently. These have argued that human rights was *the* key concept from the 1970s: its message eventually trumped Cold War divisions and created a common identity between social movements across the globe.[8] Recently, these arguments have been adopted by scholars globalizing the history of state socialist Europe, which was for a long time deemed to consist of "closed societies."[9] Whereas traditional studies typically reduced the connections between Eastern European countries and what were known as "developing countries" to official state relations and diplomacy monopolized by the regimes, more recent contributions have begun to broaden the sense we have of the scope of East-South relations during the Cold War.[10] The reception of the Third World in Eastern Europe and the various international solidarity campaigns that were staged in relation to the Vietnam War, conflict in the Middle East, and political turmoil in Latin America were not simply a matter of hollow state propaganda that aimed to buttress the legitimacy of the regimes but were part of broader societal debates.[11] The Third World inspired attempts at reforming state socialism, and vice versa.[12]

Yet this literature has largely concentrated on somewhat abstract, even imagined links, seeing the Third World as above all a mental construct and an ideological category. As a result, the debate about the global character of East European dissident movements has lacked research on substantive ties. This article seeks to shift attention to actual exchanges established in the 1980s. It will do so by examining the connections that linked Solidarność—the largest opposition movement in the Eastern Bloc—with other international issues and civil resistance movements in the Global South. Of course, Solidarność was by no means the first oppositional movement in the Eastern Bloc to draw on Third World connections.[13] Nevertheless, we should note that the Polish trade union's engagement occurred at a moment when an older, socialist, anti-imperialist internationalism was generally in decline, and new forms of global rapprochement were being forged. In particular, we will address the relationship of the Polish trade union opposition with three other causes célèbres of transnational activism of the 1980s: the civil war in Nicaragua, the Pinochet dictatorship in Chile, and the anti-apartheid struggle in South Africa. How did Solidarność react to these international issues and the international solidarity campaigns they provoked? Did the Polish trade union identify with those campaigns through the lens of the Cold War, labor issues, human rights, personal contacts, diaspora networks, or were still other elements in play? How were links established, and what was the quality of the solidarity and support sustaining these movements? How was Solidarność's international stance affected by the regime's official solidarity with these causes in the Third World? We will focus on Solidarność's official policy and explore the role of its Coordinating Office Abroad, which was created in July 1982, mandated by the trade union's underground leadership (TKK), based in

Brussels, and led by Jerzy Milewski.[14] However, we will also examine actors from Nicaragua, Chile, and South Africa, while at the same time considering how the Western European and American social movements served as intermediaries.

Nicaragua: A Paradoxical Neglect?

Shortly after its foundation in September 1980, the independent trade union Solidarność started to reach out to supportive organizations abroad—notably trade unions—in search for recognition and assistance with its struggle for human and trade union rights in Poland. As early as November 1980, a few weeks after the legal recognition of Solidarność and before Lech Wałęsa's initial foreign visit to Rome in January 1981, a first official delegation left Poland—not for Western Europe, but Latin America. The delegation consisted of just two persons: Józef Przybylski and Zygmunt Zawalski. Przybylski was a welder at the steel factory Budimor near Gdańsk who had joined the Inter-Enterprise Strike Committee in mid-August 1980, cosigned the Gdańsk Agreements on August 31, and then became a board member of the Inter-Enterprise Founding Committee Solidarność.[15] Zawalski was an electrical engineer at the Gdańsk Shipyard, the cradle of the Solidarność movement.[16] The two representatives stayed nine days in Lima and then spent seven days in Caracas. They were invited by the Central Latinoamericana de Trabajadores (CLAT), a regional confederation that united Christian trade unions in Latin America and was affiliated to the World Confederation of Labour (WCL). This small international trade union confederation, led by the Polish-born Jan Kułakowski and dependent on the financial support of Christian democratic trade unions and party foundations in Western Europe, brought Solidarność and the CLAT together. The WCL was struggling with questions of deconfessionalization and trade union unity and saw new hope in Solidarność, which it viewed as a potential template for a new kind of trade union movement that went beyond the traditional models of the West and East.[17]

Shortly after the proclamation of martial law in Poland in December 1981, a move designed to crush Solidarność, a new delegation travelled to Latin America, embarking on a tour through Venezuela, Panama, Costa Rica, Honduras, El Salvador, Colombia, Ecuador, and the Dominican Republic at the beginning of 1982.[18] The visit was steeped in a spirit of anticommunism and Catholicism. The Polish delegates went from the presidential offices of the Christian democratic Salvadoran junta leader José Napoleon Duarte and the Venezuelan president Luis Herrera Campíns to television studios, press conferences, and public meetings with trade unionists and church leaders.[19] Their major goals were lobbying for political support, providing information, bearing witness to the fifteen months of Solidarność's legal existence, and countering the official propaganda that the Polish opposition was now defeated.[20]

The visit to one country, however, cast a shadow over the Latin American tour. When the Polish delegation arrived in the airport of Managua, the Nicaraguan authorities did not allow them to leave the plane.[21] The Polish crisis had indeed had a profound impact in Nicaragua, where the Marxist Sandinista National Liberation Front (FSLN), in power since 1979, faced domestic resistance from both US-backed Contras and more moderate opposition movements. After the imposition of martial law in Poland, Nicaraguan opposition movements had been quick to present themselves as the "Poles of Central America," drawing analogies between the Sandinista government's use of violence to gain control over recalcitrant sectors of society and the military crackdown on Solidarność in Poland.[22] The CLAT-affiliated Christian democratic trade union movement Nicaraguan Workers' Centre (Central de Trabajadores de Nicaragua, or CTN) called for solidarity with Solidarność in response to denunciations of the "Polish syndrome" in Central America.[23] Nicaraguan opposition trade union leaders eventually traveled to Costa Rica and Honduras to meet the Polish delegates.[24]

Latin American trade unionists promoted the idea of a natural alliance between the Polish and Nicaraguan opposition. The similarities were obvious, since both movements faced repression from a Marxist regime. Just like its Polish counterparts, the Nicaraguan labor opposition, spearheaded by Christian democratic and social democratic trade unions, focused on a struggle over trade union and human rights. The extended states of emergency that the Sandinista government employed further reminded many of the declaration of martial law in Poland in December 1981. Above all, the Sandinistas' close relationship with the Soviet Bloc and the regime's professed backing for Jaruzelski's offensive against a "reactionary" Polish opposition cemented the comparison.[25]

Likewise, the Polish regime declared its support for the Sandinistas on several occasions.[26] Since the late 1970s Polish media and writers such as Roman Samsel and Zdzisław Antos had likewise publicized the struggle of the Sandinistas against the Somoza dictatorship.[27] The Polish People's Republic also developed amicable bilateral relations with the new regime.[28] Nicaragua's ties with the Polish People's Republic and the hostility of the Sandinista regime toward the Polish opposition therefore simply led some Solidarność supporters to entertain the idea of a common anticommunist struggle. In 1983 during his official visit to Nicaragua, the pope's criticism of the government and his public rebuke of the liberation theologian and Sandinista minister Ernesto Cardenal were broadcast internationally. The next year, a young Polish migrant living in Costa Rica, Robert Czarkowski, published an account of his disillusionment with what were called the "communist paradise[s]" of the Polish People's Republic and Nicaragua.[29] In his book *De Polonia a Nicaragua*, Czarkowski—who fled Poland in the 1970s and took refuge in Spain and Costa Rica—detailed what he discovered when visiting Nicaragua in June 1982: accused of being a "spy of Solidarność," he was jailed and interrogated for six months before being expelled from the country.[30] His message of communist infiltration in the Third World and his paeans to the Catholic church as a bulwark of resistance and unity resonated among Christian trade unionists in Latin America and Europe. They continued to use their solidarity with the Polish and Nicaraguan opposition as a means to presenting themselves as a "third way," distinct from both the social democracy associated with the United States and Soviet communism.[31]

Yet it quickly became clear that the interest in such a common "anticommunist" struggle was not reciprocated: Solidarność leaders distanced themselves from both the Nicaraguan opposition and the CLAT. Already in early 1981, their visits to Christian democrats in Latin America had provoked fierce criticism from the social democratic International Confederation of Free Trade Unions (ICFTU) and some leading members of Solidarność, who considered these trips to be an attempt by Christian democrats to appropriate the cause of the Polish opposition for the right.[32]

In 1982 Tadeusz Konopka, one of the two delegation members traveling to the region in December 1981, grasped that the Latin American partners—particularly the CLAT—were making use of the Polish case for their own purposes.[33] In 1983 the WCL transferred Zygmunt Zawalski to the headquarters of the CLAT in Caracas (Venezuela) to establish a branch of the Solidarność Coordinating Office Abroad, but the cooperation quickly broke down. Zawalski complained that his Latin American colleagues "are more concerned about the Falklands and about how to stop American imperialism than about our issues."[34] The CLAT's anti-imperialist criticism of US involvement in countries such as Nicaragua and its competition with social democratic trade unions ran counter to the interests of the leadership of the Solidarność Coordinating Office, which was much closer to the United States—both the Reagan administration and the American Federation of Labor and Congress of Industrial Organizations (AFL-CIO)—whom they viewed as their potential allies. Its president Jerzy Milewski did not want Solidarność either to ally itself with a single trade union confederation or to be seen as excessively committed to a particular ideological viewpoint; rather, it should continue to be seen simply as a force for social rights that transcended the left/right divisions of the Cold War. As a result, the CLAT's avowedly anticommunist message and its association with the Nicaraguan opposition were unwelcome. Solidarność had little interest in joining the anti-Sandinista cause, and delegations of the Coordinating Office visiting Latin America avoided Nicaragua throughout the 1980s, traveling instead to countries such as Mexico, Venezuela, and Argentina.[35]

There were still other obstacles impeding Solidarność's contact with the opposition in Nicaragua. The Sandinista regime attempted to block the forging of links, the country lacked a substantial Polish diaspora (in contrast to countries such as Peru and Venezuela), and there were few exiled Nicaraguan oppositionists in the West. Most important, however, was the fact that the regime in Nicaragua enjoyed international sympathy, not only in radical leftist quarters, but also among various supporters of Solidarność, such as the Socialist International, social democratic trade unions, and Third World solidarity groups.[36] They drew parallels between the sufferings of Poland and Nicaragua in a manner that differed markedly from the tone adopted by the Nicaraguan opposition. In a remarkable twist of irony, many Western observers drew comparisons between Poland and Nicaragua in support of the Sandinistas. For many pacifists and antimilitarists combating the installation of American missiles on their soil, the battle against American inference in Nicaragua mirrored the struggle of Solidarność against the Soviet Union and their own struggle against Reagan's vision of the Cold War. On a visit to Nicaragua, the West German novelist Günter Grass ventured a comparison that would become widely popular in Western Europe when he equated the Sandinistas' struggle against American interference with the Polish opposition's stand against the Soviet-backed Jaruzelski government.[37] Similarly, some Western European social democratic trade unions, such as the Swedish Trade Union Confederation (LO), saw no contradiction between their financing development projects of the Sandinista regime in Nicaragua and their support for Solidarność.

The leadership of Solidarność, however, balked at efforts to link their cause with the Sandinistas. They fiercely rebuffed Grass's comparison[38] and opposed plans of Western European peace activists to involve Polish and other Eastern European dissidents in campaigns against Reagan's Central America policy.[39] An alignment with the Nicaraguan regime was impossible for the Solidarność leadership: it would have placed them in the same ideological camp as the communist government and alienated them from some of their backers in the West (especially Reagan, Thatcher, and Christian democrats). Yet an alliance with the Nicaraguan opposition was not an option either. For it carried the risk of polarizing the cause of Solidarność and of jeopardizing frail Western left-wing sympathies by seemingly confirming accusations—made both by state propaganda in the East as well as radical leftist groups in the West—that the Polish opposition was a plot of the Contra-supporting CIA program. The murder of the Italian banker Roberto Calvi in 1982 provoked disquieting rumors in the media about financial connections between Solidarność and the Contras through the Vatican, the CIA, and secret networks of right-wing organizations.[40] All of these elements are crucial for understanding why Solidarność, despite the possibilities for a common struggle against "red dictatorships," dodged the issue of Nicaragua and avoided association with either the Nicaraguan opposition or the Sandinistas.[41] Conversely, these factors help explain why resistance to a right-wing regime in the Third World, namely Pinochet's Chile, became the most important international cause embraced by Solidarność during the 1980s.

Chile: The Struggle against the Generals and the Search for the Left

No single issue in the Third World became as important to Solidarność as the resistance to the Pinochet dictatorship in Chile. This is another paradox. It is true that Poland and Chile were both governed by a general with dark glasses who used state repression against opposition and, in particular, trade union movements. But apart from that, little seemed to link the two countries. In contrast with Poland, Chile had a right-wing anticommunist regime, while the opposition identified with Salvador Allende, the former president who had forged closer ties with the Communist Bloc and who was now remembered as a martyr of socialism.[42] A large faction of the opposition structures set up in exile since the 1973 coup across the world were run by members of the banned Chilean Communist and Socialist parties, whose main headquarters were located in cities such as East Berlin and Moscow and received support from Eastern European regimes, including the Polish government.[43]

Yet it was precisely this connection with the communist camp that caused the Polish crisis to leave so deep an impression on the Chilean opposition.[44] The rise and subsequent suppression of Solidarność developed into a major flashpoint for debates about the relationship between socialism and democracy and about strategies for fighting Pinochet. These debates increasingly divided the Chilean opposition at home and abroad during the 1970s. Chile's Socialist Party—the most important of the political groups in exile—witnessed a split late in the decade between a pro-Soviet tendency that advocated cooperation with the Communist Party and so-called "renovated" socialists under the leadership of Carlos Altamirano, which tied Marxism to democracy instead of armed struggle and advocated a broad alliance with Christian democrats. This latter group became dominant in Western Europe's Chilean exile organizations.[45] Whereas pro-Soviet socialists and the Communist Party leader Luís Corvalán celebrated the Jaruzelski coup as a means of protecting socialism in Poland against "counterrevolutionary forces" and of continued cooperation with the Soviet camp,[46] these "renovated" socialists were keen to identify with Solidarność, whose rapid rise and fall they associated with that of the Chilean Popular Unity government under Allende.[47]

As early as 1981 Carlos Altamirano traveled to Warsaw to meet with Wałęsa, express solidarity with the Polish opposition, and emphasize their common belief in the power of democracy, nonviolent resistance, and a broad-based opposition.[48] Chilean exile cadres living in Poland who supported Altamirano sympathized with Solidarność and even participated in its activities, to the point that some of them were forced to leave the country.[49] The crisis of December

1981 and the subsequent repression in Poland were closely followed by the major exile organizations of the "renovated" socialists, Christian democrats, and other exile organizations for whom the fate of Solidarność offered a means to distance themselves from pro-Soviet exile organizations and to reject the communist label that Chilean state propaganda (and Pinochet apologists in the West) was keen to confer on the Chilean opposition as a whole.[50] Yet solidarity with Solidarność proved contentious, not only because it widened the gulf with pro-Soviet socialists and communists and ran counter to efforts at unity, but also because the Pinochet regime had publicly condemned the Jaruzelski government and utilized the Polish crisis within its anticommunist discourse. All of this stimulated the Chilean opposition to make solidarity with Solidarność as much an anti-American cause as a critique of Marxism-Leninism. After the declaration of martial law, *Chile-América* and *Convergencia*, two major opposition journals published by Chilean Christian democratic and "renovated" socialist exiles, attributed the defeat and banning of Solidarność to the global stalemate imposed by both the Soviet Union and the United States, which had sacrificed national self-determination to "peace" and imperialism.[51]

The parallels drawn between Chile and Poland were not merely ideological but also became rooted in the changing reality inside Chile. As opposition parties were outlawed and restricted under a state of emergency, trade unions—most notably the National Union Coordination (Coordinadora Nacional Sindical, CNS) led by Chilean Christian workers—took a more central role in the domestic opposition against Pinochet in the late 1970s and early 1980s. The government's neoliberal policies and restrictive labor legislation, together with the economic crisis of the 1980s, created a fertile breeding ground for the trade unions to rally broad sectors of society behind a program for democracy and human rights that radically differed in its nonviolent character from that of marginalized Marxist opposition groups advocating armed resistance.[52] This restructuring of opposition around trade unions, along with the increased repression, changed the nature and orientation of the international campaigns against Pinochet set up by Chilean exiles and their allies in Western Europe from a struggle for socialism to a struggle for workers' rights and made the parallels with the Polish trade union opposition against Jaruzelski more obvious. Not surprisingly then, it was mainly through the Chilean trade union opposition that the most potent and persuasive link with Solidarność emerged.

A few days after the ban on Solidarność, the Christian textile worker and leading oppositionist Manuel Bustos sent from his prison in Santiago a message of solidarity with Lech Wałęsa to the ICFTU meeting convened in Brussels to discuss campaigns in support of Solidarność.[53] In November 1982 the CNS planned to stage a meeting of solidarity with the Solidarność leader, which was eventually prohibited by the Chilean government.[54] Poland remained a powerful symbol for the Chilean trade union movement: Rodolfo Seguel, the young leader of the National Workers' Command (Comando Nacional de Trabajadores, CNT) who mobilized thousands of citizens in mass demonstrations and national strikes from 1983 onward, became both internationally and domestically celebrated as a "Chilean Lech Wałęsa."[55] This referred not only to the iconic moustaches and charisma of both Catholic trade unionists, but also to Seguel's fulsome praise of Wałęsa, whom he celebrated together with Gandhi as an example of nonviolent resistance.[56]

The Polish side paid attention to the opposition against Pinochet too. Indeed, Chile became the international cause most fully embraced by the Polish opposition after December 1981. In early 1982 Wałęsa answered the declaration of solidarity from Manuel Bustos by professing his support for the Chilean labor opposition and by denouncing the imprisonment of Bustos and the communist trade unionist Alamiro Guzmán.[57] One of Wałęsa's symbolically most powerful acts was his invitation to Rodolfo Seguel to attend the awarding of the Nobel Peace Prize in December 1983.[58]

Yet more sustained and direct cooperation emerged between Polish and Chilean exiles in Western Europe. Some months after the establishment of the Solidarność Coordinating Office Abroad in the summer of 1982, the Chileans set up a similar organization to function as a coordinating organization for international solidarity campaigns with the Chilean trade union opposition. The Chile Labour Committee was created in Rome in early 1983 by CNS leader Manuel Bustos. The Polish connection is obvious: in December Bustos had met in Brussels with Jerzy Milewski, who in that period also saw Rodolfo Seguel in Rome.[59] The Chile Labour Committee's headquarters were soon transferred to Brussels, where it was given an office by the Belgian socialist trade union known as the General Federation of Belgian Labour (ABVV/FGTB), whereas the Solidarność Coordinating Office Abroad was sharing an office with the Belgian Confederation of Christian Trade Unions (ACV/CSC).[60] In Brussels a close relationship was established between Jerzy Milewski and the staff of the Coordinating Office and the Chilean social democratic unionist Luis Meneses, who had succeeded Manuel Bustos. In line with the joint solidarity declaration issued by Bustos and Milewski during their meeting in Brussels in December 1982, Chileans and Poles featured together at international conferences staged by trade union confederations, in delegations sent to the annual conferences of the International Labour Organization (ILO) in Geneva, and during press interviews in which they stressed their common identity as advocates of universal workers' rights and national self-determination against totalitarianism.

This common identity of two movements fighting regimes of differing ideological hues was used by Solidarność to present itself as a new type of oppositional movement that had gone beyond the "logics of blocs."[61] As Milewski stressed in a joint interview with Bustos, an alliance with the Chilean resistance against Pinochet had to make clear that Solidarność was far from a creature of the right or a clerical reactionary movement, still less a "CIA plot."[62] In his opinion, connecting to Chile was strategically important since it demonstrated that Solidarność was part of an antitotalitarian struggle in countries "where there didn't exist a left and right."[63] All this echoed the human rights discourse of the Soviet dissident Vladimir Bukovsky, who was released by the Soviet Union in 1976 in exchange for imprisoned Chilean communist Luis Corvalán and who uttered a phrase widely cited by Polish oppositionists, namely that "he was not of the right or left, but from a concentration camp."[64] Solidarność's stance was also rhetorical, designed to promote itself on a global stage. Its support for the Chilean opposition was limited to one subsection of the anti-Pinochet galaxy, and its relations with the socialist and communist components of the anti-Pinochet opposition were much more vexed.

Interestingly, by embracing solidarity with Chile, the Polish trade union engaged in what Serguei Oushakine has labeled "mimetic resistance."[65] After years of communist celebration of international solidarity with the resistance against Pinochet,[66] Solidarność was now able to hijack this official discourse.[67] It turned international solidarity against the Polish regime, made the Soviet camp appear as the enemy of the once-heralded Chilean opposition, and transformed its leaders from tools of communist propaganda into allies. Whereas this official propaganda had hampered any embrace of Nicaragua, the reverse was true in Chile, notably because resistance to a "fascist" Pinochet was a far less controversial and more universal symbol, one relevant to socialists, Catholics, and workers' movements alike. Chile was central to the creation of the notion of an antitotalitarian struggle for human rights and democracy. Unlike Nicaragua, it could unite the Polish opposition: diverse strands, ranging from the Workers' Defense Committee (KOR) to more leftist groups and members, converged in their sympathy with the struggle against "fascism" in Chile. It even provoked analogies with the joint resistance to the Nazi-Soviet invasion of 1939.

Chile offered the possibility of universalizing the cause of the resistance against Jaruzelski by framing it as one of many contemporaneous antitotalitarian struggles and of enhancing the international perception of the Polish crisis as "another Chile"—a propaganda move designed to undermine growing sympathy within Europe and the United States for Jaruzelski's normalization policy in the mid-1980s. Yet even if the scale and severity of the repression in Poland should not be understated, the arrests, show trials, and occasional murders paled in comparison with the thousands of deaths and disappearances that had been and continued to be perpetrated by Pinochet's regime—an observation that was also made by some left-wing Chile campaigners at that time.[68] This linking between Solidarność and Chile was also advocated by supporters of both movements in the West. International trade union confederations and NGOs such as Amnesty International simultaneously denounced human rights violations in Poland and Chile and staged meetings with representatives of both the Chilean and Polish opposition at international fora.[69] Pope John Paul II also brought the two cases together.[70] Even Pinochet's government began to recognize the interpolation of such linkages. In 1988 the Pinochet regime thus sent the rector of the Polish Catholic Mission in Chile, Bruno Rychlowski, on a secret mission to Poland to prevent, in cooperation with the Polish church, Wałęsa's visit to Chile.[71] The next year, the government even allowed the release of two imprisoned trade union leaders, the Christian democrat Manuel Bustos and the social democrat Arturo Martínez, on condition that Wałęsa's visit to Chile in October 1989 be canceled.[72] This latter event did in fact become widely celebrated as a symbol of the power of transnational solidarity.[73]

South Africa: The Problems with Anti-Apartheid

Anti-apartheid resistance was one of the largest, most resilient, and arguably most influential global social movements in the late twentieth century.[74] The system of racial segregation established in 1948 was immediately opposed by black militants and international decolonization movements. The Sharpeville massacre of March 1960 lent impetus to transnational activity in the West as well as in Eastern Europe, but the arrest of ANC leaders, the international isolation of South Africa, and the rise of other causes, such as Vietnam, sidelined the issue of apartheid for many Western European social movements.

For various Eastern European regimes, however, anti-apartheid became an important question. Forced into exile from 1960 and against the backdrop of Western European governments' disinterest in and even support for South Africa, the ANC cherished its relations with state-socialist countries, which integrated the struggle against apartheid not only within international campaigns over decolonization and anti-imperialism but also as a means to develop cooperation with Western peace and other Third World solidarity movements.[75] Communist peace movements presented the survival of the anti-communist South African regime as a symptom of the stalemate of the Cold War and used its survival to illustrate the necessity of détente.[76] The role of Third World causes in the "globalization of détente" came increasingly under pressure from the late 1970s, when the struggle against apartheid developed into a mass movement in the West, and at the same time was connected to support for dissidents in the Eastern Bloc and most notably for Solidarność. Even if communist support for anti-apartheid struggles continued, it became overshadowed by a broader antitotalitarian narrative, produced mainly in Western

Europe, that elided the distinction between apartheid, right-wing authoritarian regimes and other remnants of colonialism in the Global South on the one hand, and communism in the East on the other—all were now understood primarily as similar manifestations of illegitimate power.[77]

This shift was also partly due to the emergence of new domestic opposition forces around trade unions and churches in South Africa, which were eager to draw a contrast between their noncommunist character and the ANC's alliance with the Communist Bloc.[78] Just as in Chile and Nicaragua, sections within the South African opposition and notably the trade union movement began to identify common ground with Solidarność. The Federation of South African Trade Unions (FOSATU), for instance, allied itself with the independent Polish trade union to criticize the collusion between the ANC and the South African Communist Party (SACP).[79] Poland and South Africa were brought together by the Cold War of the 1980s: Lech Wałęsa received the Nobel Peace Prize in 1983; the black South African bishop Desmond Tutu in the subsequent year. In November 1984 Poland announced its withdrawal from the ILO following a report criticizing its policy toward Solidarność, just as South Africa had formally given up its ILO membership in 1963 in response to allegations concerning the violation of trade union rights.[80] When the Botha government intensified its repression in the 1980s, Western observers often drew parallels between Poland and South Africa and discerned in the reorganizing of trade union movements in South Africa a "new Solidarność" emerging in reaction to state violence.[81] Representatives of the Solidarność Coordinating Office Abroad and the South African trade union opposition regularly met at international fora and conferences in Western European locales, brought together—and with Chilean oppositionists—by their common allies, notably the ICFTU and the WCL.[82] Especially among social and Christian democrats, this attempt to link protest against communist repression in Poland to resistance against the apartheid regime protected by Reagan was inspired by a broader attempt to present Western Europe as a "third way" vis-à-vis both the USSR and the United States that might offer inspiration to the Global South.[83] Indeed, the resilience of what was seen as a powerful grassroots movement challenging the global Cold War on European soil offered socialists and Christian democrats in Western Europe a means to promote Europe's historical experience of resistance against fascism and communism as a model for ending "totalitarianism" across the globe.

It was therefore not a coincidence that after the victories of 1989, many figures tried to equate the two movements. Two guests of honor attended the 77th General Session of the International Labour Organization in June 1990: Tadeusz Mazowiecki—Polish prime minister since September 1989 and the first noncommunist government leader in the Eastern Bloc—and Nelson Mandela—released in February of that year. According to Solidarność, their presence together "symbolised the common achievements of the ILO."[84] In the 1990s former Polish dissidents such as Michnik were also involved in South Africa's Truth and Reconciliation Commission.[85] On December 13, 1989, on the first anniversary in democratic Poland of the proclamation of martial law, a reggae concert against apartheid was held in the Gdańsk Shipyard. The comparison to the Wembley anti-apartheid concert was evident, although the lineup in Gdańsk was much more modest.[86] Yet one should not exaggerate the actual scope of collaboration. Even if some South African trade union and church groups identified with the Polish trade union, South African opposition was largely skeptical of Solidarność. Some associated the Polish trade union with anticommunism and allies of the South African regime, such as Thatcher and Reagan, whereas the ANC had maintained close ties with the Soviet camp, which aligned itself with the anti-apartheid cause.[87] Indeed, Solidarność showed little interest in explicitly supporting anti-apartheid and only made one official declaration of solidarity with the cause between 1984 and 1989.

The communist regime's sympathies with the anti-apartheid struggle complicated Solidarność's relationship with South Africa.[88] Strikingly, Polish communists even undermined Solidarność's opportunities to work with the Western left, as they began to reach out in common cause: in March 1982, for example, several Polish governors and mayors signed a petition initiated by the mayor of Glasgow calling for the release of ANC leader Nelson Mandela.[89] And in April 1985 Polish and other Eastern European diplomats met in the Soviet embassy in London with Murphy Morobe, one of the founders of the United Democratic Front, an important anti-apartheid organization that was hosting a congress in the British capital at that time.[90]

Another element that impeded a common identity was the recruitment of Polish refugees by the South African authorities. The Polish crisis of 1980–81 had resulted in an exodus of refugees.[91] More than twenty thousand of them went to neighboring Austria, where they applied for asylum and were settled in refugee camps.[92] South Africa was interested in recruiting them for their industries, much to the vexation of the black opposition. From September 1981 onward their embassy in Austria, alongside agents from companies such as the South African electricity public utility Eskom, the steel company Iscor, and the Johannesburg-based energy and chemical company Sasol sought to recruit those Poles who were in the technical professions, opposed communism, and were still of a young age. Approximately six thousand Polish citizens moved from Austria to South Africa in 1982.[93] Most of the new immigrants settled in the industrial regions, but the South West Africa People's Organisation (SWAPO) also indicated that some of them had joined the South African army and were deployed in the war against the Namibian independence fighters.[94] Such migrants were fiercely criticized both by the ANC and the Polish authorities in Warsaw, which regularly distanced themselves from these exiled Poles, emphasizing that their recruitment took place outside of Polish territory and beyond their control.[95]

Oppositional movements tried to convince such exiles not to be tricked by the apartheid regime. In the "Letter to Polish Catholics from the Church in South Africa," issued by the Southern African Catholic Bishops' Conference in October 1982, sympathy was expressed for Solidarność, and migrants' attention was directed to the similarities between the "totalitarian" treatment of trade unions in communist Poland and under apartheid—warning them not to be deceived by higher living standards, the white privileges they would be accorded, and the impression that South Africa was a "normal country."[96]

The issue of the recruitment of Polish nationals put Solidarność in an awkward position. Its members and sympathizers who had immigrated to South Africa now served a widely condemned regime. Former allies, such as South African churches, became critical of the Polish opposition when they failed to denounce their fellow compatriots. The regime in Warsaw, in contrast, could more explicitly side with the globally acclaimed anti-apartheid movement. Under the pressure of the WCL leadership, which pointed out to Milewski that it was "unfortunate that at a moment when Solidarność called on the whole world's solidarity, it does not show at the same time its own solidarity with other oppressed people," the Coordinating Office eventually realized the importance of this issue to its international profile.[97] Jerzy Milewski traveled to Africa in April 1983 and attempted to link Solidarność and anti-apartheid ideologically in terms of trade union rights, human rights, and democratic freedoms. He also unambiguously expressed his criticism of the South African recruitment campaigns, which—he acknowledged—were in effect expressions of approval for the apartheid system.

Milewski's address caused much indignation among his compatriots in South Africa, particularly within the older Polish community, which had settled in the country during and immediately after the Second World War, and among those Poles who had left other African countries during the decolonization wave of the 1960s.[98] But the newly arrived migrants were vulnerable to the racist and anticommunist discourse of the white elite (the most famous example is Janusz Waluś, who immigrated to South Africa in 1981, joined far right organizations, and assassinated the South African Communist Party leader Chris Hani in 1993).[99]

In June 1983 Edward de Virion, the president of the Council of the Polish Diaspora in South Africa, published an open letter in leading Polish migration periodicals *Kultura* and *Słowo*, criticizing Milewski for failing to grasp that the Soviet Union was preparing a communist-led "liberation" of South Africa. The *Kultura* editorial board added a postscript to the letter, stating that they had received a huge number of letters from South Africa fiercely protesting Milewski's speech. This clearly weakened Milewski's initiative: after the summer of 1983, anti-apartheid was no longer a key issue for Solidarność. The division within the anticommunist Polish diaspora, along with Warsaw's official commitment to anti-apartheid, contributed to Solidarność's low level of engagement regarding South Africa.

Conclusion

Solidarność's relationship with other civil resistance and opposition movements in the Third World was full of ambiguity. Its struggle was connected with causes in the Global South both real and imagined. In his Nobel lecture in 1983, Lech Wałęsa explicitly stated that the Polish crisis was relevant not only to East-West relations but also to those between North and South.[100] In 1986 Bohdan Cywiński, in an interview with Jan Kułakowski and the Beninese trade unionist Dominique Aguessy, professed Solidarność's deep sympathy with trade unionists from Africa and Latin America, contrasting their openness and holistic vision on trade unionism to the lack of imagination and bureaucratic obtuseness of their Western counterparts.[101] In November 1989 Wałęsa traveled for the first time to the Americas: not only to Washington but also to Caracas, where he delivered speeches on workers' rights in the East and in the South and called for a transformation of both communism and capitalism.[102]

It was not only Solidarność, but also its supporters in the West who cultivated this East-South connection. Campaigns in support of Solidarność were to a large degree inspired by the ideas drawn from previous campaigns on behalf of national liberation movements and civil resistance against dictatorships in the South.[103] In many ways, the Polish crisis offered North-South movements in the 1980s what Czechoslovakia had provided anti–Vietnam War movements in 1968: a foothold to construct a "third way" that overcame the ideological straightjacket of the Cold War.[104]

On the other hand, although Solidarność may well have had a deep impact on contemporary struggles across the Global South, its historians have remained skeptical about the degree to which this interest was reciprocated. Indeed, few dissident movements have simultaneously been so universalized and so provincialized as Solidarność. If its leadership was keen to proclaim that "human rights have no borders" and its supporters have vaunted the Polish trade union as a universal symbol of "being at one with humanity,"[105] this was to a large degree a defensive move directed against critics who depicted Solidarność as an introverted movement. There is some truth in the objection made by contemporary critics such as Chomsky that Solidarność's scope had remained narrowly focused on the struggle in Poland while their counterparts in the South were far more globalized. Even Solidarność's allies in the West were surprised by its lack of interest in the anti-apartheid struggle and criticized the absence of an international orientation.[106]

Overall, contact with the Third World mainly proceeded through the networks of a handful of leading representatives and were preponderantly mediated by their Western allies. Indeed, Solidarność's endeavors in the Global South were mainly dependent on the goodwill and finances of its allies in the West.

Brussels, Rome, and Geneva functioned as key sites where Solidarność globalized. Furthermore, Solidarność only embraced causes that served to enhance its international profile. For instance, external pressures forced it to side with the anti-apartheid struggle. Wary of tarnishing its image as an effective trade union and becoming associated with political parties and ideologies, Solidarność notably targeted other trade union movements as partners for cooperation.[107] Strikingly, it did not seek out explicitly anticommunist struggles and refrained from alliances rooted in an earlier pattern of Cold War bipolarity. This became clear not only in its reluctance to side with the anti-Sandinista opposition in Nicaragua but also in its stance toward the Soviet war in Afghanistan. Even if allies such as the WCL and CLAT aimed at associating the Polish and Afghan opposition and on occasion brought Solidarność together with representatives of the Afghan resistance,[108] the Solidarność Coordinating Office Abroad showed great restraint on this issue.[109] Whereas other Polish opposition organizations, Freedom and Peace (WiP) among them, explicitly sided with the Afghan resistance, Solidarność kept its distance. An alignment of this sort would have stymied its efforts to transcend superpower bipolarity. It is striking that the most important issues in the Global South with which Solidarność had to deal were precisely the causes célèbres through which the Polish regime promoted its own ideological outlook during the 1980s. The degree to which Polish oppositionists could reconfigure international solidarity across the Cold War divides varied, however, and this explains to a large degree their contrasting responses to the Chilean opposition and to anti-apartheid struggles.

Yet responsibility for the evident limits to cooperation with movements lay also in the Third World: the opposition in South Africa and Nicaragua was likewise critical of Polish dissidence. Similarly, the solidarity movements that developed on behalf of these causes in the West were often more skeptical toward Solidarność than subsequent universalizing human rights histories suggested. This was partly because the idea of Solidarność ran counter to their concern to free North-South issues from the burden of bipolar East-West Cold War rivalry, which was understood to be a European conflict that obstructed Third World nonalignment and self-determination.[110] Furthermore, such links were hampered by South African organizations and the Sandinistas alike, who maintained cordial relations with the Polish communist government, received support from Eastern European regimes, and labeled Eastern European dissidents the tools of US imperialism.[111] And yet such links became celebrated in the 1990s: exaggerating the connections between a movement such as Solidarność and the Global South allowed European liberals and dissidents-turned-political leaders to integrate the story of overcoming dictatorship outside Europe in their victory over communism in the 1990s.[112]

Notes

1. Adam Michnik, *Letters from Freedom: Post-Cold War Realities and Perspectives* (Berkeley and Los Angeles: University of California Press, 1998), 99.

2. Robert Brier, "Poland's Solidarity as a Contested Symbol of the Cold War: Transatlantic Debates after the Polish Crisis," in *European Integration and the Atlantic Community in the 1980s*, eds. Kiran Klaus Patel and Kenneth Weisbrode (New York and Cambridge: Cambridge University Press, 2013), 99–100.

3. KADOC Documentation and Research Centre on Religion, Culture and Society (Leuven, Belgium), Archives WCL (hereafter WCL), 327, "Poland: From Repression to Government Terrorism?," October 23, 1984.

4. See P. Jaworski and Ł. Kamiński, eds., *Świat wobec "Solidarności" 1980–1989* (Warsaw: IPN 2013), 210–224 and Patryk Pleskot, *Solidarność, Zachód i węże: Służba Bezpieczeństwa wobec emigracyjnych struktur Solidarności 1981–1989* (Warsaw: IPN, 2011), 23.

5. Padraic Kenney, *A Carnival of Revolution: Central Europe 1989* (Princeton and Oxford: Princeton University Press, 2002), 70.

6. Filip Outrata, "In the Same Boat: Chomsky, Dissent, and the Universality of Human Rights," *V4/Revue* (July 2, 2014), http://visegradrevue.eu/?p=2821; Interview with Noam Chomsky by Zuzana Piussi and Vít Janeček, June 5, 2014, https://www.youtube.com/watch?v =H6Vcct_g_z4; *Nicaragua Today* 34 (Spring 1989): 14.

7. Paul Berman, *A Tale of Two Utopias: The Political Journey of the Generation of 1968* (New York: W.W. Norton & Co., 1996).

8. Mary Kaldor, *Global Civil Society: An Answer to War* (Cambridge and Massachusetts: Polity Press, 2003); Kim Christiaens, "Globalizing Nicaragua? An Entangled History of Sandinista Solidarity Campaigns in Western Europe," in *Making Sense of the Americas: How Protest Related to America in the 1980s and Beyond*, eds. Jan Hansen, Christian Helm, and Frank Reichherzer (Frankfurt and New York: Campus, 2015), 155–177.

9. Jacques Rupnik, "The Legacies of Dissent: Charter 77, the Helsinki Effect, and the Emergence of a European Public Space," in *Samizdat, Tamizdat, and Beyond: Transnational Media during and after Socialism*, eds. Friederike Kind-Kovacs and Jessie Labov (New York: Berghahn, 2013), 324; Robert Brier, ed., *Entangled Protest: Transnational Approaches to the History of Dissent in Eastern Europe and the Soviet Union* (Osnabrück: Fibre, 2013).

10. Sara Lorenzini, "Comecon and the South in the Years of Détente: A Study on East–South Economic Relations," *European Review of History—Revue européenne d'histoire* 21 (2014): 183.

11. Yulia Gradskova, "The Soviet Union: 'Chile Is in Our Hearts': Practices of Solidarity between Propaganda, Curiosity, and Subversion," in *European Solidarity with Chile, 1970s–1980s*, eds. Kim Christiaens, Idesbald Goddeeris, and Magaly Rodríguez García (Frankfurt am Main: Peter Lang, 2014), 329–330.

12. James Mark and Péter Apor, "Socialism Goes Global: Decolonization and the Making of a New Culture of Internationalism in Socialist Hungary, 1956–1989," *Journal of Modern History* 87, no. 4 (December 2015): 852–891; James Mark, Péter Apor, Radina Vučetić, and Piotr Osęka, "'We Are with You, Vietnam': Transnational Solidarities in Socialist Hungary, Poland and Yugoslavia," *Journal of Contemporary History* 50, no. 3 (2015): 439–464; Robert Gildea, James Mark, and Anette Warring, eds., *Europe's 1968: Voices of Revolt* (Oxford: Oxford University Press, 2013).

13. Mark, Apor, Osęka, and Vučetić, "We Are with You, Vietnam," 439–464.

14. Idesbald Goddeeris, "Lobbying Allies? The NSZZ Solidarność Coordinating Office Abroad, 1982–1989," *Journal of Cold War Studies* 13 (2011): 83–125.

15. Rafał Kalukin, "Zapluty karzeł z puszki: Rozmowa z Józefem Przybylskim," *Wyborcza.pl* (September 19, 2009); WCL, 327, Letter from Jan Kułakowski to J. E. Humblet, May 2, 1984.

16. WCL, 327, Flor Bleux to W. Canini, October 16, 1984.

17. Patrick Pasture, "Jan Kułakowski, from Exile to International Trade Union Leader and Diplomat," in *Intégration ou représentation? Les exilés polonais en Belgique et la construction européenne*, eds. Michel Dumoulin and Idesbald Goddeeris (Louvain-la-Neuve: Bruylant-Academia, 2005), 99–120; Kim Christiaens, "The ICFTU and the WCL: The International Coordination of Solidarity," in *Solidarity with Solidarity: Western European Trade Unions and the Polish Crisis, 1980–1982*, ed. Idesbald Goddeeris (Lanham, MD: Lexington, 2010), 101–127.

18. Tadeusz Konopka drafted an extensive report on this journey: "Uwagi po podróży członków Solidarności do krajów Ameryki Łacińskiej" (Rome, March 19, 1981, 16 pages), unpublished manuscript copied by the author for Idesbald Goddeeris.

19. Konopka, "Uwagi," 16.

20. Hanna Aritos, "Solidarność z Solidarnością," *Karta: Kwartalnik historyczny* 77 (2013): 130–133; on campaigns by the CLAT: WCL, 323: Letter from Jorge Cuisana Valencia and Emilio Máspero, May 19, 1982; International Institute for Social History (Amsterdam; hereafter: IISH), Solidarność Nederland, 49: *CLAT Newsletter*, September 1982.

21. Konopka, "Uwagi," 1–2 and 14.

22. "Nicaragua: El síndrome de Polonia," *Departamento de información y publicaciones, Boletín de Prensa-Radio y Televisión, CLAT*, December 29, 1981.

23. WCL, 328: *Central de Trabajadores de Nicaragua, Lech Wałęsa. Nobel de la Paz*, October 7, 1983.

24. Konopka, "Uwagi," 1–2 and 14.

25. Dieter Gawora, "Lateinamerika hier: Zur Entwicklung der internationalen Solidaritätsarbeit in der Bundesrepublik. Entwicklungsperspektiven," *GhK* 9/10 (1983): 77 and 87.

26. Harold Sims, "Nicaragua's Relation with the Communist Party States during 1984," *Conflict Quarterly* (Fall 1985): 53–77; Roman Samsel, *Dotrzeć do bunkra Somozy* (Warszawa: Książka i Wiedza, 1980); Wieslaw Górnicki, *Kultura*, February 29, 1976.

27. Carlos E. González Tejera, "La recepción en Polonia de los acontecimientos nicaragüenses de agosto-septiembre de 1978," *Estudios Latinoamericanos* 8 (1981): 131–141.

28. Mieczysław F. Rakowski, *Dzienniki polityczne 1984–1986* (Warszawa: Wydawnictwo Iskry, 2005), 141.

29. Robert Czarkowski, *De Polonia a Nicaragua* (San José, Costa Rica: Robert Czarkowski, 1984).

30. *La Nación Internacional*, July 5–11, 1984, 22.

31. Kim Christiaens, "Europe at the Crossroads of Three Worlds: Alternative Histories and Connections of European Solidarity with the Third World, 1950s–80s," *European Review of History: Revue européenne d'histoire* 24, no. 6 (2017): 947.

32. Archives Jan Kułakowski (University Archives, Louvain-la-Neuve) 72, Letter from Jan Kułakowski to members of the WCL executive board and Lech Wałęsa, January 1981.

33. Konopka, "Uwagi," 8.

34. Institute for National Remembrance (Warsaw; hereafter: IPN), 514/21, t. 2: Zygmunt Zawalski to Jerzy Milewski, Caracas, May 5, 1983.

35. Kim Christiaens and Idesbald Goddeeris, "Solidarność i Trzeci Świat. Część II. Taktyczne sojusze z kluczowymi ruchami lat osiemdziesiątych XX wieku", *Dzieje Najnowsze* 50, no. 2 (2018): 247–272.

36. Eusebio Mujal-León, "El socialismo europeo y la crisis en Centroamérica," *Foro Internacional, México* 94 (1983): 155–198.

37. Günter Grass, "Im Hinterhof: Bericht über eine Reise nach Nicaragua," *Die Zeit*, October 1, 1982, 45.

38. "Istnieją granice siły: Rozmowa Przeglądu Politycznego z Günterem Grassem," *Przegląd Polityczny* no. 3 (1984): 3–15.

39. Kenney, *A Carnival of Revolution*, 119.

40. *Controinformazione: stampa alternativa e giornalismo d'inchiesta dagli anni Sessanta a oggi* (Rome, 2006), 117.

41. "Istnieją granice siły."

42. Tanya Harmer, *Allende's Chile and the Inter-American Cold War* (Chapel Hill: The University of North Carolina Press, 2011).

43. Jadwiga E. Pieper Mooney, "East Germany: Chilean Exile and the Politics of Solidarity in the Cold War," and Yulia Gradskova, "The Soviet Union," 275–300 and 329–346.

44. Ignacio Walker, *Socialismo y democracia: Chile y Europa en perspectiva comparada* (Santiago: Cieplan-Hachette, 1990), 186–187.

45. José Del Pozo, ed., *Exiliados, emigrados y retornados: Chilenos en América y Europa, 1973–2004* (Santiago: RIL Editores, 2006); Katherine Hite, *When the Romance Ended: Leaders of the Chilean Left, 1968–1998* (New York: Columbia University Press, 2000), 47–49.

46. *Chile-América* 76–77 (1982): 56; José Miguel Insulza, "¿Polonia como Chile?" *Convergencia: Revista del socialismo chileno et latinoamericano* 5–6 (1982): 23; Luís Corvalán, "Estamos con Polonia Socialista," *Partido Comunista de Chile. Boletín del Exterior*, 52 (March–April 1982): 7–10.

47. "Declaración sobre Polonia," *Chile-América* 76–77 (January/February/March 1982): 7.

48. Heraldo Muñoz, *The Dictator's Shadow: Life under Augusto Pinochet* (New York: Basic Books, 2008), 126.

49. Walker, *Socialismo y Democracia*, 187.

50. Carlos Huneeus, "Political Mass Mobilization against Authoritarian Rule: Pinochet's Chile, 1983–88," in *Civil Resistance and Power Politics: The Experience of Non-Violent Action from Gandhi to the Present*, eds. Adam Roberts and Timothy Garton Ash (Oxford: Oxford University Press, 2009), 197–212.

51. "Nuestra solidaridad con el pueblo polaco," *Convergencia* 5–6 (November 1981–January 1982): 29–30; "La crisis polaca y la oposición chilena", *Chile-América* 76–77 (January–March 1982): 35–36.

52. Peter Winn, ed., *Victims of the Chilean Miracle: Workers and Neoliberalism in the Pinochet Era, 1973–2002* (Durham and London: Duke University Press, 2004).

53. "La Coordinadora Nacional Sindical chilena y los sucesos de Polonia", *Chile-América* 76–77 (1982): 56.

54. ILO, Interim Report, Report No. 226, June 1983, http://www.ilo.org/dyn/normlex/en/f?p=NORMLEXPUB:50002:0::NO::P50002_COMPLAINT_TEXT_ID:2900919.

55. Jorge Edwards, "Chile: El dificil retorno a la democracia," *Revista de la Universidad de México* 34 (1984): 12; "Protest mit Kochtöpfen," *Der Spiegel*, June 27, 1983.

56. Peter Ackerman and Jack DuVall, *A Force More Powerful: A Century of Non-Violent Conflict* (New York and Basingstoke: Palgrave, 2000), 291.

57. Mary Helen Spooner, *Soldiers in a Narrow Land: The Pinochet Regime in Chile* (Berkeley: University of California Press, 1999), 168; *Latijns-Amerika. Tijdschrift van CLAT-Nederland*, 1 (1982): 6.

58. Explicitly mentioned for its "decisive meaning" in an interview of Carlos Lima, the leader of the Chilean construction trade union who had remained in exile in Italy since 1974: Tadeusz Konopka, "Chile i Polska. Rozmowa z Carlosem Limą," *Widnokrąg* 6/7 (1987): 59.

59. Kim Christiaens, "The Difficult Quest for Chilean Allies: International Labor Solidarity Campaigns for Chile in the 1970s and 1980s," *European Solidarity with Chile*, 97–129; *Free Labour World* 391/392 (1983): 6. Milewski traveled to Rome in the second half of 1982 inter alia to work on the Chile collaboration: IPN 01521/2175: Wojciech Gontarski, *Biuro Koordynacyjne NSZZ "Solidarność" za granicą w Brukseli* (praca magisterska, Akademia Spraw Wewnętrznych, Instytut Kryminalistyki i Kryminologii, Warszawa, 1989), 68.

60. Goddeeris, "Ministerstwo," 343.

61. Brier, "Poland's Solidarity," 97–100.

62. *Free Labour World*, 391/392 (1983): 6–9.

63. IPN BU 01820/49, tom 4, 111 ff.: Interview with Jerzy Milewski, Radio Free Europe, February 6, 1985.

64. *D'ici—d'est: Bulletin du comité du 1er mai, pour les libertés démocratiques et les droits des travailleurs dans les pays de l'est* 18/19 (February 1983); Adam Michnik, *Letters from Prison and other Essays* (Berkeley, 1987), 91.

65. Serguei Alex Oushakine, "The Terrifying Mimicry of Samizdat," *Public Culture* 13 (2001): 191–214.

66. Early examples include Archive of New Document (hereafter: AAN), KC PZPR, LXXVI-531: "Notatka. Udział Polski w międzynarodowej solidarności z Chile. Warszawa, 17.9.1974, 6 pages" and IPN, Ld pf 13/408, t. 1, 24–24v: "Chilijscy uchodźcy polityczni w Polsce, Warszawa, 1974, 2 pages." We would like to express our gratitude to Przemysław Gasztold-Seń for pointing us to these documents.

67. Kacper Szulecki, "Hijacked Ideas: Human Rights, Peace, and Environmentalism in Czechoslovak and Polish Dissident Discourses," *East European Politics and Societies* 25 (2011): 272–295.

68. Peter Kornbluh, *The Pinochet File: A Declassified Dossier on Atrocity and Accountability* (New York: New Press, 2013).

69. Brier, "Poland's Solidarity."

70. Konopka, "Chile i Polska," 62–63.

71. Gabriel Pardo and Rodrigo Cea, "El contacto polaco del Papa en Chile," *El Mercurio*, April 10, 2005. About Rychlowski, see, for instance, Rosario Olivares, "Juventud y enseñanza de la Filosofía en Bruno Rychlowski," *La Cañada* 4 (2013): 53–66.

72. "Pinochet, to Avert a Walesa Visit, Frees 2", *New York Times*, October 25, 1989.

73. Jean-Paul Marthoz, "Bustos et Martinez sont libres: merci Wałęsa," *Le Soir*, October 25, 1989.

74. Jan Aart Scholte, "Anti-Apartheid and the Emergence of a Global Civil Society," *Acta Sociologica* 50, no. 3 (2007): 34; Wouter Goedertier, "The Quest for Transnational Authority, the Anti-Apartheid Movements of the European Community," *Revue belge de philologie et d'histoire* 89, nos. 3–4 (2011): 1249–1276.

75. Stephen Ellis, *External Mission: The ANC in Exile, 1960–1990* (London: Hurst, 2012); Klaus Storkmann, *Geheime Solidarität and Militärhilfen der DDR in die "Dritte Welt"* (Berlin: Ch. Links Verlag, 2012).

76. Christiaens, "The Difficult Quest for Chilean Allies," 105.

77. See, for instance, the common identity between Soviet dissidents, Chile, and apartheid in public human rights campaigns in the 1980s. Barbara Hendricks, *Lifting My Voice: A Memoir* (Chicago: Chicago Review Press, 2014), 256.

78. *Christabel Gurney*, "The 1970s: The Anti-Apartheid Movement's Difficult Decade," *Journal of Southern African Studies* 35, no. 2 (2009): 471–487.

79. *Black History and the Class Struggle: A Spartacist Pamphlet* (New York: Spartacist Publishing Co., 1995), 14.

80. Idesbald Goddeeris, "The Limits of Lobbying: ILO and Solidarność," in *ILO Histories: Essays on the International Labour Organization and Its Impact on the World during the Twentieth Century*, eds. Jasmien Van Daele, Magaly Rodríguez García, Geert Van Goethem, and Marcel van der Linden (Bern: Peter Lang, 2010), 437.

81. *Socialistisk Arbejderavis* 10 (June 1985): 8.

82. Christiaens, "The ICFTU and WCL," 119.

83. Kim Christiaens, "From the East to the South, and Back? International Solidarity Movements in Belgium and New Histories of the Cold War, 1950s–1970s," *Dutch Crossing: Journal of Low Countries Studies* 39 (2015): 187–203.

84. Editorial board, "The 77th Session of the International Labour Conference," *Solidarność News*, 154 (July 1990): 1.

85. Alex Boraine, Janet Levy, and Ronel Scheffer, eds., *Dealing with the Past: Truth and Reconciliation in South Africa* (Cape Town: Institute for a Democratic Alternative for South Africa, 1994); François du Bois and Antje du Bois-Pedain, "Post-Conflict Justice and the Reconciliatory Paradigm: The South African Experience," in *Justice and Reconciliation in Post-Apartheid South Africa*, eds. François du Bois and Antje du Bois-Pedain (Cambridge: Cambridge University Press, 2009), 297.

86. A record was released in the following year: Solidarność Anti-Apartheid 13.12.1989 (Gdańsk Shipyard Hall), Discogs, accessed on July 15, 2019, http://www.discogs.com/Various-Solidarno%C5%9B%C4%87-Anti-Apartheid-13121989-Gda%C5%84sk-Shipyard-Hall/release/2156251.

87. Vladimir Shubin and Marina Traikova, "There Is No Threat from the Eastern Bloc," *The Road to Democracy in South Africa*, vol. 3, *International Solidarity*, part 2, ed. South African Democracy Trust (Pretoria: SADET, 2008), 985–1066.

88. Heribert Adam and Kogila Moodley, *The Opening of the Apartheid Mind: Options for the New South Africa* (London: University of California Press, 1993), 83.

89. Archives Foreign Ministry Poland (hereafter: MSZ), Z26/85, W5: RPA 1982: Letter of the Polish Committee of Solidarity with the Nations of Asia and Africa, March 18, 1982.

90. MSZ Z18/88, W5: note of April 19, 1985.

91. Dariusz Stola, *Kraj bez wyjścia? Migracje z Polski 1949–1989* (Warszawa: PAN ISP, 2010), 303ff.; Patryk Pleskot, ed., *Za naszą i waszą Solidarność. Inicjatywy solidarnościowe z udziałem Polonii podejmowane na świecie (1980–1989)* (Warszawa: Instytut Pamięci Narodowej, 2018, 2 vols.).

92. Oliver Rathkolb, "Austria: An Ambivalent Attitude of Trade Unions and Political Parties," in *Solidarity with Solidarity: Western European Trade Unions and the Polish Crisis, 1980–1982*, ed. Idesbald Goddeeris (Lanham, MD: Lexington, 2010), 279.

93. Only 3,500 to 4,000 according to Arkadiusz Żukowski: "Republika Południowej Afryki," in *Akcja niepodległościowa na terenie międzynarodowym 1945–1990*, ed. Tomasz Piesakowski (London: Polskie Towarzystwo Naukowe na Obczyźnie, 1999), 637–638.

94. MSZ Z26/85, W5 (Notatka nt. niektórych aspektów sytuacji wewnętrznej w RPA w okresie październik 1981 r., April 1982, 11); MSZ Z27/86, W3 (dépêche from 29.1.1982); MSZ Z35/86, W5 (Notatka informacyjna dot. Polaków w Republice Południowej Afryki, 13.9.1983, 6); *Zjednoczenie Polskie w Południowej Afryce*, 340 (5.1984), 2; Arkadiusz Żukowski, "Republika Południowej Afryki," 637–638.

95. MSZ Z27/86, W3: dépêches from January 29 and February 4, 1982.

96. IISH Solidarność Nederland 6: South Africa. "The Case against Immigration: A Letter to Polish Catholics from the Church in South Africa." The letter is also mentioned (and dated) in MSZ, Z35/86: Notatka informacyjna dot. Polaków w Republice Południowej Afryki, September 13, 1983, 6.

97. WCL, 326: Letter from Jan Kułakowski to Jerzy Milewski, November 9, 1982.

98. For its official stance on apartheid, see Żukowski, "Republika Południowej Afryki," 635.

99. Martha Evans, *Broadcasting the End of Apartheid: Live Television and the Birth of the New South Africa* (London and New York: I. B. Taurus, 2014), 148–150.

100. Lech Wałęsa's lecture of December 11, 1983 is available at http://www.nobelprize.org/nobel_prizes/peace/laureates/1983/walesa-lecture.html.

101. "Związki, świat współczesny i doświadczenie 'Solidarności'. Rozmowa z Janem Kułakowskim, sekretarzem generalnym Światowej Konfederacji Pracy, Dominiką Aguessy, wicesekretarzem generalnym tejże konfederacji, i z jednym z doradców NSZZ 'Solidarność'," *Widnokrąg* 1 (1986): 25–36; "Solidarność i Trzeci Świat," *Widnokrąg* 1 (1986): 25–36.

102. Skype interview with Anna Nitosławska by Idesbald Goddeeris (Leuven and Ottawa, June 4, 2015). Nitosławska was Wałęsa's translator in Caracas, Washington, and Canada.

103. Giles Hart, *For Our Freedom and Yours: Za naszą i waszą wolność. A History of the Polish Solidarity Campaign of Great Britain 1980–1994* (London: Polish Solidarity Campaign, 1995), 14; Kim Christiaens, Idesbald Goddeeris, and Wouter Goedertier, "Inspirées par le Sud? Les mobilisations transnationales Est-Ouest pendant la guerre froide," *Vingtième Siècle, Revue d'Histoire* 109 (2011): 155–168.

104. Robert Gildea, James Mark, and Niek Pas, "European Radicals and the 'Third World,'" *Cultural and Social History* 8, no. 4 (2011): 464–466; Michael Scott Christofferson, *French Intellectuals against the Left: The Antitotalitarian Moment of the 1970s* (New York: Berghahn, 2004).

105. WCL, 328: Documents concerning the International Human Rights Conference in Krakow, August 1988; WCL, 327: Speech by Egil Aarvik in Oslo, December 10, 1983.

106. WCL, 326: Jan Kułakowski to Jerzy Milewski, November 9, 1982.

107. WCL, 326: Telegram from Jerzy Milewski, October 26, 1982; WCL, 326: *Labor* interview with Jerzy Milewski, October 26, 1982.

108. "Resolution on Afghanistan," *Labor. Monthly Review on Trade Union Information and Training* 1 (January 1983): 24.

109. Some of the rare references of the Solidarność Coordinating Office Abroad to Afghanistan: IPN BU 01820/49, tom 5, 76ff.: Interviews of Milewski for Głos Ameryki, December 13, 1985, and for Radio Free Europe, March 19, 1985; and IPN BU 01820/49, tom 11, 231–240: Letter of Jerzy Milewski to the TKK, Brussels, July 15, 1983.

110. Kim Christiaens and Idesbald Goddeeris, "Beyond Western European Idealism: A Comparative Perspective on the Transnational Scope of Belgian Solidarity Movements with Nicaragua, Poland and South Africa in the 1980s," *Journal of Contemporary History* 50, no. 3 (2015): 632–655; Dieter Gawora, "Lateinamerika hier. Zur Entwicklung der internationalen Solidaritätsarbeit in der Bundesrepublik. Entwicklungsperspektiven," *GhK* 9, no. 10 (1983): 77 and 87; V. Santiago Pozas Pardo, *Nicaragua (1979–1990): Actor Singular de las relaciones internacionales en el final de la guerra fría* (Leioa: PhD Thesis. Servicio Editorial de la Universidad del País Vasco, 2000), 232ff.

111. Kim Christiaens, "Globalizing Nicaragua?"

112. Speech of Nelson Mandela during the conference of Umkhonto we Sizwe, August 9, 1991, University of Venda, Thohoyandou; "Honecker: Glücklich und zufrieden," *Der Spiegel*, January 18, 1993, http://www.spiegel.de/spiegel/print/d-13679737.html.

KIM CHRISTIAENS is Assistant Professor and Director of KADOC, the Documentation and Research Centre on Religion, Culture and Society at KU Leuven. He is coeditor of *European Solidarity with Chile, 1970s–1980s*.

IDESBALD GODDEERIS is Professor at the Research Unit of History at KU Leuven. He is editor of *Solidarity with Solidarity: Western European Trade Unions and the Polish Crisis, 1980–1982*.

14 China Is Not Far! Alternative Internationalism and the Tiananmen Square Massacre in East Germany's 1989

Quinn Slobodian

On the night of June 3, 1989, the Chinese People's Liberation Army brought a six-week-long protest in central Beijing to an end with tanks and rifles. Several hundred people died as soldiers made their way to Tiananmen Square in what the Western media dubbed a "massacre."[1] The event sent shock waves through the Communist Bloc in the midst of campaigns of democratization and reform. In Poland it coincided with the first round of free elections, evoking unwelcome memories of the 1981 suppression of the Solidarity Movement.[2] The concern would have been even deeper for the few who knew that many Chinese soldiers had acquired antiriot training in Poland.[3] World leaders condemned the massacre. Governments in communist East-Central Europe split into critics (Hungary, Poland, and Yugoslavia) and supporters (East Germany, Czechoslovakia, Bulgaria, and Romania) of Chinese policy.[4] East German leaders were especially zealous backers, hosting the Chinese foreign minister one week after the massacre, condemning the "violent, bloody excesses of elements opposed to the constitution," and sending a delegation to Beijing within the month.[5] The East German official newspaper praised the use of force to quash what it called a "counter-revolutionary insurrection."[6] Chinese leaders thanked the GDR for their "proven solidarity" and praised their "internationalist attitude."[7]

Scholars have suggested that the audience for the East German show of support was domestic.[8] Party leaders were sending a message to the small-but-growing opposition that the government was willing to use force to defend itself against internal challenges. Fears of a "Tiananmen solution" reverberated through the autumn demonstrations that culminated in the rupture of the Berlin Wall as dissidents wondered if East German leaders would follow the Chinese example in crushing the opposition with violence.[9] Yet if the goal of party leaders was to foreclose criticism of the Chinese and East German governments, the intimidation backfired. In the six months between the fall of Tiananmen Square's *Goddess of Democracy* statue and the wall in Berlin, East Germans wrote hundreds of letters and telegrams protesting the crackdown and their own government's approval of it. Many took direct action, staging sit-ins, "drum-ins," and protests that led to dozens of arrests.[10] They carried bedsheets painted with the Chinese character for democracy, expressed solidarity (a band even called itself "Autumn in Beijing"), and organized with Chinese residents of West Berlin. In one evocative moment, dissidents in East Berlin publicized a call to protest with a woodcut flyer depicting a naked, apparently dead body over the phrase: "China is not far!" (*China ist nicht fern!*)

The following chapter explores the grassroots response to the Tiananmen Square massacre as expressions of alternative internationalism in East Germany (GDR). While international solidarity was a core governing principle in the GDR, the object of solidarity was inflexible and strictly prescribed. At different points in the republic's forty-year history, small numbers of East Germans bucked this internationalism from above and departed from the party line by forging bonds of identification and empathy with distant populations. This internationalism from below was often snuffed out quickly by police action. Though the most consequential example of such solidarity was the wave of East German solidarity with Czech and Slovak reformers in the wake of the Prague Spring, China was a recurring case in point.[11] After Mao Zedong's China broke with the Soviet Union in the early 1960s, some East Germans continued to identify with the Chinese line against Moscow. During the Chinese Cultural Revolution (1966–76), some (mostly young) East Germans wielded the Maoist critique of Soviet-style authoritarian bureaucracy against the GDR itself.[12] Alternative internationalism presented a challenge to the regime's monopoly on the language of solidarity and conjured a political geography that overlapped with and opposed that of the state.

This chapter takes the phrase "China is not far" as an aperture into the alternative internationalism of East Germany's 1989. It offers three definitions of distance—space, time, and affect—as tools of navigation for other alternative encounters in the era of the global Cold War. Evidence for the chapter is drawn from the archives of the East German intelligence service (Stasi), which gathered all letters addressed to the government and the Chinese embassy related to Tiananmen Square and investigated China-related protests with a special task force of nine officers code-named "Troublemaker" (*Störenfried*).[13] The letters of protest cannot be assumed to represent public opinion at large. People who paid attention to events overseas and penned such letters represent a self-selected group that was small relative to the entire society. Yet they came from a much broader circle than the core of activists in the major cities. Authors included party members from factories as well as married couples, church groups, mechanics, and teachers. They drew from a cross-section of East German society, proving that engagement with the events in China was not limited to those who self-identified with the alternative scene or the organized opposition movement.

The letters also show that the content of alternative internationalism was not uniform. While some critics spoke in the name of a "world public" and "the civilized world" and invoked standards of "human rights," others used the Chinese reaction as a rhetorical cudgel to swing at the GDR itself, attacking the foundations of its legitimacy as a self-described socialist state. Still others expressed no solidarity with Chinese protesters but condemned the Chinese state as backward and atavistic. If official internationalism was a clear melody, composed at the highest level and transmitted through the organs of state and society, then alternative internationalism came closer to a clamor, containing the competing claims of diverse individuals and collectives.

China Is Not Far I: The World Public and Spatial Distance

Television was the primary medium through which East Germans were sensitized to the events at Tiananmen Square. By 1989 East Germans lived in a bifurcated media world, severed from the circulation of Western print media such as magazines and newspapers but regular consumers of Western broadcast media that traveled easily through the so-called Iron Curtain. The turn of the television or radio dial moved an East German consumer from the reportage of the Eastern Bloc to the reportage of the West. The Tiananmen Square massacre was a signature moment of mediated globality. It has become a case study for the political power of images.[14] The presence of large numbers of foreign journalists in Beijing to cover Gorbachev's visit created an opportunity for prodemocracy activists to turn Tiananmen Square into what one scholar called an "information transmitter on a massive scale."[15] As one of the first "live media events" inaugurating the era of the twenty-four-hour cable news cycle—to be followed later that year by the fall of the Berlin Wall—the visual consumption of the prodemocracy movement and the massacre that followed contributed to a mediatized global "moral imaginary."[16]

A first reading of the phrase "China is not far" is that, in the era of mass media, nowhere is far. This spatial definition of distance asserts its own obsolescence. Communication technologies have shrunk the world, it claims. Contemporary observers were well aware of the power of the moving image in making history in 1989. One journalist traced a precedent when he wrote: "'The whole world's watching,' was the boast of US students when they took their lumps from Chicago police at the Democratic presidential convention in 1968. Two decades later in Beijing, this boast of television's power to astound and appall has again come true."[17]

By the late 1980s the East German state no longer actively opposed the viewing of Western television by East Germans. Some scholars argue that the lax policy meant that the leadership relied on a so-called soma effect to lull ordinary Germans into complacency by permitting a nightly escape into the dream worlds of Western entertainment.[18] If this was their strategy, the reception of the Tiananmen Square massacre proved that television could mobilize as well as sedate. Many protest letters complained of the disconnect between official GDR reportage and the televised images on West German news. A church group in Thuringia wrote that the "coverage in the GDR media is one-sided and misleading."[19] A construction worker justified watching West German media because East Germany was "misinforming its citizens."[20] More pointedly, a letter writer from Brandenburg demanded a "realistic representation" of events, saying that the GDR coverage served "the language of murderers."[21] In a memorable passage, a citizen wrote to the official newspaper, *Neues Deutschland* (New Germany):

> Opening my *Neues Deutschland* this morning I saw the headline "Chinese People's Liberation Army Crushes Counter-Revolutionary Uprising." As I read the article, I could only ask how a country can inform its citizens so falsely in this way. I can still see yesterday's images from television. And you want to scream in the face of this many lies. Let's leave aside the question of whether the demands of the students are justified or not. When a socialist country, a communist country, attacks its citizens like this, I can only wonder about this form of government. According to *Neues Deutschland*, the students' weapons of defense were "cut and thrust weapons," this is what they were attacking tanks with. I saw, and the shots were not staged or edited, how tanks simply rolled over people, how the soldiers shot at fleeing people, shot them from behind. . . . It is amazing that film footage can still be produced under these circumstances, but it is good that it can. Because when one is informed as one-sidedly as we are, one must believe what is said otherwise. And the *Neues Deutschland*'s version, in my opinion, is not fair.[22]

The letter's author drew on the authority of his own eyes. He expressed a faith in the objective mediation of West German television against that of East Germany, despite the Socialist Unity Party of Germany (SED) leaders' dismissal of the Western coverage as "horror reports."[23]

The year 1989 was not the first time that East German citizens had complained openly about the distortions of East German reportage on China. After the Sino-Soviet split in the early 1960s, East Germans complained about the one-sidedness of the official reports, which had transformed almost overnight from encomium to obloquy.[24] In the case of Tiananmen Square, scholars have argued that the low quality and unstaged nature of the video footage of the events screened on Western television counterintuitively helped to strengthen faith in their veracity.[25] Such poor production, the argument went, must be telling the truth. It is notable that the East German government sought to counter this footage with its own forty-five-minute special on "the counter-revolutionary insurrection in Beijing," which screened twice on East German television.[26] By showing images of soldiers being beaten and army vehicles set alight, they hoped to win the war of images and convince East Germans that the true culprits were the protesters.[27] As one editor for the official news service put it, "History always knows two truths."[28] It is difficult to say how convincing this counterargument was as most Germans kept silent on the issue. For the many critics who sent letters to the government, however—a self-selected small group, to be sure—Western media triumphed in the contest of truths; the gap between communist claim and Western evidence became the basis for ethical opposition.

In the discourse of critical East Germans, the idea of a world of spectators, capable of observing events in near real-time, no matter where they occurred, underwrote the more abstract notion of a category that surfaced frequently in letters—the idea of a world public (*Weltöffentlichkeit*). A master artisan from Freiberg expressed horror that "the murders continue despite worldwide protest."[29] One letter writer said that the GDR take on Tiananmen was "disrespecting the world public."[30] Another wrote that "the Chinese government has earned the contempt of the entire world."[31] A letter with nine signatures joined in "the international condemnation of the massacre" against the position of the GDR. In the language of these critics, the world public was both a space of mutual observation and a repository of shared norms and values, most commonly summarized as "human rights." China's actions had, as multiple critics put it in similar formulations, placed itself "outside of the norms applicable to civilized states" and "outside" or "at the periphery" of "the civilized world."[32]

The political geography of critics envisioned a club of the international community from which one could be banished or marginalized. The civilized world was an arena of salutary mutual surveillance. Membership in this club required embracing transparency and loosening the claims of noninterference. By conflating a nation's "civilized" status with an internationally enforceable regime of "human rights," it suggested a necessary diminishment of national sovereignty. Two critics from Potsdam wrote that "the sovereignty of China in these matters cannot be accepted because as a human, one must intervene for human life."[33] Three students at a technical institute wrote that the "events in China are not domestic affairs because human rights are clearly being violated."[34] "The GDR," another wrote, "hides behind 'non-intervention' and uses a double standard."[35] One critic appealed to the Helsinki Accords to justify this position, saying that, as a signee, East Germany was obliged to criticize China's "wave of terror."[36] In the language of international relations, critics declared the Tiananmen Square crackdown to be "intermestic," blurring the line between international and domestic affairs and not excusable through appeals to domestic autonomy. Refusing to accept the idea that human rights trumped national sovereignty meant expulsion from the civilized world.

For these letter writers, socialism and human rights were compatible languages.[37] One letter read, "It is not reconcilable with the humanist goals of a socialist society to kill people by 'legal decree.'"[38] "Death sentences," another signed by twenty-nine people declared, "are unworthy of socialist states."[39] Much criticism of China's actions rested on an invocation of the higher ideals of communism and socialism. "It's unbelievable," one person wrote, "that the heirs of Marx and Engels would act this way."[40] Whether for tactical or sincere reasons, these criticisms remained within the discursive space of socialism, projecting a world governed by shared values of human rights, norms that could and should correspond with those of socialism.

One of the more pointed forms of this critique was to invoke the abovementioned double standard. The most common points of reference were South Africa and Chile, both governed by oppressive regimes and frequent targets for the official internationalism of the East German leadership.[41] Some East Germans used China to express a solidarity that was not of the state but against the state. One factory group, called the Red October Brigade, wrote that "urged on by their party secretary [they] had to write protest letters against executions in South Africa. Today they protest—voluntarily—against the Chinese communist leadership's wave of executions."[42] Why, after all, should China be permitted to use the nonintervention alibi when these countries could not? A baker in Berlin pointed out the inconsistency by noting that "apartheid is not a domestic affair of South Africa."[43] Another critic insisted that "there is no difference if death sentences are pronounced in South Africa or China."[44] From Potsdam, a critic wrote that "human rights are recognized worldwide as the foundation of any legal order, therefore, apartheid, racial or religious discrimination, and capital punishment are anachronistic . . . the first socialist state on German soil must protest against any measure directed against life."[45] The GDR position on China would make its take on South Africa and Chile "untrustworthy," another critic warned.[46]

East Germany's stance on China made its own state discourse of internationalism vulnerable to trenchant charges of hypocrisy. Five signees from a nuclear research institute feared that the GDR position on China would undermine "its internationally recognized advocacy for peace and friendship."[47] They noted the changes in Chile, where a no vote in the plebiscite months before portended the end of the Pinochet dictatorship. Coming so soon after this progress in the Southern Cone, the Tiananmen Square massacre seemed to suggest that the communist world was losing the moral high ground. A world without distance meant that all would witness deviations from standards of "human rights" and "the civilized world." The notion of a "world public" and the phrase "in front of the eyes of the world" (*vor den Augen der Welt*), which echoed through both official and alternative internationalist discourse, suggested a world of reciprocal observation and moral evaluation—a vision of the universal public sphere that was not so different in the liberal-capitalist West and the communist East. In the minds of critics, China was not far—nor was anywhere else—and this was good.

China Is Not Far II: Oriental Despotism and Temporal Distance

Near and *far* had spatial definitions in 1989, but they also had temporal ones. At the core of both East German and larger Western narratives of civilization were theories of history that mapped patterns of state conduct onto a trajectory of progress. This was an understanding of distance measured along a historical time line, moving from barbarism to civilization, from rule based on brute force to rule based on dialogue and law. Many critics accused China of atavism or anachronism. A doctor and his wife wrote that the state's "atrocities recalled the deepest middle ages."[48] A truck driver from Berlin protested that China's executions were the "methods of a slave-holder society."[49] Another letter noted that "China offers a picture of descent into barbarity, of a degree one knows from fascist dictatorship."[50] The recurrent term was *barbarism* but also *fascism*. One East German conjoined the two by referring to the events as "fascist barbarism."[51] This was fitting as, in the communist imagination, fascism was not only a political category but a temporal one, a retrogression or backsliding on the path of history from a future politics to those of the past. Such rhetoric referenced contemporary framing of recent European politics and tapped into a deep-seated complex of culturalist and racist tropes in the German imagination, including the "Oriental" threat of Soviet communism and the idea of "Oriental despotism" in Georg Wilhelm Friedrich Hegel and Karl Marx. This political Orientalism figured China as a governmental Other: an inversion of proper statecraft.

Accusations of Chinese barbarism from East Germans in 1989 also recalled the period of the Sino-Soviet split and the Cultural Revolution from the early 1960s to the mid-1970s. Party officials at that time noted a revival of the idea of the "yellow peril," even among party members officially schooled in antiracism and internationalism.[52] They recorded extreme views, including from one East German that "there will no longer be a war between capitalism and socialism but a war between all colored and white nations. China will take over the leadership of the colored nations. To prevent the 'yellow peril,' Europe must unite under a common flag."[53] Another worker personified the threat in racist stereotype, saying: "Look at the yellow peril, smiling to your face with a dagger behind its back, that is the Asian grimace."[54] The official East German media tended toward the language of psychology, reporting on a "war hysteria" and a "chauvinist psychosis" in China during the Cultural Revolution.[55] In such texts, emotion trumped reason in a a supposedly irrational drive for expansion of Chinese power, or what one East German analysis called "the Maoist path toward the great Chinese empire as the ruler of the globe."[56]

Causing special alarm for many East German observers was the destruction of "old Chinese culture" during the Cultural Revolution, echoing many of the concerns in the West of the smashing and plundering of traditional relics and sites.[57] Like India, China was conventionally considered in the German worldview to be a civilization with an estimable history and cultural patrimony. In such acts of self-iconoclasm, Communist China was seen as performing a double depredation: first, betraying the better aspects of its own culture to relapse into despotism, and second, threatening the broader world.[58]

Sentiments such as that of one letter writer, that communism was being "bathed in blood" in China, brought such specters of culturalized violence back into circulation.[59] To announce that "China is not far" in this discourse warned that East Germany might be approaching the retrograde place on the historical time line occupied by a despotic China. Official approval for the Chinese action had driven the point home that, as one theology student put it in a letter to East German leader Erich Honecker, one could "assume that the GDR government would also use violence to uphold the existing order."[60] Twenty-nine members of a church in Angermünde expressed their fear that "in the GDR too, it may be not too long a path to calculated bloodshed among innocents."[61] A participant at a memorial service for those killed in Beijing saw the East German support for China as a "domestic political warning."[62] A similar sentiment came from Halle, where a critic saw the official position of the GDR as an "alibi for East German security forces," suggesting that approval of the Chinese techniques legitimated East German actions in advance."[63] Twenty-two people in Naumburg wrote that they "rejected the official position of the GDR which can be seen as the threat of the use of violence in similar situations in the GDR."[64] One telegram perhaps put the chain of logic most bluntly: "Today Beijing, tomorrow Berlin and Leipzig."[65]

The geography of opposition here took aim at the East German leadership by way of Tiananmen Square. As criticism, it did not inhabit the universal space of the world public but the regional space of the communist Second World. If a particular logic of rule was indigenous to the Communist Bloc, the opposition implied, one might expect technique to move from one country to the others over time. The tactics of Tiananmen might be destined for East Germany too. This was alternative internationalism in the key of alarmism, expressing less a spirit of empathy for the Chinese and more an attitude of preemptive self-care for the East Germans.

In July 1989 the underground radio show *Radio Glasnost*, which broadcast from West Berlin, reported three men in their early twenties arrested for producing the leaflet mentioned in the introduction that read "China is not far." The commentators remarked that according to the law you could receive up to three years for raising a sign that had not been approved by the officials. "China is even closer than some think," they concluded.[66] The idea of a temporal proximity between East Germany and China in a shared reversion to "barbaric" and backward forms of rule stalked the uprising into the autumn of 1989 in East Germany.[67] At the *Nikolaikirche* in Leipzig, what one historian calls the "East German Tiananmen Square," protesters wondered whether China would indeed draw painfully closer through an official decision to pit troops against the mobilized masses.[68] For China to draw near in the temporal-political sense would mean a death sentence for dissent.

China Is not Far III: Identification and Affective Distance

A third and final reading of the phrase "China is not far" relates to the question of political identification. In a notion that could be called affective distance, this definition suggests that the Chinese prodemocracy activists were legible to East German dissidents as coeval partners in an endeavor of political transformation.[69] China was not far because the dissidents claimed a shared self-understanding with the Chinese in a common cause.[70] There was both a common position of critique vis-à-vis their own government and a shared quandary—demanding genuine multiparty elections in a system whose leaders understood that acceding to these demands could mean self-destruction.

In the two weeks after the Tiananmen Square massacre, there were forty-four arrests of people approaching or protesting at the Chinese embassy in Berlin, which also received over 240 letters.[71] In one protest on June 9, forty East Germans gathered near a church in Pankow wearing white flowers as symbols of mourning. When they moved toward the embassy, plainclothes officers arrested and corralled them into waiting trucks and buses. Their fines ranged from 50 to 500 marks, the latter being roughly half of an average monthly salary.[72] Among the larger events in Berlin were a gathering at the "church from below" at the Elisabethkirche in Berlin on June 23 and another at the Samariterkirche on June 29 with over a thousand people in attendance, including journalists from all major Western wire news services.[73]

The protest language at the church events were, in the words of one news report, "directed against those in power in Beijing but also against the state and party leadership of the GDR."[74] A striking example of affective proximity was the adoption of the Chinese character for democracy by East German dissidents. In early July protesters carried a sheet painted with the character alongside its German translation in an unauthorized demonstration at the closing of the annual gathering of Protestant youth in Leipzig on July 9.[75] Alongside the character banner they carried a sign reading "No More Election Fraud," referring to protests against the most recent election in May.[76] The pairing of the signs localized the distant Tiananmen Square protest, making it part of the East German landscape of complaints and demands. Protesters also hung the character, in an adaptation of the Chinese *dazibao* (big-character poster), next to the entrance of the *Erlöserkirche* in Berlin, with signs publicizing a drum-in in support of the Chinese dead. In July Stasi agents intercepted a private letter carrying a photograph of the character, which they recognized from the Chinese democracy movement but feared was leaping over into East German circles. "It is possible it will circulate more widely," they warned.[77]

The willingness of dissidents to identify with—if not co-opt—distant struggles is partially explained by the context of the work of antiracism happening at the same time. Many of the most active protesters against the Tiananmen Square massacre came out of church circles, which were pioneers in grassroots antiracist activism in a socialist country in which the leadership denied that racism existed. When the activist pastor Almuth Berger approached officials about racism in East Germany, he was told that "in the GDR there is no racism, only solidarity."[78] The disavowal of race in official East German discourse is often noted.[79] Less often discussed, however, are the East Germans who observed this aporia themselves and sought to create autonomous institutions for antiracist work before the Berlin Wall fell. Many members of the opposition in East Germany were consciously engaged in bridging gaps between individuals of different races and places of origin, especially in light of the growing numbers of Vietnamese and Mozambican contract workers and expansion of neo-Nazi skinhead activity in the late 1980s.[80] The foundations of alternative internationalism in church groups may help to explain the currency of themes of cross-racial solidarity in the GDR absent in other state-socialist countries.[81]

The metaphor of distance was often central for antiracist activists. A prime example is the newsletter *Nah & Fern* (Near & far), published by Berlin's Ecumenical Missionary Center (Ökumenisch-missionarisches Zentrum, OMZ) beginning in April 1989. The opening essay parsed the name of the newsletter, saying that "far is not meant here as a pure concept of distance, measured in kilometers or hours or air travel, rather as a concept of foreignness." "The dismantlement of prejudice and xenophobia cannot be dictated 'from above,'" it concluded, "but can only be achieved by all of us."[82] The OMZ had two "2/3-Welt-Gruppen" (Second-Third World groups)—Xitsikwane, a working group for southern Africa, and July 19, for Nicaragua. Consistent with the politicized nature of church work at the time, these groups had no qualms about taking sides in conflict or supporting Palestinian and Namibian liberation movements. One of their primary projects of cross-cultural encounter was creating a weekly event called Cabana that drew on examples of sociability from Romania and Mozambique. In a first example of what might happen there, a participant wrote, "At the Cabana, I can ask Shiua from Beijing about the exciting developments in China."[83] At least one of the authors for *Nah & Fern* was directly involved with the Tiananmen Square protest, having been turned away from the Chinese embassy on June 8 when she tried to deliver a letter signed by fifty-four students from Humboldt University.[84]

The proposed encounter with a Chinese person at the OMZ's Cabana points to the presence of Chinese people in East Germany and nearby West Berlin, another way that China was literally "not far." Six hundred Chinese students studied in West Berlin, and about thirty Chinese people a day crossed the border at Friedrichstrasse into East Berlin. Activists in East Germany received information and eyewitness reports from these border crossers. They brought material, for example, from the demonstration of five thousand people organized by Chinese students and academics in West Berlin on June 5.[85] The West Berlin–based RIAS radio station broadcasted a protest letter written by Chinese living in West Berlin criticizing the East German support for the crackdown and its coverage in the GDR media.[86] The day after that demonstration, the Stasi found one hundred flyers in "Asian script" with images from Tiananmen Square near Friedrichstrasse.[87] A Chinese citizen who studied in Dresden was searched as he crossed the border and was found to be carrying leaflets and eyewitness accounts about the "massacre in Beijing." He was detained for eight hours before being interrogated by the police at 3:00 am and eventually released.[88]

Through gestures of affective proximity, East German protesters reclaimed the language of internationalism and solidarity from its state monopoly. Their form of alternative internationalism asserted a common struggle between the GDR and China. In downtown Berlin, dissidents stuffed mailboxes with handwritten flyers reading "Practice solidarity! Help the Chinese Students! Protest against terror in China!"[89] On July 1 a group of ten people, including seven men and three women, were caught by police putting stickers on the wall of every subway station in downtown Berlin for their band Herbst in Peking (Autumn in Beijing). The band had performed in June in Brandenburg but had incorporated messages of solidarity with Chinese students into their performance, leading to the forced dissolution of the band and a ban on further performance.[90] They would later return as one of the iconic bands of the Wende. Their most anthemic song, "Baksheesh Republic," captured their defiant rejection of official transcripts dictated from above. The song blended clips of speeches from East German leader Walter Ulbricht with these words: "Hope is a lazy dumb cow and feeds on state doctrine. . . . He who worships false gods, piss off!"[91]

Some expressions of affective proximity with China explicitly dissociated themselves from the language of both human rights and Oriental despotism. The dissident publication *Umweltblätter* wrote on June 6, 1989: "We take our distance from the human rights shrieking of Western politicians, who obviously smell losses in their China trade in the Chinese government's possible new economic policy and so gesture at the new bogeyman of the East for their own populations. We declare solidarity with the Chinese population and students because we have the same opponent: governments who take their sinecures on the backs, and against the will, of the population, and do not shy from draconian prison sentences or even murder when these are in danger."[92] For East Germans, identification with Chinese students was based on a shared sense of distance from their own governments. This sentiment had been expressed earlier by foreign students in West Germany in the 1960s, who saw the willingness to dissent from their own governments as a trait that linked the white ethnic German populations with those from the Global South. As a Cameroonian student described a German student in 1967: "Sometimes he knows a great deal about the international political situation. It keenly interests him, and he feels connected to young people on other continents. This often means fighting against those that want to endow him with their way of seeing the world. He sometimes becomes alienated from his homeland under such circumstances. Through this act of distancing, I have understood him better. We belong together at this distance."[93] East German students expressed their countersolidarity through gestures of identification. When graffiti reading "China lives" appeared on the walls of Humboldt University and the train station nearby, this was not the China of the CCP leadership but the China of the opposition.[94] China was close for some East German dissidents because they saw themselves in a shared struggle against a state that claimed to govern in their names.

Conclusion

This chapter has told the story of China in East Germany's 1989 as one of transnational identification, moral mobilization, and cross-cultural encounter. This account of a polysemic alternative internationalism from below is a marked departure from the usual role played by China in the history of the GDR's demise. While the protests discussed above often appear as footnotes, China is mostly present in the storyline of East German's 1989 as its harrowing inverse. Tiananmen Square supplies a reminder of how badly things might have gone. People ask both then and now whether the leadership ever weighed a "Beijing solution," a "Chinese solution," or a "Tiananmen solution" to the problem of protest.[95] A prayer was pinned to a Leipzig church wall in October 1989 reading: "I am afraid that 10/9/89 will be a day like Tiananmen Square in China. And that the rest of the young people will shed their blood for this senseless state."[96] Historians have concluded that in East Germany tanks and rifles were never considered seriously for use against civilians as they had been in Beijing.[97] Yet in the absence of a Chinese solution in Leipzig or Berlin, the bodies in Tiananmen Square in June still survive as counterpoint to the dancers on the crumbling wall in November. The conviction not to act "Chinese" allowed East Germany to return to West Germany, Europe, and ultimately the larger community of the West and the "international community." China serves as a point of negative comparison. It is a possible future for the GDR, mercifully unrealized—a dystopia narrowly averted.

Yet the image of Germans painting the giant Chinese character for democracy suggests that there was another China in East Germany's 1989. Affective proximity and distance suggested a deterritorialization of political problems, which were understood not as contained within a given nation but as universal pathologies to be confronted. As noted above, important geopolitical points of reference were South Africa and Chile, but in the discourse of affective distance, these were not places but bundles of problems whose roots extended far beyond their own nations. The first issue of *Nah & Fern* included a quote from the theologian Dorothee Sölle to the effect that "apartheid is not a political system in an African country; apartheid is a specific way of thinking, feeling and living, without awareness of what is happening right next to us."[98] In the translations of democracy from the Chinese character into German, the activists created a comparison and an equivalency that pointed toward a universal value.

One can hear echoes in the archives of the international influence of the Beijing Spring before it ended in a bloodbath. The Chinese prodemocracy movement inspired political identification across gaps of geography and race and sparked a transnational exchange of ideas and idioms of protest. Beyond the relatively small circles of urban dissidents on which historians have focused, the suppression of the democracy movement also summoned an outcry from East German citizens of diverse ages and backgrounds. In their reactions, East Germans did not distance China the way the current narrative of Tiananmen Square as the "89 that failed" does. Rather, they drew China close, bringing it into the East German political imagination as one point of orientation among many in a time of collective reinvention.

Notes

1. "Massacre in China," *Washington Post*, June 5, 1989. The deaths came in the surrounding city. None of the actual protesters in the square were killed. For a reconstruction of the event, see Dingxin Zhao, *The Power of Tiananmen : State-Society Relations and the 1989 Beijing Student Movement* (Chicago: University of Chicago Press, 2001), 202–209.
2. Timothy Garton Ash, *The Magic Lantern : The Revolution of '89 Witnessed in Warsaw, Budapest, Berlin, and Prague* (New York: Vintage Books, 1993), 32.
3. Maurice Meisner, *The Deng Xiaoping Era: An Inquiry into the Fate of Chinese Socialism, 1978–1994* (New York: Hill and Wang, 1996), 455.
4. Péter Vámos, "The Tiananmen Square 'Incident' in China and the East Central European Revolutions," in *The Revolutions of 1989: A Handbook*, eds. Wolfgang Mueller, Michael Gehler, and Arnold Suppan (Vienna: Verlag der Österreichischen Akademie der Wissenschaften, 2014), 107.
5. "Freundschaftliche Begegnung mit dem Außenminister der VR China," *Neues Deutschland*, June 13, 1989; "Erklärung der Volkskammer der DDR zu den aktuellen Ereignissen in der Volksrepublik China," *Neues Deutschland*, June 9, 1989; "SED Delegation in Peking empfangen," *Neues Deutschland*, July 3, 1989.
6. "Volksbefreiungsarmee Chinas schlug konterrevolutionären Aufruhr nieder," *Neues Deutschland*, June 5, 1989.
7. "Freundschaftliche Begegnung"; "China dankt der DDR für erwiesene Solidarität," *Berliner Zeitung*, July 8, 1989.

8. Gareth Dale, *Popular Protest in East Germany, 1945–1989* (New York: Routledge, 2005), 139.

9. Ingo Schulze, "1989: How We Lost Political Alternatives," *Bulletin of the German Historical Institute*, no. 52 (Spring 2013): 77.

10. See Tom Sello, "Die Reaktionen in der DDR auf das Massaker in Peking," in *Mauerkrieger: Aktionen gegen die Mauer in West-Berlin 1989*, eds. Ole Giec and Frank Willmann (Berlin: Ch. Links, 2014).

11. On Prague Spring solidarity, see Stefan Wolle, *Der Traum von der Revolte: Die DDR 1968* (Berlin: Sonderausgabe für die Zentralen für politische Bildung in Deutschland, 2008).

12. See Quinn Slobodian, "The Maoist Enemy: China's Challenge in 1960s East Germany," *Journal of Contemporary History* 51, no. 3 (July 2015): 20–23.

13. Uhlig. HA II/Stab. Maßnahmeplan. June 6, 1989. MfS HA II 26979, p. 121.

14. See, e.g., Robert Hariman and John Louis Lucaites, *No Caption Needed: Iconic Photographs, Public Culture, and Liberal Democracy* (Chicago: University of Chicago Press, 2007), chapter 7.

15. McKenzie Wark, *Virtual Geography: Living with Global Media Events* (Bloomington: Indiana University Press, 1994), 149.

16. Daniel F. Vukovich, *China and Orientalism: Western Knowledge Production and the P.R.C.* (New York: Routledge, 2012), 27. Tim Dant, *Television and the Moral Imaginary: Society through the Small Screen* (New York: Palgrave Macmillan, 2012), 54. Paul Betts adds a note of caution in interpreting local dynamics, however, observing that "televised images did not drive events in the run-up to 9 November, especially for those who elected to stay in the country." Paul Betts, "The Intimacy of Revolution: 1989 in Pictures," in *The Ethics of Seeing: Photography and Twentieth-Century German History*, eds. Paul Betts, Jennifer Evans, and Stefan-Ludwig Hoffmann (New York: Berghahn, 2018), 250.

17. John Allemang, "China in Crisis," *Globe and Mail*, June 6, 1989.

18. Woo-Seung Lee, *Das Fernsehen im geteilten Deutschland (1952–1989): Ideologische Konkurrenz und programmliche Kooperation* (Potsdam: Verlag für Berlin-Brandenburg, 2003), 39.

19. Tagesinformation. Anlage 2. (n.d.). BStU MfS-HA II 26979, p. 146.

20. Anlage 3. (n.d.). BStU MfS-HA II 26979, p. 168.

21. Anlage 2. (n.d.). BStU MfS-HA II 26979, p. 195.

22. Strobel. HA II. Abt. M. Zusammengefasster Bericht über Reaktionen der Bevölkerung zu den aktuellen Ereignissen in der Volksrepublik China. June 9, 1989. BStU Archive, MfS, HA II, 26.

23. "Nützlicher Dialog über Abrüstung und europäische Zusammenarbeit," *Neues Deutschland*, June 9, 1989; "You Could See Me in Washington . . . Bush Would Be Welcome Here," *Washington Post*, June 11, 1989.

24. Slobodian, "The Maoist Enemy," 10.

25. Sunil Manghani, *Image Critique & the Fall of the Berlin Wall* (Bristol, UK: Intellect, 2008), 51.

26. "Dokumentation im Fernsehen der DDR," *Neues Deutschland*, June 27, 1989.

27. Adam Bo, "Beim Betrachten der Bilder aus Peking," *Neues Deutschland*, June 27, 1989.

28. Tagesinformation. Anlage 2. (n.d.). BStU MfS-HA II 26979, p. 150.

29. Tagesinformation. Anlage 1. June 29, 1989. BStU MfS-HA II 26979, p. 141.

30. Ibid. On the use of the category of "world public opinion" in the opposition to apartheid, see Håkan Thörn, *Anti-Apartheid and the Emergence of a Global Civil Society* (New York: Palgrave Macmillan, 2006), 7.

31. HA II. Briefe und Telegramme, June 7, 1989. BStU MfS-HA II 26979, p. 201.

32. Ibid., p. 202; Tagesinformation. Anlage 1. (n.d.). BStU MfS-HA II 26979, p. 138; Tagesinformation. Anlage 1. June 29, 1989. BStU MfS-HA II 26979, p. 142.

33. Tagesinformation. Anlage 1. June 29, 1989. BStU MfS-HA II 26979, p. 142.

34. Tagesinformation. Anlage 1. June 27, 1989. BStU MfS-HA II 26979, p. 155.

35. Anlage 2. June 23, 1989. BStU MfS-HA II 26979, p. 167.

36. Tagesinformation. Anlage 1. (n.d.). BStU MfS-HA II 26979, p. 137.

37. Paul Betts, "Socialism, Social Rights, and Human Rights: The Case of East Germany," *Humanity* 3, no. 3 (2012). Ned Richardson-Little, "Dictatorship and Dissent: Human Rights in East Germany in the 1970s," in *The Breakthrough: Human Rights in the 1970s*, eds. Jan Eckel and Samuel Moyn (Philadelphia: University of Pennsylvania Press, 2014), 49–67.

38. Tagesinformation. Anlage 2. (n.d.). BStU MfS-HA II 26979, p. 144.

39. Tagesinformation. Anlage 1. June 29, 1989. BStU MfS-HA II 26979, p. 140.

40. Tagesinformation. Anlage 1. June 26, 1989. BStU MfS-HA II 26979, p. 154.

41. Toni Weis, "The Politics Machine: On the Concept of 'Solidarity' in East German Support for Swapo," *Journal of Southern African Studies* 37, no. 2 (June 2011). Patrice G. Poutrus, "Asylum in Postwar Germany: Refugee Admission Policies and Their Practical Implementation in the Federal Republic and the GDR between the Late 1940s and the Mid-1970s," *Journal of Contemporary History* 49, no. 1 (2014): 125.

42. Beißig. HA II. Abteilung M. Zusammenfasster Bericht. July 13, 1989. BStU MfS-HA II 25716, p. 8.

43. Anlage 1. N.d. BStU MfS-HA II 26979, p. 183.

44. Anlage 2. June 23, 1989. BStU MfS-HA II 26979, p. 167.

45. Tagesinformation. Anlage 1. June 6, 1989. BStU MfS-HA II 26979, p. 135.

46. Anlage 2. June 23, 1989. BStU MfS-HA II 26979, p. 167.

47. Anlage 2. June 26, 1989. BStU MfS-HA II 26979, p. 163.

48. Tagesinformation. Anlage 2. N.d. BStU MfS-HA II 26979, p. 148.

49. Anlage 2. June 27, 1989. BStU MfS-HA II 26979, p. 154.

50. HA II. Briefe und Telegramme, June 7, 1989. BStU MfS-HA II 26979, p. 202.

51. Anlage 2. N.d. BStU MfS-HA II 26979, p. 176.

52. See Slobodian, "The Maoist Enemy," 15. David Tompkins, "The East Is Red? Images of China in East Germany and Poland through the Sino-Soviet Split," *Zeitschrift für Ostmitteleuropa-Forschung* 62, no. 3 (2013): 421.

53. Juch. Zentrale Partei Kontrol Kommision. "Über die Auswirkungen der Spaltungspolitk der Führer der KP Chinas auf Mitglieder der SED und über einige andere Ercheinungen in der Partei." June 26, 1964. BA/DY 30/IV A 2/4/3.

54. Hinz. BPKK Halle an ZPKK Berlin. July 19, 1963. SAPMO-BArch/DY 30/IV A 2/4/3.

55. Beda Erlinghagen, *Von "wildgewordenem Kleinbürgertum" und "Weltherrschaftsplänen": Die Volksrepublik China im Spiegel der DDR-Presse (1966–1976)* (Cologne: PapyRossa, 2009), 64.

56. Peter R. Hartmann, *Wesen und Erscheinungsformen der Ideologie und Politik des Maoismus als eine spezifische Variante des Antikommunismus* (Warnemünde: Ingenieurhochschule für Seefahrt, 1976), III/21.

57. Erlinghagen, *Von "Wildgewordenem Kleinbürgertum,"* 59.

58. For a contemporary example from West Germany, see Pieter van Blättjen, *Die gelbe Gefahr hat rote Hände* (Graz: L. Stocker, 1963). For the classic analysis, see Heinz Gollwitzer, *Die gelbe Gefahr* (Göttingen: Vandenhoeck & Ruprecht, 1962).

59. Tagesinformation. Anlage 1. June 27, 1989. BStU MfS-HA II 26979, p. 154.

60. Beißig. HA II. Abteilung M. Zusammenfasster Bericht. July 13, 1989. BStU MfS-HA II 25716, p. 8.

61. Ibid., p. 7.

62. Ibid., p. 8.

63. Anlage 2. N.d. BStU MfS-HA II 26979, p. 176.

64. Tagesinformation. Anlage 1. June 6, 1989. BStU MfS-HA II 26979, p. 136.

65. Beißig, HA II, Abt. M. Tagesbericht der Abteilung M des MfS zu den aktuellen Ereignissen in der VR China, June 21, 1989. MfS-HA II 25716, p. 24.

66. Robert-Havemann-Gesellschaft, "Die Chinesische Lösung," www.jugendopposition.de/themen/herbst89/145315/die-chinesische-loesung. Accessed July 15, 2019.

67. This is the only sense in which Jarausch interprets the protest phrase "China is not far" in 1989. Konrad Jarausch, *After Hitler: Recivilizing Germans, 1945–1995* (New York: Oxford, 2006), 205.

68. Stephen Kotkin, *Uncivil Society: 1989 and the Implosion of the Communist Establishment* (New York: Random House, 2009), 54.

69. The term is inspired in part by Christina Schwenkel's notion of "affective solidarities." See Christina Schwenkel, "Affective Solidarities and East German Reconstruction of Postwar Vietnam," in *Comrades of Color: East Germany in the Cold War World*, ed. Quinn Slobodian (New York: Berghahn, 2015).

70. It is worth noting that the dead figure in the woodcut mentioned in the introduction is not overtly racialized. The recognized phenotypic marking of eye shape is ambiguous, and the monochrome of the woodcut gives the effect of either black or blond hair.

71. Tagesinformation zur politisch-operativen Lageentwicklung im Zusammenhang mit der aktuellen Situation in der VR China. June 16, 1989. BStU MfS-HA II 26979, p. 171; Müller. HA II/Stab. Rapport 170/89. "Störenfried II." July 18, 1989. BStU MfS-HA II 26979, p. 219.

72. Wolff. HA II/Stab. Rapport. 149/89. June 23, 1989. BStU MfS-HA II 26979, pp. 317–319.

73. Aktion China. June 23, 1989. BStU MfS-HA II 26979, p. 309; Kuschnierzik. HA II/Stab. Rapport. 150/89. June 24, 1989. BStU MfS-HA II 26979, p. 314. Müller. HA II/Stab. Rapport. 154/89. June 29, 1989. BStU MfS-HA II 26979, p. 288.

74. ARD report quoted in Müller. HA II/Stab. Rapport. 154/89. June 29, 1989. BStU MfS-HA II 26979, p. 288.

75. Sello, "Die Reaktionen in der DDR auf das Massaker in Peking," 123.

76. Ibid., 124.

77. Beißig. HA II. Abteilung M. Zusammenfasster Bericht. July 13, 1989. BStU MfS-HA II 25716, p. 9.

78. Paul Hockenos, *Free to Hate: The Rise of the Right in Post-Communist Eastern Europe* (New York: Routledge, 1993), 38.

79. Quinn Slobodian, "Socialist Chromatism: Race, Racism and the Racial Rainbow in East Germany," in *Comrades of Color: East Germany in the Cold War World*, ed. Quinn Slobodian (New York: Berghahn, 2015).

80. Mike Dennis and Norman LaPorte, *State and Minorities in Communist East Germany* (New York: Berghahn Books, 2011).

81. On the absence of alternative internationalism in late socialist Hungary, see James Mark and Péter Apor, "Socialism Goes Global: Decolonization and the Making of a New Culture of Internationalism in Socialist Hungary, 1956–1989," *Journal of Modern History* 87 (2015): 891. On the late socialist antiracist/ apartheid work of churches in the GDR in the 1980s, see Paul Betts, Kim Christiaens, Idesbald Goddeeris, and James Mark, "Race, Socialism and Solidarity: Anti-Apartheid in Eastern Europe," in *Global Anti-Apartheid*, eds. Robert Skinner and Anna Konieczna (New York: Palgrave, 2019).

82. *Nah & Fern: Material- und Informationsdienst zur Ausländerseelsorge* 1 (April 13, 1989), 1.

83. Ibid., 7.

84. Tagesinformation. June 15, 1989. BStU MfS-HA II 26979, p. 178.

85. Aktion "China." Lagefilm. June 5, 1989. BStU MfS-HA II 26979, p. 430.

86. Aktion "China." Lagefilm. June 6, 1989. BStU MfS-HA II 26979, p. 411.

87. Ibid., p. 410.

88. Kunschnierzik. HA II/Stab. Rapport 134/89. June 6, 1989. BStU MfS-HA II 26979, p. 444.

89. HV A. Operative-Information. July 2, 1989. BStU MfS-HA II 26979, pp. 238–239.

90. Oltn. Gerischer. Rapport 157/89. July 1, 1989. BStU MfS-HA II 26979, p. 271.

91. Quoted in Patricia Anne Simpson, *Cultures of Violence in the New German Street* (Madison, NJ: Fairleigh Dickinson University Press, 2012), 53.

92. Quoted in Thomas Klein, *"Frieden und Gerechtigkeit!": Die Politisierung der unabhängigen Friedensbewegung in Ost-Berlin während der 80er Jahre* (Cologne: Böhlau, 2007), 464.

93. Quoted in Quinn Slobodian, *Foreign Front: Third World Politics in Sixties West Germany* (Durham, NC: Duke University Press, 2012), 1.

94. Quoted in Klein, *"Frieden und Gerechtigkeit!"*, 464.

95. See, e.g., Patrick Major, *Behind the Berlin Wall: East Germany and the Frontiers of Power* (New York: Oxford University Press, 2010), 245. Dale, *Popular Protest in East Germany*, 147. Schulze, "1989: How We Lost Political Alternatives," 77.

96. Quoted in Charles S. Maier, *Dissolution: The Crisis of Communism and the End of East Germany* (Princeton, NJ: Princeton University Press, 1997), 142.

97. On the internal debates about the "Chinese solution," see Bernd Schaefer, "Die DDR und die 'Chinesische Lösung': Gewalt in der Volksrepublik China im Sommer 1989," in *1989 und die Rolle der Gewalt*, ed. Martin Sabrow (Göttingen: Wallstein, 2012).

98. *Nah & Fern. Material-und Informationsdienst zur Ausländerseelsorge.* 1 (April 13, 1989), 2.

QUINN SLOBODIAN is Associate Professor of History at Wellesley College. He is author of *Globalists: The End of Empire and the Birth of Neoliberalism* and *Foreign Front: Third World Politics in Sixties West Germany* and editor of *Comrades of Color: East Germany in the Cold War World.*

Abbreviations/Foreign Language Glossary

ABVV/FGTB Algemeen Belgisch Vakverbond / Fédération Générale du Travail de Belgique (General Federation of Belgian Labour)

Abteilung Internationale Verbindungen Department of International Relations, GDR

ACV/CSC Algemeen Christelijk Vakverbond / Confédération des syndicats chrétiens (Confederation of Christian Trade Unions, Belgium)

AFL-CIO American Federation of Labor and Congress of Industrial Organizations

Afro-Asiatische Solidaritätskomittee Afro-Asian Solidarity Committee, GDR

AIESEE Association Internationale D'études Du Sud-Est Européen (International Association for Southeast European Studies, UNESCO)

ANC African National Congress

Arcom A construction enterprise, Romania

AUC African Union Commission

BIS Bank for International Settlements

Beton "Concrete," a construction enterprise, Macedonia

CCP *Zhōngguó Gòngchǎndǎng* (Chinese Communist Party)

CIA Central Intelligence Agency, US

CIPSH/ICPHS Conseil International de la Philosophie et des Sciences Humaines (International Council for Philosophy and Humanities, UNESCO)

CLAT Central Latinoamericana de Trabajadores (Latin American Confederation of Workers)

CMEA/Comecon Council for Mutual Economic Assistance, USSR

CNS Coordinadora Nacional Sindical (National Union Coordination, Chile)

CNT Comando Nacional de Trabajadores (National Command of Workers, Chile)

CoCom Coordinating Committee for Multilateral Export Controls

Comintern Communist International

Comedor Comité permanent d'études, de développement, d'organisation et d'aménagement de l'agglomération d'Alger (Standing Committee for Studies, Development, Organization and Planning of the Agglomeration of Algiers)

COSATU Congress of South African Trade Unions

CPSU Communist Party of the Soviet Union

CPSU CC Central Committee of the Communist Party of the Soviet Union

CRUE Center of Research on Underdeveloped Economies, Poland

CTN Central de Trabajadores Nicaragüenses (Nicaraguan Workers' Centre)

CUSA Council of Unions of South Africa

ECOSOC UN Economic and Social Council

ENR *Engineering News-Record,* US

EP Energoprojekt, Yugoslav multinational enterprise

Escom Electricity Supply Commission, South Africa

EU European Union

FDGB Freier Deutscher Gewerkschatfbund (Free German Workers' Union, GDR)

FDJ Freie Deutsche Jugend (Free German Youth, GDR)

Fidesz Hungarian Civic Alliance, conservative political party

FOSATU Federation of South African Trade Unions

FRELIMO Frente de Libertação de Moçambique (Mozambique Liberation Front)

FSLN Frente Sandinista de Liberación Nacional (Sandinista National Liberation Front, Nicaragua)

FTO Foreign trade organization

G77 Group of 77, UN

GATT General Agreement on Tariffs and Trade

GKĖS Gosudarstvennyi komitet po vneshnim ekonomicheskim sviaziam (Committee for Foreign Economic Relations, USSR)

GNCC Ghana National Construction Corporation

Gorstroiproekt Institute for Town Construction Projects, USSR

Gosplan Gosudarstvenniy Komitet po Planirovaniyu (State Planning Committee, USSR)

HSWP/MSzMP Hungarian Socialist Workers' Party (Magyar Szocialista Munkáspárt)

ICFTU International Confederation of Free Trade Unions

IDEP Institut Africain de Développement Economique et de Planification (African Institute for Economic Development and Planning)

IFAN Institute Fondamental d'Afrique Noir (African Institute for Basic Research)

IIB International Investment Bank (Comecon)

IKAN Institut Kitaevedeniia Akademii Nauk (Institute for China Studies, USSR)

ILO International Labour Organization

IMEMO Institut Mirovoy Ekonomiki i Mezhdunarodnykh Otnosheniy (Institute of World Economy and International Relations, USSR)

IMESS Institut mezhdunarodnoi sistemy socializma (Institute for the Study of the Socialist World System, USSR)

IMF International Monetary Fund

INGRA A construction enterprise, Croatia

INOC Iraq National Oil Company

Iscor A steel company, South Africa

IVAN Institut Vostokovedenie Akademii Nauk (Institute for Oriental Studies, USSR)

KC PZPR Komitet Centralny Polskiej Zjednoczonej Partii Robotniczej (Central Committee of the Polish United Workers' Party)

KGB Komitet gosudarstvennoy bezopasnosti (Committee for State Security, USSR)

KOR Komitet Obrony Robotników (Workers' Defense Committee, Poland)

KÖZTI Hungarian Public Building Design Company

Limex Foreign trade enterprise, GDR

MAI Ministerium für Aussen- und Innendeutschenhandel (Ministry of Foreign and Domestic Trade, GDR)

MFA Ministry of Foreign Affairs

MfAA Ministerium für Auswärtige Angelegenheiten (Ministry of Foreign Affairs, GDR)

Miastoprojekt Biuro Projektów Budownictwa Ogólnego (General Construction Project Office "City Project," Poland)

Ministerrat Council of Ministers, GDR

NAACP National Association for the Advancement of Colored People, US

NAM Nonaligned movement

NATO North Atlantic Treaty Organization

NCR Noncapitalist road

NEP New Economic Policy, USSR

NGO Nongovernmental organization

NIEI Nauchno-Issledovatel'skii Ekonomicheskii Insitut (Economic Research Institute, USSR)

NIEO New International Economic Order

NLM National liberation movements

NPF National Progressive Front, Syria

OATUU Organization of African Trade Union Unity

OMZ Ökumenisch-missionarisches Zentrum (Ecumenical-Missionary Center, Germany)

ONI Office National d'Immigration (National Office of Immigration, France)

OPEC Organization of the Petroleum Exporting Countries

ÖGB Österreichischer Gewerkschaftsbund (Austrian Trade Union Federation)

PIM Construction company, full name Ivan Milutinović PIM, Yugoslavia

PiS Prawo i Sprawiedliwość (Law and Justice, Poland)

PLO Palestine Liberation Organization

Polservice Foreign trade enterprise, Poland

Polytechna Foreign trade enterprise, Czechoslovakia

RAD A construction company, Serbia

Rastokhez Tajikistan's opposition party

Renmin Ribao People's Daily, PRC

RIAS Rundfunk im amerikanischen Sektor (Broadcasting Service in the American Sector, Germany)

Romconsult Foreign trade enterprise, Romania

Romproiect A construction company, Romania

SAC Société Africaine de Culture (Society of African Culture)

Sasol Energy and chemical company, South Africa

SACP South African Communist Party

SED Sozialistische EinheitsPartei Deutschlands (Socialist Unity Party of Germany, GDR)

SKSSA Sovetskii komitet solidarnosti stran Azii (Soviet Committee for Solidarity with the Countries of Asia, USSR)

Solidarność Niezależny Samorządowy Związek Zawodowy, NSZZ (Independent self-governing labor union Solidarity, Poland)

SPO State Planning Organization, Turkey

SWAPO South West African People's Organisation, Namibia

TASS Telegraph Agency of the Soviet Union

TES Technoexportstroy, a construction company, Bulgaria

TKK Tymczasowa Komisja Koordynacyjna (Temporary Coordinating Commission, Poland)

UN United Nations

UNCTAD United Nations Conference on Trade and Development

UNECA United Nations Economic Commission for Africa

UNESCO United Nations Educational, Scientific, and Cultural Organization

UNIDO United Nations Industrial Development Organization

UPC Union des Populations du Cameroun (Union of the Peoples of Cameroon)

USAID United States Agency for International Development

VOKS Vsesoiuznoe obshchestvo kul'turnoi sviazi s zagranitsei (All-Union Society for Cultural Relations with Foreign Countries, USSR)

Wadeco Warsaw Development Consortium, Poland

WCL World Confederation of Labor

WiP Wolność i Pokój (Freedom and Peace, Poland)

WTZ Wirtschaftliche und Technische Zusammenarbeit (Economic and Technical Cooperation, GDR)

Index

Note: Page numbers in *italics* refer to figures. Page numbers with a "t" refer to tables. Page numbers followed by an "n" and a number refer to a footnote, e.g., 206n21 refers to footnote 21 on page 206.

Abu Dhabi, UAE, modernizing architecture, 180, *180*
Adiseshiah, Malcolm S., 256
Afana, Osendé, 152–153
Afghanistan, Central Asia and, 196–198, 203–204, 206n21; development support, 72, 172, 193; Solidarność and, 19, 303; Soviet involvement, 23, 48, 214, 222–223
Africa, Chinese policies, 87–90; Soviet attitudes to nationalism in, 232–233, 234–237, 239–240; Soviet scholarship on, 233–236, 238–239; Soviet Union and agrarian modernization, 145–147
African Institute for Economic Development and Planning (IDEP), 157–158
African National Congress (ANC), 298, 299, 300
Afro-Asian Conference, Bandung (1955), 83, 193, 211, 215–216, 235, 254–255
Afro-Asian solidarity, 211, 215, 220–221
Afro-Asian Writers Conferences, 220, 221–222, 239
Agreement on Scientific and Technical Cooperation, 105
agricultural modernization, Soviet studies on African, 149–153; in Soviet Union, 145–149
aid. *See* development aid
AIESEE (International Association for Southeast European Studies), 252, 257–258, 260–266
Albania, 253, 261
Altamirano, Carlos, 294
anti-apartheid, Solidarność's inability to support, 19, 298–301
anti-imperialism, decline in Eastern Europe, 13, 19, 21; and free trade, 36–40, 51, 52n8; and internationalism, 5–7; and nationalism, 14, 19–21, 274–278; and solidarity-based development, 49–51; and Soviet Union, 11, 81, 193–199, 205. *See also* China, relations with Soviet Union
anti-imperialist solidarity, 129, 140n6, 170
anti-Semitism, 230, 232
anticolonialism, and anticommunism in Poland, 14, 19, 274–284, 284n4; bringing it back to Eastern Europe, 17–20, 193, 204–205, 260, 273–274; Soviet policies on, 191–192
anticommunism, and anticolonialism, 19, 273–274, 278–284
antitotalitarianism, as unifying factor, 19, 296–301
Apostolova, R., 107, 112
Arab Middle-East, and non-capitalist road, 129–130
architecture, contractors, 173; individual professionals, 173–174; institutes and research centers, 172–173; and socialist worldmaking, 166–172, 175–176, 176–183, 185n32
arms industry, 50, 57n82, 186n39
Asian-African Writers Conferences, 220, 221–222, 239
Asozoda, Hudoynazar, 203
Astafiev, G.V., 93
Aswan Dam, 64, 77n24
Aytmatov, Chingiz, 204
Azad, Maulana, 215

Baghdad, Iraq, masterplan, 171–172, 174, 178–179, *179*
Balkan states, cooperation and in-betweenness, 251–256; deperipheralization and remarginalization, 251–252, 266
Balkanization, definition, 258
Bammate, N., 260, 262, 263
Bandung Conference (1955), 83, 193, 211, 215–216, 235, 254–255
barter. *See* countertrade/barter
Ben Bella, Ahmed, 240
Berza, Mihai, 258
Bhilai Steel Plant, India, 64–65, 77n24
Black African Student Union, 242–243
Bogomolov, O.T., 43
Bretton Woods system, 1, 42, 60
Buddhism, 16, 28n51
Bukovsky, Vladimir, 297
Bulgaria, architectural transfer. 180–181, *180*; Balkan relations. 253–254, 255, 256–257; computers to India. 46; nationalism versus internationalism. 21; Vietnamese vocational training. 107–108, 109t, 112, 115–116
Burma, 61, 72, 74, 214
Bustos, Manuel, 295, 296, 298
Butenko, Anatoliy, 20, 149

Cambodia, 73, 74, 85
capitalist globalization, 2, 6, 9, 43, 59–62. *See also* socialist globalization
CCP (Chinese Communist Party), 82–83, 86
Central Asia, agricultural modernization, 151–156, 159–160; continuing colonial relations, 199–202; critique of Soviet system, 202–205, 208n56; showcasing Soviet anticolonialism, 190–199
Central Asian State University, Uzbekistan, 222
Central Latinoamericana de Trabajadores (CLAT), 290–291, 292
Chile, 50, 294–298, 299
Chile Labour Committee, 296
China, claiming leadership of developing world, 6, 14, 38, 84–90; cultural solidarity and historical materialism, 214–219, 221–223; foreign aid policies, 84, 85, 88–89; relations with Soviet Union, 7, 9, 17, 80–84, 94–95; Three Worlds theory, 11, 90–94. *See also* Mao Zedong; Tiananmen Square Massacre
Chinese Communist Party (CCP), 82–83, 86
Chomsky, N., 288
Christian democrats and nonviolent "third way," 290–292, 294–295, 299
cinema and film, global contact through, 106, 189, 196–197, 231, 236
CIPSH (International Council for Philosophy and Humanities), 252, 259–260, 262–263
Clark, K., 192
CLAT (Central Latinoamericana de Trabajadores), 290–291, 292
CMEA (Council for Mutual Economic Assistance), 120n18; Eastern Bloc integration, 45, 53n19, 132; integration of non-European countries, 42, 44, 46; practice labor, 103; solidarity-based development, 49–50; technical assistance, 41, 175–176; Vietnamese labor migrants, 108, 109t, 112–113
CNS (National Union Coordination/ Coordinadora Nacional Sindical), 295–296
Cold War, and Soviet antiracism, 229–235, 241–245; and Soviet relations with Global South, 59–62, 67–68, 75–76, 236–241
colonial world, development strategies, 69–70, 78n38, 78n46
Comecon. *See* CMEA (Council for Mutual Economic Assistance)
Comintern (Communist International), 146, 147–148, 229
Communist Party of the Soviet Union (CPSU). *See* CPSU (Communist Party of the Soviet Union)
compulsory monetary withholdings, 115–117
Conakry, Guinea, 167–168
Condurachi, Emil, 257, 258, 262, 265
Connely, M., 190
Constantacopoulos, G., 258
Coordinating Office Abroad, Solidarność, 289, 292, 296, 299, 301, 302, 303
Corvalán, Luís, 294, 297
cotton complex, 192, 200

Council for Mutual Economic Assistance (CMEA). *See* CMEA (Council for Mutual Economic Assistance)
countertrade/barter, limitations and consequences, 44–47, 75, 137; principle of, 46, 48
CPSU (Communist Party of the Soviet Union), 237; policies on China, 81, 90–91, 95; policies on Third World, 20; policy of "peaceful coexistence," 128
Cuba, development cooperation with Eastern Bloc, 23, 44, 55n47; labor migrants, 110, 115
culture, as source of international solidarity, 192, 209–215; unity versus historical materialism, 215–223
Czarkowski, Robert, 291–292
Czechoslovakia, arms exports, 50; migrant remuneration, 113–116; Soviet invasion, 85; Vietnamese labor migration, 103, 105–113, 109t; Vietnamese student migration, 105

Davidson, Apollon, 235
debt crisis, 47–48, 170–171
Deng Xiaoping, 90, 95
development, in agriculture, 149–153; in architecture, 169–170; attractiveness of "tiger states," 50; attractiveness to Third World, 11–13; case of East Germany, 127–130, 138–139; case of Vietnam, 105–113; Chinese model of, 80, 82, 84, 89, 92; Eastern European assistance for, 41–47, 51–52; and import-substitution industrialization, 67–70, 78n38; socialism as non-capitalist alternative, 1–2, 62, 118; Soviet assistance for, 62–67, *66*; Soviet planning for, 8–10, 18–20, 69–76
development aid, GDR position on, 130–132; and Soviet Union, 62–67, 71–76, *71*, *72*, *73*, *74*, 77n24, 170. *See also* labor migration
dialectic materialism, 216
Diallo, Demba, 254
Diop, Alioune, 239
Djagalov, R., 196, 243
Djordjević, Dimitrije, 260
Dmochowski, Zbigniew, 178
Doctor Zhivago, 240
Du Bois, W. E. B., 231, 236
Duara, Prasenjit, 255

East Germany. *See* GDR (German Democratic Republic)
East-West MP. *See* Major Project on the "Mutual Appreciation of Eastern and Western Cultural Values"
Eastern Europe, as an anti-colonial space, 260, 280; connections with Western Europe, 49, 56n72; engaging with global economy, 42–47, 51–52, 116–117; exporting development expertise, 7–8, 10–11, 40–42; linking with decolonization struggles in Third World, 260, 280; as periphery, 18, 23, 254–255, 257, 261–262, 266; support for UNCTAD, 38–40; vision of globalization, 35–36; "worlding" of, 167–169, 178
Economic and Technical Cooperation (WTZ, East Germany), 131–132
ECOSOC (Economic and Social Council of UN), 37
education, solution to neocolonialism, 201–202; Soviet outreach to Third World, 237–246
Egypt, Aswan Dam, 64, 77n24; and China, 85, 87; development aid to, 61, 75, 85, 131, 135–136, 168, 203; and Soviet Union, 23–24
Energoinvest, 7
Energoprojekt, 167, 173, 178
Engerman, D., 145
Erenburg, Il'ia, 219–220, 234
Ethiopia, 37, 48, 254
Eurocentrism, critique of, 2, 23–24, 59, 210–214, 222–223, 258, 261–265
Eurodollar market, 22, 42, 47
Europe, Eastern Europe's return to, 19–20, 262, 264–266
European Economic Community, Africa as source of raw materials, 53n25; attractive to Eastern Europe, 265, 269n69; concern over establishment of, 37; Greece and Turkey, 255–256
European Union, 284
Evans, C., 243
Evrigenis, Dimitrios, 257
exoticization and anticolonialism, 280–282

Federal Republic of Germany, 128, 134–135, 142n30
film and cinema as global contact points, 106, 189, 196–197, 231, 236
Flagstaff House housing project, Ghana, 177, *177*
fossil fuels. *See* oil and fossil fuels
free trade, 36–40
Frelek, Ryszard, 277–278, 286n17
FRG (Federal Republic of Germany), 128, 134–135, 142n30
Frieden, J., 68, 69
Friemand, J., 81

Gankovskii, Iurii, 195
GATT (General Agreement on Tariffs and Trade), socialist states joining, 38
Gavrilov, Nikolai I., 155, 158
GDR (German Democratic Republic), official and alternative internationalism, 311–313; recognition and aid in Middle East relations, 44, 134–140, 170; Tiananmen Square Massacre and, 313–322; trade and cooperation in foreign policy, 130–133; Vietnamese labor migration, 102, 103, 107, 109t, 110, 115–116, 320; Vietnamese student migration, 105, 121n45; views on socialist globalization, 127–130
General Agreement on Tariffs and Trade (GATT), socialist states joining, 38
German Democratic Republic. *See* GDR (German Democratic Republic)
Ghafurov, Bobojon, 193, 212, 213–214, 217, 221–222
Ghana, cocoa industry/industrialization, 200; housing neighborhoods, 171, 176–177, *177*
Gheorghiu-Dej, Gheorghe, 253–254
GKES (Committee for Economic Cooperation), 7, 62, 63–64, 73–75, 196, 199
Glissant, Édouard, 168
Global North, emergence of term, 14, 43
globalization, concept of, 4, 52n1, 168–169; multidirectional approach to, 51–52, 58n94; Western-centric view of, 1–4, 22–23, 35–36, 51–52. *See also* socialist globalization
Golden, Oliver, 148
Goncharov, Leonard V., 155
Gorbachev, Mikhail, 20, 149
Grass, Günter, 293
Greece, 253, 255–256
Grotewohl, Otto, 102
Group of 77 (G77), 43
Guber, Alexander, 211–212
guest workers. *See* labor migration

Haley, Alex, 273–274, 279, 282, 283, 286n23
Hallstein Doctrine, 132, 134, 135, 170
historical materialism, 217–219
"History of Mankind" project, 211, 219
Holzman, F., 74
Hough, J., 145
House without walls (*Dom bez ścian*), 276–277
Hughes, Langston, 189–190, 231
human rights, critique of Tiananmen Square massacre, 315–316, 321; focus of Solidarność and other trade unions, 289, 291, 295–298, 301–303
humanism, extending the concept of, 259; new, 259; spiritual, 16, 219, 221
Hungary, changing relations to Third World, 38, 43, 49; Cuban labor migrants, 110, *111*; exporting expertise, 41, 169, 178; research on China, 87, 88, 90, 91–92, 93, 94; trade relations, 44, 47, 49, 56n61, 56n72, 170; under FIDESZ, 24; westernization, 39, 42
Hussein, Saddam, 23, 138
Huxley, Julian, 211, 219
hybridity. *See* "in-betweenness"

ICFTU (International Confederation of Trade Unions), 292, 295, 299
IDEP (African Institute for Economic Development and Planning), 157–158
IIB (International Investment Bank), 44, 45
IKAN (Institute for China Studies), 218
IMEMO (Institute of World Economy and International Relations), 41, 42
IMF (International Monetary Fund), 16, 42–43, 47
import substitution industrialization (ISI), 67–70, 78n38

"in-betweenness," 252–256, 257–258, 261–263, 266, 269n69
India, industrial projects, 63, 64–65, 74, 77n24; non-Soviet development aid received, 65; planned economic development, 8, 67; relations with Bulgaria, 46, 48; relations with Soviet Union, 5, 48, *66*, 145–146, 154, 163n58, 203, 214–215
Indian Impressions, 219–220
Indonesia, 61, 74–75, 85, 168
Institute for African Studies, 150–151, 156–157, 236
Institute for China Studies (IKAN), 218
Institute for Oriental Studies (IVAN), 195, 212, 217, 223
Institute for the Study of the Socialist World System (IMESS), 43, 49
Institute of World Economy and International Relations (IMEMO), 41, 42
Interkit (China international), 91–92
International Association for Southeast European Studies (AIESEE), 252, 257–258, 260–266
International Confederation of Trade Unions (ICFTU), 292, 295, 299
International Council for Philosophy and Humanities (CIPSH), 252, 259–260, 262–263
International Investment Bank (IIB), 44, 45
International Monetary Fund (IMF), 16, 42–43, 47
International Youth Festival (1957), 235–236
internationalism versus nationalism, anticolonialism and the turn to Europe, 18–20, 21; case of German Democratic Republic, 129, 135–139; case of labor migration, 111–113, 114, 116–117; in organizations for cooperation, 37–40, 261–266; in Soviet-Chinese relations, 80–84, 91, 94–95; in trade relations, 45–47, 68; in trade union relations, 5–10, 19, 232, 288–289, 301–303
Invincible (*Niepokonani*), 277
Iran, oil exports to Eastern Europe, 44, 55n49
Iraq, Baghdad masterplan, 171–172, 174, 178–179, *179*; Chinese propaganda, 87; debt, 56n65; and German Democratic Republic, 135, 138
Islam, East German-Syrian relations, 132, 134–135, 137; Soviet promotion of, 180, 213–214; Soviet relationship with, 9, 15–16, 194–195, 197–198, 203–204, 222
Israel, 134, 135
"Istanbul at the Intersection of Balkan, Mediteranean, Slavic, and Oriental Cultures" (1973), 263
IVAN (Institute for Oriental Studies), 195, 212, 217, 223

Jackson-Vanik Amendment, 49

Kakhorov, Abdullahad, 198–199
Karamanlis, Konstantinos, 256
Karpat, Kemal, 263
Katsakioris, C., 237, 239
Khoja Abu Nasr Parsa shrine, 222
Khrushchev, Nikita, abandons economic isolationism, 36–40; aid offensive to Global South, 63–67, 77n24, 170; engagement with Third World and the East, 192–199, 200, 211, 214–215, 239, 241–242; modernizing agriculture, 8, 17, 148, 151, 158–159; reaction from Chinese to the "thaw," 9, 210–211, 216–219; the "thaw" or spiritual humanism, 15–16, 202, 222–223, 234–237
King Jr, Martin Luther, 230, 245
Kirpal, Prem, 215
Korean War, 275–276
Kowalczyk, Witold, 282
Kułakowski, Jan, 290, 302
Kuwait, 136, 180, *181*

labor migration, comparing socialist and Western, 112–117; socialist, 100–101, 105–112; to Eastern Europe, 50, 102–104; to Western Europe, 101–102, 119n7, 119n8. *See also* race and racism
Latin America, in Chinese political view, 83–84, 90; economic isolation and debt, 47, 68, 78n38; student migrants, 237. *See also* Solidarność
Lee, Andrea, 245

Lefebvre, Henri, 168–169
Leffler, M., 67
Lenin Peace Prize, 240
Lenin, V. I., 7, 10, 151, 161n24, 229
Lin Biao, 83–84, 86
literary festivals, 196–197
Liu Shaoqi, 82–83
Lumumba University, 172, 237, 240–241, 243

McKay, Claude, 231
Maheu, René, 259
Major Project on the "Mutual Appreciation of Eastern and Western Cultural Values," 209, 212, 215, 261
Malcolm X, 245
Maliţa, Mircea, 257
Małowist, Marian, 278, 283
Mao Zedong, on historical materialism, 210, 216–218, 226n43; on the "intermediate zone," 80, 82–84, 86, 90, 94–95
Mao Zedong Thought, 82, 84
Mark, J., 110
Marxism-Leninism, Africa and race, 229–231, 238, 239–240, 243–245; Chinese and Russian interpretations, 44, 82, 93–94; in German Democratic Republic, 128
Mazov, S., 236
M'Bow, Amadou-Mahtar, 251
Meillassoux, Claude, 157, 158
Miastoprojekt, Baghdad masterplan, 171–172, 174, 179, *179*
Milewski, Jerzy, 290, 292, 296–297, 301
mobility, transnational, 100, 118–119. *See also* labor migration
Molotov, Viacheslav, 209, 211, 215
mondialisation, 168–169
Moscow. *See* Soviet Union (USSR)
Mujahideen (Afghanistan), 19, 303
Mukhitdinov, Nuritdin, 220–221
Mulekezi, Everest, 242, 244–245
multistructurality, 148, 161n24
"mutual advantage," as Chinese policy, 14, 84; in East German-Arab relations, 135–139; as Soviet policy, 49–50, 62, 67, 75, 154, 170. *See also* labor migration.
Myahoza, F., 154

NAM (nonaligned movement), 6, 167–168, 211, 253–256. *See also* UNCTAD
Nasser, Gamal Abdel, 83, 254
national liberation movements (NLMs). *See* NLMs (national liberation movements)
National Progressive Front (Syria), 137, 139
NCR (non-capitalist road), 129–130, 141n11, 148
N'Daw, Alassane, 259–260
Nicaragua, 24, 290–294, 297, 303, 320
NIEO (New International Economic Order), 11–12, 36–44, 251–252
Nigeria, Eastern European architecture, 178, 186n39; Soviet criticism of, 233
Nikolopoulos, Christos, 254
Nkrumah, Kwame, 54n31, 171, 176–177, 232–233, 236, 240, 254
NLMs (national liberation movements), and Chinese policies, 83, 87–88, 93; East German approach to, 128–132; and Soviet policies, 59, 236
non-capitalist road (NCR), 129–130, 141n11, 148
nonaligned movement (NAM). *See* NAM (nonaligned movement)
North Korea, 85, 275
Novopashin, Yuriy, 20, 149
Nuchovich, Eduard, 157–158
Nurek Dam, Tajikistan, 197, 203
Nyerere, Julius, 89

oil and fossil fuels, Eastern Europe and Third World, 44, 55n49, 170–171, 173, 176, 178; German Democratic Republic, 133, 136–138; Soviet Union, 11, 73, 74–75
Orientalism, 273, 278, 317–319

Padmore, George, 231, 233, 238
Pasternak, Boris, 240
Patrice Lumumba University, 172, 237, 240–241, 243
peaceful coexistence, principle of, 61, 128, 211, 214–215, 217
People's Friendship University, 172, 237, 240–241, 243
People's Republic of China (PRC). *See* China

peripheralization, alternative globalizations and, 1–4, 17–18, 22–24, 178; as basis for alliances, 6–7, 12, 43, 58n94, 254–255, 257, 264–265; concept of, 9, 278; and deperipheralization, 50, 261; development aid and, 130–133; and reperipheralization, 19–20, 251–252, 265. *See also* Balkan states; Central Asia
ping pong diplomacy, 88
Poland, anticolonialism and anticommunism, 19, 278–284; and Chile, 294–298; and China, 311; links to Europe, 21–22, 38; and Nicaragua, 290–294; provides expertise for development, 41, 172–173, 177; scholarship on postcolonialism, 273–276, 284n4; and South Africa, 298–301; and Vietnam, 276–278, 286n17
Polónyi, Charles, 178
Potekhin, Ivan I., 150–151, 232–233, 234, 236, 239
PRC (People's Republic of China). *See* China
Prebisch, Raúl, 39
proletarian solidarity. *See* socialist solidarity
Przybylski, Józef, 290
Pugachenkova, Galena A., 222

race and racism, African students in Soviet Union and, 15–16, 146, 230–232, 234, 237, 238–246; in Eastern Europe, 15, 320; in German Democratic Republic, 320; and migrant labor, 113–114
Rakhmanin, Oleg B., 90–91, 94
Rashidov, Sharof, 193, 195, 197, *198*
Rastokhez (Tajikistan opposition party), 204
Reagan, Ronald, 43, 292, 293, 300
Recovered Territories, Poland, 274–275, 285n7
remittances of migrant laborers, 115
"renovated" socialists, Chile, 294–295
Robeson, Paul, 231–232, 236
Robinson, Robert, 148, 231
Roerich, Iurii, 219
Roman, M., 229, 234, 237
Romania, 171, 176; and AIESEE, 263–264; architecture and design, 173–174, 175, 176, 179; links to Europe, 21, 30n69; relations to Balkan and Global South, 14, 43, 252–256, 258; trade agreements, 39, 171
Roots, The Saga of an American Family, 273–274, 279, 282, 283, 286n23
Rosenstein-Rodan, Paul, 41

Salazkina, M., 196
Schwenkel, C., 118
SED (Socialist Unity Party of Germany, GDR), 107, 128, 137
Seguel, Rodolfo, 296
Sékou Touré, Ahmed. *See* Touré, Ahmed Sékou
Selatile, Tsiu, 153
Senghor, Léopold Sédar, 9, 239
Sinaia colloquium, 257, 263
Sinda, Peter Mahende, 153
Singh, V.B., 154
Skachkov, Semyon, 62, 67
"socialism in one country," 6, 10, 13, 36
socialist ecumene, 23, 58n94
socialist globalization, bilateralism or pluralism, 10–11, 44–47, 51–52, 130, 253–254; creating a new world order, 5–10, 13–14, 36–42; and labor migration, 101–102; legacy of state socialism, 20–24, 181–183; role of socialist states, 4, 167–169; state control of, 14–16
"socialist mobilities," 117–118
socialist solidarity, 5, 128–133, 136–137, 140, 140n6, 229, 258, 275
Socialist Unity Party of Germany (SED, GDR), 107, 128, 137
solidarity, culture as source of, 209–214, 216, 222–223; decline of, 16–17, 20, 21, 49–50, 170; East German emphasis on, 134–136; history as source of, 18–19, 258, 262, 275, 282–283; idea of, 15, 16, 19, 275; and labor migration, 102–103, 105–108, 115; limits of, 10, 39–40; people's solidarity, 320–322; Soviet and Chinese views of, 9. *See also* Solidarność; Nurek Dam
solidarity-based development, 49–50

Solidarność, and anti-apartheid resistance, 19, 298–301; balancing domestic and international resistance concerns, 19, 288–289, 301–303; and Chilean trade union solidarity, 294–298; difficult relations with Nicaragua, 290–294; solidarity with Afghanistan, 19
Solidarność, Coordinating Office Abroad, 289, 292, 296, 299, 301, 303
South Africa, anti-apartheid struggle, 19, 298–301
South Korea, 22, 50, 56n61, 58n92, 69, 78n46
Southeast European states. *See* Balkan states
Soviet Union (USSR), on agricultural modernization, 145–153, 154–160; aid to developing countries, 62–67, 71–76, *71*, *72*, *73*, *74*, 77n24, 79n58; arms exports, 50, 57n82; competition with China, 11–12, 14, 80–90, 312; coordinating responses to China, 90–95, 210; creating a new world order, 42–44; credit and debt, 44, 48, 56n66, 56n71; development model, 7–10, 40–42, 168–172, 177; establishing trade relations, 36–40, 45–47, 67–70; ideology and outreach to Third World, 5–6, 12–13, 60–62; imperialism and the Soviet periphery, 16–20, 189–192, 202–205, 273–274, 279–280; as imperialist/ colonist, 11, 85-87, 203-5, 273-274, 279-280, 283, 312; limitations to globality, 10, 11, 12, 13, 42. 60, 75, 79 n58, 170-171, 245; oil subsidies, 44, 55n48; race and racism, 15–16, 146, 230–232, 234, 237, 238–246; Third World's impact back in, 17, 18, 19, 158-60; Vietnamese student and labor migrants, 104, 107, 108–110, 109t; westward economic integration, 49–50. *See also* Khrushchev, Nikita
Speich, D., 61
Stalin, Joseph, agricultural transformation, 147, 148; autarkic development, 6, 36; emphasis on material development, 212–213, 218, 225n14; purges, 232, 233; and Soviet Union-China relations, 82; and Third World, 193
Staszyszyn, Zbigniew, 277
state socialism, attempts at adjusting, 288–289; global relations and fall of, 16–20, 21; impact of labor migration, 15, 105; rise and extent, 1–2
student migration, African students in Soviet Union, 230, 237, 238–246; as form of labor migration, 103–104; Vietnam to Eastern Europe, 104–105
Syme, Ronald, 259
Syria, 132, 134–135, 137
Szelenyi, B., 117
Szelenyi, I., 117

Tagore, Rabindranath, 219
Tálas, Barna, 92
Tanzania, Chinese relations with, 89
Tashkent Film Festival, 196–197
Tashkent international conference on agriculture (1972), 154–155
technological transfer, 40, 84, 103, 105, 110; architectural, 169–172, 172–175, 181–183, 185n32; Eastern Europe to Third World, 40–42, 51–52, 100–101, 111, 154–159; and German Democratic Republic, 130, 131–133, 138–140; to China, 7–8, 82–84. *See also* student migration
Thatcher, Margaret, 43
Third World, China's position on, 80–82, 95n2; import-substitution industrialization policies, 68–70, 78n38; solidarity, 5, 128–130, 137, 140, 140n6, 229, 258. *See also* peripheralization
Tiananmen Square Massacre, 311; East German identification with dissidents, 319–322, 326n70; human rights and double standards, 315–316; media globalization, 313–315; threat to East German dissent, 316–319
Tibet, 9, 218, 223
Tito, Josip Broz, 253–254, 256
Todorov, Nikolai, 264
Tolmár, B., 110
totalitarianism, building an international campaign against, 19, 296–301
Touré, Ahmed Sékou, 168, 239
Touré, Mamadou, 158, 164n81

trade union movement. *See* Solidarność
"transferable rouble," 45
tropical architecture, 172–173
Turkey, 253, 255–256, 257
Tursunzoda, Mirzo, 194, 196, 199
two-camp approach, 167, 210, 211, 216–217, 220

UNCTAD (United Nations Conference on Trade and Development), and Comecon integration, 53n19, 55n45; founding principles, 36–40, 133; North-South division of the world, 14, 43
UNESCO (UN Educational, Scientific, and Cultural Organization), 148, 209, 211, 215, 222; linking the Balkan and Third World, 256–260, 261; membership, 251–252. *See also* AIESEE
UNIDO (United Nations Industrial Development Organization), 40
United Nations Conference on Trade and Development (UNCTAD). *See* UNCTAD (UN Conference on Trade and Development)
United Nations Educational, Scientific, and Cultural Organization (UNESCO). *See* UNESCO (UN Educational, Scientific and Cultural Organization)
United Nations Industrial Development Organization (UNIDO), 40
United States, countering Soviet influence, 58n92
urbanization and global architecture, 13, 147, 167–168, 176–183, 202
Uzbekistan, 197, *198*, 222

Valkenier, E., 73
Vietnam, extent of labor migration, 100–101, 106, 108; government control over migrants, 113–116; labor migration to Eastern Europe, 102–104, 105–113, 109t, 116–117; and Polish postcolonial struggles, 276–278; student migration, 104–105; workers' experiences in host countries, 113–114
vocational training, 105–108

Wałęsa, Lech, 296, 302, 307n58
WCL (World Confederation of Labour), 290, 292, 299, 301, 303
Weiss, Gerhard, 135
Wight, Martin, 254–255
workers' rights, building international alliances, 5, 19, 295–297, 302; influence of China, 92–93. *See also* labor migration
World Bank, 16, 42–43, 47
World Confederation of Labour (WCL), 290, 292, 299, 301, 303
World Congress of Intellectuals in Defense of Peace (1948), 274–275
"world public," 313–316
"worldmaking," 167–169, 181–182
Wright, Richard, 233
WTZ (Economic and Technical Cooperation, East Germany), 131–132

xenophobia, dismantlement, 320; and migrant labor, 113–114

Yamamoto, T., 260
Youth Festival (Moscow, 1957), 235–236
Yugoslavia, architecture and construction, 167–168, 172–173, 177–178; Balkan states and non-alignment, 253–255; economic links, 7, 41, 48, 52; and NIEO, 43; Tito-Stalin split, 6; and UNCTAD, 37, 39; and UNESCO, 252

Zakharov, Nikolay, 230
Zambia, 88, 89, 200
Zawalski, Zygmunt, 290, 292
Zhenbao Island, 86
Zhivkov, Todor, 21, 253–254
Zhou Enlai, 83, 84, 216
Zhukov, Georgii, 193
Żukrowski, Wojciech, 276–277

www.ingramcontent.com/pod-product-compliance
Lightning Source LLC
LaVergne TN
LVHW040756070826
844660LV00025B/1167

* 9 7 8 0 2 5 3 0 4 6 5 1 2 *